This book is dedicated to my wife, Carole, and my children, Joseph and Jessica. Their support and understanding during their many lonely evenings is greatly appreciated.

Contents

PART II   BUSINESS CASE ANALYSIS

The real key to convincing people to move to a reuse culture is its impact on the bottom line.

PART III   OPERATIONAL TRANSITION

Making reuse work requires time, talent and attention to detail especially in the process area.

Foreword

My very first programming job involved reuse; it was in 1964, and I was an undergraduate student at MIT, looking for a summer job. Digital Equipment Corporation offered me the princely sum of $3 per hour to write the FORTRAN subroutine library for their new PDP-5 minicomputer, a task that I managed to finish by the beginning of the fall semester. Total cost: a little under $1,500, plus whatever modest corporate overhead I might have incurred; it's hard to imagine a better return-on-investment justification for reuse.

There were no books on software reuse to guide me in those days, nor would there be any for many years to come. I've always found it curious that while *everyone* in the software field acknowledges reuse as a Boy Scout virtue 1996 roughly on the same level as loyalty, bravery, and thrift 1996, very little in the way of practical advice has been available in order to help individuals and organizations actually accomplish it. However, by the late 1980s and early 1990s, that situation began to change, and there is now a fairly rich collection of articles and research papers focusing on reuse, together with a few books. But when it comes to books on reuse, there are only a few—and that's why it's so important to see this new book from Don Reifer, *Practical Software Reuse.*

Many of the authors, consultants, and researchers in the reuse field seem to focus their energies on theoretical and academic issues; others are doing their best to promote silver-bullet technologies, such as CASE tools or object-oriented methods. Having been a CASE and OO enthusiast myself, I can still remember asking Reifer a few years ago whether he had begun using an OO-CASE tool for the work that he was doing for the NASA Space Shuttle project. "There aren't any industrial-strength OO methods or tools I could risk using on a system this big," he replied. "People's lives are at stake." I found the remark sobering and realized that he was probably right.

After several years as a successful consultant, during which he worked with a number of organizations in the U.S. and abroad to initiate reuse practices, Reifer was drafted to head up the Software Reuse Initiative (SRI) for the U.S. Department of Defense. If the problems and opportunities at the NASA Space Shuttle project were large and complex, the DoD situation was a few orders of magnitude larger and more complex. And as he points out in the preface to the book, Reifer learned that the political issues are more complex—and this coincides with my experiences with reuse: Technical issues associated with reuse are indeed complex, but the managerial and organizational issues are usually far *more* complex.

And thus, while *Practical Software Reuse* certainly does cover the technical aspects of reuse, most of its focus is on the strategies and techniques for actually *introducing* reuse into a large organization. It's interesting that he devotes an entire section of the book, three full chapters, to the task of creating a *business case* for reuse; as he points out, senior executives will be convinced of the need to support reuse and deal with the associated problems only if they can see a credible argument for bottom-line improvements.

And while some organizations don't even get that far in their efforts to implement reuse initiatives, many more fail in the next step: the "operational transition," as Reifer calls it. The fact that senior management firmly supports reuse, and is prepared to make a long-term investment over a period of two to three years before they see the payoff, is fine; but if the project managers and the software engineers don't have the right tools, processes, and incentives, then reuse can still fail. As noted earlier, many organizations pin their hopes on silver-bullet tools and processes, and are often frustrated to learn that they don't work: "We've written three million lines of C++ in our division," one manager lamented to me a couple years ago, "and so far, we've gotten *zero* reuse. What's wrong?" The answer to a question like this is probably not a simple one—but if this manager had had Reifer's new book *before* he launched his C++ initiative, he might have succeeded.

Working in a DoD environment (from which he has since retired, in order to return to private practice), Reifer has also seen some *special* issues associated with reuse; among these are COTS (commercial off-the-shelf software), the practice of reuse in a contractor/subcontractor relationship, and the issues of measuring performance in a reuse-oriented environment. These are all explored in the final chapter of the book, and they are equally applicable to software organizations in the private sector.

There is a handful of books that every software engineer, systems analyst, and software manager should have on his or her bookshelf. I've published a list of such books on my Web site at www.yourdon.com, and I update it whenever something new and important comes along. Unfortunately, there's been very little to recommend in the area of reuse, but I'm delighted to say that I can add Don Reifer's *Introducing Software Reuse* as a must-read item on the list.

Ed Yourdon
New York City

Preface

INTRODUCING SOFTWARE REUSE: A PRACTICAL APPROACH

During the past six years, I have been tasked with the job of making software reuse happen in several large firms and government organizations. As a change agent, my job has been inserting technology into firms that were ready to try something new. To introduce change, I had to devise strategies and implement tactics that let me demonstrate convincingly that the technology would yield positive benefits under a wide range of circumstances. I had to sell new ideas to advocates and critics alike based upon their merits. To implement change, I had to determine how to cope with a myriad of technical, managerial, and political issues. I had to analyze emerging technologies and decide if and when they could be used productively by my clients. Most importantly, I had to devise practical approaches that worked when constrained by tight schedules and budgets.

During the last two years, I stopped writing this book and took on the job of managing the Department of Defense's Software Reuse Initiative (SRI). The challenge I faced was similar to what I encountered in the corporate world. However, the scale was much larger and the politics thicker. To make things happen and succeed, I had to become a change agent. Deploying strategies for change within such a large bureaucracy was a difficult job. It required tact, diplomacy, and most importantly teamwork. Probably the most critical thing I learned in all of my experiences within government is that when push comes to shove, the thing that makes believers is a solid business case. I have therefore changed the emphasis of this book to help build such a case for my readers.

Undoubtedly, you have read the hype in the literature about the merits of object-oriented methods, CASE, and a host of other new technologies. We seem to be continuing our quest for the silver bullet. Are these techniques really ready to be used? Are they stable and can they be introduced into your organization with a minimum of effort? What are the shortfalls and how do you address them? What lessons have others learned using them? These and a host of related questions probably have crossed your mind. Hopefully, this volume will address these and other issues that will undoubtedly arise when you initiate efforts to start a reuse program within your organization.

Even if you have answers to your questions, any major change in the way your organization does business is dangerous. Although the technology may look good, your firm may not be ready to use it. The technology may not be mature enough for your application, or scalable to your projects. Time, talent, and funds may not be available when you need them to make the change. Management may decide on other priorities, or may not be willing to make the necessary investments. Your people may be scared or uncertain of what to do when faced with change. Even if you get commitment, you may not be able to produce results according to desired timetables, because they are too aggressive or key staff is just not available when you need it. If you don't deliver what you promised, you know you may not get the future resources you need to continue your quest (and your reputation) during the next budgetary cycle. Lots of things can happen (and will) when you take on the role of a change agent. You are probably thinking, Life in the fast lane sure can be fun and exciting. It can be. However, remember that it can be dangerous as well. Use the safety tips in this book to help avoid the crashes.

When all the smoke clears, it will become apparent that the underlying motivation for using technology is to save time, effort, or dollars. All the other reasons people give are poppycock. The easiest ways to accomplish these goals include one of the following:

- Improve your staff effectiveness (get more output with the same input)
- Decrease your workload (require less new output through reuse, therefore less input)

Because systematic software reuse is relatively new, proven management approaches for introducing reuse to organizations like yours are just now emerging. What works in one place may not work in another. In other words, you have to be flexible. More importantly, you have to be pragmatic and go with the flow.

Based upon my experiences, I wrote this book to provide some practical guidance for managing introduction of software reuse within a medium-size to large firm. The examples I've chosen are aimed at providing you the advice you may need to deal with a wide range of situations. The book was written to be issue based and action oriented. I have focused this book on resolving the many conflicting managerial, technical, political, and psychological challenges that often can make or break the success of a software reuse initiative.

The three specific goals I have set for this book are:

- Provide a sound understanding of fundamental concepts, processes, and management challenges associated with putting software reuse to work within production organizations
- Facilitate creation of a management infrastructure that enables advocates to manage software reuse as they introduce it incrementally
- Provide operational and management concepts that permit advocates to exploit emerging reuse technology in the most cost-effective manner

Fortunately, I have had the opportunity to test these reuse strategies in several forward-looking commercial organizations, and within early adopter programs within the Department of Defense. Their experiences and the lessons they learned form the foundations of the advice that I offer in the chapters that follow. When there are alternatives, I will discuss them. When there are issues, I will describe them and identify solutions for you if they exist. By no means have all of the problems associated with this emerging technology been resolved. Therefore, you might feel that some current issues have been left open. I apologize in advance if this proves troublesome. But, telling you that an issue has been identified and is being studied may be the best advice that I can offer you at this time.

Although pragmatic, the concepts presented in this book are based upon proven management theory. These techniques stress the need for innovation, sound planning, consensus, teamwork, and follow-through. They build on modern organization and motivation theory. They stress process maturity and take advantage of the many theories and lessons learned in the new field of change management.

The book is intended to be read by anyone who is interested in the topic of introducing software reuse into an organization. Executives, managers, engineers, programmers, researchers, professors, and students all can derive benefits from its study.

It is my sincere hope that this book will stimulate you into action. The ultimate compliment for me would be for you to try some of the ideas presented within this volume within your organization. I am also interested in results. Don't be afraid to write me to tell me the good, the bad, and the ugly. I am interested in putting what you learn into future versions of this volume.

As a final thought: Have fun. Remember, introducing change in an organization is exciting. While there will be difficult moments, it can be a rewarding experience.

Donald J. Reifer
Torrance, California

Acknowledgments

I would like to acknowledge the many organizations that let me put my reuse vision into action. From government, I would like to thank the Department of Defense (DoD) Software Reuse Initiative (SRI) team. Under my leadership, they rose to the occasion and helped craft a strategy that will permit systematic reuse to become a reality within the DoD services and agencies. Within industry, I would like to thank those who put a corporate software reuse program into place in such firms as AT&T, CAE-Link, Hewlett-Packard, Hitachi, IBM, Loral, Magnavox, Motorola, Waste Management of North America, and Westinghouse. These early adopters provided the models upon which success can be built by others. Finally, within the universities, I would like to thank the many researchers who are providing the results that government and industry need to overcome the many obstacles associated with reuse.

There are just too many people who contributed ideas that I have included within this book to thank by name. However, I will single out three who had a profound influence on my thoughts during the last few years. First, I would like to acknowledge the contributions of my dear, departed friend Fred Joh. He had the foresight to put a software reuse program into place within Westinghouse years before it became fashionable to do so. He did it because it was the right thing to do. I would next like to thank my deputy, Linda Safford, who kept me on the straight and narrow path during my two years as Chief of the DoD's Software Reuse Initiative. I can never thank her enough for helping me cope with the "broken bureaucracy" and the "system". Finally, I would like to thank my mentor, Dr. Barry Boehm. His vision and support during the past 20 years have helped me mold many of the ideas in this book.

A special thanks goes to my editor, Marjorie Spencer, for her encouragement and attention. Thanks also go to Professor Gertrude Levine, of Farley Dickinson University, for her detailed review comments and many helpful suggestions. Finally, thanks go again to my wife Carole. She proofed the book, helped me rewrite the rough segments, and made the document readable.

Fundamental Concepts

Understanding reuse technology and how it fits into your culture is key to effective use.

Introduction

1

WHAT IS SOFTWARE REUSE?

Software reuse is defined as the *process of implementing or updating software systems using existing software assets*. Reuse can occur within a system, across similar systems, or in widely different systems. The term *asset* was selected to communicate that software can have lasting value. Reusable software assets include more than just code. Requirements, designs, models, algorithms, tests, documents, and many other products of the software process can be reused.

Software reuse is really a simple concept. Your task is to identify high-leverage software that has the potential to be reused across applications, acquire it, and make it easy for your users to take full advantage of it as they develop their systems. However, as in many cases, taking a simple idea and making it happen in reality often is not as easy as it sounds. Details have to be worked out before the concept can be made to work in practice. For example:

- How do you identify assets with high reuse potential?
- Should you employ an opportunistic approach?
- Should you use architectural considerations to drive selection?
- When do you build and buy reusable assets?
- What are the issues associated with using third-party products?
- How do you make these reusable assets readily available to potential users?
- How do you document assets and certify their quality?
- What legal and contractual positions do you have to take when dealing with suppliers?

- Do you need special facilities and tools for reuse?
- Does your current organization structure support reuse advocacy?
- What skills, knowledge, and abilities must be built in order to institute systematic software reuse?
- Which world-class organizations have adopted reuse and what has been their experience?
- How long will it take to realize payback?

These questions and many others like them must be answered before you can successfully introduce software reuse into your organization. *Just having a good idea is not enough.* Often, good ideas mean organizational change. Always remember, any change, good or bad, will be resisted. As a change agent, your job is to understand the issues people in your organization face, and figure out how the change helps them overcome any problems that occur. As you will find out, most of these issues are managerial and political, not technical. A lot more will be said on the topic of change management throughout the book, although it is not specific to reuse.

WHY IS SOFTWARE REUSE IMPORTANT?

Systematic software reuse revolves around the planned development and exploitation of reusable software assets within and across applications and product lines. Its primary goal is to save you money and/or time. It succeeds when the amount of resources required to deliver an acceptable product are reduced. It tries to take advantage of software that exists or can be purchased off the shelf. Its conduct forces you to decide in advance what reusable software to build or buy. It makes you rethink the processes and paradigms you use to acquire your software. It motivates you to address the myriad management, technical, and people issues that inhibit reuse, especially in organizations where risk taking is not part of the culture. Most importantly, it forces you to view reuse from a business-case viewpoint. When you get down to basics, software reuse is motivated by the desire to get the job done cheaply and quickly.

At this point, you are probably wondering, Why make so much fuss about software reuse? Aren't most firms doing it? Don't most developers build their software to be reused? Aren't your engineers making informed make/buy decisions early in the life cycle? Hasn't the underlying technology needed for reuse been around for years? Aren't the processes known and guidelines for its systematic practice available? Aren't there examples that illustrate the success stories and lessons learned? Don't we already know how to exploit reuse opportunities as we build systems?

As you probably expected, the answer to each of these questions has been No! until recently. The type of software reuse I'm talking about has just begun to be put into practice by forward-thinking firms. Although many leaders in the industry have talked about software reuse for years, most practitioners haven't figured out how to do it in a repeatable and systematic manner. The reason is simple. The technology needed to put it into practice just wasn't available until recently. The arrival of object-oriented approaches and languages, domain engineering methods, integrated software environments and CASE, and new process paradigms make broad-spectrum software reuse possible. Advances in software architecture provide us with the foundation for software reuse, while a consensus on related standards provides us with the building codes.

This book was written to permit you to take advantage of these advances, and put software reuse into immediate use in your organization. It shows you how to build on the successes early adopters have had with the technology. To help you deal with resistance to change, it focuses on the management and people issues. It helps you develop the business case needed to convince the skeptics that software reuse makes good business sense. It shows you how to identify, manage, and mitigate the risks associated with transferring the technology into operations. The key to putting software reuse to work in any organization is perseverance, persistence and belief in yourself and your cause.

ECONOMICS OF REUSE

With the recent push to downsize or outsource, most of us are trying to look for ways to cut our software costs. The majority of improvement strategies being pursued today try to either *reduce the inputs needed to do the job (people, time, equipment, etc.)*, *or increase the outputs generated per unit of input.* A Chinese friend of mine once explained the dual nature of productivity to me using the following story: In ancient days, the emperor wanted to reduce the travel time between cities by digging a tunnel through a mountain. Like most emperors, he was in a hurry. To speed up things, his chief engineer suggested that they start two teams digging at either side of the mountain. "When they meet in the middle," he said, "productivity will increase and you will have your tunnel in half the time." If they don't meet, he thought, productivity will still improve because you will have two tunnels through the mountain.

This dual nature of software productivity can be represented notionally using the following equation:

$$\text{Productivity} = \text{Outputs/Inputs Used to Generate the Results}$$

When focusing on the equation's input side, you could arm your people with CASE tools, workstations, mature processes, and the like. Using this approach, you try to get more output from your people (your input) using an automation strategy.

Just the reverse happens when you focus on the output side of the equation. Instead of concentrating on improving staff efficiency, you emphasize reusing existing assets to get more output per unit of input. In either case, the strategies you employ tend to be complementary. For example, increased automation can lead to increased reuse. As another example, increased reuse can reduce the need for further automation, thereby reducing the costs of software development even further.

WHAT ASSETS DO YOU REUSE?

Software reuse has existed for years. Early software reuse practices were focused on code. They were done ad hoc and were opportunistic. However, reuse changed as the industry matured. Reuse became planned and was done systematically. Currently, *any product of the software life cycle can potentially be reused.* This means that in addition to third-party software packages supplied commercially, architectures, requirements, designs, code, tools, utilities, test cases, test scenarios, databases, database schemas, documentation, and user manuals are all candidates for reuse.

The trick to understanding what to reuse is to understand what I call the 20:80 rule: 20 percent of your assets are responsible for 80 percent of your reuse. In addition, you should realize that software reuse doesn't come free. It will cost you more to build software to be reusable, because you will have to package it to address broader variability. Asset designs must be done more carefully, and testing must be more comprehensive. If you reuse existing off-the-shelf software assets, you may have to give up some functionality or performance. If you reuse modified off-the-shelf assets, you probably will be saddled with their costs of maintenance.

WHERE HAS SOFTWARE REUSE PAID OFF?

Industry has realized a significant payoff by instituting systematic software reuse practices. For example, Wayne Lim of Hewlett-Packard reported the following benefits attributable to their software reuse initiative in a recent set of articles in *IEEE Software* magazine [1]:

- *Quality*—The defect density for reused code was one-quarter of that needed for new code.
- *Productivity*—Systems developed with reuse yielded a *57 percent increase in productivity* compared with those constructed using only new code.
- *Time to market*—When development efforts were compared, those exploiting reuse took *42 percent less time to bring the product to market.*

Other organizations have also reported similar results. For example, Computer Science Corporation developed the Upper Atmospheric Research Satellite (UARS) telemetry simulator for NASA Goddard Space Flight Center using a design that was highly reusable. Reuse of UARS software assets on three other NASA projects has resulted in the following quantifiable benefits [2]:

- The Extreme Ultra Violet Explorer (EUVE) telemetry simulator reused 89 percent of the UARS code without modification. *Costs as measured in staff hours were reduced by 67 percent.* Productivity was three times that of the original UARS development project.
- The Solar, Anomalous, and Magnetospheric Particle Explorer (SAMPEX) reused 85 percent of the UARS telemetry simulator architecture. Costs as measured in staff hours were 30 percent less than that of the EUVE project.
- The WIND/POLAR telemetry simulator reused 55 percent of the UARS telemetry simulator architecture. Again, costs went down and quality improved.

Such examples are not isolated instances taken to prove a point. Other forward-thinking firms, such as AT&T/Bell Labs, Boeing, Hewlett-Packard, and IBM, have published positive results [3]. However, most examples in the literature are early adopter or pilot projects. Unfortunately, most of the firms I have talked with have yet to institutionalize the practices proven on these projects across business units. Taking the practices, packaging them, adapting them, and scaling them up to achieve comparable results across organizations present a wide range of challenges. What works in the small, undercontrolled situations does not always work in the large. What works in one site cannot always be exported to multiple sites.

UPON WHAT CONCEPTS IS REUSE BASED?

Before we assess the state-of-the-art of software reuse in the next section, we must cover some of the fundamental concepts upon which reuse is based. For *reuse* to occur in practice, *reusable* software assets must be acquired that are *reused* by others in their applications. This sentence is instructive. Let's examine the concepts that surround the three forms of usage of the term reuse within the sentence (*reuse, reusable,* and *reused*).

Reuse implies a known process exists for all those activities related to finding, retrieving, and using software assets of known quality within your application. When talking about reuse, the following three types of processes are typically involved:

- *Application engineering*—The processes/practices firms use to guide the disciplined development, test, and life-cycle support of their applications software. These are the processes your software engineers normally use to develop/maintain your products.
- *Domain engineering*—The reuse-based processes/practices firms use to define the scope, specify the structure, and build reusable assets for a class of systems or applications. These activities are typically conducted to figure out what to build to be reusable.
- *Asset management*—The processes/practices firms use to manage their assets and make them readily available in quality form to their potential users.

These are the processes your engineers use to search libraries to find the reusable assets of interest. The quality of the assets is maintained along with the integrity of their configuration using some online mechanism that is part of your software engineering environment.

Figure 1.1 illustrates how these processes are related. The software development approach depicted in this figure is called the two-life-cycle model, because domain and applications engineering activities are conducted in parallel when it is used. As shown, domain engineering uses the architecture it develops to identify the reusable software assets that applications engineering develops and uses. Asset management links these activities and makes these assets available.

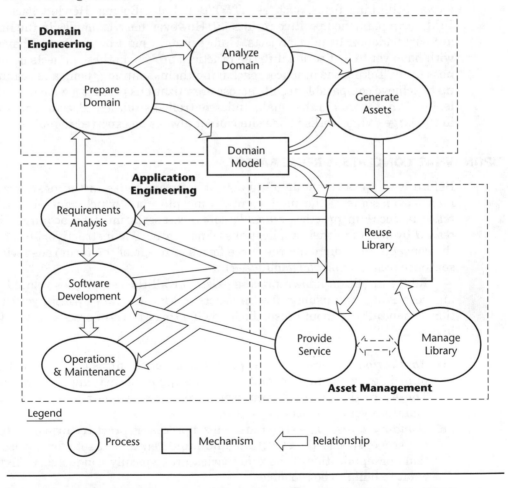

FIGURE 1.1 Dual Life-Cycle. *Source:* Reifer, Software Reuse: *Making It Work For You,* Report RCI-TN-494A, 12/91.

Assets of interest can be newly developed or acquired from others (other projects, third parties, or commercial suppliers). Just having reusable software assets available does not provide any benefit if potential users do not know what exists or can't find what they need when they need it. In addition, having the wrong assets is worse than having nothing. Users must have some way to judge the worth of the assets. You must make sure that the assets available provide the capabilities that your users both need and want. Finally, you must make it easy for potential users to find and access things of value. This takes specialized tools, software reuse libraries.

The term *reusable* refers to the product and its basic features. To have value, the asset must have high reuse potential and be packaged with reuse in mind. If the asset is hard to understand or adapt, users will abandon it. Product-line software architectures are now in favor because they let users identify and acquire the 20 percent of the assets responsible for 80 percent of the reuse across families of like systems. Ease of reuse should be a design consideration for each of the assets that are part of the product line. Finally, the asset's quality must be known and users must feel satisfied that it won't break.

The term *reused* has a value-added connotation. An asset built to be reusable does not take on value until it is reused with some advantage by someone else on another application. Typically, incentives must be provided to make this happen. All too often, reuse is avoided because of deadline pressures or a desire to keep the costs to the bare minimum. In such scenarios, developers are rewarded when they cut corners and limit functionality. The reward structure must be changed to overcome reluctance to address the broader needs of the organization. In other words, reuse must be sold to both the managers and the programmers.

Undoubtedly, some of you have probably noticed that the software reuse field has developed a vocabulary all its own. For example, I use the terms architecture and product lines in my explanations, thinking everyone knows what I am talking about. For those of you interested in definitions, let me ask for patience, as I will cover each of these major topics in detail in later chapters. If you can't wait, let me refer you to the glossary that appears as an appendix.

STATE OF THE ART

A great deal of research is underway under the banner of software product lines, domain-specific software architectures, domain engineering, and software reuse. International, national, and company-sponsored programs abound. In the United States, the government has mounted several software reuse initiatives. It is issuing policies that call for and give preference to the use of commercial off-the-shelf and third-party software. In Asia and Europe, major initiatives are underway that have reuse thrusts.

The reason for all of this interest in software reuse is primarily economic. Government is looking for ways to cut their spiraling software costs. As they downsize, they can no longer afford to build all of their software as new. In contrast, industry is looking to increase the speed in which it brings products to market. They need to provide the features and functions their users are looking for quickly in order to maintain their competitive advantage. As a complementary strategy to productivity improvement (remember the story of the emperor who dug the tunnel through the mountain), software reuse is viewed as a reasonable way to accomplish these goals quickly and with a minimum of disruption.

Throughout the world, significant progress has been made in software reuse technology. Early adopters have demonstrated the feasibility of reuse concepts under controlled situations on a number of pilot projects. Probably the two most significant large-scale reuse programs that I am aware of in the United States are the STARS [4] and DoD Software Reuse Initiative [5]. STARS (Software Technology for Adaptable, Reliable, and Maintainable Systems) is a just completed research initiative that focused on megaprogramming (i.e., developing software using large building blocks instead of single lines of code) [6] and developed related reuse technologies (reuse libraries, frameworks, etc.). In contrast, the DoD Software Reuse Initiative is trying to take the reuse technology that STARS and others in the community have developed, and institutionalize it across the Department of Defense so that its Program Managers (project managers) and Program Executive Officials (product line managers) can take full advantage of it.

As its finale, in its last two years, the STARS program sponsored three early adopter projects that applied advanced reuse concepts to build software for the Air Force's mobile command center (command and control), rebuild software for the Navy's T-34C Flight Instrument Trainer (crew training system), and reengineer software for the Army's Improved Guardrail V (intelligence system). Both generative and constructive approaches to reuse were used in these projects. The results achieved on these pilot projects are impressive. For example, the Air Force project cut delivery time almost in half, improved quality by a factor of two, and lowered costs by about 70 percent using a product-line approach to reuse. The STARS experiences have been published [7, 8] and their lessons learned form an integral part of guidance provided by this book.

Many firms throughout the world are also pursuing software reuse. For example, AT&T has instituted a major reuse program to lever its investments in telecommunications software assets within and across domain-specific product-line architectures. They have developed a set of best practices that many of their business units have adapted and are using to foster wide-spectrum reuse [9]. Hewlett-Packard (HP) has focused on developing and deploying software reuse concepts into its product divisions via a corporate program [10] aimed at gaining a competitive advantage. The strategy uses a software bus and glue language to interface reusable software building blocks together to build application systems quickly for a range of client applications. Others have also instituted reuse programs that also have an architectural flavor.

In 1989, I conducted a study [11] to assess the current state of the art of software reuse within the United States. I have updated the major findings of this study, which follow, to reflect today's situation. Other recent studies have been conducted, which validate my findings and lead to similar conclusions:

- *Many efforts are underway to build a technical infrastructure for reuse.* With the introduction of object-oriented methods and languages such as Ada 95, C++, and Smalltalk, the technology exists to package software for reuse. Many efforts are currently underway that capitalize on this technology, attack known reuse barriers, and develop a reuse infrastructure. International programs, such as the European REBOOT [12] effort, are starting to realize benefits as they transfer technology to industrial firms. As already noted, the DoD is pursuing reuse as part of its STARS and SRI efforts. Government think tanks, such as the Software Engineering Institute (SEI) [13], and industry consortia, such as the Software Productivity Consortium (SPC) [14], have active reuse programs that address architecture, product lines, and domain engineering methods in addition to other reuse issues. Many research centers (HP Labs, etc.), colleges, and universities (University of Southern California, etc.) are pursuing aligned investigations.
- *The hot research topics in software reuse are product-line management, software architectures, and domain engineering methods.* Domain-specific reuse is in. Most current research focuses on reusing software assets that populate architectures designed for families of systems with like characteristics (product lines). Many efforts underway are developing methods, notations, and languages used to model and analyze domain experience. The methods foster the expanded use of product-line architectures that foster reuse across projects and organizations. These architectures are used to identify which assets need to be acquired to populate product lines. The methods are used to analyze domain experience and develop a responsive architecture.
- *Object-oriented techniques are starting to be viewed as reuse enablers.* Many of the reuse efforts I've looked at are toying with the use of object-oriented methods, languages, and tools. Most agree that these techniques help package software for reuse. When used in conjunction with domain engineering approaches, object-oriented methods are viewed as enablers for reuse primarily based on their class abstractions. In addition, more reusable software is being brought to market as the popular object-oriented methods (Booch [15], Coad/Yourdon [16], FODA [17], etc.) become more widely used. Framework and class libraries containing both fine-grain (data structures such as queues, etc.) and coarse-grain (communications handlers and subsystems, etc.) components are being marketed to support developers who use one or another of the popular techniques.
- *Several prototype software reuse libraries that serve as models for the future are operational today.* Several industrial strength software reuse libraries that provide their users with the ability to search, browse, and retrieve assets of interest are in operational use. These serve as models for what organizations can do when they want to make reusable software assets readily available. Assets are also becoming increasingly available to populate these libraries

(class libraries, etc.). Standards for interoperating these libraries across the Internet are being devised by such groups as the Reuse Library Interoperability Group [18]. Three of these reuse libraries have been interconnected in a seamless manner [19]. Unfortunately, not a lot of people are using these libraries. The major lesson the DoD has learned is that just having a reuse library is not enough. Users need to agree on the architecture so that they know how to use the library to get to the parts that matter. Without such a framework (the architecture), few will use the library in a cost-effective manner.

■ *Lots of software assets exist that can be reused.* A great deal of off-the-shelf, public-domain software exists that has the potential for wide-scale reuse. However, finding what you need when you need it continues to be a challenge. In addition, knowing the software exists doesn't motivate you to use it. One of the biggest barriers to software reuse is the lack of trust potential users have in the capabilities and quality of public-domain software. That is the main reason users don't take advantage of the many bulletin boards and data banks that provide free software to those interested. In addition, concerns over such computer maladies as viruses may place limits on what can be reused. However, some firms are hoping to change this situation and make a business out of marketing such assets [20, 21]. Their view that reuse makes business sense and that much more than code can be reused is similar to mine.

■ *Reuse tools are being put into the software engineering environments.* Several efforts are integrating software reuse tools and library capabilities into the next-generation software engineering environment using backplanes or Java-based servers as mechanisms for tool connectivity [22]. The philosophy being pursued is to make software reuse a natural part of the way firms do their business. Tools are the natural means to implement this philosophy, because they automate tedious manual processes and often act as technology transfer agents. A lot of attention is being placed on generative tools [23] for reuse, because they can generate the assets needed directly from an architecture specification. Work on a variety of metrics, measures, and performance evaluation tools is being pursued, because they are needed to analyze the cost effectiveness of the reuse program along with the quality of the assets. Browsers are being built to allow users to view both text and graphics objects of interest. Object managers are being examined to see if they control the information that flows between repositories that are part of a virtual environment.

As can be seen, there is a great deal of activity being pursued in software reuse-related areas. Considerable progress has been made by the early adopters and reuse technology seems ripe for the picking.

Let's now look at the state of the practice and see how it compares with the state of the art. Let us also try to answer the difficult questions: Where are most organizations when it comes to the reuse-adoption cycle? and, What are organizations doing to try to take advantage of the reuse technology that is available?

State of the Practice

The state of the practice always seems to lag behind the state of the art. This was true for the UNIX operating system, which took 15 years to make the transition from inception to widespread use [24]. It is also true for software reuse.

The curve shown in Figure 1.2 displays the four phases of technology adoption. Software reuse should be viewed as an emerging technology, because most experience with it reported to date is from the early adopters. Their experiences are important because the early majority relies heavily on this input when it makes the decision whether the rewards associated with technology adoption are worth the risks.

The following findings provide insight into the current state of the practice of software reuse. Although significant progress has been made in the past few years

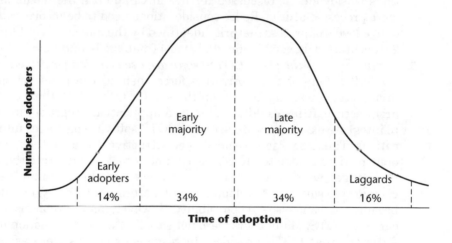

Early adopter	Early majority
• High risk, high returns	• Moderate risk, moderate returns
• Trend setters	• Innovative
• Advance emerging technologies	• Harness maturing technologies
• Limited risks, limited returns	• Low risk, low return
• Conservative	• Ultra conservative
• Exploit new technology	• Only use proven technology
Late majority	**Laggards**

FIGURE 1.2 The four phases of technology adoption.

in the state of the art, there still is a lot to do to make software reuse part of our corporate culture:

■ *For the most part, reuse tends to be done ad hoc in most firms.* As illustrated in Figure 1.3, most of the firms whose software reuse processes have been evaluated using a reuse maturity model [25] are not using the state of the art. Reuse processes are not well defined and practices are not institutionalized in the majority of the firms studied. This analysis assumes that the processes organizations use to manage product lines, architectures, and software reuse should be part of their business practice framework. Perhaps reuse will be considered as a key process area in some future revision of the SEI process maturity model [26]. Being part of the SEI model is important, because this powerful tool is being used extensively to assess the software process capabilities of organizations worldwide. As discussed further in Chapter 4, the model assesses software process maturity. Reuse considerations need to be incorporated into each of five levels of process maturity identified by the model: Level 1 (*ad hoc*), Level 2 (repeatable), Level 3 (defined), Level 4 (managed), and Level 5 (optimizing).

■ *Commercial off-the-shelf (COTS) software use is no longer perceived to be a silver bullet.* One of the motivating forces behind the push for open systems architectures was commercial off-the-shelf (COTS). With the advent of layered architecture, firms could use standard application program interfaces (APIs) to integrate existing third-party and COTS software packages into their applications. These packages seemed very attractive. Because they existed, development time translated to whatever time it took to integrate them, assuming no changes were required. Licensing costs were but a small fraction of the comparable software development costs. More importantly, maintenance now became someone else's responsibility. However, many problems arose when it came to COTS. Many users were not satisfied with the functionality and performance that COTS provided. In response, vendors were asked to modify COTS, and maintain custom packages. Costs then started to escalate, because such packages were expensive to keep up to date. In addition, many firms did not want to put their core competency in the hands of third parties (e.g., mining companies wanted to maintain the software used to manage mines, not software that could be purchased to manage payroll taxes). The focus was placed on such competencies because these were areas where competitive advantages existed. As a consequence, many firms have backed off the use of COTS. Most have devised policies and practices aimed at determining the long-range cost/benefits of use of COTS, not the immediate attraction.

■ *Most projects don't have the time or skills to do a domain analysis and develop a product-line architecture.* Because most software projects are schedule driven, they don't seem to have the time or budget to perform a domain analysis or develop a product-line architecture. Methods for domain analysis are relatively new, immature, and unproven. In addition, most of the engineering staff is unskilled in their application and in modern, standards-based, open

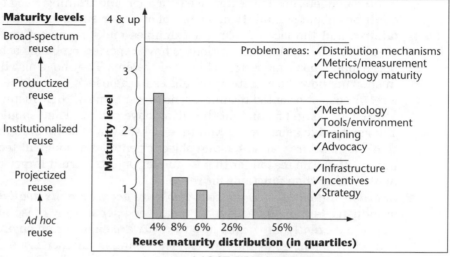

FIGURE 1.3 Process maturity models.

Maturity level	Name	Characteristics
1	*Ad hoc* reuse	• Reuse occurs *ad hoc* • Reuse is neither repeatable nor managed
2	Project-wide reuse	• Reuse is a product of a project, not a process • Reuse is repeatable on a project-by-project basis
3	Organization-wide reuse	• Reusable assets are a product of the process • Reuse is part of the way the organization does business
4	Product-line reuse	• Reusable assets are a product of the process • Reuse is viewed as a business unto itself
5	Broad-spectrum reuse	• Reuse is an integral part of the corporate culture • Processes are optimized with reuse in mind

software architectures. As a result, most projects focus on narrow views of the problem. Typically, the best that they can do is some form of project-wide commonality analysis. No reuse opportunity analysis across projects is done, because there just isn't time, talent, or budget to do it. There is nobody in charge of validating the architecture, and nobody looking out for the long-term interests of the organization.

■ *The jury is still out on object-oriented methods.* While many organizations are trying to use object-oriented techniques, few production shops have adopted them as their primary methodology. The change in mindset, tight schedules, limited budgets, need for extensive education and training, need to retool, and questions about scalability make use of object-oriented technology risky. Past failures and the lack of relevant examples make many software managers suspicious. In addition, practitioners have reported problems achieving tight performance goals for certain classes of systems. They have also had difficulty in showing how the architecture relates to the user's view of the problem. As a result, object-oriented techniques have lost some of their luster in the literature. This doesn't mean that they don't have potential and shouldn't be used. You can't make gains unless you take risks. Even with its problems, I believe that the risks are warranted and object-oriented development techniques are here to stay. The reason for this is simple. Objects permit larger-scale components rather than functions for reuse.

■ *Sharable industrial-strength reuse tools are not yet readily available.* The lack of industrial-strength reuse tools (analyzers, generators, reuse libraries, etc.) that are currently integrated into the software engineering environment, and shared by members of the development team, is another issue. Many of the reuse tools available today are primarily prototypes neither designed nor intended for large-scale use, because the market for such tools has not yet materialized. In response, the vendors are pouring their limited resources into other areas where the market potential is known. As a result, the reuse tools they are working on as part of their next-generation software engineering environments have not yet been brought to market. Based upon past experience, the widespread adoption of proven reuse concepts will not occur until industry markets more supportive tools. Without better tools, the technology may lay fallow as engineers avoid the toil associated with doing reuse tasks manually.

■ *The many nontechnical barriers to software reuse must be overcome.* The most pressing software reuse issues are nontechnical [27]. Based upon these, a number of cultural, organizational, management, and infrastructure changes are needed to make reuse work in most organizations. In other words, firms will have to change the way they do business in order to reap the benefits of reuse. Table 1.1 provides a list of potential barriers. Do not let the list scare you off. You can overcome any of these barriers if you want to. Unfortunately, others can use them to justify why you should not waste your time on reuse. I do not believe that there are any showstoppers on the list. As discussed later in the book, there are ways around each of the obstacles.

■ *There are still technical issues that need to be tackled.* The most pressing technical issues in the field are associated with architectures. Agreement on standards to be used for representation are important. So are tools. It is important to realize that architectures are models used to synthesize product lines. They do this by letting us frame, optimize, and converge the operational, technical, and system views of what the system should do. To develop the models, you must be able to relate what you are building to your user's requirements, and exploit the knowledge base of applicable experience. To decide if you are

TABLE 1.1 List of Nontechnical Barriers to Reuse

Barriers	Explanation
Legal and Contractual Issues	Many people are worried about the liability issues. If they build something that proves faulty, can they be held liable? How do they protect and recoup their investments? Those in the game know that the legal and contractual issues are workable. Many legal positions have been formulated, model contract agreements developed, and lots of guidance published [28].
Lack of Incentives	Because reuse makes the software job smaller, cheaper, and more manageable, you would expect people to flock to it. Many haven't, because reuse doesn't result in promotions, raises, or prestige in their organizations. In response, the reward system needs to be modified to show management fully supports reuse goals and achievements.
Project-by-Project Mindset	Most organizations fund software projects one at a time. Little time and few resources are provided to determine if software assets can be reused. Some opportunities for reuse appear, but systematic reuse does not occur, because deadlines are short, funds are not available, and little emphasis is placed on reuse by project management. As product-line concepts catch on and standard architectures become more prevalent, the line of business manager and chief architect may be able to correct this trend.
Not-Invented-Here Syndrome	Many engineers feel uncomfortable using the work of others. They don't trust it. Instead of investing effort in reengineering existing software, they feel more comfortable building applications anew. This problem can be attacked with advocacy, rewards, education, and training. Making your corporate commitment to reuse highly visible through the payroll and promotion system also goes a long way.
Few Meaningful Metrics	Part of the problem is, there are few accepted metrics for measuring whether reuse has actually occurred. Devising a reward system is impractical when there is no easy and fast way to determine if reuse goals have been realized. Several efforts are underway to address this issue. New estimating models [29] that address reuse cost/benefits have been devised to help quantify the benefits.
Limited Investment Capital	Lack of suitable tools is also hindering reuse adoption. A chicken-and-egg situation seems to exist. Because there is little current market, there are few investment dollars. However, because there are few tools, the market languishes. Things aren't as bleak as they seem. Several computer manufacturers and tool vendors are developing needed tools to act as differentiators for their offerings.

finished, you must understand what constitutes a good architecture. As reported, research is underway to resolve these and other technical problems. We should see results soon.

The situation described seems normal. Adoption of other major software technologies takes a lot of time, effort, and perseverance. While the SEI and SPC have efforts aimed at streamlining the technology transfer process, results with these new paradigms may still be years away. As the change agent, you will have to figure out what makes sense for your organization, and how to make the necessary improvements.

LESSONS LEARNED

What lessons have the early adopters learned as they have introduced software reuse into their organizations? To answer this question, I conducted yet another study [30] in 1992, whose updated results are summarized in the following section. Although seemingly somewhat repetitious, the advice still seems useful:

- *Lesson 1—Reuse is not a silver bullet.* It should be apparent that reuse is only part of the solution to what many in the industry have labeled the software crisis. Beware those promising simple solutions. In my experience, simple solutions to difficult problems, such as improving productivity, don't work. Introducing software reuse into an organization is difficult. Realize that if it were easy, we would have done it already.
- *Lesson 2—Emphasize product-line architectures.* Probably the most important lesson learned during the past three years is that product-line architecture is where the action should be. The architecture creates the foundation for systematic reuse to occur. It becomes very difficult to figure out what to buy or build to be reusable without an architecture to serve as a decision framework.
- *Lesson 3—While technical issues exist, reuse remains a management problem.* While technical problems still exist, most of the barriers facing reuse adopters are cultural, managerial, psychological, and political. Deal with the people and process issues head on and you will be successful. Don't, and you will probably fall flat on your face.
- *Lesson 4—For reuse concepts to work, new processes and paradigms must be introduced organization-wide.* Changes in management infrastructure (organization, policies, processes, practices, etc.) are needed to support the introduction of reuse into your firm. To increase your chances of success, address the people, processes, and technology issues when you make needed changes. Make it easy for your people to do their jobs by providing them the structure and tools they need to get products out the door quickly and expertly.
- *Lesson 5—Even though industrial-strength reuse libraries are available, none that currently exists fills the bill.* Most of the reuse tools that exist either do not have the required capabilities or just don't scale up sufficiently to meet the demands of the using organization. Even if they did, they currently don't

integrate with your other software engineering tools and repository. Be prepared to put the kludges in place to make them help you simplify the work.

■ *Lesson 6—Case tools need to be reoriented to model the solution space in addition to the problem domain.* Most CASE tools define what should be built without considering available reusable assets. As a result, reuse opportunities are not fully considered as systems are synthesized. Be prepared to analyze your models to determine where reuse makes the best sense.

■ *Lesson 7—New, innovative, contractual/legal models are needed to overcome buyer resistance to reuse.* Current contracts do not provide those who develop and reuse software assets with adequate financial rewards. As a result, many have found it to be more profitable to redevelop software rather than reuse it. Use award-fee provisions of contracts as an interim fix.

■ *Lesson 8—Software must be viewed more as an asset than an expense by management in the future.* Viewing software as an asset would encourage management to capitalize its software research and productize its software development efforts. The firm would be able to recoup its initial investment over a multiyear time period using depreciation as it captures market share and makes a profit through sales of reusable assets.

■ *Lesson 9—Pay attention to technology transfer issues.* To succeed with reuse requires you to pay attention to the technology transfer needs of your organization. Ready your people for the technology. Gather the hard data you need to sell management and discredit the critics. Plan demonstrations so that they are in step with the budgetary cycle. Innovate and push the edges of the envelope. When things turn out well, you'll be glad that you did these things.

Additional specific lessons learned appear throughout the book. I think they are important because they let you take advantage of the experiences of others. Remember, each of these lessons was derived from the experience of those who tried to introduce reuse into their organization. Try not to relearn the lesson.

Based upon the nine lessons in this chapter, the list of success prerequisites for a software reuse program, which appears in Table 1.2, can be derived. Each item in this list will be addressed in the noted chapter. Examples will be provided along with guidelines, whenever possible, to help you understand the implementation details.

WHO SHOULD READ THIS BOOK?

This book is written primarily for software professionals and students. Both novices and experienced engineers can derive benefits from reading it:

■ For the *student,* the book provides insights into what reuse is and how it helps you do your job quicker, better, and cheaper.

■ For the *change agent,* the book provides strategies that you can use to insert reuse into your organization in a more structured manner.

TABLE 1.2 Prerequisites for Reuse

Prerequisite	Expansion	Where Addressed
1. Defined process	Business planning	Chapter 7
	Domain engineering	Chapter 10
	Applications engineering	Chapter 10
	Asset management	Chapter 10
2. Sound business case	Benchmarking results	Chapter 5
	Business case development	Chapter 6
	Measures of success	Chapter 6
	Business measures	Chapter 6
3. Well-defined approach	Vision and strategy	Chapter 2
	Operational concepts	Chapter 3
	Business case	Chapter 6
	Business plan	Chapter 7
	Transition approach	Chapter 8
4. Facilitating infrastructure	Advocacy organization	Chapter 4
	Incentives and rewards	Chapter 4
	Planned evolution	Chapter 8
5. Management control	Project management	Chapter 10
	People management	Chapter 10
	Product management	Chapter 10
	Intergroup coordination	Chapter 10
	Reuse management	Chapter 10
	Transition management	Chapter 9
	Technology management	Chapter 11
6. Skilled practitioners	Skilled staff	Chapter 11
	Educated management	Chapter 11
	Knowledgeable consumers	Chapter 11
	Motivated producers	Chapter 11
7. A grasp on the technology base	A view of the future	Chapter 11
	Impact of new technologies	Chapter 11
8. Handle on legal, contractual, and acquisition issues	Supplier management	Chapter 12
	Subcontractor management	Chapter 12
	Contracts management	Chapter 12
	Patents management	Chapter 12

- For the *software and information systems engineer,* the book shows you how to take advantage of architectures, product lines, and reusable software to build your products quicker, cheaper, and better.
- For the *software process engineer,* the book defines the key process areas you should pay attention to when you revise your activity structure for reuse.
- For the *project manager,* the book describes how to create an infrastructure for managing reuse. It also identifies incentives you can use to motivate your

software staff to develop reusable software and take advantage of assets others have created.

■ For the *executive,* the book identifies the strategic and investment issues associated with reuse, and provides a business case that justifies pursuit of an initiative.

This book is suitable for use in undergraduate and graduate courses, and for individual study. Since it deals primarily with management issues, it could serve as a supplement to the more technical texts written on these topics.

HOW THIS BOOK IS ORGANIZED

I have identified many issues and promised you a lot in my introductory remarks. To deliver, I have divided this book into three sections:

■ *Fundamental Concepts*—understanding the reuse fundamentals
■ *Business-Case Analysis*—making the case for reuse
■ *Operational Transition*—putting reuse to work in practice

Part I examines the motivation for and the technical concepts upon which software reuse is built. I define reuse, show what it can do for you, assess the state of the art and state of the practice, share my vision, and hone in on scenarios you can use to introduce reuse into operational use within your organization.

The four chapters that comprise Part I include:

Chapter 1 Introductions—Introduces you to software reuse and discusses how the book can help you put the concepts to work operationally.

Chapter 2 Reuse Vision and Strategy—Provides you with a high level vision and strategy for reuse. Lets you understand what needs to be done in the long term to change the culture.

Chapter 3 Reuse Operational Concepts—Discusses the concepts of operation that you can use to realize the vision and strategy.

Chapter 4 Elements of a Successful Reuse Program—Identifies the elements of a successful reuse program. Highlights the process, people, product, and technology relationships.

Part II addresses the business issues associated with reuse. It focuses on reuse economics and business planning tools and techniques, and shows you how to build a business case to justify reuse. It describes models for determining reuse cost/benefits, and focuses on developing a solid business plan. I have placed a lot of emphasis on this section because it provides ammunition to make your case for reuse.

The three chapters that comprise Part II include:

Chapter 5 Competitive Benchmarking—Summarizes techniques you can use to assess and figure out how to improve your current competitive position.

Chapter 6 Business-Case Development—Describes how to develop a business case for reuse, which justifies expenditures based upon cost/benefits or investment opportunities.

Chapter 7 Business Planning—Shows you how to take advantage of market opportunities and come up with a reuse business plan.

Part III discusses ways to manage the transition of software reuse into your organization. Focus is placed on what is needed to make and manage the transition to a reuse culture. Domain engineering, asset management, and applications engineering processes are described in detail from a technical point of view. Emphasis is placed on how to tap the benefits of reuse. Finally, a look into the future is provided to identify technologies that may revolutionize the way we do reuse.

The five chapters that comprise Part III include:

Chapter 8 Making the Transition—Discusses how you can use different approaches to make the transition to reuse in a planned and orderly manner.

Chapter 9 Managing the Transition—Describes controls you can use to ensure that you meet expectations and deliver what you promised when you sold your reuse initiative.

Chapter 10 Key Reuse Process Areas—Summarizes the practices that comprise key process areas for reuse-based software development paradigms that perform domain engineering in parallel with applications development activities.

Chapter 11 Future Directions—Looks at technology developments that have the potential to revolutionize the way we do reuse in the future.

Chapter 12 Special Topics in Software Reuse—Discusses special topics pertinent to reuse primarily in the area of government contracting and acquisition management.

A considerable amount of supplemental information is provided in the text. Every chapter has sidebar boxes to show how others have addressed the issues raised. I have also included as appendices:

■ Pointers to information sources
■ A bibliography and a glossary

HOW THIS BOOK CAN HELP YOU

This book was written to arm those interested in making software reuse happen within their organizations with the information/ammunition needed to:

■ Understand the issues associated with software reuse and what you can do to address them

- Develop a software reuse vision and workable strategy for your organization
- Generate a concept of operation that makes software reuse part of the way you conduct your software business
- Develop a plan you can use to incrementally insert software reuse into your organization
- Prepare a business case you can use to justify your investments in software reuse
- Provide your management with the controls they will need to ensure that expectations you have set for software reuse have been fully realized
- Address the issues associated with changing your culture to one that emphasizes product lines, architecture, and reuse
- Provide the examples, facts, hard data, and case studies you will need to sell a reuse initiative to your management

SUMMARY

- Software reuse is defined as the process of implementing or updating software systems using existing assets.
- The motivation for reuse is economic—it saves money.
- Software reuse is aimed at exploiting more than code.
- The state of the art in software reuse is advancing rapidly. Emphasis is currently being placed on populating domain-specific, product-line architectures.
- The state of the practice lags behind the state of the art.
- The barriers to harnessing reuse are primarily managerial.
- This book identifies the issues and helps you figure out how to address them.

Those seeking more general information on reuse and the technologies it builds upon are referred to the bibliography at the end of the book.

REFERENCES

1. Wayne C. Lim, "Effects of Reuse on Quality, Productivity, and Economics," *Software,* IEEE Computer Society, September 1994, pp. 23–30.
2. DoD Software Reuse Initiative, *Software Reuse Executive Primer,* May 1995.
3. Jeffrey S. Poulin, *Measuring Software Reuse,* Addison-Wesley, 1997.
4. Defense Advanced Research Projects Agency (DARPA), *STARS 1991 Proceedings,* available from STARS Technology Center, December 1991.
5. DoD Software Reuse Initiative, *DoD Software Reuse Initiative Strategic Plan,* available from the Defense Information Systems Agency, 1995.
6. Barry B. Boehm and William L. Scherlis, "Megaprogramming," *Proceedings DARPA Software Technology Conference,* April 1992, pp. 63–82.
7. Loral Federal Systems, *AF/STARS Demonstration Experience Report, Version 2.1 (Update),* Contract F19628-93-C-0129, March 1995.

8. Unisys Corporation, *Army / STARS Demonstration Project Experience Report,* Contract F19628-93-C-0130, February 1995.

9. Larry Bernstein, "Politics of Reuse," *Proceedings AT&T Symposium on Software Reuse,* May 1995.

10. Brian W. Beach, Martin L. Griss, and Kevin D. Wentzel, "Bus-Based Kits for Reusable Software," *Proceedings of 2nd Irvine Software Symposium,* University of California at Irvine, March 1992, pp. 19–28.

11. Donald J. Reifer, *Findings of the Software Reuse Survey Task,* available from Reifer Consultants, RCI-TN-410A, August 1989.

12. DoD Software Reuse Initiative, *Software Reuse Benchmarking Study,* available from Defense Information Systems Agency, February 1996.

13. Gibbie Hart and Sholom Cohen, "Domain Engineering and Product Lines," *Proceedings 8th Annual Software Technology Conference,* April 1996.

14. Art Pyster, "A Product-Line Approach," *Proceedings 8th Annual Software Technology Conference,* April 1996.

15. Grady Booch, *Object-Oriented Design with Applications,* The Benjamin/Cummings Publishing Co., 1991.

16. Peter Coad and Edward Yourdon, *Object-Oriented Analysis (Second Edition),* Yourdon Press, 1991.

17. Kyo C. Kang, Sholom G. Cohen, James A. Hess, William E. Novak, and A. Spencer Peterson, *Feature-Oriented Domain Analysis (FODA) Feasibility Study,* Software Engineering Institute, Report CMU/SEI-90-TR-21, November 1990.

18. Jim Moore, "Reuse Library Interoperability Group (RIG)," *Presentation of status to DoD Reuse Executive Steering Committee,* available from Defense Information Systems Agency, September 1995.

19. DoD Software Reuse Initiative, *Virtual Reuse Library Assessment and Library Infrastructure Report,* available from Defense Information Systems Agency, September 1994.

20. Elena Wright, *Library Business Fee for Service,* available from Defense Information Systems Agency, February 1993.

21. Central Archive for Reusable Defense Software (CARDS), *Franchise Plan,* STARS-VC-B010/001/00, February 1994.

22. Bob Hennan, *NASA Electronic Library System (NELS) Future Plans,* available from NASA Johnson Space Center, August 1994.

23. Don Batory, *Validating Component Compositions in Software System Generators,* TR-95-01, University of Texas at Austin, 1995.

24. Sam Redwine, personal communications.

25. Software Productivity Consortium, *Reuse Adoption Guidebook,* SPC-92051-CMC, November 1993.

26. Mark Paulk, "Survey of major changes proposed for CMM v2," *CMM Correspondence Group Correspondence,* Software Engineering Institute, April 1996.

27. DoD Software Reuse Initiative, *Software Reuse Metrics Plan (Version 4),* available from the Defense Information Systems Agency, August 1993.

28. Craig A. Will and James Baldo, Jr., *Proceedings of the Workshop on Legal Issues in Software Reuse,* Institute for Defense Analyses, Document D-1004, July 1991.

29. John Gaffney, Jr. and R. Cruickshank, "A General Economics Model of Software Reuse," *Proceedings 14th International Conference on Software Engineering,* IEEE Computer Society, 1992.

30. Donald J. Reifer, "Software Reuse: The Next Silver Bullet?" *American Programmer,* Volume 6, Number 8, August 1993, pp. 2–9.

Reuse Vision and Strategy

VISION AND STRATEGY

I hope by now that you want to introduce software reuse into your organization. Because reuse represents a culture change in most organizations, you will need a vision and strategy. To start, goals for your reuse program need to be defined along with how you are going to demonstrate that they have been realized. Then, tactics must be devised so that the strategy can be put into action. Next, operational concepts that are compatible with the way you do business must be put into place. Investments then must be delineated and budgeted. Finally, all sorts of plans must be developed, executed, and kept up to date.

The primary vision to consider revolves around the consumer-oriented model of reuse that I introduced in the first chapter. This model, which is shown in Figure 1.2, is architecturally based, market driven, and consumer oriented. Using this model, products are built to support architectures developed for families of similar systems, called product lines. Market forces are used to define the priorities for the products that are built to be reusable, and establish the application domain boundaries. Consumers define the standards to which the products will be built and any aligned reuse services that they will be willing to pay for (training, consulting, etc.). Market windows are established based upon consumer opportunities, and outside competition is used to keep suppliers lean and mean. The principle of equal partnership dominates. This concept is a win-win strategy, in which everyone who participates in your reuse program derives positive economic benefits from it. In total, reuse should be viewed primarily from a business perspective: If what you do does not provide you, your suppliers, and your consumers with some financial rewards or tangible advantages, you should abandon your reuse program.

There are many approaches you could use to attain my architecturally based, market-driven, consumer-oriented vision. The strengths and weaknesses of the four most popular of these are listed in my preferred order in Table 2.1:

TABLE 2.1 Strengths and Weaknesses of Alternate Reuse Strategies

Strategy	Strengths	Weaknesses
Product-line architecture	Product-line oriented Investments are limited to what is needed by the architecture Reuse of COTS and third-party software is emphasized Economies of scale and breadth are possible Systematic approach	A major culture change is needed to make it work A new infrastructure must be created (policies, processes, organizations, etc.) Investments are large Suppliers might rebel Switchover takes a lot of time and effort
Megaprogramming	Product-oriented Reuse becomes a natural part of the way you do your business Participatory No central group or taxes needed to fund reuse	A major culture change is again needed The infrastructure must be built (processes, etc.) Investments are large as you cut over to reuse as you build systems
Library	Service oriented Opportunistic by nature Simple and easy to implement Costs are reasonable Can make an impact in the very near term Provides those services the users are willing to pay for	Often bureaucratic because access must be protected Taxes on users are both possible and probable Users are often directed to use library or else General versus domain-specific parts populate the library
Electronic shopping mall	Market based (forces brokers to focus on business issues) Partnerships are possible (to reduce costs) Makes money or you go out of business	Market may not be strong enough to justify up-front expenses Startup costs are high Focuses attention outside, not inside, thereby causing user dissatisfaction

Note: The first two strategies are systematic and the latter two opportunistic by their very nature.

Product-Line Architecture Strategy

Define product lines revolving around a line of business concept. Structure each line of business so that it has profit and loss responsibility. Then, define the family of products, market, and customer base for each line of business. Within each product family, make the effort to develop an architecture aimed at satisfying consumer demand. Next, take the time needed to define the standards that will permit you to open the architecture and exploit the use of COTS hardware and software in the future. As part of this effort, make sure that you define the 20 percent of the parts that are responsible for 80 percent of the expected reuse. Then, acquire/develop these components and use them to populate the architecture of those products that are part of your product lines. For legacy products, develop a migration strategy to upgrade the products so that they are compatible with the architecture. Finally, modify your management infrastructure so that your organizational structure, processes, and reward structure support the product line architecture approach you use to do your business.

Megaprogramming Strategy

Make software reuse an integral part of your software development and maintenance activities. Arm those doing the work with the processes, methods, tools, and decision framework they need to incorporate any number of reusable assets (architectures, designs, algorithms, code, tests, etc.) into their deliverables. Use either fine-grain (i.e., small building blocks, such as some object taken from a framework library) or coarse-grain (i.e., larger building blocks, such as an entire communications application) components. Train your people in the use of domain architectures, application generators, COTS/third-party software, and reusable building blocks. Automate your reuse processes to make it easy for those doing the work to get their jobs done. Make sure your tools support your reuse paradigm. Do everything possible to focus on improving the productivity and efficiency of your software workforce. This approach is called component-based development when systems are built by combining and integrating pretested/preengineered fine-grained software objects.

Library Strategy

Pursue a more opportunistic approach for reuse. Create a core group to champion reuse, perform domain analysis, provide education and training, and support technology insertion into projects on a centrally funded or fee-for-service basis. Set up a central software reuse library to store, qualify, distribute, and maintain reusable assets and COTS components. Make these assets and information about them readily available to those doing the work (via online catalogs, newsletters, fliers, etc.). Modify your reward system to provide a variety of incentives (financial, career progression, etc.) to stimulate use of the library. Encourage your staff to browse and withdraw your holdings by making the library easy to understand and use.

Electronic Shopping-Mall Strategy

Extend the reuse library concept into the world of the Internet and World Wide Web (WWW). Create an electronic mall for ordering reuse goods and services. As part of the mall, set up a central reuse library to store, qualify, distribute, and maintain reusable assets and COTS components. Provide training online and a variety of linkages to search engines that allow your users to access other nodes of interest on the network. Market those reuse goods and services that appeal to your consumers on a fee-for-service basis. Broker information and other people's products. Use market demand to define what you provide, your timing, and pricing. Modify your internal management infrastructure to enable projects to pay for reuse goods and services. Consider marketing goods and services externally. In reality, set up a small business within your business, and force it to operate in either a breakeven or profit mode.

Of course, there are other strategies being pursued and there are variants of the four mentioned in the preceding. If there is a better option, go for it. I believe in pursuing whatever works.

SELECTING A STRATEGY

You are probably saying that all four preceding strategies seem to make a lot of sense. Any of these options could work if the circumstances are right. Selecting your strategy revolves around many factors and I use the following five criteria.

Consistent with Your Firm's Future Plans

Select the option that fits with your firm's future plans and investment strategies. If it is downsizing, don't create new organizations (even temporary ones). If it is centralizing, marry the strategy with the central services organization. If centralized organizations are not popular, make software reuse one of the themes for your centers of excellence. If the firm is defining new products or product lines, make architecture and upwardly compatible migration strategies for existing systems your primary concerns. Under such conditions, I would join the product development team and get them to endorse my software architecture strategy. I have found that being consistent with corporate initiatives will make it much easier to sell reuse concepts to those in positions of power. It also ensures that your strategy is consistent with that of other engineering groups who are working on aligned hardware and systems engineering issues.

Compatible with Your Level of Process Maturity

Select the option that matches with your process improvement tactics. Using this approach, you will be able to insert software reuse into your processes as they are being developed. No retrofit will be required if things are done *just in time* (JIT).

Marrying reuse to your process improvement program has lots of advantages. Chiefly, this approach helps you make reuse part of the overall improvement plans. It reduces risk because it tackles the difficult task of inserting reuse practices into your business and technical processes. It makes it simpler to justify the investments involved, because they are viewed as part of the broader process improvement effort. It makes tracking and reporting simpler, because they can be done in concert with all of the other improvement activities you have underway.

Consistent with Your Corporate Culture

Don't be a revolutionist when it comes to selecting a strategy. Pick the approach that seems to work best with a business-as-usual-at-first concept. Else, you will have to fight harder to introduce reuse, because you will be fighting those who resist change just because they are afraid of trying something new. Make it easy for the critics to agree with you that change is necessary. Create an atmosphere conducive to change. Incrementally develop the ammunition you'll need to convince the critics that the change is not bad. Sell change under the banner of natural evolution. If you can, try to make the critics think the changes you are proposing were their idea. Praise them and give them credit for the idea. I have always been surprised to see how easily egos can be swayed and support can be developed in this manner.

Compatible with Your Investment Strategies

Select the option that is compatible with your organization's current five-year investment strategy. If money is tight, go with a more near-term, opportunistic strategy. For example, if you are already planning to invest in methods, tools, and workstations, emphasize the megaprogramming option. Purchase the libraries in addition to the tools to make this approach feasible. Avoid making your software reuse investments a separate target during the battle of the budget. Align with a winner and you will survive. Understand that you must adjust your plans so that they are synchronized with key budget events. For example, demonstrating a capability one month prior to putting in a budget request for the next phase of the effort helps your supporters justify why you, and not your chief competitors, should be funded.

Achievable within the Desired Time Period

Make sure that you can successfully fulfill expectations you've set in both the near and long term. Hopefully, you can establish expectations so that they are aggressive but realistic. Don't sign up to something you know can't be done even when pressured to do so. Remember, your reputation will suffer if the team doesn't deliver. Many times you can declare success and move on when you deliver a prototype that has most of the features you have promised. I have often seen people trying to get out of commitments by making excuses. This approach does not work. However, delivering something that provides 80 to 90 percent of desired functionality and works goes a long way toward developing management confidence in your ability to deliver.

Improving software productivity has proven to be enigmatic in the past. Software reuse represents one of many available approaches you can take to realize such improvements. To be successful with your reuse initiative, you need to get agreement on what your vision for the future is and what strategy should be adopted. Then, you can figure out how to implement your strategy and realize the vision. Last, you must set realistic expectations and get everyone involved to buy into them.

In this section, I have tried to offer some criteria you can use to guide your selection of strategy. In the next, I will provide insight into why you need to write a vision and strategy document, and how you should structure it.

WHY YOU NEED A VISION AND STRATEGY

Many people make the mistake of trying to implement a reuse initiative before they define what they are really trying to do, and why. They try to develop some grand plan of attack before they convince upper management that such an initiative is needed to remain competitive, and the money requested will be well spent. Misunderstandings result and the process often becomes bogged down because nobody seems to be able to agree on what needs to be done, when, and why. The situation gets even more confused when management thinks that their software people already do reuse. They must be convinced that systematic reuse approaches need to replace the more opportunistic tactics that most software organizations currently practice. They must be persuaded that the money they spend on their reuse initiative is justified in terms of its potential impact on the bottom line. They must be told what the competition is doing, and shown that they have no alternative but to move aggressively.

The vision and strategy document is written to communicate these points in a manner that anyone can understand. It is an important document to generate when you are starting up a software reuse program, because it gets all affected stakeholders to agree on the goals they are trying to achieve. In smaller organizations, a well-written white paper can achieve a similar purpose. However, white papers don't seem to work in larger organizations, because they often pit one organization against another, especially when they battle for their piece of the limited engineering or research and development (R&D) budget. To avoid such infighting, the vision statement must be written from the top in a manner independent of whatever organization(s) will be put in charge of execution. The goal underlying the vision statement's development should be getting agreement on what you are trying to do before fighting over how to do it, or who does it.

When I was running the Software Reuse Initiative (SRI) for the Department of Defense, we went in circles for almost a year because nobody had concisely and crisply stated to our upper management what we were trying to do. How could they champion a set of programs when they and those on their staffs didn't know what they were trying to do? Reaching agreement on goals, terminology, and a plan of attack was made more difficult by the fact that I had to get representatives from the Joint Chiefs of Staff, the three services, the Ballistic Missile Defense Organization, and five agencies (Defense Information Systems Agency, Defense Intelligence Agency, Defense Logistics Agency, Defense Mapping Agency, and National Security Agency) to reach consensus. To deal with these and many more political issues, I devised the document hierarchy [1] illustrated in Plan of Action 2.1. Then, I convinced the representatives that the hierarchy was their idea. Next, I generated draft documents for their review and approval. Then, after I got their input, I asked them to help me by getting their organization (e.g., the Air Force, Navy) to approve publication. While the approval process seemed long and tedious, it worked.

The DoD vision-and-strategy document communicated what we were trying to do, and the strategies we planned to use to achieve our goals in terms anyone could understand. We needed a document that developed a consensus picture of what all of us were trying to accomplish so that there would be no confusion on the part of anyone as to the intent of our effort. The document created a roadmap and a top-level set of requirements for our program. Each of the activities in the subsidiary plans were ultimately traced back to the vision document to ensure that they were justified.

To implement our vision, we developed the strategic, tactical, and organizational plans illustrated in Plan of Action 2.1. Each of these documents served a specific purpose. Each was important because it represented the consensus opinion of all of the affected organizations. Designated representatives from the DoD services and agencies worked hard over a period of 18 months to draft these documents. Each representative coordinated with their operating divisions and commands to ensure that the DoD's and their interests were properly addressed. Of course, there were arguments and disagreements during the process. However, agreements were reached and we generated what we thought was the best plan of attack for the DoD at large.

In retrospect, I believe we should have produced an operational concept document in addition to the planning documents. Such a document would describe the management and technical operational concepts we would use at the department level to implement the plans. We addressed some of the processes needed in our operational procedures documents. However, these did not provide the comprehensive guidance needed to pull the initiative together across all of the organizations involved. The service and agency representatives argued that they should each separately address their operational concepts in their execution documentation, because they each had a somewhat different way of doing business. There was merit to this argument, and we at the initiative level backed off.

WHAT GOES INTO A VISION-AND-STRATEGY DOCUMENT?

Most of you have never produced a vision-and-strategy document. What goes into it? At what level do you write it? Who should write it? Should it have a sales or

PLAN OF ACTION 2.1   The SRI's Document Hierarchy

LONG-RANGE VISION

| DoD Software Reuse Initiative Vision and Strategy |

Vision and Strategy

Summarizes what you are trying to achieve and why it is important.

FIVE-YEAR STRATEGY

| DoD Software Reuse Initiative Strategic Plan |

Strategic Plan

Sets in place the strategy you will use to achieve your goals.

TWO-YEAR STRATEGY

Management Plan

Highlights the execution tactics that you will use in the near-term.

| DoD SRI Operational Management Plan |

OPERATIONAL PLANNING PROCESS

Procedures

Puts the processes into place that you will use to implement your plans.

| DoD SRI Procedures |

EXECUTION PLANS

Software Reuse Plans

Tells how the Services and Agencies will implement reuse in a manner consistent with the overall DoD approach.

| Service and Agency Software Reuse Plans |

engineering orientation? These and a host of other questions are probably on your mind.

I have provided an outline for a vision-and-strategy document in Plan of Action 2.2. This builds on what was produced for the DoD Software Reuse Initiative [2] and several other reuse initiatives. I have also provided a somewhat sanitized version of an executive summary that I prepared for one of my telecommunications clients who wanted to pursue an architecturally based initiative, as shown in Plan of Action 2.3. Hopefully, these outlines will provide you some useful insights into what should be put into such a document.

As you have probably noticed, the example executive summary shown in Plan of Action 2.3 is crisply written and results oriented.

In smaller organizations, you can do away with much of this paperwork. Instead of producing reams of paper, a well-written white paper that explains what you are trying to do and why should suffice. Such a paper can be organized into the following five sections and an executive summary:

- *Executive Summary*—Provides a short, well-written summary of the white paper for the executive to read.
- *Challenges or Opportunities*—Summarizes either the challenges (normally competitive, etc.) you face or the opportunities that you see are available to your firm. Tells why what you are proposing to do is important to accomplish in no uncertain terms.
- *What We Can Do About It*—Briefly describes the alternatives that are available. Make sure that you include *do nothing* as one of your options, because maintaining the status quo is something you should consider.
- *Recommended Solution*—Rates the pluses and minuses of each of the options being considered in terms of the business-related evaluation criteria you think are important (maintaining technology leadership, increasing market share, etc.).
- *Feasibility Demonstration*—Outlines your plan to demonstrate the technical and economic feasibility of your recommended solution. Asks for funds to demonstrate feasibility. This approach appeals to management. And next budget cycle, you will find it easier to continue an ongoing project than get a new one started.
- *Anticipated Cost/Benefits*—Includes a high-level business case that shows what you plan is smart to do. Quantify the benefits in terms of cost avoidance or quality improvement. Never promise anything during the first year of the program because of startup costs. Don't promise more than you think you can deliver.

The white paper should be short (not exceed 20 pages) and well written.

SELLING YOUR STRATEGY

Now that you have a vision and strategy or white paper, what do you do with it? Whom can you get to take and run with it? Often, many initiatives do not get off the ground because the ground work needed to sell the program did not get done in a timely fashion. The moment you start writing, start selling your strategy. The best way to do this is to get someone in upper management to champion your cause during the right times during the budget cycle.

How do you find your corporate champions? Most times, they will find you. However, you will have to arm them with the ammunition they need to deal effectively with the politics that often dominate discussions at their level. I have used sales presentations similar to the one portrayed in Figure 2.1 to gain support. If you look at it closely, you will realize that the presentation basically says that you

PLAN OF ACTION 2.2   Vision-and-Strategy Document Outline

Executive Summary

1. Introduction
    1.1 Purpose and Scope
    1.2 Background
    1.3 Definitions
    1.4 Document Overview

2. Reuse Vision
    2.1 Where We'd Like to Be
    2.2 Basic Concepts
    2.3 Underlying Principles
    2.4 Plan of Attack

3. Strategy
    3.1 Develop domains where the greatest opportunities exist to apply reuse techniques
    3.2 Identify the assets to populate domain-specific architectures
    3.3 Establish criteria for deciding the ownership of reusable assets
    3.4 Integrate reuse into the overall system/software life cycle
    3.5 Modify the current acquisition process to foster reuse
    3.6 Develop and apply new business models that incentivize both government and industry to practice reuse
    3.7 Define a process to evaluate reuse success
    3.8 Pursue those technology-based investments that support appropriate reuse-oriented process and product technologies
    3.9 Define and implement a technology transition plan to a reuse-based paradigm

4. Necessary Prerequisite
    4.1 Develop operational concepts that enable use of third-party and commercial off-the-shelf software to populate the architecture
    4.2 Develop requirements for the architecture based upon domain knowledge
    4.3 Develop a project plan to define what work needs to be done, when, and at what cost to build the desired capability
    4.4 Develop a business case, tied to business plans, which justifies investments

5. Measures of Success
    5.1 Competitiveness measures (time to market, price/performance, etc.)
    5.2 Financial measures (cost, contribution to overhead and profit, etc.)
    5.3 Market measures (market share, customer satisfaction, etc.)

6. Summary and Conclusions

7. References

PLAN OF ACTION 2.3   Example Executive Summary

Challenges

The manner in which systems are built is changing. As more and more firms adopt open systems concepts, custom systems are being replaced by those composed primarily of commercial off-the-shelf hardware and software components. This trend creates a variety of new challenges as the work of most engineering organizations changes to become integration instead of development oriented. No longer can firms develop systems from scratch. They can't remain competitive if they pursue this approach any longer. They must instead develop architectures that enable them to execute their and third-party software on multiple platforms, reusing existing off-the-shelf assets whenever possible to reduce time to market and cost. New processes and paradigms must be introduced to define these architectures and put product-line management concepts into operation. Personnel must be trained to work in such environments, and new decision frameworks must be used to take advantage of new technologies and new engineering paradigms.

Opportunities

Luckily, several early adopter organizations in government and industry have developed approaches to deal with these challenges. These groups have demonstrated convincingly that the new architecturally based, product-line paradigm can improve a firm's profitability by shortening time to market, reducing cost, and increasing customer satisfaction. However, as expected, such gains don't come for free. They ask management to champion the change and make the required investments. Patience is also cautioned, as payback may take three to five years.

Basic Concepts

While firms have been trying to reuse software supplied by their completed projects or third parties for years, success has been elusive. The reasons for this are simple. First, the software was designed as a point solution. Nobody seemed to look at its broader applicability across products that comprised the product line. Second, open system standards that enabled software to be portable across workstations supplied by different vendors did not exist until recently. Third, software engineers did not trust the hand-me-down software and felt it would take less time to rebuild than reengineer the application. Experience has shown that these barriers can be overcome when suitable, standards-based, product-line architectures are introduced for a specific application domain. The 20 percent of the software that is responsible for 80 percent of the reuse across the product line can thus be identified and built one time. Standard building blocks that run on top of some common operating system, such as POSIX, can be built to bind applications across platforms to embrace common services. Processes can be introduced to increase the software engineers' trust in the existing reusable components, and make sure new products adhere to the architectural frameworks.

PLAN OF ACTION 2.3   *(Continued)*

Underlying Principles	The six principles upon which high levels of software reuse are founded include:

- *Domain-specific reuse*—Reuse occurs within well-bounded areas aligned with lines of business where application expertise is available and market potential/requirements are known.
- *Product-line architectures*—The assets to be reused are a natural fall-out of an analysis of the architecture developed to grow families of similar products for both vertical and horizontal markets.
- *Layered architectures*—The product-line architectures developed are structured to support industry-wide standards (POSIX, CORBA, etc.) and the definition of the services needed to support the OSI reference model and other evolving communications standards.
- *Off-the-shelf components*—The product-line architectures will be populated with compliant and proven off-the-shelf hardware and software components whenever possible.
- *Process-supported reuse paradigm*—Software reuse is an integral and transparent part of the systems/software engineering processes and related toolsets used within the firm.
- *Product-line management concepts*—The management infrastructure (organization, decision processes, business and technical practices, etc.) used by the firm supports exploitation of reusable software assets within and across product lines.

Plan of Attack	The firm plans to demonstrate the superiority of its product-line architecture concepts in one or more domains. Pathfinder projects will be used to develop an appropriate product-line architecture and put a responsive engineering and management infrastructure in place within selected business units. Then, emphasis will be placed on transitioning the results achieved to different lines of business organizations in a planned manner.
Goals	The five goals set for this five-year initiative are:

- Reduce the amount of time needed to bring a new product to market from years to months.
- Reduce the cost of fielding a new system by a factor of five.
- Improve the quality of new systems by at least a factor of 10.
- Improve the level of customer satisfaction with the firm's products and product lines.
- Be perceived as the industry leader for systems by your customers.

Vision	To achieve these goals, we see the firm establishing a high-performance, affordable, distributed architecture built to take full advantage of standards-based, commercial off-the-shelf hardware and software components for the designated product lines.
Strategy	The approach to realize these goals is based upon the following seven strategic elements:

- Develop a layered, domain-specific, product-line architecture that builds on experience to satisfy market requirements.

PLAN OF ACTION 2.3   *(Continued)*

- Ensure that the architecture takes advantage of existing standards so that it can use proven, commercial off-the-shelf components.
- Acquire those architectural components with high reuse potential across the product line, and qualify them for widespread use.
- Rework both the managerial and technical processes to provide needed support for an architecturally based reuse paradigm.
- Acquire the tools (building, development, operations) used to automate the disciplined development, maintenance, and support of products.
- Develop the metrics and measurement strategies that can be used to determine whether the initiatives have been successful.
- Pursue technology-based investments that support architecturally based reuse processes and product line developments.

Necessary Prerequisites

The following five prerequisite actions need to be completed in the near term in order for this vision to become a reality:
- Develop an operational concept that enables use of third-party software to populate the architecture.
- Develop a high-level set of requirements for the architecture based upon existing domain knowledge.
- Develop a project plan to define what work needs to be done, when, and at what cost to build up the desired capability.
- Develop a business case, tied to business plans, which justifies the investment outlined in the project plan.
- Develop a demonstration testbed as a show-and-tell facility.

Measures of Success

The following three measures of success will be used to demonstrate that the goals established for this effort have been satisfactorily fulfilled:
- Use of the architecture and product-line management concepts result in significant reductions in time to market and cost.
- Use of the architecture and product-line management concepts play a major part in winning new business and increasing market share.
- Use of the architecture and product-line management concepts contribute directly to reduced overhead and increased profitability.

Summary & Conclusions

This document summarizes a vision of how the firm can take on the leadership role in the telecommunications marketplace. It suggests that large reductions in cost and time to market can be achieved when product-line architectures are used as the basis for system developments within the specified domain of interest.

will lose your competitive edge unless you mount a reuse initiative that makes it possible to use third-party packages. Who would not agree with this argument?

There are other messages that will help you sell your initiative and solicit high-level support for your reuse initiative. The three that I have had the most success with are: *Economies of scale*—Sell your initiative based upon levels of

Software Reuse Checklist

Some guidelines that I suggest you follow when you write this document include the following:

- ✔ If you cannot say what you have to say in 20 pages or less, don't write it.
- ✔ Make sure the executive summary is well written, as many senior executives may opt to read nothing but this digest.
- ✔ Make the document both factual and sales oriented (i.e., a well-written proposal). Achieve the required balance by focusing on what can be gained if the strategies outlined are successful, not on the current situation.
- ✔ Give pertinent information about the history of the initiative under background. Discuss the challenges your organization faces from a matter-of-fact viewpoint. Tell readers what you want to achieve, and why it is important to them.
- ✔ Establish measurable objectives for the initiative, and paint in the vision section the picture of where you would like to be. Make your statements succinct. Don't overwhelm or overburden the reader.
- ✔ Summarize your thrusts and tie them together so that the reader sees how they help to achieve objectives. Don't confuse tactics with strategy. Strategies are long term, while tactics are nearer term.
- ✔ Use the prerequisites section to discuss what management must do at startup to make sure the initiative will be successful. This is an important section, because it lets you tell management what changes must be made to set the stage for the initiative.
- ✔ Develop your measures of success to answer the question, So what? Management always seems to want to know: If I did not do this, what would happen?
- ✔ Make sure any facts you cite in the document can stand up to close scrutiny.
- ✔ Make sure that what you say in your summary and conclusions agrees with your executive summary. Often, they are written at different times by different people.

reuse in the order of 50 to 90 percent. Of course, the only way to achieve this is to pursue an initiative where assets can be reused across a well-defined product-line architecture; *New markets*—Sell your reuse program by showing how assets you develop for internal use can be sold externally for a profit. Be sure to scope your dual-use program so that it does not give away any of the elements that contribute to your core competency; and *Technical leadership*—For those in more of the services and consulting end of the business, sell your initiative based upon the skill sets it provides the workforce. Such skills, knowledge, and abilities would be prized in any client setting. The presentation in Figure 2.1 can be easily modified to support any and all of these sales strategies. I hope it serves you well. In any case, you probably should supplement it with a competitive assessment to let your management know what the firms with whom you directly compete in your marketplace are doing, and how you expect to take the lead.

SUMMARY

■ A vision and strategy document communicates what you are trying to achieve with reuse over the long haul.

SETTING THE STAGE

- Our products are software-intensive
  - More than 50% of our engineering costs are for software

- Our users continue to want more features and functionality
  - That is the primary reason why we have software

- Software cost, quality and time-to-market continue to be issues
  - While competitive, we need to continue to improve

- New software technology is becoming available which addresses these issues
  - Use of COTS, object-oriented techniques and rapid proto-typing paradigms

Copyright RCI, 1996

THE OPPORTUNITY

- Exploit the use of new software technology to reduce costs and time-to-market

- Systematically reuse third-party packages and commercial off-the-shelf software

- Make our products more open in terms of their standards-base

- Make our products more portable across platforms

- Respond to user requests more quickly with the features and functions they desire

APPROACH - DEVELOP A SOFTWARE ARCHITECTURE FOR EACH OF OUR PRODUCT LINES

Copyright RCI, 1996

FIGURE 2.1a Sales presentation.

WHY IS ACTION NEEDED?

- We need to tap this technology to remain competitive
  - Our major competitor is getting a leg up on us
  - They have a major initiative under way to insert software architecture and reuse technology
  - They are starting to strategically partner with many of our suppliers
  - They are starting to talk about their initiatives to our key account representatives
  - If successful, they could gain substantial market share at our expense
- We need to be thought of as a market leader
  - Must maintain technology leadership is addition to maintaining an edge in price/performance

WHY WE NEED YOUR SUPPORT?

- Putting technology to work takes a lot of time, patience and effort
  - We need 1-2 years of sustained effort to catch-up
  - We need another 2-3 years to develop a leadership position
- We need a champion at the corporate level
  - Understand what we are trying to do
  - Explain why it is important to other executives
  - Help us overcome the resistance from the middle
  - Help us win the battle of the budget
- We believe you want to be our champion
  - Appreciate your support in the past
  - Need your support in the future

FIGURE 2.1b Sales presentation.

- You must sell your vision and strategy to management in order to get them to commit the resources you will need to make your initiative work.
- Vision should be long range and related to factors that influence your ability to compete and realize a profit.
- Strategies need to be selected to be consistent with your firm's plans for the future, and its corporate culture.

OUR PLANS

- Focus on software architectures in the long term
  - Consistent with our product-line orientation
  - Provides us with a transition path for our existing products
  - Lets us design our products to take advantage of COTS and third-party software to the maximum degree possible

- Take advantage of near-term opportunities to increase reuse
  - Will acquire a COTS reuse library to make reusable assets widely available as a first step
  - Will promote the reuse of software assets we already own

- Get our users and suppliers involved as we figure out what to do to get ready for the future

Copyright RCI, 1996

THE EXPECTED BENEFITS

- Market leadership
  - The right products with the right features and functions
  - The best price/performance on the market
  - The highest perceived quality for the price

- Improved customer satisfaction
  - Good value for their dollar
  - Great responsiveness to problems

- Enhanced image
  - Viewed as the industry leader

- Reduced software engineering costs

- Quicker time to market

Copyright RCI, 1996

FIGURE 2.1c Sales presentation.

- A well-written white paper that explains the vision and why it is important to pursue it will suffice for small organizations.
- The document should be aimed at selling your reuse initiative to both your champions and critics.

You are probably thinking that generating all of the documentation illustrated in Planning Guide 1 is overkill. You are absolutely right for small organizations. Under such situations, I would generate a white paper and lay out my plans in it. However, I would generate more and more paper as my organization grew bigger and bigger. Organizational plans could then be mapped to an overall strategy that implemented my vision using such a documentation framework.

WHAT ARE THE NEXT STEPS?

- Get our reuse library operational
- Perform feasibility demonstration for selected product line
  - Start small, build big
  - Develop an architecture and migration path
  - Figure out how to address known risks
  - Incrementally demonstrate capabilities
- Take advantage of lessons others have learned
- Learn from our users, teammates and suppliers
  - Involve them and gain their commitment
- Catch up and take a leadership position

SUMMARY & CONCLUSIONS

- Our competitors have launched a major initiative aimed at increasing market share
- We need to counter by taking the initiative
- To gain support, we need your help as our corporate champion
- We believe we can mount a successful counterattack
- We need your help in selling our program
- We believe in starting small, building big
- We are open to your suggestions

FIGURE 2.1d Sales presentation.

REFERENCES

1. Donald Reifer, "DoD Software Reuse Initiative: Status, Achievements, and Lessons Learned," Defense Information Systems Agency, August 1995.
2. DoD Software Reuse Initiative, *Vision and Strategy,* November 13, 1995.

Reuse Operational Concepts

OPERATIONAL CONCEPT DOCUMENT

Now, you must translate your vision and strategy into action. To do this, you must have an understanding of *what* you are trying to achieve, and *how* you are going to achieve it. The *what* should be part of your vision statement. The *how* must be captured in your operational concept document (OCD) and business plan (BP). These key documents justify the initiative and define how you will make the transition from concept into reality within the target domains of interest. Because of its importance, I devote Chapters 5 through 7 to the topic of business planning and business-case preparation.

The OCD defines the set of operational concepts you will use to implement a cost-effective reuse program. It identifies the changes you must make to your management, and technical process to stimulate widespread adoption of the reuse throughout your organization. An example OCD outline is shown in Plan of Action 3.1. This outline reflects the experience that I gained developing such a document. Guidelines that I suggest you follow when you prepare this document include:

- As with all important documents, place special attention on the executive summary. Many of your readers may not take the time to read more.
- Provide a roadmap so that your different classes of readers (engineers, program managers, executives, etc.) can logically pick their way through the document.
- Summarize your reuse vision and strategy right up front. It is probably wrong to assume that your readers have read this document beforehand.

PLAN OF ACTION 3.1 Operational Concept Document Outline

Executive Summary

1. Introduction
   1.1 Purpose and Scope
   1.2 New Operational Concepts
   1.3 Vision Overview
   1.4 Definitions of Key Terms
   1.5 Document Overview
   1.6 Reader's Roadmap

2. Architecture Overview
   2.1 Client/Server Concepts
   2.2 Layered Architectures
   2.3 Service Model
      2.3.1 Common Support Applications
      2.3.2 Infrastructure Services
   2.4 Networking Concepts
      2.4.1 Internet
      2.4.2 Intranet

3. The Product-Line Paradigm
   3.1 Product-Line Concepts
   3.2 Standards Framework
   3.3 Customer Involvement/Satisfaction
   3.4 Key Process Areas
      3.4.1 Architecture Management
      3.4.2 Integrated Product Teams
      3.4.3 Resources Management
      3.4.4 Reviews and Approvals
      3.4.5 Strategic Partnerships

4. Technical Concept of Operations
   4.1 Domain-Specific Architectures
   4.2 COTS and Third-Party Reuse
   4.3 Internet/Intranet Exploitation
   4.4 Key Process Areas
      4.4.1 Domain Engineering
      4.4.2 Architectural Engineering
      4.4.3 Applications Engineering
      4.4.4 Asset Management
      4.4.5 Interface Management
   4.5 Integrated Tool Environment
   4.6 Demonstration Testbed

5. Management Concept of Operations
   5.1 Organizational Roles and Responsibilities
   5.2 Architecturally Based Process Model
   5.3 Operational Scenarios/Use Cases

PLAN OF ACTION 3.1   *(Continued)*

NOTE: Many of the key process areas (KPAs) identified are the same as those identified in the Software Engineering Institute's Capability Maturity Model [1]. Practices under these KPAs need to be modified to address reuse considerations. The Software Engineering Institute is currently considering ways of accommodating such revisions.

- If you are embarking on a paradigm shift, explain the new approach you have selected and outline the paths different groups within the organizations will take to make an orderly transition to its use.
- If you are embracing an architectural reuse strategy, discuss your concepts and provide models that give the reader insight into what you are trying to do.
- Explain your technical and managerial concepts of operations from a process point of view. Discuss what processes need to be changed. Provide use scenarios to show how these processes will be used operationally to get the job done.

- Don't be afraid to recommend needed organizational changes in the document. Make sure you justify the changes and identify who should become the process owners.
- Be sure to discuss how you plan to address technology transfer in the document. Because of its importance, I recommend treating it in a separate section.

The business plan (BP) that often accompanies the OCD supplements it with target opportunities, potential returns, a description of the work to be done, the resources required, the schedules, and management practices to be followed. Specifically, the BP identifies:

- The near-term business goals and the projected returns, should they be realized
- A summary of the work required to achieve these goals, along with task statements
- The organizations who will do the work, along with the scope of their activities
- A detailed plan of action and milestones for getting the work done in a timely manner
- A summary of the budgets established for each of the tasks in the action plan
- A master milestone schedule and task relationship diagram for the effort (PERT chart)
- The controls established to determine the status of the effort, and measure its progress
- The management review strategy and any reporting requirements
- Any metrics and measurements that will be used to provide added visibility

Don't be scared by this list. Although it looks formidable, it is really content, not bulk, that's desired. You don't need to prepare lengthy, formal documents. In some cases, you can get by with an annotated briefing. In others, you can include most of this information in the white paper you develop to communicate your reuse vision and strategy. Again, the larger and more distributed the organization, the more paperwork involved. Such growth is understandable because the paperwork is being developed as a communications and consensus-building tool. The important message is that you write down what you plan on doing, so your thoughts can be made visible and can be shared with others involved in the effort.

For corporate-wide reuse initiatives, a business plan/case may be produced in addition to the OCD. The documents may be separated to convey different information to different audiences. The OCD will probably be written for engineering groups. In contrast, the business plans may be used to communicate proprietary or privileged budgetary information to the financial community. Because the languages and needs of these two communities diverge greatly, it may make a lot of sense to prepare separate documents.

SELECTING YOUR REUSE PARADIGM

There are several reuse life-cycle models that you might want to consider when you frame your operational concepts. Such models consist of the steps involved in software development, their products, and the rules that govern how you determine whether you are finished. The three most popular life-cycle reuse models or paradigms that I've seen put into use include: Dual-development, middleware/component-based and the rapid prototyping approach.

Dual Development Life-Cycle

As discussed in Chapter 1 and shown in Figure 3.1, applications and domain engineering functions are cleanly separated from each other and performed in parallel. The applications engineering function concerns itself with building the product, while the domain engineering function focuses on defining the architecture and populating it with the right reusable software assets.

The reuse library is a mechanism the two groups use to manage their assets and handle their distribution. The beauty of this approach is that architecture activities can be performed by specialists without adversely impacting the software development process. In addition, each group can select the paradigm best for it. For example, applications can be developed using a spiral development model [2], while domain engineering is performed using an iterative process [3] that emphasizes rapid prototyping. The focus of this approach is on developing the architecture, because most adherents feel it creates the framework for figuring out what is reusable.

Middleware/Component-Based Approach

As an alternative, the middleware/component-based reuse approach [4] shown in Figure 3.2 has a dedicated following. Here, reusable software components are spawned/used during each stage of the software life cycle in a planned and systematic manner. No major change to the way you do business is required. Standard application program interfaces (APIs) are used to glue pretested components to a middleware layer designed to isolate programmers from platform and architecture-specific peculiarities. Legacy applications can be interfaced to the middleware without change by using wrappers.

Software developers build their applications by taking fine-grained components from their class libraries, and integrating them into working systems using templates or frameworks. When behavior is well defined, generators may be used to produce the application directly from specifications. Reviews are held throughout the life cycle to identify the assets needed to populate the libraries. When a market exists, vendors may be convinced to develop other needed components for sale as COTS products. Under some situations, firms may develop the components

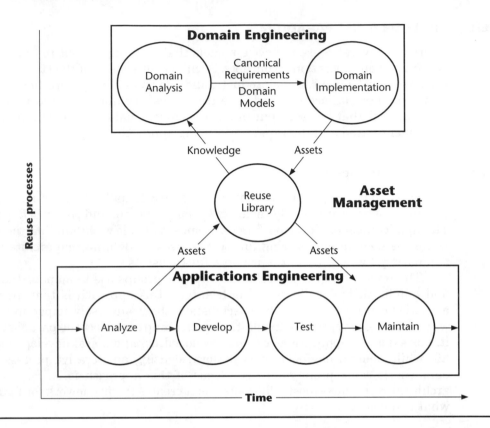

FIGURE 3.1 Dual development paradigm. This work was developed in part under a grant from DARPA to the Software Productivity Consortium NFP, Inc., who owns the copyright thereto. The content of the information does not necessarily reflect the position or the policy of the Government and no official endorsement should be inferred.

themselves, especially if they relate to one of their core competencies (i.e., a mining firm would develop its own components for mining applications if it provided its users with some advantage over COTS). Because this approach focuses on the use of middleware as the glue, it is sometimes referred to as the *middleware approach* to software reuse.

Rapid Prototyping Approach

The rapid prototyping paradigm shown in Figure 3.3 serves as our third and final option. Reusable assets are prototyped anytime during the life cycle that a reuse opportunity is identified. The philosophy is to try the components before you buy or build them. Again, the emphasis is on cost containment. Only those components

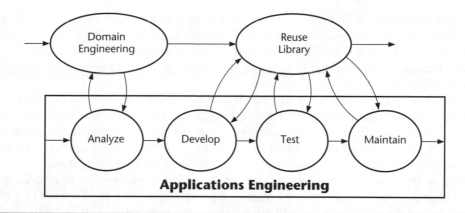

FIGURE 3.2 Middleware/component-based approach.

that withstand the test of fire are raised to product status. If it is hard to reuse, it won't be used, is the rule used to make decisions.

Engineers are tasked to look for opportunities as they perform their jobs. Often, rewards are provided to those who are successful (bonuses, prizes, time off with pay, etc.). Reuse occurs in an *ad hoc,* not a systematic, manner. Instead of

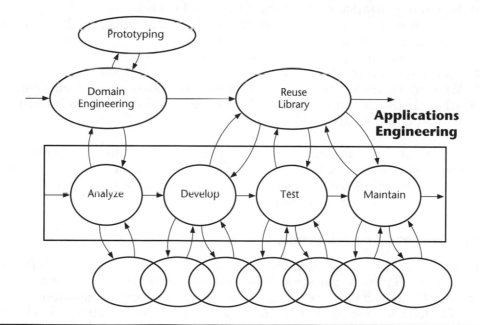

FIGURE 3.3 Rapid prototyping paradigm.

being a planned function, reuse relies on the tenacity of the engineers tasked to perform it. This approach does have some redeeming virtues. High levels of reuse can be achieved using rapid prototyping without a major infrastructure change when engineers are properly trained and motivated to handle the additional responsibilities.

Each of these approaches has merit because each has been made to work in practice. Selection of the right approach is not easy. Yet, to succeed, you must make a decision. Because the paradigm impacts your process framework, you won't be able to refine your operational concepts without it. Of course, you could create a hybrid that takes advantage of the strengths, and overcomes the weaknesses of the available options. While not perfect, my preference is middleware/component-based development, because it permits you to use the dual life-cycle approach to develop your architecture, and rapid prototyping to develop components. It really lets you employ a hybrid or compromise approach that takes the best from all of those covered.

Questions that need to be answered as you select an applicable paradigm include:

- Is the approach consistent with your vision and strategy?
- Can expected results be achieved within the expected time period?
- Is your budget sufficient and do you have a multiyear commitment?
- Is your organization ready to adopt the paradigm selected?
- Are your customers willing to accept the selected paradigm, or will you have to convince them to waive their requirements?
- Is management supportive of introducing a new paradigm?
- Can your existing infrastructure sustain a paradigm change?
- What education and training will be needed to make the approach work?
- What are the risks involved and what processes are you using to reduce them to acceptable levels?

As you can see, many trade-offs exist that must be evaluated. Other questions come to mind that will need to be answered as you implement your process framework. You must have the answers in your pocket, because someone will ask for them as you brief your recommendations up the line.

TECHNICAL CONCEPTS OF OPERATIONS

There are a number of technical issues you must consider in your OCD, including the selection of a reuse paradigm. The additional issues to address seem to be a function of your current state of process maturity, your technical workforce's overall skills, knowledge, and abilities, and your organizational readiness for change. I will explain each of these factors as I relate the items in the OCD outline in Plan of Action 3.1 to each of the issue categories I have listed in the preceding.

Paradigm

As illustrated in Plan of Action 3.1, the way you develop software will change radically because you selected the dual life-cycle paradigm for use. As your first step, introduce the concept of domain-specific software architectures in your OCD. This concept requires you to model your past experience to develop a reference architecture for the domain. This architecture becomes your framework for deciding what you make or buy for the product line.

Reusable COTS components, along with those developed by third parties, can then be used to populate the architecture if they satisfy the requirements you are trying to satisfy. Architecture reviews must be held to make sure that products that evolve comply with the reference architectural standards as they are built, tested, and brought to market. Existing policies, standards, processes, and practices must be changed to be consistent with the technical changes needed to support the conversion to this product line-oriented way of doing business.

State of Process Maturity

As part of the change, you will notice that five key process areas have been identified in Plan of Action 3.1. The Software Engineering Institute (SEI) defines a key process area as a cluster of related activities that, when performed collectively, achieve a set of goals considered important for establishing process capability [5]. Because the dual-development and the other reuse paradigms are so new, few firms have factored its process requirements into the practices they use to describe their key process areas. These practices need to be institutionalized in the more mature organizations (i.e., SEI Level 3 and above), and tailoring guidelines must be generated so that projects/product-line organizations can adapt them to their unique requirements. If your state of process maturity is low, you will probably have problems because you will have to insert new practices slowly into your organization project by project. If your state of process maturity is high, you will also have problems because you will have to change a set of practices that are widely used, accepted, working, and being optimized across organizations.

Skills, Knowledge, and Abilities of the Technical Workforce

You must develop the skills, knowledge, and abilities of your technical workforce to perform the work described in the OCD. Again, because reuse technology is new, there are few books and university courses on the topics. Many of those available have often been produced by researchers who have limited practical experience with problems of scale. Luckily, several excellent courses are being taught by government organizations that make their courseware available free to the general public [6,7]. For example, the Army Reuse Center gives a terrific free course on domain analysis monthly at its Fort Belvoir, Virginia, site. In addition, several seminars are being taught by experienced consultants who have real-world experience.

There are four simple things you can do to make your training program more effective. First, develop your training requirements and prepare a skill inventory for your staff. Next, take the time to tailor needed courseware (i.e., materials you can buy or get off the shelf that meet your requirements) to reflect your processes, culture, and folklore. Third, use a real and relevant project as a focusing tool to illustrate the points about which you are talking in your OCD. Finally, arm your people with the desired skills, knowledge, and abilities by training in a just-in-time manner as they start to put the concepts to work operationally.

Organizational Readiness for Change

Many organizations are neither ready nor willing to use state of the art. Independent of the reason why, it would be a major mistake to try to insert technology that these organizations are unprepared to use. You must match the technology you are trying to transfer to the readiness of the organization to take and use it. For example, it would be inappropriate to bring tools into an organization when the workforce did not understand why they were being introduced, what methods they supported, and when and how they could be used. Such tools would become shelfware under such conditions. Because much of the technology for reuse is new and immature, make sure that you prepare those who are going to use it for its idiosyncrasies. If you don't, you will find that introducing the architectural and process concepts that permeate the OCD outline will create a shock wave that will disturb normal operations. So will the use of immature tools if your staff is not warned to be wary of them. Do the simple things first. Then, build toward technical superiority and sophistication.

Example Technical Concepts

Let us look at how you would write up some of the technical concepts that appear in the OCD outline. The tendency normally is to provide a lot of stuff you can sink your teeth into. I think this is a mistake. Your practices are where you put the details. In contrast, your OCD is where you outline the concepts and high-level requirements for your practices. What follows is a writeup that illustrates the point. This writeup was taken from an OCD that I recently prepared for one of my clients.

COTS and Third-Party Reuse   The domain-specific architecture we've developed contains a domain model, reference requirements, and a reference architecture for the product line within the target application area. The reference architecture was developed ultimately to reduce the amount of work and thereby the time and effort associated with product development. This will be accomplished by using the following three approaches which are part of this concept of operation:

- *Increased Reuse*—Use of the reference architecture and the qualified components that are acquired to populate it should reduce considerably the resources (time, talent, etc.) required to get a product out of the door. To facilitate large-scale reuse, the current reward structure will be changed so that raises, bonuses, and promotions will be based at least partially on achievement of reuse goals.
- *Increased Use of Standard Metatools*—Use of application generators and GUI (Graphical User Interface) builders as part of the architecture to accommodate development of those reusable assets that often vary from customer to customer (screens, bindings to client libraries, database population tools, etc.). The architecture proposed for the product line contains a developer's kit to house such tools as reusable software assets. It also uses standard interfaces to bind service layers to both the user and the machine.
- *Increased Use of Third-Party and Commercial Off-The-Shelf (COTS) Components*—Use of standards-based architectures should enable existing third-party and COTS components to be reused as is. Each component acquired will be tested prior to its incorporation into a production build. If needed components designated reusable in the referenced architecture are not readily available, we will try to form strategic partnerships with our suppliers, both hardware and software, to develop them. Such partnerships by design will provide both parties with strong incentives for development.

The operational concepts employed will encourage the development and reuse of pretested and qualified components. As will be elaborated in subsequent paragraphs, an index of these components will be available online via the Internet. The components will be classified and stored in our software reuse library, which has been established at the line of business level to make holdings visible and easily accessible. These libraries are extensions of those used for software development, and are part of our software engineering environment. Assets in such libraries are subjected to various levels of testing, depending on their intended levels of reuse.

Key Technical Process Areas

Now, let us look at one of the key process areas (KPA) that appears in our OCD outline to get some insight into how it should be written. I have chosen architectural engineering because it is not a KPA that is presently part of the Software Engineering Institute's Capability Maturity Model. The level of writeup is illustrative of what I recommend for an OCD.

Architectural Engineering   Architectural engineering performs the processes/practices you will use to develop a reference architecture for their product line. The reference architecture is a high-level, basic design for the range of related applications included within the scope of your domain model. It should be communicated using the three architectural viewpoints illustrated in Figure 3.4. It should be provided in the form of a use case or usage scenario (the operational architecture), connectivity block diagram represented using a standard domain engineering notation (the technical architecture), and your standards profile, list of design principles, list of constraints, and qualified/preferred parts list (the systems architecture).

Operationally, the reference architecture and customer requirements will provide the starting point for all future product designs. First, an architecture will be developed by mapping requirements to a proposed technical solution and overlaying the operational and systems architecture on top of it to ensure that it satisfies usage needs and design constraints. As shown in Figure 3.5, once a suitable design has been developed, both engineering (form/fit/function) and management (cost/schedule/function) trade-offs should be performed to refine the design and develop alternative solutions that satisfy packaging, delivery, and programmatic restraints. Based upon the results of this analysis, product proposals can be formulated. Each will be evaluated on its merits by product-line management before they will consider issuing a work permit to authorize work on the product to commence.

The following building codes need to be in place to ensure that architectural engineering processes used by the project incorporate architecture, product-line, and reuse considerations:

- Practices make sure the architectural elements are mapped to the reference requirements and the domain model upon which they are founded.
- Practices make sure that all three architectural views have been captured and correlated in the product design.
- Practices make it easy to use the reference architecture to develop an architectural design.
- Practices are compatible with those adopted for architectural engineering, applications engineering, and asset management.

MANAGEMENT CONCEPT OF OPERATIONS

There are also a number of management issues you must consider as you prepare your OCD. These tend to be more difficult to get agreement on because they may impact your management infrastructure (organizations, decision structure, management processes, etc.). Yet, such changes are often essential, especially if you are trying to motivate some culture change. As illustrated in our OCD outline in Plan of Action 3.1, the primary management issues you need to treat include organizational roles and responsibilities, user involvement, necessary process changes, and

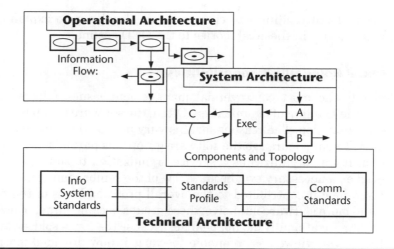

FIGURE 3.4 Three views of an architecture.

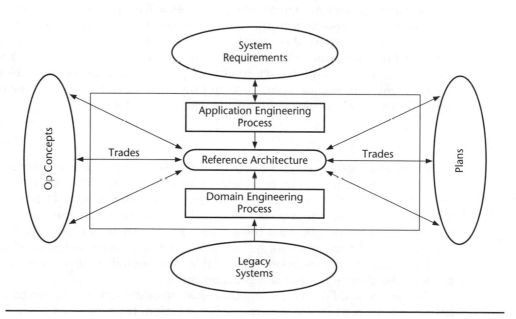

FIGURE 3.5 Architectural trade-offs.

organizational readiness to change. Again, I will try to explain these factors by relating issues in these categories to the OCD outline.

Organizational Roles and Responsibilities

Probably the most controversial management issues I have experienced come under the heading of organization. Often, the software group is buried deep within the organization. The reasons for this vary but for the most part are the result of history. Twenty years ago the software group was part of some engineering organization. It was organized as a service organization to some product group. It was viewed as a necessary evil, because few of the senior managers understood what it did and how it contributed to the overall profit and loss of the firm. As products became more software intensive, these groups became larger. However, their placement organizationally did not change, because the firms sold systems not software. Software was viewed as an enabler because it now provided most of the product's features.

Some software managers were promoted into executive ranks, but few of them have made it into the line-of-business or product-line organizations. The reason cited for this was that few software engineers had manufacturing experience, and that was where most of the profits were made. Many firms are reevaluating this position now that manufacturing has changed into an integration business. Because many of the current issues they face are software oriented, they are looking to place software people into the executive ranks. As you can imagine, there is a lot of opposition to this movement primarily from the powers that be. Many senior executives do not talk the same language as software engineers. Many feel that software engineers do not make good managers, because they cannot address the many multidisciplinary compromises that go into a product development. One compromise solution is to bring a chief software engineer into the line-of-business organization to provide vision and integration.

Customer/Users Involvement

Whatever changes you make need to be understood by your customers/users. This can ease their pain as your organization makes the transition to a new way of doing business. Often, the change can provide an opportunity to improve your level of service and increase customer satisfaction. In some cases, such changes may have little impact because the software group's customer interface is handled through a third party, such as systems engineering or some program office. However, when such improvement is desirable, you should involve your customers/users in the change process and get their inputs.

You also should determine whether existing customer-oriented processes need improvement (distribution control, documentation, training, etc.). If they do, you can try to accommodate such change as you revamp your processes. This becomes easier when you have done the proper planning and adequately prepared those involved with the change. I have found working with the customers/users to develop usage scenarios or use cases to be very valuable. I thought I knew how they used my products until I sat down and found out the truth. Modeling what they did and how they did it was very revealing. In addition to improving understanding, these models can be used to verify the sequence, flow, timing, and control logic of the operational architecture.

Necessary Process Changes

You cannot help but notice that we identified 15 management key process areas in Plan of Action 3.1 that need your attention. Luckily, most of these already exist in the SEI Capability Maturity Model (CMM). All you will need to do for existing KPAs is rewrite them so that they address reuse concerns. The only two new KPAs proposed are patents and supplier management. The General Agreement on Tariffs and Trade requires firms involved in international commerce to provide protection for software innovations. Patents, trademarks, and copyrights are the primary techniques firms use to provide such protection. Determining who owns the rights to technical data and computer software becomes important when you use or plan on selling COTS and third-party software.

Electronic commerce/electronic data interchange is another new area where further process guidance is necessary. With regard to supplier management, you must define practices that enable you to get your suppliers to provide you with the necessary functions in their COTS and third-party software products. There are many more management issues to tackle under this heading. We will address most of them in the remainder of this book.

Organizational Readiness for Change

As stated in the previous section, many firms are neither ready nor willing to make changes. Management has different reasons for their reluctance. Why change what we are doing when we are making money? is often the cry. If the system is not broken, why mess with it? is often the response. Middle management is by its very nature resistant to change. After all, change to them represents the risk of the unknown.

To overcome the opposition, you can employ many strategies. You can have senior management tell them to do it. You can plead and try to convince them that the change is warranted based upon its merits. You can show them why what you propose makes sense, and work with them to overcome their objections. Spend the time and do something that you know will work. Middle management support is essential. You must have it to be successful. You must figure out how to overcome the resistance.

Example Management Concepts

Now, let us look at how you would write up some of the management concepts that appear in the OCD outline. Often, the tendency is to gloss over and try to avoid the tough political issues. Many think focusing on them will jeopardize your initiative and make your OCD unacceptable. I do not agree with this line of reasoning. Senior management needs to know what they must do for you to become successful. It is your responsibility to tell them in the OCD, but you have to word it in such a way that it is both sensible and nonthreatening. The following writeup on a proposed organizational change in a large firm illustrates the point. This writeup was taken from an OCD that I prepared for one of my clients.

Organizational Changes   The firm we are talking about is decentralized and composed of many companies that are organized in a line-of-business organization. While its companies may be geographically clustered by nation (France, Germany, etc.) or national market area (Latin American, Pacific Rim, etc.), its product and product lines are generated by teams whose players may come from many organizations. Line-of-business organizations are delegated profit-and-loss responsibility. Software organizations are traditionally part of the engineering groups of these companies. Customers are mostly operating companies, such as your local telephone service provider.

Because accountability is at a low level, there are few centralized organizations reporting at the corporate level. The major exception is the research-and-development (R&D) budget and the central R&D laboratories. Fundamental research is done at the laboratories. Product research is typically done by the operating company. Vision, coordination, and research ranking are handled by a central R&D council.

The firm manages the development of its products using a classical matrix management scheme within its line-of-business organizations. Engineering organizations are tasked by project management groups with product developments. Customer requirements are gathered and used as the driving force behind product developments. Marketing, manufacturing, and other groups contribute as needed during the entire product life cycle. Products under such a scheme are separate entities. Each is funded based on its own merit. Project managers are rewarded for delivering products that satisfy specified requirements on time and within budget. As currently structured, the system provides few incentives to those who build components that will be reused by others. Instead, focus is placed on making the delivery at hand, and little attention seems placed on levering projects to address future requirements for products or product lines.

There are several approaches others have put into place to address architecture, product line, and reuse in similar organizations. Most call for creation of some centralized organization whose job is to take advantage of reuse opportunities that exist in licensing, partnering, and cross-group component developments.

The issue with such organizations is always who pays the bill. Resistance mounts whenever a tax is levied across all product lines to pay for a central organization. Product-line organizations always feel the money would be better spent locally instead of by a group outside their span of control. Funds could be better directed, they argue.

For the firm to reap the benefits of systematic reuse, the organizational realignment displayed in Figure 3.6 is recommended. This scheme represents the minimum change necessary to put the operational concepts in this document into practice. The scheme calls for assignment of a chief software engineer

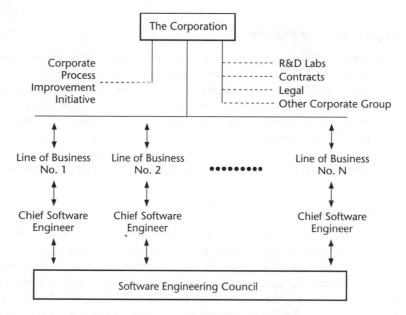

Council roles and responsibilities

- Owns architecture, product-line, and reuse software initiative
- Coordinates product-line needs with corporate groups
- Addresses common asset development proposals
- Works any corporate-wide engineering issues
- Coordinates enterprise-wide licensing requirements
- Arranges technical aspects of strategic partnerships
- Addresses interoperability needs across product lines
- Chairs corporate-wide shared asset change control board

FIGURE 3.6 Recommended organizational realignment.

to each line-of-business organization. This individual would own the architecture and be responsible for ensuring each product within the product line complied with the building-code requirements. Each chief software engineer would sit on a software engineering council. The software council would coordinate corporate-wide product-line needs in the areas of process improvement, technology development, and licensing and partnering initiatives with those centralized groups currently tasked to accomplish them. It would form working groups as needed to address specific engineering issues that might require a consensus to pull off or have company-wide impact (e.g., selection of a standard middleware component).

Key Management Process Areas

Now, let us look at one of the key process areas (KPA) that appears in our OCD outline to get some insight into how it should be written. I have chosen supplier management for two reasons. First, it is an important element of a COTS/third-party software reuse strategy. Second, because it is not a KPA that is presently part of the Software Engineering Institute's Capability Maturity Model. I have also included a writeup on configuration management, because it is illustrative of the changes you will have to make to support whatever reuse paradigm you select. The level of writeups are illustrative of what I recommend for an OCD.

Supplier Management

Suppliers are firms who provide third-party and commercial off-the-shelf software under some form of contract or licensing agreement. Typically, these firms supply the tools and specialized libraries that you use to generate your products. Like subcontract management, the purpose of the supplier management KPA is to make sure the processes used lead to selection of qualified software suppliers, provide motivation for reuse, permit effective management, and ensure timely delivery. Unlike subcontractor management, what you buy is what you get unless you pay to have it modified. What you get is no longer an off-the-shelf product, and you must be prepared to fund its continued maintenance if you elect to purchase a one-of-a-kind option.

Supplier management is a KPA not currently discussed in the CMM writeups. Processes put into place here deal primarily with management of COTS. In addition, partnerships are sometimes used to motivate suppliers to put new features into their products. This is especially true when suppliers can get paid for making their products more marketable. In response, you should consider the following procedures for use as part of your supplier management KPA:

■ Whenever possible, acquire the metatools to generate third-party or COTS software rather than the software itself.

■ All third-party and COTS software should be fully evaluated before it is acquired to make sure it is compatible with your reference architecture and preferred middleware.

■ All third-party and COTS software should be thoroughly tested to make sure it does what it is supposed to do, and is free of potential software hazards (viruses, worms, etc.).

■ All third-party and COTS software should be baselined, archived, and placed under configuration control once it is received. Vendors may be asked to place a current copy of their source code in escrow when the product is used to implement a crucial function/component in the product-line architecture.

■ Whenever possible, use buying power to motivate the supplier to incorporate desired features/functionality. If required, partner and pay as long as the supplier agrees to incorporate the enhancement into commercially available versions.

The following building codes must be in place to ensure that supplier management processes used by the project incorporate architecture, product-line, and reuse considerations:

■ Practices address selection of software that complies with your reference architecture.

■ Practices reinforce legal, contractual, and ownership considerations put in place by the patents management KPA.

■ Practices provide suppliers with financial incentives to support your requirements.

■ Practices encourage strategic partnering and joint investments.

■ Practices focus on making commitments to do business together now and in the future.

Configuration Management

According to the IEEE Computer Society [8], software configuration management is a discipline that applies technical and administrative direction and surveillance to identify and document the functional and physical characteristics of configuration items, control changes to these characteristics, record and report change processing and implementation (both hardware and software) status, and verify compliance with specified requirements.

Configuration management is an SEI CMM Level-2 key process area. The goals outlined in the CMM description for configuration management seem to adequately address architecture, product lines, and reuse in their current scope. However, current processes will have to be modified to address reuse of both shared and reusable assets:

- *Reusable Software Items*—Software designed and implemented for the specific purpose of being reused within a product line. Change impact is within one business unit, and can be addressed by a local change-control board chaired by that unit's chief software engineer.
- *Shared Software Assets*—Reusable software that is shared across line-of-business units and product lines (class libraries, bindings, tools, etc.). Change impact must be addressed across multiple business units. Therefore, some corporate-level change-control board must be set up to perform this function.

With these distinctions in mind, at least the following three levels of boards will need to be established under this concept of operations to control changes that affect products:

- *Product/Project Change Control Board*—Chaired by the project manager or his/her representative; membership comprised of engineers affected by change within the work center; change impact is constrained to be within project/product boundary.
- *Product-Line or Line-of-Business Change-Control Board*—Chaired by the chief software engineer; membership comprised of engineers representing each project/product that is part of the product line; changes have impacts across the product line.
- *Shared Software Change-Control Board*—Chaired at the corporate level; membership comprised of chief software engineers representing each line of business; changes have impacts across lines-of-business organizations.

Care must be taken as the charters for these boards are written, because, as more boards are created and become involved, requests take longer to process. In addition, the configuration management practices set up to handle third-party and commercial off-the-shelf software will have to be strengthened to maintain the integrity of these assets.

There are many known issues that must be addressed as these practices are devised. For example, you should, as part of its licensing agreements, require its software suppliers to place a copy of the source code in an escrow account to provide them with access should the firm go out of business or decide to discontinue its support for the asset. Finally, procedures must be put into place to address the interface between the configuration management and software reuse libraries. Automated tracking is needed to ensure that when versions of reusable assets change, projects are notified so that they can decide when and how to incorporate the update into their next release. Copies of previous versions of components from both libraries must be made and archived in case they have to be rebuilt. Distribution controls must be put into place to ensure customers get proper versions of the releases.

The following building codes must be in place to ensure that configuration management processes used by the project incorporate architecture, product-line, and reuse considerations:

- Practices make clear distinction between how shared and reusable assets are managed.
- Practices address the configuration identification, control, and accounting relative to all designated reusable software assets, not just code and documentation (domain models, reference architectures, designs, etc.).
- Practices address new, reused, third-party, commercial off-the-shelf, and legacy software.
- Practices discuss interfaces between change boards established at different levels.
- Practices take advantage of any opportunities to improve the customer's perceptions of the efficiency of change-control practices, including defect tracking and reporting.
- Practices address interfaces between libraries and how one tracks versions in the other.
- Practices address archiving and distribution-control procedures used for releases.

TRANSITION/MIGRATION CONCEPTS

The third and final set of issues in your OCD revolves around the topic of technology fanout. I have been saying again and again that change management is the name of the game from both a technical and managerial perspective. The technology associated with architecture, product lines, and reuse is relatively new and untested. While the technology has been used effectively on some early adopter programs, it hasn't been fanned out for general-purpose use except in one or two cases. As such, its transfer represents a degree of risk for those projects that are just starting to embrace these new techniques. Some refinement and maturing of the technology must go on in parallel as the product is developed. Such activities in turn require time and resources (people, funds, etc.). Unfortunately, most projects never seem to have enough of these two commodities to spare as they race to bring products to market ahead of the competition. As a result, fanout of the technology, once proven, to other product-line organizations often fails because it is neither adequately planned nor funded. This operational concept document remedies this situation. As shown in Plan of Action 3.1, it does this by asking you to address the topics of technology transfer, knowhow engineering, and cutover techniques/migration paths. Again, I will try to explain these factors by relating issues in these categories to the OCD outline.

Technology Transfer

Crossing the chasm [9] between the early adopter projects and early majority organizations is a topic that has been frequently addressed. Needed innovations often sit on the shelf and go unused. Project managers are afraid to be the first ones to try to use them because of the risks involved. They fear all sorts of problems could occur (the technology won't scale, it will cause performance to degrade, etc.). Yet, technology change within industry represents the competitive edge. To grow a business, you need to be able to put innovations to work quicker than your competitors. You need to be able to use technology to improve the processes you use, the products you market, and your manufacturing techniques. The chasm that exists at each gap in the technology-adoption life cycle is often depicted by the bell-shaped curve you saw in Figure 1.2. Based upon this discussion, this figure should be updated as follows to put innovators as one of the tails:

INNOVATORS>
    EARLY ADOPTERS>
        EARLY MAJORITY>
            LATE MAJORITY>
                LAGGARDS

The goal established for technology fanout is to eliminate these gaps and put architecture, product-line, and reuse technology into operational use more quickly than the competition. This means that you will have to take the innovations other firms have made and put them to work immediately in your line-of-business organizations. Processes to bridge the gap have been devised by the SEI and Software Productivity Consortium [10]. You should plan to take advantage of lessons learned to shorten the process, using the guidelines these think tanks have developed as a means to cope with the barriers that exist.

Knowhow Engineering

As a prerequisite to technology transfer, an organization must be readied to accept change. Unfortunately, many firms haven't realized this and don't seem to manage the processes involved in transferring the knowhow from one project to another. The team that worked on the early adopter project gets reassigned, and their experience is rarely leveraged for the good of the company. How many of you have worked on a project in which the technology resided in the heads of one or two key individuals? As things got underway, these people soon became the choke points. There was no mechanism put into place to transfer their knowledge to others. They became indispensable and everybody suffered as a result.

Knowhow engineering [11] overcomes these obstacles by putting into place processes that enable you to tap the experiences of early adopter engineers assigned to your project in a straightforward and structured manner. Knowhow in this sense refers to your workforce's ability to use the technology to get its work accomplished. It transfers the skills, knowledge, and abilities needed to do the job using the technology at hand.

Knowhow engineering's goal is to put the processes in place that allow firms to transfer innovation from their early adopter to their early majority organizations quickly and with a minimum of fuss. As a result, new work processes may need to be developed, or existing ones reengineered, to take full advantage of new technology [12]. Changes suggested may be pervasive.

I have found the writings on this topic to be enlightening. There are a number of approaches you could use to transfer knowhow. You could acquire a firm with the needed expertise, hire experts to transfer technology (i.e., develop your people's skills, not the expert's marketable experience), or use a concept that I used when I worked in government, called *technology transfer kits,* in which everything you need to make the transition is put on a CD-ROM in multimedia format (video, audio, text, and graphics).

Cutover Techniques/Migration Paths

Let us assume that processes for the technology's use on a wide range of products, along with guidelines, examples, lessons learned, tools, and libraries of reusable assets, are available for use. How do you take this knowledge base and fan it across your line-of-business organization? How do you package technology for widespread dissemination? What makes sense and what doesn't? As part of the OCD, you must plot out the course of action to be used to support the orderly fanout of architecture, product-line, and reuse technology.

You must also address how you will migrate your legacy to be compatible with your future architectures while maintaining upward compatibility. Flexibility must be provided in your operational concept to allow organizations to pursue innovations that are self-directed or customer focused. The goal should be to harness technology for business reasons. You should innovate and use technology to gain the edge in a growing marketplace, in which those who introduce products with the features and functionality customers desire faster and cheaper than the competition win market dominance.

As this and the previous paradigms emphasize, there are a lot of issues you need to address in your OCD. Our emphasis so far has been to map your operational concepts to the product life cycle. This approach has the advantage that it both provides a logical organizational structure and lets you develop your operational concepts when you need them. The next paragraphs discuss what tactics to use to make this switch in an action-oriented way.

TACTICS TO INTRODUCE REUSE

There are many approaches that you could use to introduce software reuse into your organization. As already stated, each of these require changes to the way you currently do your business. Such changes are often fiercely resisted by those charged with making them happen. The reasons for this opposition are many and include apprehension, complacency, and fear of failure.

Change must be closely managed. To do this, your OCD must address the many relevant social and psychological factors. Your management plans should therefore be structured to introduce change incrementally. When you mechanize your plans, you must treat change as a risk element and monitor it closely so that it doesn't get the upper hand. You also must educate all those involved in the process to overcome their opposition. Remember, it is results that count, because management will judge your success or failure based on them.

Roadmap to Success

The 11 principles that follow can be used to effectively deal with the changes brought on by the introduction of software architectures, product lines, and reuse:

1. *Change only if it makes good business sense.* In other words, don't make investments in architecture, product lines, or software reuse unless you can reasonably expect to show some positive results within a meaningful time period. Senior management gets restless easily, especially when expectations have not been set properly.
2. *Don't become enamored by the technologists.* Don't believe the technologists when they tell you how wonderful it will be when you use their wares. Immature technology can often result in your expending effort to refine new methods and tools instead of using it to develop the product. Be sure to evaluate such hazards when you develop your plans and make your commitments to schedules. Focus on getting the product out.
3. *Get your people involved at all levels.* The best way to get your people to buy into your initiative is to get them involved as you define it. Listen, act, and factor their inputs into your plans. Address their concerns and let them know their opinions count. When you do this, your plan will become their plan. Then, they will become your allies.
4. *Focus changes on product-related improvements.* Focus your energy on making your products better. Make improvements visible where it counts, where the customer sees them. You will create bastions of support that will help you deal with the critics.
5. *Look to the future, not the past.* Don't worry about past mistakes. Instead, learn from them as you plan for the future. Set realistic expectations. Then, claim success in everything you do and focus on being successful.

6. *Don't reinvent the wheel.* Build on the successes of others. Many are publishing their experiences [13, 14]. Take full advantage of what they have learned, your experiences, and the information that is being published about architecture, product lines, and reuse to build the bastions of support you will need to sustain your initiative.

7. *Remember, Rome was not built in a day.* Be patient. Make incremental impact. Build momentum slowly but steadily. Move ahead smartly, gaining speed on every straightaway. Take detours as necessary but continue along your planned path. Establish credibility along the way by making your results visible for all to see. Remember, trying to do too much too quickly often leads to failure.

8. *Do the easy things first.* Make an immediate impact by doing the obvious things right at the start. This maneuver will buy you time to figure out how to attack the harder things. It will also create the impression that you are successful. Because success breeds success, such perceptions can go a long way to keep you out of trouble.

9. *Identify and manage risks.* Figure out the five things that can cause your effort to go astray, and then figure out what to do about each of them. Worry about the really important issues. That's where you should focus because that's where the action is. Realize that situations change. Be on the lookout for new risks.

10. *Keep focused.* Most of the failed initiatives that I have studied got off track because they took on added responsibilities midstream. They did not have a chance because they were trying to do so many new things, they could not do anything right. Fight the urge to couple other needed changes with your initiative. There will be time for them later, after you meet expectations and deliver a working product.

11. *Buy the initiative based on the facts.* Separate fact from friction as you examine the business case. Believe those numbers and those facts that can be justified. Most of the others are nothing more than smoke and mirrors. Separate *hard* numbers from *soft* data. This approach can be used to illustrate the tangible and intangible benefits.

While seemingly common sense, these principles can help you deal with change. They emphasize the need to develop and implement sound tactics. They build on many of the fundamentals already shared with you in this chapter. Most importantly, they create a framework you can use to build your plan of action and milestones.

Tactics that I have used in the past to put these principles into action include the following:

■ *Define a vision and strategy.* As stated in Chapter 3, a vision and strategy that upper management can understand and relate to is needed. Tell management what you are trying to do and why it is important to them. Identify how this fits into their plans, and how it complements the corporate vision.

- *Document your operational concepts.* As stated in this chapter, document your proposed technical, management, and technology fan-out concepts of operations. Provide senior management with some insight into the changes needed in order to use these concepts to achieve your long-range goals.

- *Assign responsibility to a dedicated leader.* You can't institute change without leadership. Using part-timers or teams, even when they are competent, has not worked in the past. Someone has to take charge of the initiative, motivate the troops, sell management, focus energy, generate products, and publicize results. With part-timers, progress will be slow and things just won't get done as scheduled.

- *Establish a plan of attack based upon my 11 principles.* Supplement your vision and strategy with a management plan and an operational concept. Show everyone concerned how you will manage the realization of your business-case goals.

- *Let people know what you are doing and get them involved.* Let people know what's going on, why it is important, and how they can contribute. Else, they will feel like mushrooms and avoid making the necessary commitments. Listen to their suggestions, act upon them, and keep everyone informed about your progress. Be viewed as a winner.

- *Baseline your current norms.* Get the historical cost, productivity, and quality data you need to show you have made a positive impact. Numbers can be your ally, especially when they show you have delivered as promised. Articulate them and explain what they mean very carefully. Else, they will be misinterpreted and used against you.

- *Make a positive impact as quickly as possible.* Avoid ivory towerism. Prove your worth under controlled conditions on a pilot project, or by conducting a live demonstration. Choose your early projects carefully. You will be surprised at how well you will be received when you can provide proof of your value to both your supporters and critics.

- *Publicize successes and encourage exchange of ideas.* Make what you are doing and what you have done visible. Publish a monthly newsletter, articles, and press releases. Set up a bulletin board. Have your people make briefings and present their experiences. Encourage the exchange of information. Deal from a position of power, not weakness.

- *Expand the initiative as you learn.* Start out small and expand slowly. Use your metrics data to decide on your next course of action. Beware of becoming a threat to those in power. Provide support to other organizations that can help you best win the battle of the budget. Make them your allies, not enemies.

- *Establish ways of changing midstream.* Continuously monitor the feedback you are getting on how well you are doing. Take suggestions, listen, and make changes when they are warranted. Keep in touch with your customers/users and keep them satisfied.

SUMMARY

- Define the operational concepts you will use to make your vision and strategy happen in practice.
- The predominate issues relative to operational insertion of product lines, architectures, and reuse in most organizations are change and change management.
- The technical concepts that seem impacted most by the shift to product lines includes the selected paradigm; your state of process maturity; the skills, knowledge, and abilities of your workforce; and your organization's readiness for change.
- The management concepts that seem most impacted include organizational roles and responsibilities, user involvement, necessary process changes, and readiness for change.
- Making needed organizational changes will prove to be the most difficult item on your agenda, especially if existing empires are threatened.
- Scope how you will handle technology transfer and migration issues in your operational concept document.
- Many of your technical, managerial, and technology fanout processes will have to be changed to deal with issues involved in putting this technology to work operationally.
- The major trick to putting new technology to work is to develop the knowhow in a planned and systematic fashion.

You are probably thinking that generating the OCD illustrated in Plan of Action 3.1 is overkill. In most cases, I do not believe so. You really must figure out how you are going to get the job done before you venture forth to do it. Project plans are not broad enough in scope to identify all the needed changes. Many concepts developed at the project level may not scale across line-of-business organizations. However, a white paper is better than no paper. If what is proposed seems too much, scale it down. The important thing is not the form of what is produced, but the essence.

REFERENCES

1. Mark C. Paulk et. al., *The Capability Maturity Model: Guidelines for Improving the Software Process,* Addison-Wesley, 1995.
2. Barry W. Boehm, "The Spiral Model of Software Development and Enhancement," *Computer,* IEEE, May 1988, pp. 61–72.
3. Niklaus Wirth, "Program Development By Stepwise Refinement," *Communications of the ACM,* April 1971.
4. Dan Kara, "Object-Oriented and Component-Based Development," *Application Development Trends,* Vol. 3, No. 6, June 1996.

5. Mark C. Paulk, et al., The Capability Maturity Model, Addison-Wesley, 1995.

6. U.S. Army, *Reuse Training Brochure,* Army Reuse Center, 1996.

7. Defense Information Systems Agency, *Reuse Training List,* Reuse Information Clearinghouse (ReuseIC), 1995.

8. IEEE Computer Society, *Software Engineering Terminology,* IEEE Std 610-12-1990, December 1990.

9. Geoffrey A. Moore, *Crossing the Chasm,* HarperBusiness, 1991.

10. Software Productivity Consortium, *Using New Technologies: A Software Engineering Technology Transfer Guidebook,* SPC-92046, December 1992.

11. Karl Sveiby and Tom Lloyd, *Managing Knowhow,* Bloomsbury, 1987.

12. Michael Hammer and James Champy, *Reengineering the Corporation,* Harper Business, 1993.

13. James O'Connor, Catharine Mansour, Jerri Turner-Harris, and Grady Campbell, Jr., "Reuse in Command-and-Control Systems," *Software,* IEEE Computer Society, September 1994.

14. Emmanuel Henry and Benoit Faller, "Large-Scale Industrial Reuse to Reduce Cost and Cycle Time," *Software,* IEEE Computer Society, September 1995.

Elements of a Successful Reuse Program

4

WHAT ARE THE ELEMENTS OF A SUCCESSFUL REUSE PROGRAM?

You have developed your vision and strategy and operational concepts. Now, you must put these concepts into action. Plans are needed to identify what must be done, when, and by whom. Controls are needed to assess status, measure performance, and track progress. It has been my experience that you can successfully introduce reuse when you employ a classical approach that is issues based, action oriented, and scoped based upon the following concepts:

Project Management Tips

✔ Be success oriented and goal driven

✔ Limit the scope to something everyone thinks is meaningful

✔ Ready the organization for reuse by defining the barriers and ways to overcome them

✔ Define a reasonable, activity-oriented plan to realize reuse goals

✔ Break down activities into work tasks, and define deliverables for each of them

✔ Provide management with visibility into progress, and control over the work in progress

---

> ✔ Put controls in place to ensure product quality and integrity
> ✔ Focus on risk management and mitigation
> ✔ Identify the key management issues and how you will address each of them
> ✔ Demonstrate success on highly visible, meaningful projects
> ✔ Exploit the technology base and makes it work in practice

The preceding project management principles work in practice. I strongly recommend that you consider incorporating them as you develop your plans.

Let's assume you develop your plans using the guidance in Chapters 5 through 7. What are the issues that management needs to be concerned with as they develop their action plans? The eight major management issues that early firms have had to deal with relative to inserting product lines, architecture, and reuse operationally include:

- *Policies*—How do product lines, architectures, and reuse impact your existing decision-making framework? How will you go about changing your management policies and practices to support the introduction of these technologies?
- *Processes*—How do architecture and reuse tasks impact your process framework? How will you change them to address new activities and key process areas? Will new standards (documentation, etc.) have to be introduced along with new reviews and milestones?
- *Organizational Structure*—How do product lines impact your organizational structure? Are modifications in order to accommodate new functions? Will these changes positively impact communications and span of control? Are lines of business the norm?
- *Staffing*—How does the new work impact your current staffing levels and labor mix? Will you have to hire new staff? Where will you get them? What skills, knowledge, and abilities will they need? How will you develop these skills?
- *Budgets and Schedules*—How will you pay for architecture and reuse taskings? Will infrastructure modifications be expensed or covered via a form of a charge-back scheme? What reuse incentives will be offered to motivate project and product-line managers?
- *Management Methods and Tools*—How does the work impact the methods and tools you use for project management? Will you have to change the approaches you use to monitor progress, manage risk, control changes, and ensure quality?

- *Legal and Contracts*—How do architecture and reuse considerations impact your contract requirements? Will new legal guidelines be needed to limit liability and secure rights to reusable assets? Will financial incentives be offered to motivate your suppliers?
- *Metrics and Measures*—How will success or failure be measured? Are new metrics and measures needed? How are they related to your charge-back schemes? Who will take the measurements? In what form and how often will these measurements be reported?

Many of these issues are a consequence of organizational change. To effectively cope with change, you need to attack the issues head on. This issues-based approach is preferable because it provides you with the answers you need to get the critics of change off your back.

While the barriers to putting product lines, architectures, and reuse to work are primarily managerial, there are also a number of significant technical issues that will have to be resolved before you can successfully introduce reuse into your firm. The six major issues that have a profound effect on your tactics include:

- *Languages*—Are modern languages, such as Ada, C++, Java, and Smalltalk, more amenable to software reuse? If so, which of their features enable reuse (inheritance, class hierarchies, generics, etc.)? How do you move to a new language? What steps do you follow and what conventions do you observe? How can you make sure that software written in other languages is upward compatible? How will you take advantage of the inventory of software that you have written in other languages? What about the use of fourth-generation and scripting languages such as Visual Basic? When do you use generators?
- *Packaging Standards*—Are different design, coding, and test standards and conventions needed to package software assets to be reusable? Can you purchase off-the-shelf assets packaged to these standards? Can you retrofit your existing software to these standards? How do you convert? Are innovations becoming available to address these issues?
- *Methods*—How will you represent the results of architectural engineering and domain analysis? What methods will you use to identify elements of the architecture that are potentially reusable? What methods will you use to build reusable assets? How do these methods relate to those you are already using for problem and solution space modeling? Can they adequately address performance, interoperability, and security expectations?
- *Tools*—What tools will be needed for reuse? Are they compatible with the new methods and packaging standards you adopted? Are they readily available, mature, and reasonably priced? Can they be easily integrated with your other tools into your software engineering environment? Can a single repository be used or will separate software engineering, data, and reuse repositories have to be integrated?

■ *Libraries*—Will you need a separate reuse library? If so, how will you integrate it with the other libraries you've established as part of your software engineering environment for configuration management? What features should the library tool provide? How does this library relate to your repository strategy? How do you interconnect your library with others to expand your inventory? How do you classify and certify components and ensure quality control? What standards should you establish for the library tool itself?

■ *Technology Fusion*—How will you integrate emerging technologies so that they complement each another? Will you be able to resolve the structure clashes that occur as products of often conflicting methods are linked together at different times throughout the life cycle? What approaches do you use to consider reuse as you construct an architecture? What frameworks exist and how do you take advantage of them?

Technical issues such as these are direct results of the technological explosion we are experiencing in the fields of computer science, information engineering, and software engineering.

PROCESS AND PRODUCT RELATIONSHIPS

To take advantage of the lessons learned and address the issues identified in earlier chapters, you'll need a framework. The one that has worked for me in the past is what I call the three Ps [1]. Simply stated, the three Ps are the *processes, people,* and *products/product lines* that populate today's software *projects* and *lines of business.* Each of these three Ps must be carefully and painstakingly managed. Conflicts between the three Ps need to be reconciled in order for you to be successful, which suggests that just focusing on process improvement is not enough. The people and product aspects of the process are considered just as important. They must be addressed along with the trade-offs and the technology that exists as the process is executed. Else, failure will result. In other words, the process must be humanized and focused on products in order for it to work in practice.

I have already spent some time discussing process and process issues. I explained the dual-development approach and showed how architectural considerations get introduced into a traditional product development cycle. The area I intend to emphasize is applications engineering. My reason for this is simple. To get your interest, I must show you how to take advantage of reuse opportunities within the context of how you currently do business. Figure 4.1 displays the three popular applications development process models. These build on the product line, architecture, and reuse concepts discussed in earlier chapters. In each, the major software reuse opportunities are identified. Notice that they include much more than just code.

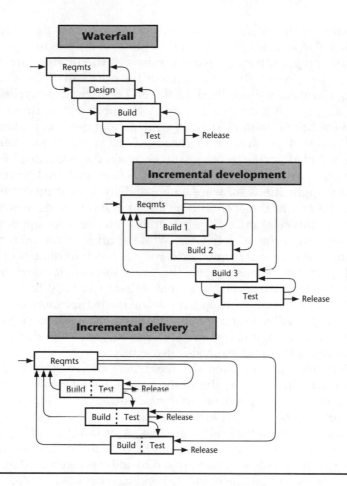

FIGURE 4.1 Applications development process models.

The waterfall option models the software development process as a series of sequential activities. Each phase of the process needs to be completed before you are permitted to move on. Reviews terminate phases and act as quality gates [2]. Management inspects the products of each phase (specifications, models, plans, code, tests/test cases, manuals, etc.) at these reviews, and makes decisions relative to their quality prior to giving permission for the staff to move ahead with the next phase. The waterfall model has been severely criticized in the literature [3] as not being representative of how people actually produce software. The most common criticism revolves around its lack of iteration and feedback during each of its cycles.

The incremental development option assumes that applications are being developed in a series of increments or builds. This staging reduces integration risk on large projects, because early versions of the product are available for testing early in the process. It also overcomes the criticism of the waterfall model by providing iteration and feedback at the end of each of its cycles. Reviews are again used as gates. Management samples the products at these reviews, and makes decisions based upon predefined measures of *goodness*. Many variations of this model exist, depending on the needs of the organization using it. Prototyping is often included during the early stages, when there is a need for models, and to pin down user requirements. The model is often anchored by having friendly users test the applications software under realistic operating conditions (beta testing). The popular spiral model [4] is a variant of iterative development.

The incremental delivery option models the applications development process as a series of deliveries. While similar to the incremental development option, it delivers increments to users to get feedback and provide a phased buildup of operational capability. Each increment must be tested and documented. In contrast, only the final delivery is fully tested under the iterative development option. This option's downside is that more coordination is required to manage feedback and maintain control over released products that come in many versions. Again, reviews are used as gates and decision points, and many variations of this process model also exist.

Maintenance is viewed as a recurring activity by each of the three options. It can be thought of as a replay of the basic model. Of course, the work that goes on during maintenance may be different. Instead of developing applications software, the staff may be involved in making repairs, enhancing capabilities, and inserting changes into the fielded releases. Most agree that the differences are not substantial enough to warrant construction of yet another process model. However, balancing of workloads may be required to address conflicts that arise when trying to satisfy users and handle scheduled and unscheduled changes to baselines.

Asset Acquisition Mechanisms

Let us look at the applications engineering processes you could use to acquire products that will become your reusable assets (architectures, designs, code, etc.). You could: Develop assets to be reusable, purchase reusable assets from third parties, and/or mine existing libraries for reusable assets.

To be reusable, assets must embody the desired form, fit, and function. They must do all the things they are supposed to do for the full range of desired capabilities. They must be packaged properly, comply with standards, and be built to the level of quality desired. If they are built to a reference architecture, they must comply with any constraints it may impose on them.

Purchased assets require you to pay attention to details. In addition to testing them to be sure that they meet your standards and perform the functions desired, you may have to establish legal rights and negotiate licenses for their use. You also must consider the responsiveness and staying power of vendors. If they go out of business, who will keep the asset up to date? As stated in Chapter 3, you might want to partner with the vendor to add the features you desire.

Mining reusable assets involves making the conscious decision to reengineer existing products to satisfy form, fit, and function requirements set for them. Reengineering often means extra effort because of the rework required to bring the assets up to your minimum standards of quality. A yes decision should be made only when the estimated costs of reengineering are justified. If they aren't, you should be asking, Why put up with all of the headaches?

Desirable Asset Properties

Let's now look at the following six desirable properties for software products that could become your reusable assets. These properties can be applied to any artifact (design, code, tool, etc.) considered for inclusion in your software reuse library (your distribution mechanism):

- *Domain Specific*—The assets you develop should be aimed at satisfying the applications needs of a specific class of user. Users in this sense could include an architecture or an operating system. For example, a framework library designed to provide icons for use by financial analysts working with spreadsheet applications could be the target.
- *Generalized Form*—The software should be packaged in canonical form (i.e., templates). Care should be taken to ensure that standard import/export interface mechanisms are used along with the principle of separation of concerns. Data used should be standardized and separated from any processes so that it can be changed with minimum effort. Product-line considerations should dominate so that specialization can be performed by product teams.
- *Fixed Functionality*—The functionality of the product should be fixed, along with its preconditions and postconditions. In this manner, users will know exactly what the asset is supposed to do, and under what circumstances. For example, standard algorithms should be specified, along with their range of applicability and initialization and exception (e.g., divide by zero) conditions.
- *Known Performance*—Performance expectations should be defined explicitly. For example, timing, loading, and latency should be specified along with boundary conditions. Poor performance is the most cited reason users reject assets. To overcome this bias, users must know what to expect. For example, algorithm performance should be specified as a function of an iteration rate to make any slowdown visible to the user.
- *Well-Bounded Interfaces*—Interfaces are other important considerations. They should be designed to minimize coupling and maximize cohesion [5]. Such focus will allow you to minimize dependencies between components, and

implement information-hiding concepts [6]. In addition, table-driven concepts should be used to make your products easy to modify. This becomes very important when your variables are expected to change frequently.

■ *Demonstrable Quality*—Quality is the final consideration. Your users must be able to trust the quality of your product, or they won't use it. Product quality in this case is defined in terms of attributes of user satisfaction (ease of use, maintainability, etc.). These attributes must be specified along with the criteria used to demonstrate their satisfaction.

Because of their importance to reuse, let's examine packaging concepts in more depth, keeping the properties we just reviewed in mind.

Asset Packaging Concepts

Packaging refers to a logical design that has been shaped to accommodate the target environment (machine, operating system, etc.). You develop a package by first defining the associations and relationships between structural elements (classes, modules, and other forms of building blocks) in an environment-independent manner. Next, you adapt the design to the environment by iteratively taking into account restrictions that occur in the solution space (time limitations, language dependencies, hardware shortcomings, etc.) It has been likened by many to an optimization process. As I've heard Ed Yourdon say, "It is easier to make a working system efficient than make an efficient system work."

A package can be viewed as a black box with a group of objects or functions in it. Groups of packages bound together by control and data structures form an application. The architect arranges these boxes so that user-defined class, functional, interface, and performance requirements can be met. There may be other constraints that limit the design options available (e.g., operating system restrictions, such standards as SQL, etc.). The architecture that evolves is important because it governs how data is communicated, and how sequencing and control are handled. Packaging is viewed as arranging encapsulations (boxes, class hierarchies, etc.) into a structure designed to achieve specified performance goals. From a reuse perspective, the four most important goals that the packaging should achieve include:

■ Minimize the coupling or dependencies between packages (i.e., allow one package to be replaced with another easily)
■ Maximize the cohesiveness or information content within a package (i.e., ensure the integrity of what's in a package based upon predefined rules)
■ Ensure the computational resources (time, I/O bandwidth, memory, etc.) needed to perform are available (i.e., ensure the package owns the resources it needs to do its job)

- Ensure the package behaves properly under nominal and stress conditions (i.e., critically examine the interactions that govern performance under realistic scenarios)

To accomplish these goals, the architect should pay attention to the following factors as the design is developed:

- The overall topology of the architecture (static structure, number of connections, types of connections, etc.)
- The operational and system architectural constraints
- The application-to-application interface mechanisms
- The data architecture (types of data, dependencies, etc.)
- The mechanisms used by the package to access the database and pass data
- The control logic and state behavior of the architecture
- The dynamic behavior of the architecture under various load conditions
- The information content of the packages (data, algorithms, etc.)
- The resources needed to execute the package (memory, timing, etc.)

Structure clashes will undoubtedly occur as the architect tries to mate reusable assets to the architectural design. Approaches to resolve these clashes and trade-offs must be explored as the process unfolds. To develop designs, many firms use one of the many popular model-based requirements methods and related CASE (Computer-Aided Software Engineering) tools. A modeling method embodies the processes, representations, and the decision logic for moving from problem to solution space specifications. Mappings from requirements to design are also provided as an output, so there will be traceability from user's need to implementation. Reuse should be an integral part of this specification methodology, because existing packages (designs, algorithms, code modules, library routines, etc.) may constrain the design options available as the requirements are analyzed and the design is produced.

Candidate Methods and Tools

The methods and tools that applications engineers use to design, develop, and deploy their products are also important considerations. In addition to addressing packaging concerns, they make the application development job easier because they automate many tedious, labor-prone activities. The methods and tools you use should provide the following support for reuse:

- Processes that incorporate reuse considerations within their steps should be employed
- Notations should note what the architecture is and when reuse opportunities arise

- Completion criteria and example products should be provided for each defined reuse step
- Rules for identifying high-payoff reuse opportunities and risk areas should be provided
- Approaches to resolve the structure clashes that occur when existing packages are being fit into the design should be part of any methodology
- Guidelines for taking reuse packaging considerations into account in behavioral models should be provided by the tools

Both functional and object-oriented methods have been successfully used in the past to develop reusable software assets. When you select a method, you should consider the availability of guidelines, rules, and predefined completion criteria as your primary selection criteria. It is much more important to have such support than the representation and other technical considerations most people argue about as they make their tool decisions. The reason for this is simple— applications engineers need structure and guidance to get the job done. Without it, they often falter and revert back to their old ways of doing business. You want to avoid this trap at all costs, and be able to use the tools to their full capabilities.

The software reuse tools that you should consider for incorporation into your Software Engineering Environment (SEE) are pictured in Figure 4.2. The most important of these tools is your software reuse library because it stores your reusable assets and serves as your primary reuse distribution mechanism. This library should be selected because it provides your applications engineers with the following minimum set of user-oriented capabilities:

- Provide seamless access to available library capabilities and populations for authorized users (may consist of several libraries networked together)
- Be able to quickly search, browse, and retrieve quality reusable assets (or abstracts) that satisfy your user's requirements
- Be an integral part of the SEE (permit engineers to promote assets from one library to another using common service modules—configuration management, SQL queries, etc.)

PROCESS AND PEOPLE RELATIONSHIPS

Let's now look at how people influence reuse process and product decisions. No matter how well the process works, it won't be followed unless those who have to use it believe it is a smart and reasonable way to get their jobs done. It will not be used if the staff building the applications thinks that it creates a lot of unnecessary extra work. To successfully introduce these concepts, you must match your process and product expectations to the skills, knowledge, abilities, and temperament of the people who will be tasked to use them. Make sure that you do not ask your staff to do more than is absolutely necessary. Desire must be tempered by

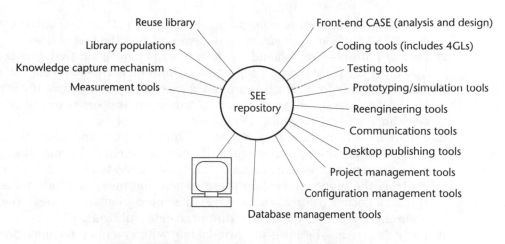

Software Reuse Library Capabilities

• Access control	• Metrics reporting
• Account management	• Performance measurement
• Asset classification	• Query by example
• Database search, browse, storage, and retrieval	• Database administration and auditing

FIGURE 4.2 Candidate software reuse tools.

realism as you ask your people to do what everyone must believe is the right thing. You must make reasonable demands of sensible people when you address the barriers to change.

As stated in Chapter 1, the following psychological and political barriers must be dealt with as you introduce reuse into your firm:

- *Apathy*—Why change, we're successful? is a question that you're bound to hear. You can counter this argument by using your business case and making technical arguments for reuse. You must convince your critics that it makes sense and is in everyone's best interests, including theirs, to change. Else, they will fight everything you do just because they are comfortable with the old ways.
- *Not-Invented-Here (NIH) Syndrome*—Just because it works there, why do you think it will work here? is another question you're bound to hear. You can use success stories to counter their criticisms. Positive results can be used to con-

vince anyone that reuse concepts work in practice. Demonstrations can show critics the value of approaches that have survived the test of fire.

■ *Fear of Failure*—Why should we do it now? is a question that smells of fear. You must convince those in charge that the time is ripe and that the organization is ready for change. You must convince all those people involved that your plans are sound, your upper management support is unwavering, and they have a high probability of success.

■ *Tribal Chieftains and Turf Battles*—Who will do it and how will they be funded? is another question you will hear. As Machiavelli said, "Beware the prince when empires are at stake." You must understand who is in power and controls the money to resolve these issues. You must build alliances, make treaties, gather political support, get the voters registered, and avoid being embroiled in the tribal warfare that permeates all firms.

■ *Ivory Towerism*—Because you are dealing with emerging technologies, many practitioners will argue it is premature to try to use them at the present time. What researchers discuss does not always work in practice. The technology will drain resources from those using it when it is immature. You can counter these arguments with proof that the technology is ripe for the picking. Show the critics it works using real examples from projects from their own backyards.

■ *Who Is in Charge*—Who is in charge anyway? is another common question you will hear. People tend to distrust anybody outside of their immediate realm of acquaintance. As a result, some form of internal advocacy organization must be built to act as a bridge between those building the applications and those working reuse. Communications must be managed and teamwork emphasized as the advocacy structure is deployed.

Dealing with these people issues is difficult. People are not always logical or rational. They do the strangest things. Your challenge is to keep them focused and build teams. Your desire is to channel their energy toward the accomplishment of common goals. Involvement is required, as is leadership and direction. A solid management infrastructure can help because it makes your focusing on the job easier. This management infrastructure is nothing more than a decision framework established to help you with your planning and control activities. The critical elements of the infrastructure include: software reuse policies and procedures, product standards, processes, organizational structures, distribution mechanisms, incentives, and measurement approaches.

Let's turn our attention toward organizational options for reuse. It is through these organizations that the reuse job gets done.

Organizational Options

You can address many of the psychological and cultural barriers associated with inserting this technology through your organizational structure. High-level advocacy, teamwork, well-defined roles, and dedicated responsibilities go a long way to reduce the confusion associated with the movement to product lines. Both authority/responsibility and ownership/accountability relationships need to be addressed as parts of the organization. Clear lines of communication through the organization help make interfaces clear and reduce confusion.

The following three popular advocacy organizations for software reuse are displayed in Figure 4.3 and briefly discussed as follows:

- *Centralized Group*—A group is formed to address architecture and reuse concepts at either the corporate or line-of-business level. The group defines the architecture, develops a migration strategy, and searches out reuse opportunities. Personnel assigned to this group work with business units to help transition to the concepts from theory into practice. The group maintains the software reuse library and provides support to business units. It makes sure training opportunities are available to those who need them. It is led by the chief software engineer, and staffed by a band of skilled professionals.

- *Coordinating Committee*—A committee is formed with representation from each of the affected business units. The representatives act as advocates for change within their separate business units. The committee chair serves as the corporate champion and chief engineer. Roles and responsibilities are decentralized and allocated to different units based upon their ability to perform. The champion often has a small staff that monitors actions, tracks progress, and reports to corporate management.

- *Strategy or Integrated Product Team*—A team is formed with representatives from each of the affected business units. The team's function is to develop a plan that each unit can live with and follow. Each business unit will then implement the plan to get the job done. A strategy is devised to pull things together by the corporate champion or chief software engineer. Although some duplication may occur, autonomy is preserved as each unit does what makes sense for its operation. This approach is often used in firms where business units are held accountable for profit and loss.

For any of these options to work, a dedicated champion must be assigned to lead the adoption effort. Assigning someone part-time to this position does not seem to work. There just is too much to do and too many conflicting priorities. Where this person resides organizationally really doesn't seem to matter as much as the reputation of the individual, and whether he or she is fully empowered to get the job done. People must perceive the champion as someone who knows the culture, understands what current organization does, how it works, and what needs to be done.

There are many organizational variations to consider as well. Of course, the option that is best for you is the one that is compatible with your corporate culture. For example, one firm I worked with chartered its software process group [7]

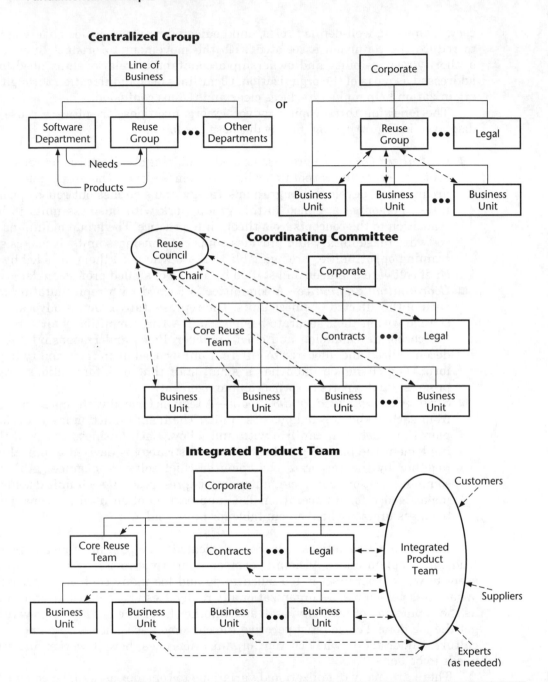

FIGURE 4.3 Candidate advocacy organizations.

with the responsibility of devising the reuse processes. This group then became the reuse group because it had completed its process development task and was looking for new challenges. Another firm I recently worked with assigned the reuse responsibilities to its tools group. Management reasoned that it should focus on the reuse library as a primary mechanism for implementing reuse. The tools group provided a range of support to its users, along with library services. This combination of functions (reuse support, tools, systems administration, etc.) was very economical. Finally, one firm I am currently working with delegated the responsibility to an integrated product team made up of the perceived technical leaders from all affected disciplines. This is the approach I like best because it gets the perceived technical leaders into the picture.

Distribution Mechanisms

Integral to any reuse initiative are the mechanisms used to distribute reuse information and assets. Vehicles to let people know what exists and where to get staff are essential parts of the infrastructure. The primary means used by firms is some form of reuse library and catalog. While similar to a software development library, a software reuse library differs because it provides the following additional capabilities:

- *Asset Classification*—A way to classify assets that permit users to quickly find reusable software components of interest.
- *Asset Browsing*—The ability to browse reuse library abstracts or the actual assets themselves. Most users want to examine the asset before they extract it from the library.
- *Library Interoperability*—A seamless and controlled exchange of information between reuse libraries interoperating across a network providing access to a wide range of assets (may be configured with either homogeneous or heterogeneous libraries).

You could employ either a manual or automated reuse library system to perform these functions. Depending on the volume and frequency of use, it might be overkill to put a powerful but infrequently used reuse library system into place. It might be more efficient and economical to use manual procedures along with some database management system.

While logically a separate entity, there is no reason why your reuse library couldn't be physically integrated with other libraries and your configuration management system via the software repository or backplane. Unfortunately, most of the reuse library systems implemented to date have been mechanized as stand-alone systems. However, this phenomenon will probably change in the very near future as more and more firms demand some form of integrated software reuse capability from their CASE vendors.

Finally, a reuse newsletter serves a very beneficial purpose. It can let people know what you're doing and can get them interested. It educates the uninformed, communicates helpful information to your users, and serves as a marketing tool for new services. I suggest that you circulate one monthly online and as a stand-alone paper publication.

Incentive Approaches

You should consider introducing incentives to motivate your people at all levels of the organization to expend the extra effort needed to achieve high degrees of reuse. These incentives don't necessarily have to be financial. Nonmonetary rewards (prizes, plaques, etc.) and recognition function just as well when they are packaged to provide the proper appeal. That's why software engineers like to have their work put online, why there are so many Web sites, and why there are code and Java applets to download. The types of incentives firms use and their target audience include:

Audience	*Incentive(s)*
Executive	Increased profitability
	Improved competitiveness
Product-line manager	Improved customer satisfaction
	Reduced time to market
	Improved price/performance
Project manager	Increased probability of providing an acceptable product on time and within budget
	Reduced cost (time and effort)
	Improved quality (fewer errors)
Software engineer	Ability to get the job done
	Increased recognition
	Career growth and bonus
	Prizes (especially gadgets and toys)

Just saying these words without showing people how they can be realized won't buy you anything. Your job is to make them real. For example, software engineers will believe architectures and reuse are important when they see that they influence their ability to be promoted or get a raise. They will become converts when they receive recognition or a cash award. Project managers will become believers when they see percentage reuse as a factor in their bonus plans. Executives and product-line managers will be convinced when their profits go up and their market shares grow as product lines are introduced and architectures solidified.

Of course, simpler things can be done in parallel as well. Recognition of stellar performance through award programs or ceremonies can go a long way. Putting up posters that show relative reuse performance of organizations goes a long way. The important thing to do is to send the signal that upper management feels that reuse is important.

Candidate Metrics and Measures

Reuse metrics close the feedback loop. They provide insight into how well your reuse process is working, whether the products you are generating are reusable, and how well your people are performing relative to their reuse plans.

Several candidate reuse metrics are shown in Table 4.1. These are segmented to represent the following viewpoints:

TABLE 4.1 Candidate Metrics

Viewpoint	Measurement Issues	Metrics/Measures
Executive	Overall profitability	$ profit/$ sales
	Organizational effectiveness	Win ratio or return on investment
	Capital expenditures	Return on capital
Product-line or Line-of-Business Manager	Customer satisfaction	Satisfaction index
	Costs of goods sold	$/source line of code
	Market share	$ sales/$ market
	Time to market	Months
Project Manager	Budget performance	$ actual/$ planned
	Schedule performance	Time actual/planned
	Requirements volatility	Change request frequency
	Product quality	Customer complaints or first-pass test yield
	Cycle time	Process downtime
Software Engineer	Size	Source lines of code
	Complexity	Cyclomatic number or Halstead ratio
	Reliability	Error density or rate
	Productivity	Source lines of code/staff month of effort

Notes:
1. The metrics in this table are just examples. One useful approach to develop those metrics of interest to your firm is to use the goal-question-metric paradigm. Using this approach, you would start by defining the reuse goals your firm feels are important (e.g., reduce cost). Then, you would use different viewpoints to develop questions pertinent to achieving these goals (e.g., how do I estimate cost or improve predictability). Finally, you would identify the metrics helpful in answering your questions (e.g., we estimate using $/source line of code and we improve predictability by inserting a process that calibrates our estimating models using actuals to reduce the variances).
2. Two excellent references on the topic of metrics are Robert B. Grady and Deborah L. Caswell, *Software Metrics: Establishing a Company-Wide Program,* Prentice Hall, 1987 and Robert B. Grady, Practical Software Metrics for Project Management and Process Improvement, Prentice Hall, 1992.

- *Executive*—Reuse metrics of interest address financial measures, such as return on investment and profitability.
- *Product-Line or Line-of-Business Manager*—Reuse metrics of interest address marketing measures, such as market share and customer satisfaction.
- *Project Manager*—Reuse metrics of interest look at the impact of reuse on schedule, budget, and technical performance.
- *Software Engineer*—Reuse metrics of interest examine the reusability characteristics of the product, and their impact on such production activities as degree of testing.

As shown in Table 4.1, the most meaningful metrics seem to be the ones that are hardest to quantify. These address such terms as *goodness, profitability, efficiency,* and *effectiveness*. To deal with this issue, both hard and soft numbers must be developed to show improvements in performance for each of the viewpoints noted previously. Your metrics program should be designed to collect, normalize, analyze, and report measures that are useful in this regard.

Many people try to avoid collecting the data needed to quantify metrics of this sort. They argue it is too hard or meaningless. However, these are the same people who freeze when senior management asks them the difficult questions and for proof that they are making progress. Metrics are essential and I recommend you make the effort. They make your progress visible and are worth the pain.

Obviously, many of the metrics in Table 4.1 should be collected and analyzed independently of reuse. They support good software engineering and can also be used to help determine whether software assets are reusable. When defining metrics with reuse in mind, there are many measurement issues that must be addressed that don't appear at first glance. For example, stringent metrics requirements on complexity might serve as a barrier to reuse, because they force producers to spend more time and effort on qualifying assets. As another example, measuring size of reusable assets will require you to decide between use of actual, modified, or equivalent source lines of code. Needless to say, such issues are pervasive and must be addressed as you set up your metrics program for reuse.

PUT THE TECHNOLOGY THAT EXISTS TO WORK

To this point, we have viewed new technology as a risk. We have taken the project manager's viewpoint to temper the natural tendencies of those working pilot projects to run with the latest innovation. We understand that technology can make the difference if its insertion is managed carefully. That is why we put an entire section on technology fan out in the OCD discussed in Chapter 3.

Promising Technologies

There are a number of emerging technologies that can have an enormous impact on software reuse. Many of these technologies have been made possible by the ever increasing availability of high performance, cheap hardware. The important technologies include the following:

- *Domain-Specific Software Architectures*—The world of architectures is going through a revolution. Methods, tools, and approaches for building systems within limited domains are taking advantage of the drive to make systems more open and standards based. Advances are being made so rapidly that you will find it difficult to keep current.

- *Architectural Description Languages*—A lot of research is being devoted to this topic. Very high-level languages are being proposed to develop architectural models that allow you to look in depth at the many design trade-offs. This is another hot topic to follow.

- *Knowledge-Based Systems*—Many are banking on the use of knowledge-based systems to provide the rule base needed to automate decision support within limited application domains. Scaling of concepts continues to present an obstacle that limits the widespread use of the technology. However, the use of inference engines, knowledge databases, and a host of related technology will continue to creep into support systems that you will use.

- *Visualization and Animation*—The use of high-resolution, 3D graphics and virtual reality makes it easier for users to model and understand complex phenomena and situations. Animation can add to this the element of humor or realism. It is very conceivable that these technologies will be used in the future to permit your customers to look at, review, and exercise models of their future systems before they are built.

- *Multimedia*—The ability to communicate via sound, video, graphics, and text in color helps the human interface designer determine how best to mechanize the man/machine interface. As voice recognition becomes more prevalent, workstations will become more an office tool than an office machine, because users will not have to know how to type. This will make it easier for designers to converse with users and scope their needs.

- *Network Servers*—The days of the PC are numbered if you believe the literature. Network servers tied to cheap home servers sold like appliances will do most of the work in a manner invisible to the user. Use of such networking connections for system/software development will permit globalization of the enterprise in the sense that all of the corporation's assets will become available to those employees with proper authorization.

- *The Internet (and Intranets)*—Distribution of information via high bandwidth digital networks is making it easier for consumers to access a wealth of knowledge. Using a TV model, suppliers of goods and services are starting to push information to those interested using channelized pipelines instead of broadband networks. These pipelines pave the information highway and make electronic commerce feasible in the future.

- *Electronic Commerce/Electronic Data Interchange*—The information highway is promulgating the biggest revolution in the industry, because it is changing the way business is conducted. Those who take advantage of the change the earliest will reap the largest rewards. That's why so many people are flocking to the Web. For reuse, the Web will act as a distribution and sales hub. It provides those who wish to market their assets broadly with marketing opportunities unthought of just a year or two ago.

Take Advantage of Them

Taking advances being made in these areas and putting them to work will remain a challenge. It is relatively easy to get a pilot or showpiece project to use new technology. However, the real trial for most organizations is taking the technology the next step. I recommend you take the following approach in your quest to fan out technology:

- *Prove it works.* Make sure the technology you are interested in works by using it on a pilot or showpiece project, or to build a piece of a larger system. Make sure you select the right project, or credibility might become an issue.
- *Demo it as you prove it.* Make the project visible by demonstrating results continuously to potential supporters. Do not wait until you are finished to start to develop a potential customer base for the technology.
- *Synchronize reviews with the business cycle.* Show your bosses you are making progress just before you submit your next year's budget request. You will be surprised about how much good will this generates as the seniors slice the budget pie.
- *Get your ducks in line.* As the project is unfolding, gather the data you need to build a convincing case for the technology. Get the most conservative person you know to list his or her concerns. Then, collect the data and develop the arguments that counter them. Try out your case on this person before presenting it to your senior management. You'll be glad you did.
- *Have seniors management help you.* Persuade your senior executives and line-of-business managers that the benefits of the technology outweigh the risks. Get them to ask those in the middle why they are not planning to use the techniques. Such questions generate interest at the middle, where most of the opposition to change lies. Now, you can use the data you have collected to substantiate your arguments.
- *Make your requests reasonable.* Take small steps instead of one big one. If you ask for everything all at once, you will fail. Do as kids do. Ask for a quarter from mom and a dollar from pop, but ask in such a manner that both mom and pop know what you are up to. They will think it is cute. Pretty soon you will get all that you want from management.
- *Build the support of the working troops.* Make sure that you get the working troops on your side. Get them to endorse the technology and stimulate them to play with it and use it on other jobs. If they like the technology, they will support your case. If they don't, they might sabotage your efforts by inadver-

tently telling your management that what you are proposing doesn't make technical sense.

■ *Get the line-of-business or product-line manager behind you.* Target your transition at the line-of-business level. This person has the power to stimulate reuse across projects in most organizations. Select your pilot carefully and build your justification accordingly. Such transitions are feasible, especially if you take the preceding advice.

While you may think these steps are nothing more than common sense, many times they are not followed. The results are often disastrous. My experience has been that if you set reasonable goals, remain focused, and are persistent, you can transition the technology.

PUTTING IT ALL TOGETHER

Your reuse adoption approach should take advantage of the three Ps and the tactics outlined in Chapter 3. The 10-step process I recommend for doing this is shown in Figure 4.4. Each of these steps is briefly explained in the following sections.

Define Your Vision and Strategy   Discuss what reuse is and why it is important to your firm. Identify the benefits and the downside risks. As explained in Chapter 2, describe what your strategy is and how it will realize these benefits. Summarize how the applications developers will benefit. After all, they are the people who are important because they are your reuse customers. Address the viewpoints of all those affected (executive, product-line manager, project manager, and contributing software engineer).

Determine Where You Are   Benchmark your current levels of software cost, productivity, and quality [8]. Conduct reviews to get the *hard* data and gather your experience and lessons learned. You'll need this information to prepare the business case that justifies your proposed investments and computes your return on investment. You will also need it to provide your supporters with positive reinforcement so that they will not waive their commitment.

Establish Your Operational Concept   As explained in Chapter 3, define how your users will take advantage of reuse opportunities within the context of how you plan to run your business now and in the future. Define the players and the usage scenarios. Identify the technical and management issues and how you will address them. Decide how you will handle the social and psychological change issues in any operational concept you develop.

Prepare a Business Case   Use the data you collected to develop a business case that gives your management a compelling reason to invest in software reuse. Highlight the financial benefits via a detailed economic or cost/benefit analysis.

Get your management to sign up by showing them how reuse helps them to increase their market share and develop a competitive edge. Provide the numbers to substantiate the claim that reuse is a good business decision.

Develop Your Business Plan   Identify how you plan to manage the many activities you will have to undertake to introduce reuse into your firm. Prepare your business case. Use a work breakdown structure to show how the products and people relate to your process. Involve those affected and get them to buy into and become owners of the plans. Address change as you develop your risk-management tactics and schedules.

Focus Early Effort on Infrastructure   While you've got the support of upper management, make any needed organizational changes and investments in management infrastructure (processes, standards, guidelines, tools, etc.). Allocate six months to a year to complete this activity. Later, when your support erodes and times get tougher, this firm foundation will help you to get through the many crises that will plague you.

Make an Initial Success   Focus your efforts on making an immediate impact. You can do this by concentrating on doing the simple things first. For example, publish a catalog identifying reusable assets and where to get them. As another example, put components that will be reused repeatedly (mathematical routines, database bindings, etc.) into a library and publicize their availability. As stated earlier, do the easy things first. Build momentum and support. Buy time to do the more difficult things later. Once you start rolling, you will be surprised by how much you can get done.

Try Your Ideas before You Try to Sell Them   Don't blindly adopt product-line, architecture, and reuse concepts just because people make them sound good. Try them before you buy them in demonstrations or on pilot projects. Perfect them and iron out the wrinkles before you venture forth to institutionalize them. You will be surprised how your standing will increase when project and product-line managers stand up and support you by saying: He is right based upon our experiences with the concepts.

Be Perceived as Being Successful   Continue publicizing your successes. Remember, success breeds success. This perception does wonders for you when you're fighting for people or budget. Reinforce the perception by making successes out of failures (we failed but took advantage of the lessons we learned). Publish or perish. This tactic lets you communicate your successes on your own terms, not your critics'.

Iterate and Refine Your Approach Based upon Results   Devise a process to perfect your process. Gather pertinent information and make it work for you. Iterate based upon results. Define ways to change, and use them to implement necessary product-oriented improvements. Be flexible. Listen to both your suppliers and customers; act and respond promptly to their concerns. Change your process only when you must, when the change is justified and supported by the facts.

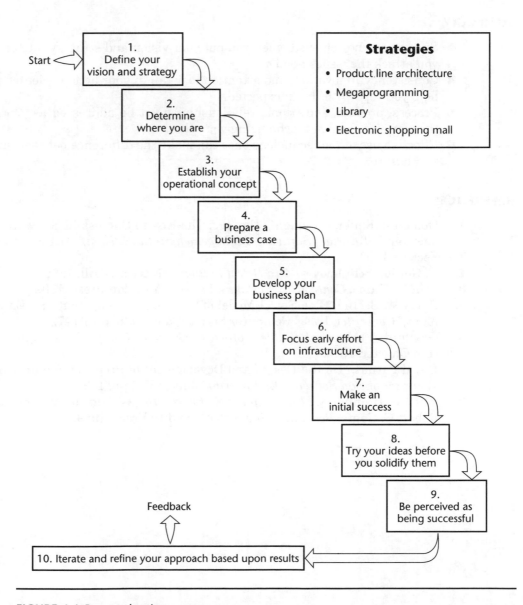

FIGURE 4.4 Reuse adoption process.

This process will be amplified with examples throughout the remainder of this book. These examples were selected to serve as models to help you introduce reuse into your firm. They contain both positive and negative experiences, and communicate lessons often learned the hard way. Examples were selected so that each represents a different stage of introduction for reuse.

SUMMARY

- Success can be achieved when you put your vision and strategy into action if you attack the issues head on.
- Consistency, innovation, and attention to detail in your action-oriented plans help you cope with the unexpected.
- Process, product, and people relationships must be addressed as you scope the work involved in mechanizing your plan.
- Effective use of the technology base can make the difference between success and failure.

REFERENCES

1. Donald J. Reifer, "Managing the 3Ps: The Key to Success in Software Management," *Tutorial: Software Management (4th Edition),* IEEE Computer Society, 1993.
2. G. Gordon Schulmeyer, *Zero Defect Software,* McGraw-Hill, 1990.
3. Tom DeMarco, *Controlling Software Projects,* Yourdon Press, 1982.
4. Barry W. Boehm, "The Spiral Model of Software Development and Enhancement," *Computer,* IEEE Computer Society, May 1988, pp. 61–72.
5. Glenford J. Myers, *Reliable Software Through Composite Design,* Petrocelli/Charter, 1975.
6. David Parnas, "On the Design and Development of Program Families," *IEEE Transactions on Software Engineering,* June 1976, pp. 1–9.
7. Watts S. Humphrey, *Managing the Software Process,* Addison-Wesley, 1989.
8. Robert C. Camp, *Benchmarking,* ASQC Quality Press, 1989.

Part II

Business Case Analysis

The real key to convincing people to move to a reuse culture is its impact on the bottom line.

Competitive Benchmarking

YOUR ORGANIZATIONAL CAPABILITIES

You must figure out where you are before you determine how to get where you are going. To do this, you should determine your position relative to your competition. The reason for developing such measures is simple. To win support, you will have to show those who are in the approval chain for your plan what you are trying to do, and how it will generate value for your firm. Such promotion requires you to quantify your software organization's capabilities and capacity to perform relative to some accepted norm. To build a case for change, you should consider baselining some of the following factors within your organization.

Hard Factors (Measurable)

- Workload (functions performed/month, including application development)
- Backlog (number of applications in the queue for development)
- Software cost (total $ spent/year, $/function, $/line of code and/or $/function point)
- Staff productivity (lines of code or function points/staff-month)
- Product quality (complaint rate, customer returns, etc.)
- Time to market (months until release from a project start)

Soft Factors (Discernable)

- Process maturity
- Degree of customer satisfaction

- Goodness of fit (did you build the right product, right, the first time)
- Overall competitiveness (measured by sales growth and market share)

There are various ways to ascertain how your organization rates relative to these factors. You can talk to people to get a feel for where you are. You can be more scientific and have a team assemble the data you need to quantify your current position. You could sample several projects to develop the experience database you need to conduct your analysis. Of course, the more quantitative you can get, the more believable your output. Don't discount war stories and lessons learned either. Both can be used effectively to improve the credibility of any proposal you may make, especially if you are requesting money to put your reuse strategy into action.

To assess your current position, you could perform a process assessment, benchmarking exercise, and/or a capability evaluation. A process assessment is directed at determining the maturity of the processes you use to develop your software and define where improvements are needed. Benchmarks are used to assess best practices and how you compare to best-of-industry or world-class organizations. Benchmarks can also be used to determine competitive position and figure out whether your costs, productivity, and quality are in line with your industry norms. Capability evaluations are reviews held to assess your capability and capacity to generate products. They focus primarily on product-directed recommendations for improvement. All three approaches recognize the importance of the development, maintenance, management, and technology transfer processes you use as an indicator of performance and source of competitive advantage.

Let's now look at experience with each of the three approaches before we turn our attention to your readiness to initiate your adoption activities.

Process Assessments

One of the most significant advances made in the field of software engineering during the past decade is the process maturity model [1], which is shown in Table 5.1a and 5.1b. The model was prepared by the Software Engineering Institute (SEI) in the late 1980s to assess the maturity of the processes that firms use to develop their software. The five levels shown in Table 5.1a and b are used to portray where an organization needs to make improvements. Key process areas were added to identify where to focus improvement efforts. To develop a rating, a structured approach is followed, which is based upon assessment findings taken from the sources using a variety of instruments (questionnaires, interviews, etc.). Although chiefly qualitative in nature, the findings of the assessment are valuable because they show how your organization compares with similar firms within your industry. They also help you to identify fundamental weaknesses in your process, which you can plan to correct in the near term.

TABLE 5.1a CMM Architecture

Level	Focus	Key Process Areas
5 Optimizing	Continuous process improvement	Defect prevention Technology change management Process change management
4 Managed	Quantitative control and predictability	Quantitative process management Software quality management
3 Defined	Common engineering processes	Organization process focus Organization process definition Integrated software management Software product engineering Intergroup coordination Training program Peer reviews
2 Repeatable	Project management, commitment processes, and baseline control	Requirements management Software project planning Software project tracking Software subcontract management Software quality assurance Software configuration management
1 Initial	Heroes	

M. C. Paulk, et al, (1995). The Capability Maturity Model: Guidelines for Improving Software Process. Reading, MA: Addison-Wesley.

A software process, as we have already learned, is a set of activities, practices, and decision rules that guide a staff in the generation and maintenance of software products. An effective process is one that people actually employ because it makes sense and is the right thing to do, not because management tells them to use it.

Let's look more deeply at the process maturity model to understand the characteristics of each of the SEI levels more fully.

Level 1 (Initial)   The process you use is *ad hoc* and not well defined. Instead of having common processes, each project must figure out how it will get the job done. Project managers are encouraged to document their processes in their software development plans. However, this is rarely done. Training in the process is on a project-by-project basis, and there is little or no commonality in software methods, tools, and management approaches. Essentially, every project is on its own. Projects must invest in defining, implementing, and deploying processes;

TABLE 5.1b Characteristic Behaviors at CMM Levels

Level 1	Level 2	Level 3	Level 4	Level 5
Success depends on heroes and overtime	Success depends on controlling commitments and baselines	Success enhanced by using common well understood processes	Success made more predictable by bringing processes under quantitative control	Competitiveness enhanced through continuous process improvement
Fire fighting is common-place	Problems are identified and managed	Processes designed to handle problems	Problems causing variation in performance are eliminated	Common causes of problems are prevented
Processes are sacrificed to schedule pressure	Processes are repeatable on similar projects	Common processes defined from best practices used across the organization	Variation in performing processes brought under quantitative control	Everyone engaged in continuously improving processes
Imported cultures	Commitment culture	Professional culture	Culture of precision	Empowered culture
Unstable results	Capability to meet schedule	Capability to meet cost and function-ality targets	Capability to predict quality results	Capability to continuously improve critical measures of success

Personal communication from Bill Curtis. Jan. 1997.

and experience gained in their use is rarely shared amongst them except in rare cases.

Level 2 (Repeatable) Processes exist on the showpiece projects (i.e., the big, risky, and important ones). However, they differ and there is little effort to pool knowledge and come up with a standard process for everyone's use. There is some consistency with regard to the software management infrastructure, but the wide latitude permitted allows project managers to do just about anything they wish relative to tool, methodology, training, and technology investments. Best practices are passed to people from people, not organization to organization. Small projects tend to be on their own. As a result, there is a breakdown of process discipline, especially when people are under the gun to meet a delivery date (i.e., the norm in most firms where I've worked).

Level 3 (Defined) A single software process is institutionalized for use across the firm. Of course, tailoring is permitted to adapt it to the varying needs of projects and the requirements of the customer. Management practices are standardized as well, and there is a single investment strategy in tools, methods, training, and technology. People understand the process and believe in its use. As a consequence, the firm reaps a lot of benefits from the process, especially when its people are transferred from one area to another (i.e., the learning curve is minimized and there is consistency across projects). Best practices can be applied as experience in their use is analyzed and built upon. Experience is capitalized upon as lessons learned are taken to heart.

Level 4 (Managed)   The institutionalized process takes advantage of an aggressive measurement program to determine what works best under which conditions. Effort is placed on doing the right tasks right the first time. Problem prevention instead of repair becomes the norm as emphasis shifts from process institutionalization to improvements in product quality. Technology is continuously infused to make the process better. Attention is placed on instituting a process management feedback and control system. Concerns over efficiency dominate as process improvement activities get attention.

Level 5 (Optimizing)   Utopia is realized as focus moves to continuous process improvement in a total quality management sense. Optimization is achieved via a feedback system, in which measurements taken are analyzed and results are fed forward to continuously improve the processes used by the firm. Advanced statistical controls are employed as product quality and productivity gains are made when the process is enhanced and strengthened. While no organization that I have worked with has yet achieved this level of maturity, I believe achieving level 5 is a good goal.

From 1987 to March 1996, the SEI has gathered the data shown in Figure 5.1 from 477 participating organizations who had conducted process assessments. Collectively, these assessments examined about 2,500 software projects that involved thousands of software professionals in discussions of process-related issues within their organizations. While most of these organizations were at the initial level of process maturity, the results show that many firms have made steady progress toward the goal of achieving higher maturity levels [2]. Such findings are similar to those reported several years ago at the project level when the initial findings of the SEI were published [3].

During the past five years, the SEI has been enhancing its process assessment methodology to include the concept of Key Process Areas (KPAs) discussed in Chapter 4. The Capability Maturity Model (CMM) [4] for software that has evolved, whose architecture is illustrated in Figure 5.2, makes heavy use of these KPAs to provide the detail necessary to understand the content of each of the maturity levels. While relatively new, the CMM resolves several known inconsistencies with the questionnaire approach used in the past to quantify process maturity, and provides better links between assessment results and improvement

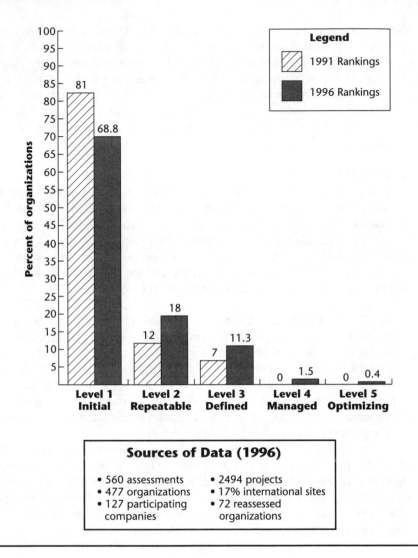

FIGURE 5.1 Process maturity rankings and ratings.

activities. It is currently trying to determine how to incorporate architectures, product lines, and reuse in its rating schemes.

The SEI has also defined in detail the process you would use to conduct an assessment. This process gathers data from projects using your software practices to determine where they fit relative to the CMM. Management gets involved early so that their expectations can be set and commitments can be extracted. The key product of the assessment is an improvement plan, not the rating score received, along with the findings and recommendations.

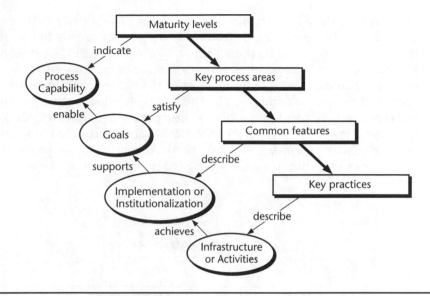

FIGURE 5.2 CMM structure. *Source:* M. C. Paulk, et al. (1995). The Capability Maturity Model: Guidelines for Improving the Software Process. Reading, MA: Addison-Wesley.

The SEI has done a lot to promote the process maturity model. It has conducted seminars, run conferences, published reports, and provided valuable assistance to firms on the how-to. In addition, it has transferred its methodology to the commercial sector by authorizing lead assessors after they receive required training and experience in conducting internal assessments.

The firms I have worked with, who have conducted process assessments using the CMM, have found them extremely valuable because:

■ They provide a consistent framework for assessing the maturity of their processes.
■ They accurately identify organizational strengths and weaknesses.
■ They focus attention on making the investments necessary to improve the software process.
■ They identify an implied order for what must be done to move up the maturity ladder level by level through their definition of relevant KPAs.

From a reuse point of view, process assessments are valuable because they can help you determine whether your firm is ready to adopt reuse technology using any of the strategies we have described. Several attempts have been made to rate reuse process capabilities [5, 6] using the SEI process maturity model as the basis. Conceptually, the mapping between reuse process capabilities and the five levels in the SEI maturity framework could be similar to that shown in Figure 5.3. The five groupings of reuse factors shown in this figure are characterized in Table 5.2 and in their original form in an SPC guidebook [7] on the subject. You would use these factors to assess the relative effort needed to implement your reuse strategy. Of course, once the reuse capabilities are agreed upon, the CMM framework employed by the SEI to develop maturity ratings will have to be revised. Several proposals to incorporate architecture, COTS, and reuse have been made for version 2 of the CMM [8], and the SEI is seriously contemplating taking action based upon them. As you will see, you will have to use approaches like that devised by the SPC to determine if you are ready to adopt reuse.

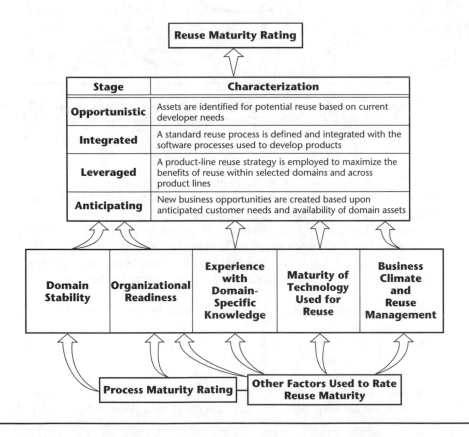

FIGURE 5.3 Reuse process maturity model. This work was developed in part under a grant from DARPA to the Software Productivity Consortium NFP, Inc., who owns the copyright thereto. The content of the information does not necessarily reflect the position or the policy of the Government and no official endorsement should be inferred.

TABLE 5.2 Reuse Factor Characterizations

Domain Stability	*Organizational Readiness*	*Experience with Domain-Specific Knowledge*	*Maturity of Technology Used for Reuse*	*Business Climate and Reuse Management*
Domain age	Organizational stability	Years in this business	Research investments	Market share and dominance
Number of products and product lines within domain	Motivation for reuse	Experience in building products and product lines for the domain	Maturity of domain engineering technology used	Availability of capital and R&D funds for reuse
Volatility of customer requirements	Scope of the planning done for reuse	Experience of customers and consumers	Maturity of asset packaging technology used	Availability of partnering opportunities
Availability of domain models	Identification of candidate reuse opportunities	Experience with the domain model	Maturity of asset management technology used	Availability of incentives for reuse
Availability of domain experts	Management commitment to reuse	Experience of the domain experts	Maturity of application development (with reuse) technology used	Existence of contractual, legal and other management barriers to reuse
Availability of reference architectures	Level of reuse advocacy	Experience with the reference architecture	Maturity of reuse methods and tools used	Depth of domain management
Availability of off-the-shelf assets to populate the architecture	Development process capability maturity (SEI)	Experience with the available reuse processes, tools, and assets	Maturity of reusable assets used (high quality, etc.)	Breadth of support for domains
Supplier commitment to maintain assets	Development environment support for reuse	Effectiveness of domain asset classifications		
Potential for rapid change within marketplace	Reuse education and training opportunities	Effectiveness of suppliers in servicing needs		

This work was developed in part under a grant from DARPA to the Software Productivity Consortium NFP, Inc., who owns the copyright thereto. The content of the information does not necessarily reflect the position or the policy of the Government and no official endorsement should be inferred.

Indeed, the process maturity model has proven to be so valuable a tool that the Department of Defense and several other government agencies regularly expect firms responding to their solicitations to demonstrate that they are rated at least an SEI Level 3 before they are considered eligible for a competitive award. They also have developed a people- and systems-oriented CMM to provide structure for assessing the maturity of processes in these critical related areas. It is likely that these agencies will consider product lines, architecture, and reuse when appropriate practices are considered for inclusion under either an existing or new KPA in the future.

The commercial sector is doing a similar thing when they require the use of the International Standards Organization's SPICE [9] to determine a firm's software process maturity before the award of a contract or subcontract. This model identifies 34 processes, each of which can be independently measured according to six capability levels. In addition, the ISO has also released its 9000 series standards for making sure firms certified under it are using a gated process.

Benchmarking

Benchmarking is defined as the search for those industry best practices that lead to superior performance [10]. Your goal is to identify those firms, regardless of industry, that demonstrate superior performance relative to those factors you feel are important to your customers (price/performance, quality, etc.). During a benchmarking exercise, you would also look for firms that you feel are leaders or world class within your industry, especially if you were conducting a competitive evaluation. For example, if you decided to switch to product lines, you might look to the telecommunications industry for best practices. Products within this industry (switches, wireless, etc.) are organized in this manner using a line-of-business orientation. You might look for practices that lead to reductions in time to market if this is the goal you have set for improvement as part of your benchmarking investigations.

As described previously, benchmarking is basically an objective-setting process. As shown in Figure 5.4, the process starts with planning and ends with action. Benchmarking's focus is on figuring out what practices within an industry lead to goal fulfillment. The process goes through the following five phases in 10 steps.

Planning   To start with, you want to identify what factors should be benchmarked and why. Then, you must figure out which firms in your industry have successfully addressed these factors in their current practice. Although it helps, firms whom you perceive as doing this well do not have to be your competitors. They could be firms in totally different fields, whose processes not products are comparable to yours. Next, you should identify which firms your customers (not your marketing group) feel are the best in your industry, against whom you can make the most meaningful comparisons. You can endeavor to benchmark at many levels: best of breed, industry leader, national class, or world class. Finally, you need to figure out how you are going to get the data you need to create your benchmarking baseline. You could get this either from industry associations or from the firms you selected directly as industry leaders (benchmarking partners), as long as you have some carrot to offer them for their help.

Analysis   Data gathering and analysis begins right after you figure out what, why, how, and who will be benchmarked. You should first get the data you've identified internally; it is the easiest. Then, go after your benchmarking partners' inputs. Make sure that you validate the data against industry norms before making any judgments, or your critics may discredit your efforts before they get off the ground.

The data validation step is often difficult because people fear measurement. Instead of providing reasonable data, workers may alter or discolor it to make themselves look good. Once resistance is overcome, thorough analysis of the validated data permits you to point to what leads to superior performance. You can then examine the relative strengths and weaknesses of your benchmarking partners' practices to determine why they are performing better than you are and what process changes are needed, where, in what order. You need to answer the question: Will these practices, if adopted, have a positive impact on my future performance?

Integration   Assuming that change appears necessary, you will next have to gain acceptance of the benchmarking results by those who can empower change and fund implementation. In addition, findings must be communicated throughout the organization to get the commitment, agreement, and support needed for change from all those impacted by it. The key to success in this venture is the integration of the benchmark results into a number of possible change targets. These targets must be ones that your operating units think are needed and are willing to commit to make happen. Remember, change should be done specifically to attain superiority, not because it sounds like a good idea or pacifies some critic.

Action   Targets must now become implementations. Plans should be developed to pinpoint the actions required to make improvements happen operationally. Measurement is needed to assess performance relative to these plans. As progress is made, detours will become apparent. Changes must be incorporated, when needed and justified, and activity refocused on achieving results. Progress toward superior performance based upon your benchmarks should be periodically reported to all concerned in order to retain their commitment and support. Iteration based upon results is essential, especially when you are counting on others to assist you to perform the implementation.

Maturity   Maturity is realized when the best industry practices finally become part of the way you conduct your business. However, you can become truly world class only when you recognize that benchmarking is a continuous process. Keeping ahead of the competition may force you to adopt a continuous improvement process. You should rely on the Japanese principle of Kaizen [11] to strive always to do things better, make things better, and improve even when it seems you can no longer. If you do not, you will not keep up with the firms that do.

Other benchmarking processes have been proposed using variations of the *plan-act-do* approach [12]. Each of these calls for collecting the necessary data to determine performance gaps and enablers. Each calls for you to integrate the results with other competitive information to provide you with an accurate picture of the options available for your firm's future.

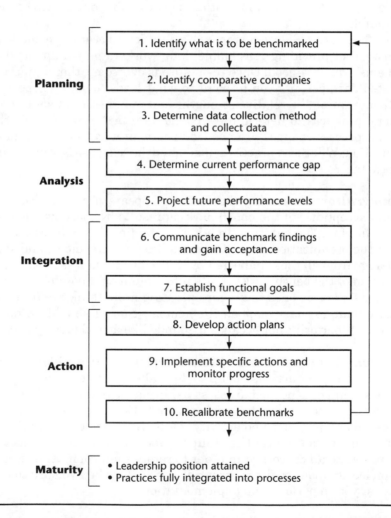

FIGURE 5.4 Benchmarking process. *Source:* Robert C. Camp, *Benchmarking,* ASQC Quality Press, 1989.

You can pursue different kinds of benchmarks. The three most popular forms of benchmarks that I worked with include: internal, competitive and industry-wide.

Internal Benchmarks   These measurements are used to rate the comparable performance of organizations within the same firm. They may be taken across operating units, divisions, or geographical businesses. Often, management's goal in pursuing such benchmarks is to raise the overall performance of its units to the level of its highest producers. This leveling strategy builds upon existing strengths, and is relatively easy to make work in practice.

Competitive Benchmarks   These yardsticks are used to compare competing organizations that generate like products within similar industries. They assume that competitors will cooperate to develop industry norms. Results can then be packaged to motivate management to make those investments needed to raise the level of performance to industry norms. It was surprising to me on my first benchmarking exercise how cooperative competing firms can be when you explain to them how everyone who participates will benefit from the benchmarking effort. The American Society of Quality Control propagates this win-win theme in many of its publications on the topic.

Industry-Wide Benchmarks   These standards are used to compare general business functions that remain constant across industries (beta testing, distribution, inventory control, marketing, etc.). Investigation outside of one's industry often leads to innovative ideas that can be used to improve performance above those levels achieved by the industry leader. Your problems are not unique. Solutions tried and tested elsewhere may work within the context of your application. Industry-wide benchmarks enable you to search across industries for such innovations.

Once completed, you must present the results of your benchmarking study to management. Proper preparation and packaging can add greatly to how well they are received. The approach I've used is to focus benchmark results on the practices that work for others within my industry, and then describe how you can put them to work within your firm. Talk alternatives and results achieved as part of the effort. Remember, doing nothing is always an alternative. You must show management why they should take action. Give them a compelling reason to buy into your recommended action plan. Tell them what they are going to gain. Permit them to make the important decisions. Give them the bait and then hook them when they come after it. You will be amazed by the enthusiasm management displays when they think they were responsible for coming up with the idea.

Benchmarks can be used very effectively by those introducing software reuse. As shown in Figure 5.5, they can be used to supplement SEI process maturity assessments with the hard data on relative performance that seems to count when briefing senior management. Providing management with the data that shows how investment in reuse strategies reduces cost, improves quality, and increases your competitive ability to deliver on schedule always seems to get their attention. Again, be careful with such data, because it can come back to haunt you. Remember, managers never seem to forget a number. Use such numbers only when you are sure that you can live with them.

Benchmarks definitely get management's attention. Just see what happens when you tell them how well their competition is ranked and rated using hard data. Benchmarks have the advantage that they define what has to be done in quantitative terms. They are hard hitting because they tell management what others in similar situations have done to make necessary improvements. Investments required tend to be acceptable because they are competitively oriented and market based. Because benchmarks permit goals to be set, measured, and acted upon, it is no wonder that many *Fortune*-500 firms, such as American Telegraph & Telephone, General Electric, and Westinghouse have embraced and used them to implement change for the better strategies. Once during an executive briefing, I remember seeing a senior vice president standing on a chair in the back of the room to see the numbers more clearly. It is a good thing he did not fall, because he

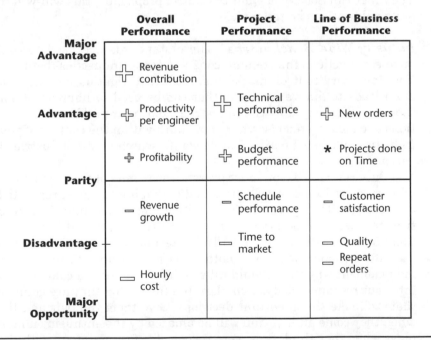

FIGURE 5.5 Benchmarking results. Note: Results of analyzing 47 projects done by three lines of business over the past two years, and comparing them against industry norms compiled from 25 firms involving 876 similar projects' worth of data.

became one of my greatest supporters later on when I was implementing the process improvement plan justified by the benchmarks I was presenting.

Capability Evaluations

Capability evaluations are our third and simplest option. Typically, such evaluations of current position are made by conducting some form of structured review. Such reviews often focus on critical success factors, defined as those characteristics, conditions, or variables that have been shown to have a direct influence on your customers' satisfaction with your products and/or services, and have been designated as critical to the success of your business. Such factors represent the measurable or observable aspects of the important processes you use to run your business. Examples of such factors include price/performance, perceived quality, and performance.

As can be gleaned by their name, capability evaluations investigate more than just process. In addition to process variables, they examine the following other critical success factors that have a direct impact on an organization's capability and capacity to perform:

- Financial health of the firm, borrowing capability, and ability to secure venture capital
- Marketing and distribution channels available within different geographic locales
- Strategic relationships that exist between this firm and its suppliers and customers
- Innovation, experience, skills, knowledge, and abilities of the software workforce
- Management capability to deliver products acceptable to key client accounts
- Overall capability of the firm to retain technical leadership over the competition
- Degree of capitalization and availability of modern facilities, tools, and resources
- Degree of burden and availability of necessary support staff (editors, etc.)
- Capability of the firm to perform in all areas deemed core competencies

By no means is this list complete. The critical success factors chosen were selected to illustrate the wide range of variables you must consider when assessing an organization's capability and capacity to perform, especially in such an area as software where innovation is prized.

The U.S. Department of Defense has led the way with such reviews. They have been conducting Software Development Capability/Capacity Reviews (SDC-CRs) [13] since the mid-1980s to ensure that their contractors have the capability to produce quality software for their weapons systems. Such reviews are held prior to the award of a contract, and are used as factors in source selections. The requirement to hold SDCCRs is explicitly called out in solicitations via the following Notice to Offerers:

> A Software Development Capability/Capacity Review (SDCCR) will be conducted as an integral part of the (program name) source selection. The SDCCR is intended to review the offerers ability to develop software. This review encompasses all aspects of the offerers software development capability, and is organized in eight major areas: management approach, management tools, engineering development process, personnel resources, Ada technology, flight-critical software, artificial intelligence technology, and complex hardware development (Modify based on areas included). The SDCCR will be a factor in the basis for award. The SDCCR will be based on the review areas, factors, and questions attached herein.

Like the DoD, I have found such reviews extremely valuable when I have been evaluating contractors' capability to perform. If you are looking at teaming or using third parties to develop software, you might consider conducting such a review to provide useful insights.

An effort has recently been mounted to merge the SDCCR with the SEI CMM. Evaluations of this sort, however, are much more extensive than process assessments, because they have third-party inspectors instead of internal assessors examining the many additional variables that may impact a software organization's capability and capacity to perform.

ARE YOU READY TO ADOPT REUSE?

Now that you have assessed your current position, you are probably asking the following questions: Am I ready to adopt reuse? How do I take the assessment or benchmarking data that I have gathered and use it to sell the vision and strategy I came up with along with my operational concepts? Is it time to start putting strategies into action?

To develop answers to these questions, let's review where you are in the change process. You have done most of the prework needed to define your plan of attack. You have formulated a vision and strategy, and developed an operational concept document. You have interested management in the topic, and gotten its support to pursue taking the next step—developing your business plan and case. You have performed an assessment, evaluation, and/or benchmarking exercise to gather the data needed to quantify your competitive position. You have developed a lot of interest, but for the most part generated paper as products instead of immediate results. What do you do now to maintain your momentum?

The output of your assessment or benchmarking exercise presents you with a unique opportunity. You will brief senior management on your findings, conclusions, and recommendations. You will be able to quantify your competitive position and provide them with hard data that substantiates the need for a paradigm switch to reuse. You can hammer home the need to adopt the strategies you have developed. You can do this in conjunction with the action plan you have or are in the process of developing to improve your firm's software capabilities and capacity.

The timing for the briefing could not be better. Management has started to work on other issues since you visited them last. Rekindling their interest in reuse and support for the changes you are recommending will be to your advantage. Remember, being out of sight and out of mind often results in being out of the picture, especially when the budgets for next year are being formulated.

WHAT DO YOU PUT IN AN ACTION PLAN?

As noted, an assessment, evaluation, or benchmarking exercise tells you your competitive position within your industry. However, just knowing where you are and what the problems are is not good enough. You must also figure out where you are going and make a business case for change. Action planning is therefore a necessity, as is its presentation to management. Based upon my experience, briefing a problem without a solution tends to be suicide. As a result, many questions should be entering your mind about what you should put in your action plan, and how to package it so that it sells your reuse strategy. Let me answer some of these questions in the following paragraphs, and show you how to take your assessment results and use them to support your reuse strategy.

Action Plan Formulation

You're probably asking how to take your assessment results and turn them into an action plan that supports your reuse vision and strategy. The nine-step process is shown in Figure 5.6. It starts with a goal and ends with a set of actions that, when completed, demonstrate that you've achieved the goal in no uncertain terms. It identifies the problem you're attacking and shows how it will be corrected. It defines tasks and details the resources (equipment, time, staff, money, etc.) needed to complete them. It provides near-term results while it focuses on long-term payoffs. It shows how your investments in reuse will contribute to improving the overall health and well-being of your firm. A typical action plan outline is shown in Plan of Action 5.1. As so structured, the plan focuses on the actions you must complete to achieve the goals you have set and fully address the issues raised during the assessment, evaluation, and/or benchmarking exercise you just completed.

The reason you are pursuing product lines, architectures, and software reuse is probably economic. You most likely want to reduce your time to market, improve quality, or reduce your software costs. You are interested in how software reuse contributes to your overall improvement goals. You want to pinpoint the risks so that you can try to avoid them. Your action plan must therefore be structured to address all of the issues and justify the investments. The numbers in the business case that will accompany the plan must be able to sell reuse as part of an overall improvement plan based upon its merits. As you can see, I believe that making reuse part of a broader plan has benefits.

My experience in action planning differs from that written about by others. Many suggest that you take several weeks to develop your action plan after you have completed your assessment, evaluation, and/or benchmarking exercise. In my opinion, managers do not want to wait. They want to know how to solve a problem the moment they hear about it. When briefed on the results of an assessment, they are not willing to let a team go off, study the problem, and come back later to tell them what to do about it. They want action proposals during the out-briefing.

You would be foolish not to take advantage of the opportunity and strike when the iron is hot. The reason for this is simple. If you wait too long, you may

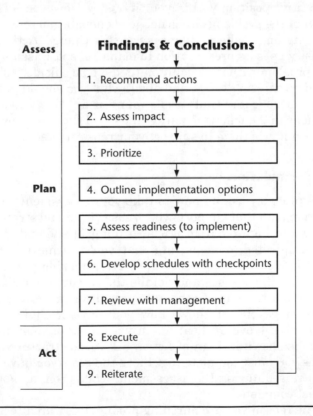

FIGURE 5.6 Action planning process.

PLAN OF ACTION 5.1   Action Plan Outline

Executive Summary

SECTION 1: INTRODUCTION
  A. Purpose and scope
  B. General background
  C. Business goals (summary)
  D. Business case (summary)

SECTION 2: ACTION PLAN
  A. Summary of assessment findings
  B. Alternatives
  C. Recommended actions (prioritized)
  D. Readiness to perform
  E. Work plan
  F. Schedule (with checkpoints)
  G. Deliverables
  H. Budget
  I. Risks
  J. Measures of success

APPENDIX A   GLOSSARY OF TERMS
APPENDIX B   DETAILED ASSESSMENT FINDINGS
APPENDIX C   MAPPINGS BETWEEN FINDINGS AND RECOMMENDATIONS
APPENDIX D   DETAILED ANALYSIS OF OPTIONS
APPENDIX E   ASSESSMENT OF PRIORITIES
APPENDIX F   BUSINESS CASE DETAILS
APPENDIX G   OTHER BACKUP MATERIALS

never get another opportunity to make your case, because management will divert its attention to deal with the other fires as they erupt.

Be careful, it may be premature to make recommendations on the spot for a number of reasons. First, you may need to examine the situation more closely to understand the consequences of the recommended actions more fully. Simple solutions to difficult problems do not work in my experience. Many people treat the symptoms of a problem, not its root cause. Next, you may need to get a lot of organizations to buy into the solution, especially if they will be expected to implement the remedy in the near term. Finally, you may need time to study the alternatives more deeply to figure out what will work best under what circumstances. As a consequence, you may have to temper management's desire for immediate results by taking small steps in the interim to buy time and demonstrate that you've got things under control. Some of the things you could do include:

■ Identify the major issues identified in your out-briefing, and recommend at a high level the actions that could be taken to address each of them. Separate your actions by timing (near term, midterm, and long term) and priority (essential, critical, and priority). Get management involved by soliciting their feedback to alternatives. You might even consider planting someone to ask questions to stimulate discussion on the options. Be sure to address the near-term issues and windows of opportunity in your briefing. As an output, try to get management to form a team to address how to make the culture change to product lines, architectures, and reuse that you are proposing.

- In addition to handling the near-term issues, propose doing something you can do that is simple and generates visible products right away (publish a success story, prepare a catalog of your reusable assets, etc.). Broker information, because it is something tangible that is easy to get your arms around. You will be perceived as being successful if you get something done quickly. It does not seem to matter how big or small the success is on which you are working. What matters is, you did something that had value. Remember, you are always being tested and you need a passing grade to get the okay to continue.

- In parallel, build a business case that justifies your proposed action plan and creates the notion that any investments made this year will not yield returns until perhaps the second or third year in the future. Temper management's desire for immediate payback by presenting large returns in the long term. Justify investments in terms of the factors management thinks are important. Be aggressive but realistic with your plans. Be sure to set expectations that you have a reasonable chance of realizing.

- Prepare your plan to detail the initial steps, products, schedules, and resource requirements. I have found providing a five-year strategic and two-year tactical plan works well. View briefing management as an opportunity to get their commitment and support for your initiatives. Be assured that management wants to know the issues and what to do about them. They also want to know how they can help get the job done cheaper, quicker, and better. Help them help you. Be prepared or be sorry. Rehearse your pitch, get your backup together, and be ready to handle the questions. Be assured that management will test you. Brief your champions beforehand. If they approve, they will protect you.

There are many other techniques you can use to rate and rank the goodness of the alternatives. The trick is to pick the things with high value about which you can do something. Chapters 6 and 7 offer suggestions on the things you can do to justify alternatives. In any evaluation, make sure that you pick criteria that management understands, feels is important, and is concerned about. Otherwise, you will be wasting everyone's time when you make your recommendations and brief the results.

Make sure you show management that you can deliver what you have promised by implementing your plan and producing results. When briefing management, you must be specific about how you will get the most value for the least cost. The best way to be successful is to deliver. Even when you fail, claim success (Yes, we didn't do everything we planned, but look at the lessons we've learned). Plan for success and publicize your results. Do the things that you know you can do and avoid wasting time studying the problem to death. You will be surprised how well these strategies work.

Your immediate challenge is to get management to approve your action plan. Part of the plan will provide the hooks for the business plans and cases you will need for reuse. Your longer-term challenge is to be able to deliver what you promised. Never forget the proof of the pudding is the pudding. Realize, if you do not deliver, your critics will never let you (or management) forget it. Remember that change agents are always viewed as threats. Never let down your guard. Do not let the naysayers, want-to-bes and do-nothings get you down.

Change Tactics

Action plans should result in change. Otherwise, why pursue them? To harness change and make it work for you, different tactics can be considered. The five most popular of these tactics that I have been exposed to include pull-push, push-pull, rolling wave, win small–win big, and big bang.

Pull-Push   As part of this approach, a corporate champion agitates for change and gets upper management to commit to a plan of action. Those in the middle of the organization often actively resist the change and try to enlist those at the bottom in their cause. When those at the bottom support the champion, they can put pressure on those in the middle to make the desired changes. This tactic is something called the *visionary strategy* because the champion sometimes acts as the forcing function for the change.

Push-Pull   Here, support for change comes from both the top and bottom at the same time. Those in the middle must battle both extremes as they try to resist change at all costs, because they truly view change as a risk to their ability to deliver. Both sides pressure and wear the middle down in their quest for improvement. This tactic is sometimes called the *squash* approach, because those in the middle often feel crunched when they are pushed and pulled at the same time. It is the most difficult tactic to pull off, because advocacy at the middle is really where the action is in most organizations.

Rolling Wave   This approach feeds experience gained during one spiral (minidevelopment or step in your action plan) into the next. It spawns skills that are then used during the next spiral to reduce the learning curve and implement a *do a little, learn a lot* philosophy. The staff from one spiral often spins off and spreads the gospel to other areas. It is an evolutionary approach that relies on phasing to overcome many of the barriers that plague the more revolutionary approaches that rely on change agents to break down the resistance and develop champions. It is an incremental strategy, in which results are staged to make progress visible. It relies on success to breed success. However, the tactic typically takes years to unfold. As a result, those wanting results quickly may grow impatient.

Win Small, Win Big   This tactic revolves around the belief that a large number of small victories are themselves a large victory. To gain momentum and support, you plan on doing a large number of highly visible, real, short-fuzzed, practical low-risk, high-payoff things very quickly as part of your action plan. As previously stated, being perceived as being successful is synonymous with being successful in most people's minds. What counts is perception. Generating a lot of activity, being highly visible, and producing useful results make you appear to be a winner. This buys you the time and reputation to do the really important things later when your program is solidified and not too tightly scrutinized.

Big Bang   This is a more revolutionary approach, in which change is introduced quickly before any resistance can be mounted. Here, the organization commits to making the shift and absorbing the budget and schedule hits as it implements needed changes all at once instead of in a just-in-time manner. Those who resist those changes are either removed or placed in parking positions. Action dominates, especially when the consequences of the alternatives are severe. Typically, an outsider is brought in to be the ax man. Radical change is possible because past friendships, relationships, and loyalties do not enter into the decisions. They are made based on merit alone. However, to pull off this approach, the ax man must be empowered by those at the top of the organization to make radical changes even when they make people angry. Else, the strategy will fail as politics dominate and nothing gets done.

Selection of the most appropriate change strategy for reuse from this set depends on many factors, chief among these includes:

- Perceived urgency or need for change (this is where your benchmarks and process assessment data will pay off because they justify the recommended changes)
- Maturity of the organization (reuse may be secondary to more pressing problems, such as lack of configuration or project management)
- Degree of management commitment and support (without such backing at all levels of the organization, you're dead before you start)
- The cost in terms of investments and schedule delays your projects will incur as you implement the change (they have to be acceptable)

■ Degree of acceptance and support for change by those impacted by it (without backing, no change is possible because critics may resist every attempt to do something different)

When it comes to a switch to a reuse paradigm, those who oppose it will think of at least a hundred reasons why it shouldn't be done. This is a natural phenomenon, so don't get overly excited when people start complaining. Your job is to channel this emotion and gain favor for the changes contained in your action plan.

Remember that product lines, architecture, and software reuse represent change. No matter how well you plan it, people will fight the change because it scares them. To succeed, your tactics must deal with the psychological and cultural factors in addition to the managerial and technical ones. If you are not willing to put up with all the heartburn, recommend something else; because the changeover to reuse, although worthwhile, has been found by early adopters to be hard.

CASE STUDY

When I started to write this book, I wondered how to communicate the lessons learned as I worked with clients to put reuse into practice under a variety of circumstances. The first things that immediately came to mind were case studies. However, getting approval from organizations for release of case study materials proved to be a long and difficult process. To overcome these clearance problems, I decided to disguise and build upon real cases to convey my points. I have also modified the cases somewhat to make them more issues based and action oriented. The cases cover the wide range of situations that I have encountered across many industries. I believe they are relevant and present you with a number of learning opportunities.

The first case deals with a large software house developing a persistent object-oriented database for the POSIX/workstation marketplace. This is a high-growth company that is under a great deal of pressure to produce to keep its investors (mostly venture capitalists) happy. The company currently has about 300 professional employees, of which 150 are in software engineering. Their marketing workforce is small (about 50) because they market their products through OEM (original equipment manufacturers) and distributors. Their existing relational database management and data warehouse products are viewed by many as providing the best value for the money. Because they are competing against several much larger and more entrenched database management system vendors (Oracle, Software AG, Sybase, etc.), they have to do it right the first time or face the possibility of going out of business.

The new vice president of software engineering had been disturbed about the perceived quality of the firm's products. Complaints about latent defects from key OEM account managers had become frequent and troublesome. It was taking his staff an average of six weeks to fix a defect. The vice president asked one of his senior staffers to conduct a benchmarking study to determine:

- Defect rate norms within the POSIX/workstation market
- How long did it take on average within the industry to fix a defect
- Practices that could be used to bring defect rates and turnaround time in line with industry averages

The staffer did not know where to start, so he began by placing a call to a friend in a larger firm's quality assurance department to get some advice. The friend suggested that he call the American Society of Quality Control (ASQC) to get literature on benchmarking, and get in touch with me to provide help.

The first thing we did was more precisely define the object of the benchmarking exercise. We needed to define exactly what defect rates were, how we were going to measure them, and the average time to fix them. We initiated a literature search to try to determine how firms within the database software industry measured these items, coming up with the following conclusions:

- *Defect* was any problem the user experienced with the product, independent of cause, that resulted in a written complaint being received by the firm or its marketing distributor
- *Defect rate* was the number of complaints recorded per month once a product had been released for sale
- *Defect turnaround time* was the number of days it took for a fix to be received by the customer

Armed with these definitions, we developed a questionnaire to collect normative data for the industry. Usually at this time, I seek out an industry association to help get competing firms involved in the benchmarking exercise. Unfortunately, I could not find one. I resorted to working with a consortium of firms acting together on common object-request broker architectures, called the Object Management Group. I used the network of contacts that I had developed through this group to generate interest in finding out the industry norms.

Next, I distributed the questionnaire. Before long, I started to get phone calls from potential participants. They wanted to know what I was going to do to protect their data and to mask the identity. I told them that was what my firm did as a business, and sent them an agreement that I had used in the past, which provided legal remedies should I release proprietary data (any data other than the composite norms). We overcame the resistance to filling out the questionnaire by providing our advocates with such an agreement and an understanding of how the data was to be used.

We were not finished. We initiated an effort to validate the data after we received the completed questionnaires. To do this, we checked each questionnaire for omissions and obvious errors. Using 14 surveys, we then computed the norms and looked for data outliers and inputs that did not seem to make sense. Next, we got on the telephone and worked with those who filled out the questionnaires to figure out whether corrections were necessary or if we just needed more information to understand the situation.

Finally, we prepared an executive briefing that summarized the results of our data analysis, and provided lessons learned. The briefing was developed in annotated form, with text explaining the bullet charts on facing pages. We did this because this briefing was what we promised each firm as its reward for participating in the exercise.

The numbers we presented were very interesting because they built on what we learned during the benchmarking exercise. Several participating firms asked us to modify our questionnaire to collect data on the average time to market (as measured in the number of days from a project start until product release). As will be shown in Chapter 6, this number proved very valuable to us as we formulated our business case, because it allowed us to develop additional justifications for improvement projects. The industry norms were couched in ranges as follows:

Rate (Defects/Month)			Turnaround Time (Days)			Time to Market (Days)		
Min	Norm	Max	Min	Norm	Max	Min	Norm	Max
2	8	26	1	5	93	180	400	1,005

You are probably wondering how the company fared relative to these norms. Their numbers were as follows:

Rate (Defects/Month)		Turnaround Time (Days)		Time to Market (Days)	
Firm	Norm	Firm	Norm	Firm	Norm
17	8	42	5	365	400

This data says that although this firm was turning products out quicker than the industry norm, their quality as measured by the defect rates and turnaround times experienced was inferior when compared to industry norms.

Remember, I said not to brief a problem without a solution in the chapter. Well we did not. We made several suggestions in this brief to improve the practices used for testing, quality assurance, and customer support. We justified these improvement activities based on reduced cost of quality as measured by abbreviated cycle times and lower defect rates.

Of course, the firm's performance and the specific suggestions for improvement were not released in the executive briefing that was shared with all benchmarking participants. However, I have been led to believe that several participating firms used the data to justify improvements.

At the time, I did not recommend that the firm focus on reuse. I felt that it had more fundamental problems primarily with its processes and customer support infrastructure. However, today I would. Software reuse could help this firm improve its quality immediately. As stated in Chapter 1, industry data indicates that reusable assets have as much as ten times better quality than new ones. Increasing the percentage of reusable assets in this firm's product releases could therefore help this firm to overcome its apparent quality problems. With regard to the relative impact on turnaround time, I believe improved procedures could be put into place to address this issue as software processes were being changed to incorporate support for increased reuse.

SUMMARY

- You must figure out where you are before you can figure out how to get where you are going.
- Process assessments, benchmarking studies, and capability evaluations can help you identify issues and determine your competitive position.
- Management believes hard data; use it to your advantage.
- You are ready to show how product lines, architectures, and reuse contribute as part of your overall improvement plan.
- Reuse in an action-planning context should be viewed as part of a broader improvement program.
- Your next step is to use the data you have gathered to help prepare your business case.

REFERENCES

1. Watts S. Humphrey, *Managing the Software Process,* Addison-Wesley, 1989.
2. Software Engineering Institute, *The Evidence for CMM-based Software Process Improvement,* May 1996.
3. David H. Kitson and Steve Masters, *An Analysis of SEI Software Process Assessment Results: 1987–1991,* Software Engineering Institute, CMU/SEI-92-TR-24, July 1992.
4. Mark C. Paulk, Charles V. Weber, Bill Curtis, and Mary Beth Chrissis, *The Capability Maturity Model: Guidelines for Improving the Software Process,* Addison-Wesley, 1995.
5. Harris Corporation, *Reuse Maturity Model,* briefing on topic, 1992.
6. Donald J. Reifer, *Software Reusability: Making It Work for You,* Reifer Consultants, Inc., RCI-TN-494A, December 1991.
7. Software Productivity Consortium, *Reuse Adoption Guidebook,* SPC-92051-CMC, November 1993.

8. Mark Paulk, *Survey Results: Proposed Major Changes for SWW-CMM v2,* Software Engineering Institute, memo to CMM Correspondence Group, June 1996.

9. International Standards Organization, *Baseline Practices Guide,* Version 1.01, December 1994.

10. Robert C. Camp, *Benchmarking,* American Society for Quality Control, Quality Press, 1989.

11. Masaaki Imai, *Kaizan,* McGraw-Hill, 1986.

12. Gregory H. Watson, *Strategic Benchmarking,* John Wiley & Sons, 1993.

13. Department of the Air Force, *Software Development Capability/Capacity Review,* ASD Pamphlet 800-5, June 1991.

Business-Case Development

6

SCOPE THE MARKET FOR REUSE

In Chapter 5, you looked inward. You assessed your capabilities and benchmarked your relative performance against industry norms. You identified your change tactics and developed an action plan to ready your organization for reuse. In essence, you figured out how to create an environment conducive to adopting your reuse vision and your operational concepts. You have also defined the strategies and tactics you will use to make a difference once you've received go-ahead.

In this chapter, you will look outward. You will assess the impact of your reuse vision and strategy on your organization's business, and develop a business case that justifies your projected expenditures. This business case can make or break you. While your critics can argue the merits or demerits of your technical proposal, they will have a difficult time discrediting you when the numbers speak strongly for your proposition.

A long time ago I learned that focusing on the financials is the key to success when dealing with executives. They are most interested in the impact of your proposals on the bottom line. Executives want to do the right thing, but their ability to act is limited and there is always so much that needs to be done. They will listen to technical and emotional arguments, and give you support and sympathy. However, executives seem always to choose those alternatives with a strong business case when presented with alternatives. My goal in this chapter is to help you to scope and develop such a winning business case.

To sell reuse, you must show that it has positive impact on your organization's primary business goals. For example, you might emphasize how reuse improves your ability to get products to market quickly if you are in a highly competitive, commercial field in which additional functions and features sell merchandise. You might, as an alternative, focus on improved customer satisfaction and build a convincing argument that improved quality improves your ability to market. However, you must show how these improvements translate to improving your organization's bottom line for either of these cases, or your arguments may fall on deaf ears.

The approach I advocate for scoping the potential market for reuse is relatively simple. First, find out who your customers are and where you can have the largest potential impact using the grid shown in Table 6.1 [1]. The easiest way to scope the potential market is to conduct a market survey aimed at determining what products and services your customers desire. You could complete the survey using internal marketing resources, or by hiring a professional market research firm to tabulate results using questionnaires, focus groups, or any of a number of vehicles for generating the desired output. Internally led surveys tend to work best when management trusts marketing inputs, and they can get at customer data that outsiders have difficulty accessing. When trust doesn't exist, management tends to put more trust in a market survey generated by a credible outsider. No matter how you generate the output, you should make sure that both existing and new customers are polled. As Plan of Action 6.1 illustrates, both represent potential markets that should be analyzed.

While acquiring new business is great, you should not discount exploiting your existing customers to sell your reuse program. Many times, you can quickly increase your sales by working with existing clients to show them how your proposal implements their suggestions. Then, you can lever these improvements to acquire new business through existing marketing channels. To do this, get the data you need to determine if indeed this sales approach will work from your marketing organization. Review their marketing plans, revenue charts, and demographic data to get a clear picture of whom to target (i.e., which of your customers are responsible for what proportion of your sales). If, like most organizations, 10 to 20 percent of your customer base is responsible for 80 to 90 percent of your sales, your search will be easy.

Next, you must do some homework. Start by quantifying how your reuse program will directly benefit your customers, and segment your analysis a number of ways: by customer, product line, industry, and geographical region. To understand the data you have at your fingertips, talk with your potential consumers and mar-

TABLE 6.1 Potential Reuse Markets

Sell old products to old customers	Sell old products to new customers
Sell new products to old customers	Sell new products to new customers

PLAN OF ACTION 6.1   Business-Case Contents

SECTION 1: MARKET ANALYSIS
A. Target markets and customers
B. Market projections
   1. Worst case
   2. Most likely case
   3. Best case
C. Demographic projections
   1. By market, product line, etc.
D. Improvement opportunities
E. Key success factors

SECTION 2: FINANCIAL ANALYSIS
A. Sources and applications of funding
   1. Internal funding
   2. External funding
B. Capital equipment list
C. Budget projections
D. Income projections
E. Cash flow projections
F. Tax impact analysis
G. Cost/benefit analysis
   1. Net present worth
   2. Benefit/cost ratio
H. Value tree analysis
 I. Breakeven analysis
 J. Reuse opportunity analysis
K. Financial forms
   1. Income statement
   2. Balance sheet

SECTION 3: COMPETITIVE ANALYSIS
A. Market position and share
B. The competition

SECTION 4: SUPPORTING DOCUMENTS
A. Market survey
B. Benchmarking results
C. Assessment findings
D. Revenue charts
E. Cost-estimating model runs

keting people to figure out what products are needed and what their worth will be when they are provided. As you conduct your fact finding, focus your attention on identifying what is needed to keep your customers satisfied. Try to understand enough about the future to anticipate and accommodate their imminent requirements. The results will be worth the effort. When asked to justify your proposal to management, nothing beats your saying: We could increase sales within this region for these products by 20 percent this year alone if we adopted our reuse strategy based upon my projecting existing sales taken from our existing quarterly reports and my conversations with key representatives from these three firms, who represent 60 percent of the current business base.

Many software organizations I have dealt with service internal customer needs. Determining what their needs are is just as important as determining what the final consumer desires are in terms of the goods and services you produce. Such internal customers may be other departments (systems, engineering, etc.), divisions, marketing organizations, and/or program offices charged with taking the software you build and integrating it with the work of others to generate products for some external client. In some situations, marketing and the program office may act as a filter because they interpret the customer's requirements. Under other circumstances, they act as a management agent charged with ensuring an acceptable product is delivered per the customer's requirements, on time and per the negotiated budget. No matter what their role, you must keep these internal customers happy by providing them with value for their money and with ideas on how to make the improvements their clients want. Else, they might seek external sources for the goods and services you provide, or align politically with others in a manner that will hurt you, especially when you are lobbying for either funds or support internally.

To assess the potential impact of your proposal, look at your internal customers' sales forecast or marketing plan. Then, educate these customers about what you are trying to do and work with them to generate figures they feel are reasonable. I suggest bounding the potential market impact of your reuse strategies in terms of the least likely, most likely, and best estimates. Using these bounds, you can project the returns in terms of ranges of what is possible. Using ranges will protect you from others misquoting your numbers or using them inappropriately. When you complete your analysis, it might be useful to get your internal customers to bless your numbers. It might also be valuable to have them support your arguments for change, especially when they are the only ones who can testify to what it will take to satisfy the consumers' needs.

Your final step is to use your benchmarking and assessment data to show how your strategy addresses the competition. These numbers provide added justification that can solidify your business case for reuse. Use any and all the ammunition you can gather when fighting to get the budget and go-ahead for your reuse program. The more solid your business case, the better your chances are for success.

WHAT IS A BUSINESS CASE?

As already inferred, the business case provides your management with a compelling and sound reason why they should pursue your reuse proposal. The business case provides the financial, competitive, and/or other forms of rationale that justify why the firm should invest time, talent, energy, and internal funds in your reuse proposals at this point in time, instead of in other worthwhile ventures. It assumes that you have analyzed the options and have laid out a feasible, thorough, and low-risk plan that will allow you to deliver as promised.

Organizations do not invest in technology for technology's sake. They make such investments only when the resulting innovations provide them with some positive returns (increased profitability, improved efficiencies, etc.). Your business case must convince management that the potential returns justify the risks inherent in your plan. To do this, you must investigate the costs and the benefits, and examine the relative return you will realize on your investment.

You might also search for ways to acquire external financing. Cost sharing across divisions, partnering with other organizations, and external research and development contracts represent ways to offload some of your costs for reuse, and make the returns higher and therefore more acceptable. Often, management will perceive the value of an alternative to be higher when someone else is willing to put up the funds as a show of support.

By this point in the cycle, you should have lots of data. The trick now is to put it together so it paints the justification picture you want management to see. The typical contents of a business case are summarized in Plan of Action 6.1. As illustrated, the case provides management with insight into the results of your market survey and a look at the details of your financial analysis. Many of the terms in this guide, such as cost/benefit, breakeven, and reuse opportunity analysis, will be more fully explained in the next paragraph. Let's now look at the process you need to follow to paint an acceptable picture.

DEVELOP A BUSINESS CASE

You now must figure out how to justify your improvement proposals to your management. You must develop strong business arguments to get management to open their wallets and fund your recommendations, especially when times are tight and money is hard to get. A solid and defendable business case must be developed to get the chance to move ahead and execute selected options in your action plan.

The approach many use is to develop a white paper that is submitted alongside of their action plan that provides justifications for proposed expenditures. Regardless of how you present the information, you must detail your alternatives and present the results of your financial analysis. It is here that your assessments, evaluations, and benchmarking exercises pay dividends. They provide the justification that management will pay attention to as you make your pitch. Once the case is accepted, a go-ahead for your plans in some modified form will be assured.

A white paper is an essential first step because it can get everyone to agree that reuse represents an opportunity. It sets the stage for action by elevating reuse to the appropriate level of concern within the organization. It gets senior management talking about reuse, and helps you build support when and where you need it to get everyone excited about the prospects for change. Your white paper should be short and to the point. It should describe in high-level terms the reuse opportunity, how you propose to take advantage of it, and why it's important to your firm. It should be well written, compelling, and, most important, focused on the actions that must be taken to realize some measurable improvement. Its acceptance can be enhanced if you presell someone in your upper management chain to act as your champion and sponsor for your next step, the development of a business plan. This plan must be prepared if the proposed actions impact more than one of your line-of-business organizations.

The business case looks in more depth at the opportunities that you have identified in your action plan. It identifies alternatives and assesses their relative strengths and weaknesses. It looks at competition, market, and a host of other factors that may influence which of the options is best for you. It assesses the numbers and financial trade-offs, and performs the accompanying cost/benefit and investment analysis. It builds on your benchmarks and assessment results. In essence, it conveys the business and technical arguments that are used to justify the desirability of change. It too should be short and sweet. If it is not, management won't read it. To develop a business case, you could use the following seven-step process:

1. *Define your objectives.* Start by briefly describing the opportunity, then define what you are trying to do about it in terms that anyone reading the document will understand. Focus on what you believe your target audience needs to hear to make an informed decision. Be as specific as possible about your goals, explaining as you go why they are important. Use the results of your assessments, evaluations, and benchmarking studies to strengthen your arguments in the paper. Make sure the proposals you present reference your reuse vision and strategy and operational concepts. Summarize the important parts of these documents, because management probably has not read them yet.

2. *Identify scope and boundaries.* Bound the scope of the opportunity tightly so that you can hone in on the solutions recommended in your action plan (specific markets, products, windows of opportunity, etc.). Be sure to identify organizational interfaces and recommend who should be responsible so that the reader will know what is included in the scope.

3. *Establish the business-case strategy.* Summarize the business-case strategy you are using and discuss why you chose this alternative. Tie your business-case strategy to your goals, and show how they facilitate making the improvements identified as part of your assessment, evaluation, and/or benchmarking exercise.

4. *Identify the windows of opportunity and alternatives.* Define the timing of your alternatives, and relate each of them to their potential market windows. Focus your actions on exploiting the windows of opportunities. That is where the action is in most organizations. Don't forget that doing nothing is a feasible option that should be considered.

5. *Perform economic analysis.* Develop cost/benefit and/or investment opportunity analysis for your primary option(s). If you need help in developing your numbers, read the paragraphs that follow. They will give you insight into how to generate accurate estimates. Be cautioned that problems with numbers have a way of resurfacing. Check the mathematics for accuracy before you present the results. Any mistakes will be used to discredit you.

6. *Assess the perceived risks.* Conduct a risk analysis to identify those factors that can negatively impact your primary option. Rank these risks by potential impact and tell management how you plan to deal with each of them. Discuss how these risks affect your numbers and summarize the consequences of them in your figures. Emphasize the negative side of risk to get management to buy into the things you need them to do to be successful.

7. *Let the numbers speak for themselves.* Present the numbers as ranges (e.g., the gain expected in productivity will be between 10 and 20 percent during the first year). This will prevent senior management from pinning you down to a single number. Make sure you suggest that your action proposals should be shelved if the numbers do not show them to be a wise investment. Let the numbers speak for themselves and you'll be surprised how much management support, commitment, and interest you'll garner.

Information needed to develop your business case, along with its sources, is summarized in Table 6.2. Much of this information should be gathered internally via questionnaires and interviews to prepare your business case. The reason for this is simple; most outside sources for information are not always considered credible. Your critics will argue that these sources do not know your firm, your marketplace, your customers. Even if they did, someone would still need to determine your current levels of cost, productivity, and quality. No outsider but you can get your baseline performance data. Such data must be gathered at the source from those who do the work, or the meaning of the data will be continually questioned and its use will have marginal value.

As part of your business case, prepare a hard-hitting management briefing that summarizes your findings, conclusions, and recommendations. This sum-

TABLE 6.2 Information Needs

Type of Information	Source of Information
Business Planning Fundamentals:	
Format of acceptable plans	See Chapter 7
Timeline for their submission	Look for division or corporate practice
Examples of what is acceptable	Ask colleagues or go to your asset library
Business Case Fundamentals:	
Format of a case	This chapter of the book provides all the information you need to
Process for preparing the case	prepare a case
Guidelines for success	
Marketing Data:	
Competitive analysis	Ask your customers, not marketing people
Benchmarking data	See Chapter 5
Demographic information	Ask your marketing department
Market position	Ask your marketing department
Sales projections	Ask your marketing department
Marketing plans	Ask your marketing department
Finance and Accounting Data:	
Accounting guidelines	Look for division or corporate practices
Balance sheet	In a copy of your current annual report
Business metrics	Look at the footnotes in the annual report
Income statement	In a copy of your current annual report
Tax tables	Look for division or corporate practices
Discount tables	Look in most textbooks on statistics
Legal Requirements:	
Ownership guidelines	Talk with your legal department or attorney
Licensing guidelines	Look at one from one of your software packages, and then talk with your attorney
Estimating Guidelines:	
Cost-estimating models	Look at one of your proposals to see what is used and what the
Cost-estimating conventions	conventions are
Sales Pitch to Management	Look in Chapter 7 for an example pitch that pulls things together

mary should be short and pointed like the one shown in Plan of Action 6.2. The summary should amplify the points in your action plan, and provide the evidence needed to justify your recommendations. Understand, upper management will rarely read the full document. Instead, they'll have their staff analyze every inch of it. That is why you must check and recheck the numbers, as they are often the source of most of the controversy. Skeptics will argue the numbers until they are blue in the face to discredit your findings. The following guidelines can help you prepare your findings:

- Define your terms precisely. Use examples to communicate meaning whenever possible. If you do not, others may ascribe other meanings to your numbers (e.g., the difference between lines of code defined by nonblank, noncomment carriage returns and those defined as terminal semicolons can vary as much as ten to one).
- Be very conservative with your numbers, or your financial analysis will be discredited for being overly optimistic.
- Assess the tangible benefits of your alternatives in dollar terms in your analysis. Then, factor in a dollar gain for intangibles to show how they will provide added value to your preferred option (customer goodwill, etc.). Keep the numbers separate.
- Present your numbers as ranges of values; the worst, most likely, and best cases. These numbers will permit you to derive a statistically valid composite figure.
- Discount the value of your dollars in the out years using the statistical concept of net present worth, assuming a very conservative cost of money (i.e., this concept assumes that you could take the money you are investing, deposit it in a bank, and earn interest at some favorable rate as an alternative to your proposal). This will show the accountants that you know how to count the beans according to their rules.
- Focus on the business issues. Executives view technical and managerial problems as workable when there is money to be made. Tell them what can and cannot be done. Be honest about the challenges. Solicit their advice in addition to their support. They wouldn't be in their positions unless they had a lot of savvy advice to offer.

Let us look at how to develop the numbers that make up your business case. These are important because they are what you will use to really sell your action plan to management. However, do not assume that is all you will have to do to sell your initiative. Make sure that your technical approach is sound, low risk, and supported by the practitioners who will eventually have to implement it. Check to make sure that your management approach is well thought out, detailed, and puts you in control. Finally, get your corporate-level reuse champion's insights and blessings before you pitch your action plan/business case to his cohorts (i.e., you must develop such an advocate if you haven't already done so).

PLAN OF ACTION 6.2   Example Business-Case Summary

The Market	Several independently conducted market surveys support the contention that the largest growing market for wireless products in the world is the People's Republic of China. Projections indicate that this market will grow by a factor of ten within the next five years. If projections hold true, this market will account for one of every two sales of wireless products in the year 2000.
Market Penetration	As you already know, the firm has successfully penetrated this market by teaming with several major Chinese telecommunications manufacturers, distributors, and retail establishments. We have invested more than $600 million in capital equipment and facilities, and have trained over 2,000 Chinese workers in modern engineering and production techniques. We currently supply more than 30 percent of the equipment that the Chinese telephone operating companies use to provide service to businesses in fourteen of sixteen provinces in the country.
The Opportunity	The largest growth market within China in the future will be aimed at consumers. Wireless sales are projected to be a $2 billion marketplace by the beginning of 1998. We have products that we could sell through distributors to the local population. However, their price/performance will not satisfy the low-end needs of the market. We need to restructure our product line to fill this gap within the next year.
The Solution	We can develop a competitive product line that would sell in China and Europe if we move forward with our reuse initiative. We believe that we could replace our existing wireless product line with five new offerings that would permit us to capture between 25 and 40 percent of the market by the year 2000. This product line would build on our existing experience to provide the functions and features customers have stated they want and are willing to pay for. A new architecture will be developed that will allow us to bring new products to market every six to eight weeks. This architecture will allow us to capitalize on off-the-shelf hardware and libraries of software building blocks specially developed to accommodate all of the anticipated growth options.
The Numbers	We estimate that it will take us about 18 months to develop this new product line and will cost about $10 million. Based upon our sales models, we anticipate breakeven to occur in less than a year. The net present worth of the benefits that will accrue over a five-year planning horizon is estimated at more than $50 million, assuming a very conservative income stream. The after-tax income projections for yields for this business unit are well in excess of 40 percent.
The Competition	We are not the only major telecommunications firm viewing this market. We believe we can bring products to market two years ahead of the competition by moving ahead with our reuse approach. However, the window of opportunity is short and we need your immediate approval to start in order to be successful.

Cost/Benefit Analysis

Financial analysts use various methods to determine the cost effectiveness of a business-case proposal. Cost/benefit analysis is recognized as the most widely accepted approach used for this purpose. It is straightforward to prepare, quantitative, and simple to understand. Most importantly, it presents financial numbers to upper management, and their staffs, in a form that they are used to dealing with. When two alternatives are equal, these same managers will base their decision upon these numbers. Therefore, you should pay considerable attention to what the numbers say and mean before presenting them to management.

To perform a cost/benefit analysis, use the worksheet shown in Plan of Action 6.3. Reuse costs on this worksheet are grouped into nonrecurring (one time) and recurring (ongoing). Similarly, reuse benefits are grouped into tangible (easy to quantify) and intangible (hard to quantify). Both costs and benefits must be expressed in current years' monetary terms to make any resulting analysis meaningful. For example, training costs could be estimated based upon the number of people you would have to send to two public seminars on the topic. As another example, the gains derived from reducing your time to market could be estimated based upon the royalties derived by selling a license for an upgraded version to 70 percent of a product's existing customer base.

The capital costs associated with installing the software reuse infrastructure should be assumed to be part of the overhead (i.e., amortized across your direct costs). This will make the bottom line of your cost/benefit analysis look better, because these costs will not appear as a negative spike in the first few years of operation. For this reason, the costs associated with inserting the reuse processes, tools, and management oversight are not listed as an entry on the worksheet.

You can now take a hard look at the numbers. Because you are dealing with economic quantities, the net present worth of the investment must be summed over the projected life of the investment using the following formula, which takes into account discounted cash flows:

$$\text{NET PRESENT WORTH (NPW)} = \sum_{t=0}^{T} (B_t)\,(1/(1+i)^t)$$

where: B_t = net benefits for each time period considered in the investment decision (may be negative); i = cost of money (attractive rate of return); T = number of time periods included with the investment (typically months/years).

The NPW computation takes both time and the cost of money into account. It assumes that today's dollar is worth more than tomorrow's because of the effect of inflation. The NPW also assumes that as an alternative you could put the dollars you are requesting in some bank account and receive the current interest rate as your minimum attractive rate of return. Many economic analysts use NPW alone to analyze the relative financial performance of alternatives. Because your rate of return assumption is subject to scrutiny, I recommend you use either the prevailing interest money market or the prime interest rate (the rate banks charge their preferred customers) for i in the formula.

PLAN OF ACTION 6.3   Cost/Benefit Analysis Worksheet

Nonrecurring Costs		*Tangible Benefits*	
Acquisition	_____	Cost avoidance	_____
• Assets		• Less time	
• Methods/tools		• Less effort	
Process adaptation	_____	Added capability	_____
Documentation	_____	Added capability	_____
Architecture establishment[1]	_____	Reduced cost of quality	_____
Education & Training	_____	Cost savings	_____
• Development		• Less staff	
• Conduct		• Less equipment	
• Beta test		• Less overhead	
Other	_____	Other	_____

Recurring Costs		*Intangible Benefits*	
System administration	_____	Increased customer satisfaction	_____
Asset reengineering	_____	Fitness for use (did the right	
Asset maintenance	_____	job right the first time)	_____
Library operations	_____	Reduced time to market	_____
Continuing education	_____	Increased market penetration	_____
Total Costs	_____	**Total Benefits**	_____

[1]Includes costs associated with domain and applications engineering support.

Let's determine the cost/benefits using the following figures based upon our best engineering estimates for what we believe it would take to establish a product-line architecture:

Nonrecurring Costs			*Recurring Costs*		
Domain engineering	=	500,000	Asset maintenance	=	25,000
Architecture formulation	=	250,000	Asset reengineering	=	25,000
Reusable assets acquisition	=	200,000	Asset development	=	100,000
Education and training	=	50,000	Continuing education	=	50,000
Marketing costs	=	500,000	System administration	=	50,000
Library software acquisition	=	250,000	Library operations	=	250,000
Infrastructure development	=	0			
		$1,750,000			$500,000

Let's assume that you experience a cycle-time reduction of six months, and your complaint rates drop from an average of nine to three per month in the second year per product. Assuming that rework costs an average of $8,000 per complaint, the annual savings you would accrue due to the adoption of architectures and reuse would be $1,800,000, assuming five products in the product line.

Let's look at the cost benefits over a five-year time period assuming an attractive rate of return of 6 percent (i):

	Year 1	Year 2	Year 3	Year 4	Year 5
Costs	2,250,000	500,000	500,000	500,000	500,000
Benefits	0	2,880,000	2,880,000	2,880,000	2,880,000
Net Benefits	<2,250,000>	2,380,000	2,380,000	2,380,000	2,380,000
NPW(6%)	<2,122,650>	2,118,200	1,998,248	1,885,198	1,778,574
SUM(NPW)	<2,122,650>	<4,450>	1,993,798	3,878,996	5,657,570

During the first year, we assumed that we would not derive any benefits whatsoever in the example. As suggested, we also assumed that the infrastructure costs were capitalized and did not influence the analysis we were performing. The breakeven point for the option is toward the start of year three. Over the course of five years, we would develop $5,657,570 worth of benefits for our investment of $1,750,000. This yields a 223 percent return on investment, or about 45 percent a year. This return seems very attractive and we would probably recommend pursuing this option, especially when we factored the reduced cycle time into the decision analysis.

Another figure of merit that your management may ask you to compute is the benefit/cost ratio (BCR). This ratio can be computed simply using the following formula:

$$\text{BENEFIT/COST RATIO (BCR)} = \text{NPW/PW(NRC)}$$

where: $PW(NRC)$ = present worth of accumulated investment outlays taken from your worksheet (nonrecurring costs only), and NPW = net present worth of the investment alternative figured using the equation displayed as the formula presented earlier.

Looking at our example, the BCR would be computed as follows over our five-year planning horizon:

$$\text{BCR} = \$5,657,570/\text{PW}(\$1,750,000) = \$5,657,570/\$1,346,625 = 4.2$$

Although NPW can be used effectively for financial analysis, the use of BCR has certain distinct advantages. Given two alternative investments differing only slightly in NPW, the one requiring the minimum nonrecurring cost outlay would be preferred by management. Realize that given the same two alternatives, management would view the option that pays back the initial investment quickest as part of the same analysis. In our example, the payback occurred during the beginning of year three.

Investment Opportunity Analysis

Many other standard financial measures of interest can be used to assess the attractiveness of a range of alternatives. For example, the return on capital or after-tax effective rate of return could be calculated and used to assess the merits of alternative investment strategies. Both of these measures make sense to the money people, who will be called upon to determine the financial merits of your action planning proposal. Both measures assume the items acquired as part of your improvement recommendations will be carried on the firm's books as capital items, and will be written off over time as capitalized expenses. Both are sensitive to the depreciation methods you use, and both provide insight into the effects of investments after taxes on profits.

Return on capital looks at how much money the raw investment is making over its useful life. It is computed by dividing the investment's cumulative return over the planning horizon by the one-time investment. For example, the nondiscounted return on capital for reuse library software that cost you $250,000 would be 4:1 if you saved $1 million in equivalent development costs over the tool's effective life span.

After-tax effective rate of return reduces the projected revenue stream associated with an alternative by its potential tax liability. The investment is then divided by these altered revenues to compute the effective rate of return. This rate is then compared to some minimum attractive rate to assess whether the option is appealing. For example, an investment that provided a 4-percent after-tax yield would be considered a bad deal if you could get 5 percent from tax-free municipal bonds.

When dealing with the financial community, I have found it important to do a complete and thorough analysis. In addition, I always check to make sure I have done the mathematics correctly. In anticipation of the accountant's questions, I suggest that you take taxes, scheduling of tax payments, depreciation, tax credits, and other matters related to amounts and timing of cash flows into account as you analyze your options. Under certain conditions, you may be able to sell your proposal based upon the tax merits of the alternative.

Other financial performance measures, such as return on investment (ROI) and return on capital, can also be used effectively to determine the desirability of your alternatives. I recommend that you select whichever measures your financial people think are appropriate in order to establish credibility with those who will be called upon to independently review them. Seek help from internal consultants within your finance department if you do not understand how to create, compute, analyze, or use these measures. They probably have specialized software that you could use to perform these and your present worth calculations. They are most often willing to provide expert help.

You are probably asking: Do I really have to worry about the numbers? Most times you don't. However, the numbers can become sales tools when you are trying to get reluctant managers to commit to a reuse program. Engineering managers believe formulas and numbers when they are certain that the mathematics are correct and the assumptions upon which they are based are reasonable.

Value-Tree Analysis

The simplest technique that I have found valuable for quantifying the financial impacts of the action plan is value-tree analysis. This technique can be used to assess the impact of each option using a form of decision-tree analysis. As shown in Figure 6.1, the expected value for each alternative represented on the tree is computed using the formula:

$$\text{EXPECTED VALUE}_i = (Hv_i + 4MLv_i + Lv_i)/6$$

where: Hv_i = highest possible value for option i; MLv_i = most likely value for option i; Lv_i = lowest possible value for option i.

This decision tree can be used to show the projected financial impact of each alternative in one glance. The formula used to perform the analysis creates a sort of weighted average around the statistical mean of a bell-shaped curve, because it assumes the range of expected values between the two extremes, Hv and Lv, is normally distributed as shown in Figure 6.2. The accuracy of the value-chain output is only as good as the relative goodness of the inputs used to quantify the financial gain associated with each alternative. The old saying, Garbage in yields garbage out, seems quite applicable.

There are many other techniques that you could use to rate and rank your action planning alternatives. The trick is to pick the options with high value that management understands, feels are important, and is concerned about. Don't waste management's time by focusing on things that won't make a difference in their eyes.

Reuse Cost Estimation Models

As an alternative to value-chain analysis, several software cost-estimating models can be used to forecast the time and effort associated with your improvement proposals. These models take heuristic relationships (e.g., it cost us $25 for each line of code) and modify them to fit actual experience using those number of factors to which costs have been shown to be sensitive (e.g., this is more complex; add 25 percent to the cost).

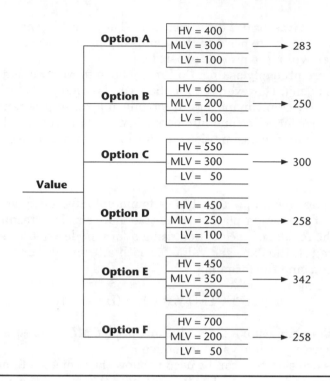

FIGURE 6.1 Value-tree analysis.

The Software Productivity Consortium (SPC) has developed one such estimating model [2] to assess the impact of reuse at an organizational level. As shown in the Figure 6.3, the model can be used to graphically portray the projected benefits as a function of the number of reuses expected to occur. The more reuses, the more benefits that accrue. The graphics generated by the model are easy to understand and to brief to management. The model uses ranges to show the potential payback for families of options. Because of its simplicity, I suggest that you use it especially if you are trying to quantify the returns of your improvement options at a macro or high level.

At the project level, several cost models exist that can be used to look at the overall cost and schedule impacts due to reuse. The most popular of these is the COCOMO model [3]. Fundamentally, the model estimates effort and duration based upon past experience heuristically using linear regression formulas. These formulas are so simple that you can compute results using an inexpensive hand-held scientific calculator. Cost/schedule drivers are used to adjust the results to reflect such parameters as product complexity, requirements' volatility, and programmer experience.

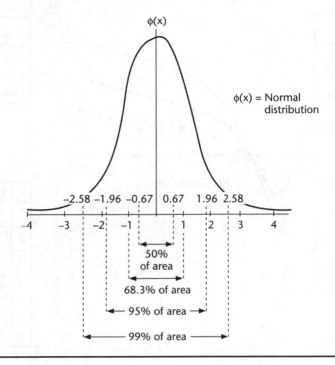

FIGURE 6.2 Value-tree probability distribution.

I suggest you consider using version 2.0 of the COCOMO [4] software cost model, whose structure is shown in Table 6.3, for estimating the financial returns of your reuse options, because:

■ It is easy to understand, learn, and use.

■ Its mathematics remain simple and are in the public domain.

■ It has been recently updated to incorporate stronger reuse and reengineering estimating mathematics.

■ It permits you to estimate costs associated with fourth-generation languages (4GLs).

■ It has been restructured to address applications composition, early design (and prototyping), and postarchitecture phases of the software development life cycle.

■ It has been subjected to a very broad public review and validation process.

■ It has been made upward compatible so that its large, committed user base can move easily from previous versions.

■ It can be easily automated and made part of your software management toolset.

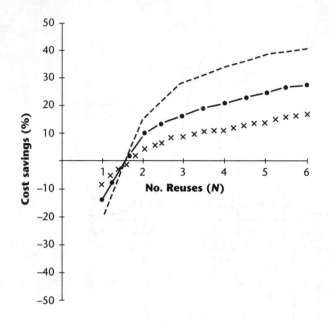

	R = 0.2	R = 0.4	R = 0.6
1	1.07	1.14	1.21
2	0.95	0.89	0.84
3	0.90	0.81	0.71
4	0.88	0.77	0.65
5	0.85	0.74	0.61
6	0.81	0.72	0.58

Simple Reuse Model

This simple model works as follows: Let *COST* be the cost of software development for a product, assuming all new code (*R* is the proportion of reused code in the product ® ≤ 1). Let *b* be the relative cost to reuse software (then *b* = 1 for new software) and *E* represent your estimate of the relative cost of developing reusable software assets. Then, *COST* can be estimated based upon the number of reuses, *N*, using the simple formula:

$$COST = (1 - R) + R(b + E/N)$$

where: *COST* = cost of software development; *b* = relative cost to reuse software; *R* = proportion of reused code in the product; *E* = relative cost of developing a reusable asset (*E* > 1); *N* = number of reuses over which the asset development costs will be amortized.

FIGURE 6.3 SPC reuse cost model.

Either of the two types of models can be used effectively as tools to estimate the costs of your action planning options. Selection of the most appropriate model depends on how big your effort is and how much detail your management expects you to provide along with your recommendations. I would use the SPC model if I were determining the cost impact of reuse at an organizational level. The reason for this is that the SPC model lets me build a business case across several organi-

TABLE 6.3 COCOMO 2.0 Estimating Model Structure

	COCOMO	COCOMO 2.0 Application Composition	COCOMO 2.0 Early Design	COCOMO 2.0 Postarchitecture
Size	Delivered source lines of code	Object Points	Function points and language or SLOC	Function points (FP) and language or source lines of code (SLOC)
Reuse	Equivalent (SLOC) linear function of reuse %	Implicit in model	Percentage reuse	Equivalent FP or SLOC nonlinear function of reuse %
Breakage	Requirements volatility	Implicit in model	Breakage percentage	Breakage percentage
Maintenance	Annual change traffic used to compute maintenance effort	Annual change traffic used to compute maintenance effort	Annual change traffic used to compute maintenance effort	Annual change traffic used to compute maintenance effort
Scale in equation: Effort = a(size)[b]	Three modes: - Organic: 1.05 - Semidetached: 1.12 - Embedded: 1.20	Linear scale or 1.0	Nonlinear scale ranging from 1.01 to 1.26	Nonlinear scale ranging from 1.01 to 1.26
Product cost drivers	Three different drivers	None	Two different drivers	Five different drivers
Platform cost drivers	Four different drivers	None	One driver: platform difficulty	Three different drivers
Personnel cost drivers	Five different drivers	None	Two different drivers	Six different drivers
Project cost drivers	Three different drivers	None	Two different drivers	Three different drivers

Note: Drivers in COCOMO 2.0 are calibrated differently. *Source:* Barry W. Boehm, "Software Reuse Economics," *Fourth International Conference on Software Reuse,* April 26, 1996.

zations and product lines. In contrast, I would use the COCOMO 2.0 model if I were assessing the cost and schedule impact of my options at the project or even product-line level.

FINANCIAL DATA

There is a lot more to learn when it comes to pulling together all of the pieces of the business case outlined in Plan of Action 6.2. So much, I could probably write a book about this one topic. So far, I have discussed what I believe are the important topics relative to reuse in this chapter. Other, more standard elements of a business case are treated in the many publications on the topic, some of which I have included within the reference section [5, 6, 7]. The two other standard tools used by management to determine an organization's financial health that you must know are the *income statement* and *balance sheet*. Because of their importance, I will spend a little time on each.

A sample format for a balance sheet is shown in Plan of Action 6.4. Balance sheets are designed to show how the assets, liabilities, and net worth of an organization (company, division, line of business, etc.) are distributed at a given point in time. The balance sheet provides a static picture of the financial health of the organization. The format never varies, as it is used to facilitate comparison. Typically, a balance sheet is completed so that it can be used by accounting professionals to analyze the relative financial performance of different profit-and-loss (P&L) centers.

A sample format for an income statement is illustrated in Plan of Action 6.5. This P&L statement complements the balance sheet by providing a dynamic picture of the organization's anticipated profitability over a multiyear forecasting horizon. Budget, income, and cash flow projections by year normally accompany the form and provide the accounting professional with needed backup details.

CASE STUDY

The economic arguments used for reuse on a large software training simulator development project are driven by competition. In order to win the job, proposal management assumed that it could lever its experience and assets from a recently completed crew trainer they built for a military aircraft. Based upon their experience, the levels of reuse they proposed in response to the solicitation were thought to be realistic and achievable. Because the firm knew the customer and what was needed to perform the job, they felt that the numbers in their proposal were believable and had a high win probability. Their strategy was to employ their existing product-line architecture and software reuse as the hook to reel in the contract. "Build it once, not many times," was one of the key themes in their proposal as was, "Build it cheaply, reusing software assets that already exist." To solidify their argument, they cataloged the assets they had already built (algo-

PLAN OF ACTION 6.4   Format for a Balance Sheet

Assets

Current Assets	$_____	Assets that can be converted to cash in a period of a year(notes, receivables, etc.)
Fixed Assets	$_____	Assets whose life is measured in years
Less Depreciation	$_____	Tax credits given to offset the cost of replacing equipment
Net Fixed Assets	$_____	
Other Assets	$_____	Intangible assets such as patents and copyrights
Total Assets	$_____	The value of what the organization owns

Liabilities

Current Liabilities	$_____	Obligations coming due in one year
Long-Term Liabilities	$_____	Obligations that are multiyear (loans, etc.)
Total Liabilities	$_____	The value of what the organization owes

Net Worth

Net Worth	$_____	The owner's equity (total assets less Total Liabilities)

PLAN OF ACTION 6.5   Format for an Income Statement

(1) Net Sales:	$_____	
(2) Less Cost of Goods Sold:	$_____	Expenses incurred to market goods and services
(3) Equals Gross Margin:	$_____	
(4) Less Operating Expenses:	$_____	Expenses incurred to develop, package, and distribute goods and services
(5) Less Other Expenses:	$_____	Other expenses such as interest
(6) Yields Pretax Profit (Loss):	$_____	Gross margin less all expenses
(7) Less Taxes:	$_____	
(8) Yields Net Profit (Loss):	$_____	Tells you how well your business is doing

rithms, models, libraries, software, etc.) and offered to provide them along with the modifications they planned in their reuse process in the draft software development plan that was submitted along with their proposal.

Management priced the software very competitively because they felt a good percentage of the job had already been done. They had confidence in the ability of their people to estimate, and believed the story they were being told relative to software reuse. They felt each delivery could provide its successors with reusable assets, because they were developing their software using an incremental delivery process. They felt that their architecture could be reused intact and that no new algorithm developments were needed to satisfy the customer's requirements. In addition, they felt the use of object-oriented methods would allow them to package at least 50 percent of the new models and 20 percent of the simulation software to be reusable within and across simulator subsystems. Of course, a high degree of optimism permeated the proposal. "You can't win by being pessimistic," was management's response to the criticism they received. Of course, management really believed the goals were realistic and could be realized, especially if the customer understood them and agreed to be flexible.

The firm has linked its competitive goals with a business case for reuse. Their motivation was to avoid cost primarily in the operations and maintenance phase of the life cycle. Management had bought the idea that investments made in process improvement, new object-oriented methods, and modern tools would result in fewer people being needed for maintenance and operational support during the trainer's anticipated 30-year lifetime. The estimated reduction in staff was substantial in the out years, when enhancements would be incorporated into the system. To prepare their bid and quantify the cost avoidance, the firm used two parametric cost models, COCOMO and POP-POP (a home-grown program that estimated based upon rules of thumb derived from years of experience in the simulator business). The parametric analysis showed convincingly that out-year costs could be reduced by factors of 20 to 40 percent if a 20-percent software reuse level were achieved. The breakeven point for the investments that had to be made was five years. This estimate assumed the quality of reusable assets would be five to ten times better than the industry norm. As expected, this improved quality translated into reduced repair and enhancement costs in the out years.

Looking at the numbers, it doesn't take much thought to realize that management was being very aggressive. They were awarded the contract because their numbers were justifiable and withstood audit. They also spent a lot of time explaining to the customer what the numbers meant and what the prerequisites for success were if they were awarded the job. Such education set the stage and created an atmosphere of understanding and joint commitments. As the contract unfolded, the customer was reminded numerous times of how the preconditions agreed upon were relative to achieving the cost goals, and what was and was not possible.

The team actually exceeded the levels of software reuse originally proposed for the job even though it was delayed due to budgetary constraints, and had yet to enter the operations and maintenance phase of its life cycle. As a consequence, it is difficult to determine whether the maintenance cost reduction goals that were originally promised were realized. Independent of these, both the firm and its customer are very pleased with the results to date, which show that reuse within and across projects can dramatically reduce effort when an architecture is reused from one project to another within the same applications domain. The architecture was the key because it provided management with a framework for tracking whether the assets (algorithms, models, software, etc.) proposed for reuse were indeed utilized.

SUMMARY

- To sell reuse, you must show management how it positively impacts their bottom line.
- The business case provides management with a compelling and sound rationale for pursuing your reuse strategy.
- Don't forget that there are both internal and external clients for your reuse program.
- Your business case should present its arguments in terms and using business metrics (net present worth, etc.) that your finance and accounting people understand.
- There are a number of software cost-estimating models that can be used to quantify the cost/benefits of software reuse.
- The SPC model provides a high-level estimate of the relative costs. The COCOMO 2.0 model provides a more detailed look at the factors that can influence your costs.
- When in doubt, consult with your finance people to understand how to present your proposal so that it is acceptable to them.

REFERENCES

1. David H. Bangs, Jr., *The Business Planning Guide,* Upstart Publishing Company, 1995.
2. John E. Gaffney, Jr. and Thomas A. Durek, *Software Reuse—Key to Enhanced Productivity; Some Quantitative Models,* Software Productivity Consortium, Report SPC-TR-88-015, April 1988.
3. Barry W. Boehm, *Software Economics,* Prentice-Hall, 1981.
4. Barry Boehm, Bradford Clark, Ellis Horowitz, Chris Westland, Ray Madachy, and Richard Selby, "The COCOMO 2.0 Software Cost Estimation Model: A Status Report," *American Programmer,* July 1996.
5. David H. Bowen, *Software Success Reference Book,* Software Success, 1992.
6. John G. Burch, *Entrepreneurship,* John Wiley & Sons, 1986.
7. A. L. Frank, *A Guide for Software Entrepreneurs,* Prentice-Hall, 1982.

Business Planning

7

ELEMENTS OF A BUSINESS PLAN

You have management's attention. They are interested in hearing your proposal. You've briefed them on your vision and strategy, and showed them the results of your preliminary business-case analysis. You've done your homework and pulled together your operational concepts, benchmarking data, and business case. You have everything you need to sell your program in hand. You are tired of planning, ready to roll, and want to get started. Now you have to glue together everything you have so that you can begin to make a positive impact.

The business plan, whose typical contents are outlined in Plan of Action 7.1, is the vehicle you will use to accomplish the desired integration. It is prepared to communicate all of the salient information about your reuse program to interested parties. This document is short, meaty, focused, and written to communicate the whats, whys, whens, and hows at a summary level to those you enlist to get the work done. Instead of presenting readers with volumes of data, the plan references the other work you have done and points to the details, whenever possible, in other documents. The plan begins by explaining what you are trying to do and why it is important to your organization from a business point of view. Next, it summarizes your goals, describes how you are going to accomplish them, provides a top-level plan of attack, and provides marketing and management information. It uses graphics to the maximum degree possible, because pictures communicate a lot better than text. It covers a lot of ground in at most 30 to 50 pages. It puts in writing everything that your management expects to see prior to giving you approval to start up your reuse program. Again, don't let the outline in Plan of Action 7.1 scare you. You can keep the document brief by putting the details in the appendices, or by pointing to them in other places by reference.

The chief aim of your business plan is to plot a course of action for making the effort successful once you have been given a go-ahead by management to start the effort. The plan puts together the pieces of the puzzle in a way that allows you to generate results in both the near and long term. It details what you must do to be successful. It takes the strategy you've developed and uses it to generate results. The plan defines how the producers and consumers of your reusable assets will work together within the context of your technical approach. It takes all of the concepts you've developed and brings them down to earth so that you can mechanize them.

Your plan of action should be both aggressive and achievable. It should provide those who will implement it with a roadmap that leads them through the maze of things you must do to achieve your goals. It should contain more than just a bunch of words and charts. It should summarize what tasks you must complete and products you must deliver to be perceived as successful. The plan should be by its very nature action oriented and issues based. It should list the risks you have identified and discuss how you plan to address them. It should provide schedules and list your primary deliverables and milestones. It should contain a budget and discuss how you are going to spend it. It should discuss how you will manage the effort, focus the effort, keep tabs on your status, maintain momentum, and make progress.

There are things that you should emphasize in your plan. You should focus your discussions on its business aspects. and use standard planning tools (work breakdown structures, milestone schedules, etc.) to illustrate that you have matters under control. You should underscore the reasons why you are doing things, what the options were, and the logic used for selection. For example, you should always pinpoint the market, identify the customers, define their needs, and discuss how you will satisfy them by your plan. Deal with risks head on by describing what they are and how you plan on keeping them under control. Don't be afraid to take chances, especially if the payback is large and the risks are controllable. Recognize that plans are working documents. As such, they will change as organizations, staff, and situations change. Be flexible and always expect the unexpected to happen. Then, if and when it does, you will be prepared to address the changes that occur that can make your plan obsolete.

You should always try to synchronize your plan with your firm's financial cycle. The reason for this is simple. If you are out of synchronization with the financial cycle, you might have to wait months for money to become available. Such money fuels your engines. Be first in the queue with your requests for financial support and you will probably get it, especially if your cause is thought worthy and you are prepared. As key milestones near, get whatever paperwork you will need to win the internal battles for money. Let the others who have waited too long panic when deadlines near. Be prepared and you will be rewarded. In addition, try to schedule a deliverable that demonstrates results one month prior to when you are expected to submit your follow-up proposals for your next year's budget. Achieving such milestones shows management that you are making progress in terms that they understand—results. Such results tend to solidify your case for continued funding and make it easier for you to win the battles for support in future years.

OPPORTUNISTIC VERSUS SYSTEMATIC REUSE

Chapter 2 discussed four alternative reuse strategies. Two of these were opportunistic (library or electronic shopping mall), while two were systematic (product-line architectures and megaprogramming). Each of these strategies greatly influences the work you would plan to accomplish as part of your business plan. For example, you would concentrate your efforts on getting your reuse library operational, and on perfecting your asset management processes if you selected either of the two opportunistic strategies. In contrast, you would focus on inserting reuse processes and tools into your applications development paradigm if you pursued a megaprogramming approach. You would perform domain analysis, develop reference architectures, and devise an infrastructure that employed product lines to maximize sharing of common assets (both hardware and software) when you pursued a product-line architecture approach.

Of course, you could decide to pursue a hybrid approach. For example, you could employ an opportunistic approach to develop results quickly as you pursued either a megaprogramming or product-line architecture in parallel. Such an approach makes a lot of sense in organizations that don't have the patience to wait several years before they see the results of your reuse efforts. If you elect to pursue this strategy, probably the first thing you should plan to pull together is some form of reuse catalog that you can use to let your engineers know what reusable assets are available.

Your use of any of these four strategies makes sense under certain circumstances. Let's look at some top-level characteristics of those organizations who might want to use one or more of these strategies in Table 7.1. You might use this table to take the results of your reuse assessment and determine what approach makes best sense for you using the following four critical success factors [1] taken from the Software Productivity Consortium's reuse capability model (with modifications):

Opportunistic

Systematic

Application Development

Engineers are aware of, can find, and have access to reusable assets (more than just code).Engineers identify and reuse high-payoff, reusable assets to implement standardized architectures.

PLAN OF ACTION 7.1   Business Plan Contents

Executive Summary

SECTION 1: WHAT ARE WE TRYING TO ACCOMPLISH?
A. Mission statement
B. General background
C. Business goals and milestones
D. Business case (summary)
E. Measures of success

SECTION 2: HOW ARE WE GOING TO ACCOMPLISH IT?
A. Vision and strategy
B. Technical approach
C. Operational concepts
D. Strategic alliances
E. Financial plan

SECTION 3: DEVELOPMENT PLAN
A. Product descriptions
B. Development approach
C. Work plan/deliverables
D. Schedules and milestones
E. Budgets and controls

SECTION 4: MANAGEMENT PLAN
A. Management team
B. Management controls
C. Supplier management
D. Quality control
E. Risk management

SECTION 5: MARKETING PLAN
A. Target market and customers
B. Marketing strategy
C. Producer/consumer model
D. Sales and distribution
E. Competitive analysis

APPENDIX A   GLOSSARY OF TERMS
APPENDIX B   BENCHMARKING RESULTS
APPENDIX C   BUSINESS CASE DETAILS
APPENDIX D   OTHER BACKUP MATERIALS

Asset Development	Identified needs are used as the basis for acquiring and/or developing reusable assets. Needs are anticipated and solutions are developed using mature reuse processes.
Management	Management commits funds and staff to implement reuse approach as part of product development effort (includes cost accounting, legal, and licensing procedures).

TABLE 7.1 Characteristics of Adopter Organizations

Strategy/ Organizational Characteristics	Product-Line Architecture	Mega-programming	Reuse Library	Electronic Shopping Mall
Maturity of adopting organization	*High*—requires a great deal of organizational commitment to change	*High*—requires processes to be well defined and institutionalized	*Low*—can be inserted easily into software development shops	*Moderate*—assumes you have a good handle on technology and what it is you want to sell
Culture	*Line of business-based culture*—product lines represent an evolutionary change	*Service culture*—software reuse put easily into the process; process group guides implementation	*Project culture*—central reuse library adds sharing and doesn't threaten project focus	*COTS culture*—reuse library points to products supplied by both internal and external sources
Degree of risk they are willing to take	*Risk takers*—willing to take risks when rewarded	*Risk neutral*—take moderate risks when justified	*Risk adverse*—not willing to tax or impact project success	*Risk neutral*—take moderate risks when justified
Primary goal of the software reuse program	*Systematic*—build only those reusable assets needed to populate/lever product lines	*Systematic*—make software reuse a natural part of the way the software organization builds its products	*Opportunistic*—make it easy for engineers to store, find, and access reusable software assets	*Opportunistic*—make it easy for engineers to store, find, and access reusable assets; sell assets when it makes business sense
Main obstacle faced by the software reuse program	Disagreements revolving around program and functional goals	The lack of agreement on what constitutes good reuse processes for the firm	Lack of sharing across projects who have limited budgets for reuse	The cost of setting up the shopping mall—who pays for it and how is it sustained
Primary state of readiness (to adopt reuse technology)	*High*—tries to figure out what makes sense to reuse	*High*—tries to figure out how to do it as part of existing processes	*Low*—tries to take advantage of existing assets	*Moderate*—tries to put sharing mechanisms in place

	Management established an infrastructure based upon product lines, which satisfies their long-term market needs and continuously refines and improves how they harness their reuse potential.
Process and Technology	Reuse needs are identified in software development, training, and tooling plans. Standard reuse processes and tools are adapted to use new reuse technology as it becomes available for widespread production use.

The purpose of these discussions is to reinforce the fact that you will have to define the work you must complete in order to put your strategy in action within your business plan. The "Pulling Together Your Plan" section provides a detailed catalog of tasks that you might consider to help you with putting your strategy into action. To supplement these descriptions, Chapter 10 provides the overarching requirements for these tasks in terms of key process areas (KPA). These tasks generate/exploit the reusable assets your engineers will use to make software reuse happen within your organization, using the two life-cycle models explained in Chapter 1 as its framework. As a refresher, this life-cycle model employs the following three major activities to insert reuse into the way you do business:

1. *Asset Management*—The processes/practices firms use to manage their assets and make them readily available in quality form to their potential users. These are the processes your engineers use to search libraries to find the reusable assets of interest. The quality of the assets is maintained along with the integrity of their configuration using some online mechanism that is part of your software engineering environment.
2. *Application Engineering*—The processes/practices firms use to guide the disciplined development, test, and life-cycle support of their applications software. These are the processes your software engineers normally use to develop/maintain your products.
3. *Domain Engineering*—The reuse-based processes/practices firms use to define the scope, specify the structure, and build reusable assets for a class of systems or applications. These activities are typically conducted to figure out what to build to be reusable.

These three activities can be viewed from either a producer or a consumer viewpoint. Both perspectives are valid and should be related to your reuse strategy, especially when you are identifying the results you hope to achieve. Both influence the techniques you would use and the processes you would set up as parts of your overall reuse infrastructure.

PRODUCER/CONSUMER MODEL

Consumers reuse the assets you have acquired to develop their products. Once they've been indoctrinated, they explore every opportunity to reuse assets to build their software systems and related documentation. They believe that software reuse has value, and create systems from scratch only as their last resort. Consumer focus is on finding, selecting, modifying/specializing, and integrating reusable assets into their products. They utilize some reuse library that their organization has set up to use as a mechanism for sharing. As a consequence, they are very concerned with how easy the library is to use, and the quality of its holdings. When set up properly, consumers view reuse as a natural part of their job, not as a culture change.

Producers acquire those reusable assets that have been identified to have a high payoff for the firm. They do this by buying, developing, and/or reengineering the components that have the potential to be shared across many projects and/or product lines. They believe that reuse of existing third-party software represents an opportunity to save time and effort. They understand that making assets reusable costs more because applications must be packaged to encapsulate support for more than one project. They strive to use generators in mature domains. They are concerned with making sure that they acquire assets with high reuse potential. That's why they perform a domain analysis and develop a reference architecture. Producers also understand they must design for commonality, and package products in a flexible enough manner to achieve variability. Once indoctrinated, producers develop a desire to address the concerns of their consumers. They understand that the best reusable assets in the world have but limited utility when they sit in some library and are not used to build systems.

Consumers often become producers and vice versa. For example, those building systems may identify assets that they believe have high reuse potential as they develop their products. Producers may suggest that these assets be enlarged in scope to address a broader spectrum of user needs once they are nominated for inclusion in the reuse library as reusable assets. Both sides start to negotiate. Consumers often view additional scope negatively because it will interfere with their ability to deliver on time and within budget. In contrast, producers take on the role of consumers as they ask for more and more capability. This give and take continues as both sides strive for equitable compromises.

Plan of Action 7.1 illustrates these roles along with those of the buyer/seller of reusable assets from both the demand and supply sides of the picture. Don't be confused by the roles, because often the producer is also the buyer and the consumer the seller. However, these roles get separated when a market-driven strategy, such as the electronic shopping mall, is used to generate revenue. As part of such strategies, the requirements of potential users from outside the firm may drive the manner in which you package and produce your reusable assets.

Let's illustrate this point further by looking at a hypothetical example. Your team is in the midst of developing routing applications for movement control of such vehicles as trucks and trains. You are using object-oriented design concepts and pursuing an opportunistic approach to reuse. One of your most talented programmers comes to you with an idea. He says that he has developed a set of object libraries that has general applicability. These libraries are currently being used by several projects to develop products. These libraries organize objects into application frameworks that are highly abstracted collections of object classes that solve a particular type of movement problem. Such frameworks have saved your organization many staff-years of development effort.

The immediate question is, Should you package and sell these libraries as products? From a pro side, you probably could derive some amount of income if you packaged these libraries for sale by your sales department, or some third-party organization through their existing marketing channels. From the con side, you might not want to sell the libraries because you might believe that they provide you a competitive edge in your business. Why give away the farm to make a little extra money? Let's assume you decided to pursue the idea after your market survey turns up a large demand for such libraries. You would probably task your producers to broaden the scope of the library developments to address the marketing requirements, or manage the effort as a separate and new project.

It is important that you clearly identify roles when you develop your business plan. The reasons for this revolve around the processes, tools, and techniques selected to implement reuse. For example, consumer tools and techniques that you might acquire as an example to make it easy for your engineers and users to rework existing objects [2] using their new processes could include:

Tools and Techniques	Benefits	Examples
Repository	Provides shared access to common objects	Unisys Universal Repository
Framework	Provides initial set of objects and interactions	IBM's SOM/DSOM
Patterns	Provides conceptual design	Coad components [3]
Version control tools	Manages sharing of objects among engineers	Intersolv's PVCS
Object browsers	Enables easy inspection of objects	Symantec's Object Master

As another example, the tools and techniques that buyers would use to define the potential market, and the producers to identify which frameworks to develop for the movement control domain, would have differed greatly. These tools and techniques could have consisted of the following:

Tools and Techniques	Benefits	Examples
Focus groups, Pareto analysis, and other marketing tools	Provides means to understand users needs and requirements	Most textbooks on marketing provide a discussion

Domain engineering methods	Enables you to model the knowledge base of experience associated with building families of similar systems	Feature-Oriented Domain Analysis (FODA) method
Knowledge capture tools	Captures knowledge base and helps you analyze it using inference approaches	KAPTURE [4]
Domain engineering tools	Captures domain information and helps you identify commonalities and variabilities	DARE-COTS [5]
Version control tools	Baselines the architecture and manages changes to it for those projects using it	Intersolv's PVCS

Needless to say, producers should treat consumers as customers and employ a buyer/seller model to ensure that the reusable software assets they plan to develop have a ready market. Such emphasis is important independently of whether the market is internal or external. Many of us in the business have found selling products internally harder because of the inherent distrust that exists between organizations in large firms. Such barriers need to be addressed as part of the business-planning process primarily in the risk management and marketing sections (see Figure 7.1).

PULLING TOGETHER YOUR PLAN

While the business plan outline in Plan of Action 7.1 covers a lot of turf, its meaty sections are those associated with the work plan and risk management (i.e., sections 3A and 4E). As mentioned earlier, the tasks you identify in the plan should be related to the reuse strategy you selected and your decision to pursue either an opportunistic or a systematic approach to reuse. These tasks are also impacted by the buyer/seller and producer/consumer roles you have decided upon, and the promises you have already made to management when you pitched your reuse business case to them. The tasks are also influenced by your customers' requirements, especially if they provide the majority of your funding (e.g., government contracts used to provide supplemental funding may force you to do tasks that you normally don't perform). Now is your chance to shine and show management how you plan to follow through and deliver.

Let's look at some typical work tasks to more fully comprehend what needs to be done in order to put your reuse strategy into action. Before you begin, let's summarize the work tasks you've completed so far and the products you have developed under the heading of reuse readiness:

FIGURE 7.1 Demand versus supply-side model.

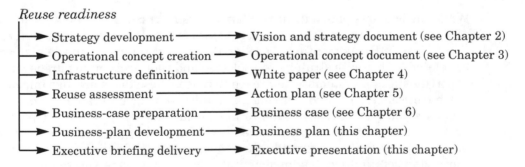

As noted, the content of each of these tasks has already been addressed by a chapter in this book. For completeness, each element of the reuse readiness activity tree is briefly discussed in the task glossary that appears as Table 7.2. Needless to say, you've done a great deal of work to get ready and now is the time to pull together everything so that you can get your plan approved and get on with the effort.

TABLE 7.2 Task Glossary (Reuse Readiness)

Activity	Task	Discussion
Reuse readiness	Strategy development	Prepare a crisply written vision and strategy for your reuse program
	Operational concept development	Define your technical, management and transition reuse concepts of operations
	Infrastructure definition	Define the success elements of your reuse program (includes your asset acquisition/packaging, methods/tools, organizational, distribution, and incentive approaches)
	Reuse assessment	Develop a reuse plan of action based upon an assessment of your organization's readiness to adopt reuse techniques
	Business-case preparation	Prepare a business case that justifies your reuse program based upon accepted financial measures
	Executive briefing delivery	Get management to commit to your reuse program by preparing and presenting a hard-hitting pitch soliciting their support
	Business-plan development	Prepare a business plan that maps in detail the path you will travel to insert reuse into your firm

Opportunistic Approach

Now you are ready to kick off your reuse effort. Using the opportunistic approach, you will try to do reuse in a manner that does not disrupt existing software production operations. As already discussed, the four major activities you will pursue when you take this approach are applications development, asset management, management, and marketing. The typical task breakouts for the applications development activity and some of its related reuse products are:

Applications development (from a reuse viewpoint)

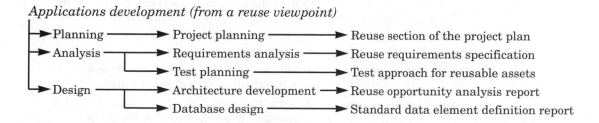

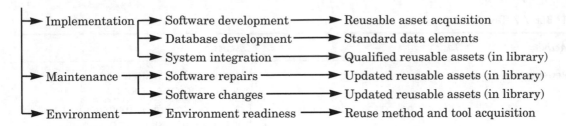

Note: The primary tool to be acquired is a reuse library. The software engineers use this tool to access reusable assets. The asset management is related because it encompasses the work involved in operating the tool and qualifying the components that populate it.

TABLE 7.3 Task Glossary (Applications Development)

Activity	Task	Discussion
Applications development	Project planning	Plan for reuse by expanding scope of existing tasks within normal project plan
	Requirements analysis	Specify reuse requirements by identifying desired level of commonality and variability
	Test planning	Define how reusable assets will be qualified prior to incorporation into system builds
	Architecture development	Analyze and identify high-payoff reuse opportunities as architecture is developed
	Database design	Design database schema to maximize the reuse of standard data elements
	Software development	Acquire reusable assets (i.e., buy, reengineer) and incorporate them into the software system as it is being developed
	Database development	Develop the common data elements and use them to populate the physical databases
	System integration	Qualify reusable assets as part of the software integration and test process, and deliver them to the reuse library in a form fit for use by other projects
	Software repairs	Modify reusable assets to correct problems identified from the field
	Software changes	Modify reusable assets to incorporate perfective or adaptive changes agreed upon by users
	Environment readiness	Acquire reuse methods and tools identified in the project plan as being needed by the project

This is a pretty standard software life-cycle process modified to take full advantage of reusable assets (designs, off-the-shelf packages, existing code, standard data, canned test assets, etc.). The preceding activities, whose elements are discussed in Table 7.3, should contain no surprises. The work identified is what you would normally do to field and sustain any operational software system. I broke out the environment as a separate task because selecting, acquiring, and getting the reuse methods and tools inserted into your organization often take a great deal of time and effort to accomplish. To save room, I defined only the reuse elements of these tasks. If you need more details on their content, there are many excellent references [6, 7, 8].

This life cycle was selected because it allows you to use just about any of the development paradigms (incremental development, spiral, etc.) and reuse strategies (generative, library, etc.) discussed in earlier chapters. It also permits you to tackle the needs of either database or process-intensive software developments. You should realize that most projects try to incorporate whatever improvements they can under the constraints of time and money. Therefore, it would be inappropriate to limit our discussion to just one approach when there are many available.

You cannot be successful with reuse by pursing applications development tasks alone. There are other interrelated activities that must be completed in order to put a repeatable system of software reuse management into place in primarily a project organization. For example, packaging standards need to be developed to guide the development of assets that you will use to populate the reuse library. In addition, an up-to-date catalog of holdings needs to be put online so that potential consumers know what's available in the library. As another example, release and distribution controls, such as those illustrated in Figure 7.2, need to be put into place if you are planning to put your electronic shopping mall online to derive added income from external consumers.

The following three additional activities define these related tasks and their work products. The task glossary shown in Table 7.4 provides a brief discussion of the work associated with each element of these activities. The first activity to be discussed is *asset management*. As shown in the following list, asset management is concerned with managing, populating, operating, and maintaining the reuse library:

Asset management

- Library management ⟶ Actions taken to manage the library effort
- Library population ⟶ Reusable assets that are available for use
- Library operations ⟶ Catalog of holdings generated, plus user support
- Library maintenance ⟶ New versions of the library software released or installed

Asset management tasks are often assigned to the configuration management group because of the economies of scale associated with having a central group perform the functions, and the need to have one party manage the libraries used

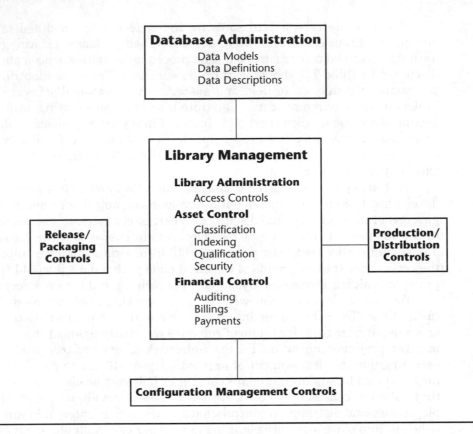

FIGURE 7.2 Electronic shopping-mall release and distribution controls. *Source:* Ian S. Hayes, "Bridging Business and Management," *Application Development Trends,* Vol. 3, No. 8, August 1996, pp. 30–37 (adapted considerably). © 1996 Ian Hayes.

within and across projects. Creation of the first release of the reuse library can be a time-consuming and expensive task if you attempt it from scratch. However, the effort can be done more quickly if you mimic the libraries that already exist and point to their holdings. This is what is meant in the table by the phrase *library of libraries.*

The next activity you are concerned with is *management* (of reuse). As explained earlier, a management infrastructure (processes, standards, etc.) must be developed to make software reuse practical. This can be done by the first project to embrace the concept, or by a team established across projects for this purpose. Once established, the infrastructure can be enhanced either by the project or by members of the team based upon the specific needs of their project(s). The management tasks delineated in the activities that follow were created to be flexible enough to handle either of these alternatives. They were also created under the

TABLE 7.4 Task Glossary (Other Activities)

Activity	Task	Discussion
Asset Management	Library management	Administer the reuse library, maintain access control, and manage the day-to-day activities
	Library population	Acquire, classify, qualify, and make assets available to authorized users via a library or library of libraries
	Library operation	Operate the library, providing products and services to users; generate catalog of holdings; support help desk; perform configuration management and quality control
	Library maintenance	Maintain the library software, installing or releasing new versions of the package whenever it is needed
Management	Infrastructure development	Develop the management infrastructure to be used by the projects, and keep it current
	Reuse management	Manage the reuse program and determine/report progress periodically to management
	Education and training	Develop and offer educational and training materials, courses, and tutorials to project/reuse staff
	Configuration management	Broaden the existing configuration management function to maintain traceability of reusable assets to project baselines (more than one)
	Quality assurance	Broaden the existing quality function to confirm that reuse requirements are satisfied, reuse considerations are addressed, and reuse processes are being followed
Marketing	Planning	Prepare the strategic marketing plan that identifies target markets and how you will penetrate them
	Partnering	Negotiate agreements with partners to develop COTS versions of product to satisfy your needs, and which potentially involve joint marketing arrangements
	Sales	Conduct the promotion campaign, develop leads, and earn revenue by closing sales

Note: Assets may be acquired via any of the following three means: develop it new, use off-the-shelf or third-party software, or reengineer existing software so that it meets standards.

assumption that there is a group that provides centralized software configuration management and quality assurance support to all projects on some fee-for-service basis. They are also based upon the assumption that the additional effort to manage reuse would be minimal if the work involved were made a natural part of what the engineers did normally to generate their products. If these assumptions are faulty, you should modify the management activities list somewhat to accommodate the changes:

Management

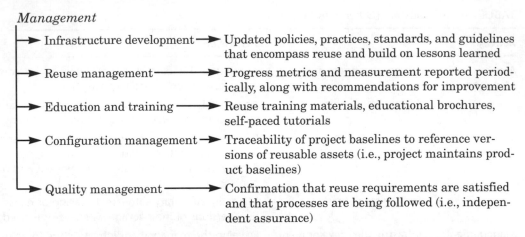

Infrastructure development	Updated policies, practices, standards, and guidelines that encompass reuse and build on lessons learned
Reuse management	Progress metrics and measurement reported periodically, along with recommendations for improvement
Education and training	Reuse training materials, educational brochures, self-paced tutorials
Configuration management	Traceability of project baselines to reference versions of reusable assets (i.e., project maintains product baselines)
Quality management	Confirmation that reuse requirements are satisfied and that processes are being followed (i.e., independent assurance)

The last of the three activities you are concerned with is *marketing*. Such an activity is needed no matter what strategy you embrace. If you are implementing a library strategy, you must sell your wares to the engineers on your programs. This requires you to get the message out to your target audience and train them on the rudiments of your system. If you are pursuing an electronic shopping-mall approach, promotion takes in an added dimension. You may need to advertise and market to sell your wares and meet your sales quotas. Marketing activities are as follows:

Marketing

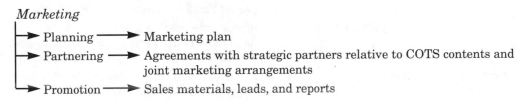

Planning	Marketing plan
Partnering	Agreements with strategic partners relative to COTS contents and joint marketing arrangements
Promotion	Sales materials, leads, and reports

Systematic Approach

The systematic approach is much more product-line and architecture oriented. As previously discussed, it adds a fifth activity, *domain engineering,* which feeds and is conducted in parallel with the applications development to figure out what assets to build to be reusable. The major difference when you implement the product-line and megaprogramming strategies is who generates the architecture and reusable assets. The product-line approach often tasks some separate group to analyze the application domain, develop the reference architecture, and generate the reusable assets to populate it. This separation can make sense in firms where the prerequisite skills, knowledge, and abilities reside in some systems engineering or architecture organization, and when the architecture involves hardware and software trade-offs (e.g., allocation of requirements in a real-time approach and landing system used to vector aircraft into an airport in foul weather). The megaprogramming strategy takes a different tack. It typically tasks the software shop to develop the architecture and populate it with the desired reusable assets. Often, this approach makes sense when the system is purely software and the architectural trade-offs can be handled by senior software engineers as part of their enterprise-wide segmentation and modeling efforts (e.g., a financial system that must interface with other software systems within the firm to refresh its data).

The activities you would pursue using this approach would encompass the two life-cycle models and add domain engineering as the fifth task to applications development, asset management, management, and marketing. The typical task breakouts for the domain engineering activity and its related reuse products might include:

Domain engineering

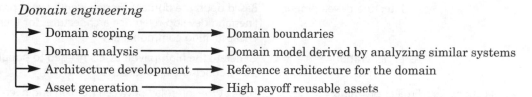

Domain scoping ⟶ Domain boundaries
Domain analysis ⟶ Domain model derived by analyzing similar systems
Architecture development ⟶ Reference architecture for the domain
Asset generation ⟶ High payoff reusable assets

The techniques used to perform these four domain engineering tasks are relatively new. Few firms have integrated these tasks into their life cycles, and even fewer have developed their product lines using them. The modeling methods they use are new and the experience base has just matured to the point where they can be used on large systems. As a result, the manner in which you practice domain engineering may differ from organization to organization. To help you understand the tasks involved in domain engineering better, a brief discussion of them is provided in Table 7.5. Because of domain engineering's importance to reuse, we have devoted a major part of Chapter 10 to provide a more complete discussion of this critical technology.

The tasks done in the four remaining activities are not much different from those identified for the opportunistic approach. While the names may appear the same, the work performed is sometimes considerably different. Again, we will cover the work involved in both applications development and asset management more extensively in Chapter 10. For now, we will summarize the differences in the paragraphs that follow and in Table 7.5.

Applications development takes on a different meaning when a systematic approach is followed. Instead of building systems from scratch one at a time, a reference architecture is used as a framework to enable your engineers to take advantage of available assets, including knowledge gained in the past when they built their systems. Make/buy decisions are made in the context of the architecture. Opportunities for reuse are identified and exploited as part of the normal processes used to design, implement, and maintain elements of your product line(s). The use of the reference architecture permits your engineers to specify a solution that can be built in half the time at a cost of between 50 and 60 percent, and covers as much as 90 percent of the requirements.

There is some debate over who should develop the reusable assets. Many papers on domain engineering include asset development in their scope because

TABLE 7.5 Task Glossary (Systematic Approach)

Activity	Task	Discussion of Changes Made for the Systematic Approach
Domain engineering	Domain scoping	Select and bound your domain precisely so that you can quickly hone in on reuse opportunities
	Domain analysis	Model the domain using knowledge gained from building families of similar systems
	Architecture development	Based upon the domain model, identify your product lines and develop reference architectures for them by encapsulating commonalities
	Asset generation	Generate the high-payoff assets needed to populate the product-line architectures
Applications development	Project planning	Look at the interplay between domain engineering and applications development; emphasize mechanisms you will use to address intergroup coordination
	Requirements analysis	Look for 90-percent solutions to problems based upon constraining the requirements to achieve high levels of reuse
	Test planning	Use the operational architecture as the basis for test planning and scenario validation
	Architecture development	Use the reference technical architecture as the basis for making design decisions
	Database design	Use the reference system architecture as the basis to make design decisions; perform opportunity analysis
	Software development	Incorporate reusable assets provided by domain engineering and own staff into your software system
	Database development	Incorporate standard data elements provided by domain engineering and own staff into your databases
	System integration	As you qualify reusable assets, coordinate fixes with suppliers, including your domain engineering group
	Software maintenance	Coordinate repairs and changes to reusable assets with your suppliers, including your domain engineering group via a central organization
Asset management	Library management	Broaden scope to encompass domain engineering as an additional asset supplier
	Library population	Coordinate new requirements for reusable assets with domain engineering group in addition to existing suppliers

TABLE 7.5 *(Continued)*

	Library operations	Relate catalog of holdings to reference architectures so that users will know what building blocks are available for their products and product lines
	Library maintenance	Remains basically the same
Management	Infrastructure development	Broaden the infrastructure to emphasize teamwork, communications, and intergroup coordination
	Reuse management	Broaden the scope to encompass domain engineering tasks and product-line architectures
	Education and training	Broaden the scope to develop additional skill sets needed to perform domain engineering and architecture tasks
	Configuration management	Broaden the scope to permit line-of-business organizations to own product-line architectures and control changes made to their key assets
	Quality assurance	Broaden the scope to encompass domain engineering tasks and product-line architectures
Marketing	Planning	Broaden the scope to better understand the customer requirements for your reusable assets, products, and product lines
	Partnering	Broaden the scope to partner to populate product-line architectures
	Promotion	Broaden the scope to promote the product line and product-line architectures

they believe that only a central group can produce software that satisfies a variety of project needs [9, 10]. However, most projects that practice product-line reuse suggest that they too can generate reusable assets. This is especially true as the project unfolds and new reuse opportunities are identified, developed, and made available via the reuse library. In response, Table 7.5 shows reusable assets being generated by both activities. If you disagree with this assumption, please remove one or the other entry when you develop your plan.

You should also notice that the environment readiness task under applications development has been removed from Table 7.5. Reuse methods and tools are typically incorporated into the infrastructure by those firms that practice systematic reuse. This is done to make reuse an integral part of the way these firms conduct their business. Under such assumptions, individual projects don't have to worry about developing a methodology or acquiring tools. Instead, they can focus their attention and energy on getting the product out quickly and economically.

As the final change to applications development, the software repair and change tasks in Table 7.4 have been combined in Table 7.5 under the heading of software maintenance. The reason for having two tasks previously was to separate reusable asset repair from perfective/adaptive actions. As both will probably be done by the same shop, there is no need to make this distinction any longer.

As illustrated in Table 7.5, asset management maintains its previous orientation under the systematic approach. The reuse library remains important even though it is not the central focus of this strategy. The reason for this is apparent. The reuse library continues to serve as the primary distribution mechanism for reusable assets being made available to a variety of projects by both your domain engineering and applications development groups. While some of the practices involved may be enlarged to encompass the broader scope of the contributing activities, the tasking in Table 7.5 remains basically the same. The one major new requirement revolves around the need to map assets to the product-line architecture. Your engineers need to know this information to identify the building blocks that they can use as they develop their applications.

Management and marketing tasks in Table 7.5 also take on a broader scope. Teamwork, communications, and intergroup coordination become important factors as groups interact to generate reusable assets that will be integrated into products and product lines. Projects are no longer king. Product-line goals may direct what a project builds and how they go about building it. New technical skills, knowledge, and abilities must be developed and new roles must be assigned. The guiding force for management and marketing is the product-line architecture. It serves as the basis for making most of the technical, management, and marketing decisions.

Cost and Schedule-Estimating Rules of Thumb

Now that you understand what it is you must do, you're probably wondering how long it will take to do it and how much money you should allocate to the job. As discussed in Chapter 6, there are several software cost-estimating models, such as COCOMO 2.0 [11], available to help you develop answers to these questions. They are recommended because they build on the knowledge base of experience within the community to provide you with responses to your queries. However, such an answer does not help you develop schedules and budgets for your plan. In response, I have included the following rules of thumb that you can use cautiously to scope the resources required to implement the strategy you've selected.

Rules of thumb are nothing more than a recipe for making an educated guess. They are an easy-to-remember set of guidelines that fall somewhere between a mathematical formula and a shot in the dark [12]. They are instructive and should be fun to read. The following 20 reuse rules of thumb are provided based upon my and others experience [13, 14] to help you to scope the time and effort involved in implementing your strategy. Use them carefully as tools.

1. *The reuse packaging factor.* The additional effort to package an asset to be reusable is in the order of 35 to 50 percent. Such costs assume that the effort required to put the reuse infrastructure into place in your organization has already been expensed and doesn't enter into the computations (i.e., to recoup the costs).

2. *Effort and time are not interchangeable.* Brook's law [15] still holds true. Just because a woman can have a baby in nine months doesn't mean that you can replace her with three women and have three babies in three months (see Exercise 8 on page 325).

3. *Leveraged software reuse.* Coding represents at most 20 percent of the effort in most software development efforts. Leverage your efforts by focusing on reusing high-payoff assets such as designs. You will thus be able to recover your costs quicker than the norm.

4. *The 20/80-percent rule.* Twenty percent of your library holdings are responsible for 80 percent of your reuse; 20 percent of your clients are responsible for 80 percent of your business; 20 percent of the staff is responsible for 80 percent of the productivity.

5. *The reuse breakeven point.* The breakeven point for a reusable software asset is three instances of reuse. Based upon this observation, make sure that there are at least three potential users for an asset prior to making the decision to build it to be reusable.

6. *There is no free lunch when it comes to reuse.* The cost to reuse an asset with no modifications whatsoever ranges from 10 to 25 percent [16]. You still need to expend effort to identify and acquire the asset. Then, you need to qualify it and integrate it into your system. No wonder people get disillusioned. The following list compares the nominal ranges of software development costs in $/source line of code for the following three categories of software for five different applications domains: reused as is off the shelf, modified off the shelf, and new. It should give you some idea of the relative costs.

Category/Domain	Off the Shelf (as is)	Modified Off the Shelf	New
Business applications (inventory, payroll, logistics, etc.)	$2–5	$12–15	$20–35
Control systems (pipeline control, etc.)	$5–15	$20–30	$40–75
Military systems (tanks, warships, etc.)	$15–25	$50–100	$100–150
Scientific applications (weather prediction, etc.)	$8–15	$18–25	$40–80
Telecommunications systems (switches, wireless, etc.)	$10–20	$25–40	$50–75

Cost Metric: $/source line of code.

7. *The 3-percent breakage rule.* Expect 3 percent of the assets you use to break when you try to integrate them into your application. Expect 10 percent to fail to compile.

8. *Generate it if you can.* Generative approaches to software reuse increase over-all staff productivity by factors of between 10 and 20. This means that generators make a lot of sense even if their usage is limited to but a small part of your application (human interface, etc.). Recognize that generator code itself can be reused at a metalanguage level.

9. *Ten times the norm in quality rule.* Reusable code assets made available via a reuse library typically exhibit 10 times the quality as measured by defects per thousand lines of code (0.2 versus the norm of two defects/KSLOC). This makes sense when you think about it, because these assets have a lot more users than normal to exercise their capabilities.

10. *Three strikes and you are out.* If you can't get the reusable asset to work in three tries, give up and try something else, because experience indicates that it will take you an average of 20 more trials to get the asset to behave as expected.

11. *Throw-away code is normally not thrown away.* Less than 10 percent of the code that is advertized as throw-away code is ever thrown away. Most of it winds up in your application and is delivered as part of the system.

12. *A few good assets (especially in a reuse library).* The bigger your reuse library gets, the less likely it will be used. Consumers will give up and go elsewhere if they have to spend a lot of time and effort trying to figure out how to get what they want from the library.

13. *The domain engineering rule of six.* It takes six experienced people six months to do a domain analysis under the assumptions that the domain is well bounded and that the methodology and tools being used are mature. The six people involved include a full-time methodologist, a facilitator/scribe, a senior software analyst, and three part-time knowledge experts who know the domain inside out and can provide you with the details of why products were built the way they were in the past. It should be noted that a limited domain analysis can be done at the boundary layer in about six weeks.

14. *An experience base of five.* Don't develop a domain model for any application for which you have fewer than five examples. It normally doesn't make sense because you will probably be working with outgrowths of the same system.

15. *Architecture reviews pay dividends.* Conducting reviews to ensure that products conform with product-line architectures can save a project about 10 percent of its total development budget. It also reduces the rework associated with nonconformance by a factor of between 20 and 30 percent.

16. *Methodology maturity rule.* It will take you three tries before you become proficient in the use of a new method such as domain analysis. To speed the technology transfer, bring in an outside expert to provide the knowhow to get the job done.

17. *Be the fourth user of a new software tool.* When acquiring software tools for a new methodology such as domain analysis, never be one of its first major users. Else, you will spend much of your time debugging the tool instead of generating your product. Don't use a tool unless there have been at least three users who have already worked the kinks out of it. Else, double your budget and extend your schedule by six months.

18. *Ninety-day rule for an idea.* You have 90 days to develop your idea and 90 days to sell it to your management. After that time, management loses patience and funds evaporate.

19. *Half your time.* Allocate half your schedule to requirements, architecture, and design tasks. Make sure you develop your schedule based upon the work you have to do. If you are handed a schedule, check its feasibility before you slice it in half to accommodate this rule. Recognize again that time and effort are not interchangeable. You may budget as much as 40 to 60 percent of your effort to be spent in the first 50 percent of your time.

20. *Six-month increments.* Plan to deliver something visible in six-month intervals. This appears to be the time it takes for management to get nervous when they don't see anything coming out of the hopper.

Hopefully, these rules of thumb will help you develop your cost and schedule estimates. They were written to supplement your existing procedures and provide some insight into where you need to add and subtract time and effort. If you like rules of thumb, I suggest you read Norm Augustine's book [17] on the topic.

ADDRESSING RISK

Now that you understand the work required to implement your strategy, you are in a better position to identify the risks that you face. Risk is defined as the probability that a software project will experience potential hazards that will adversely impact its scheduled delivery dates and budgets. There are technical risks on a project, such as those associated with trying to use a new tool or compiler. There are management risks on the same project, such as those associated with aggressive schedules or shortfalls in available personnel. There are even technological risks, such as those associated with using new technologies like Java to host your reuse library. Independently of what the risks are, you must show management you have a handle on them in your business plan. You must talk intelligently about how you will manage them and show your assessment of their potential impact on the work you have planned, and the cost and schedule estimates in your plan.

I don't believe your business plan will be accepted unless you show management that you've performed a risk assessment. Such a review identifies possible risks, assesses their potential impact (i.e., primarily on your costs and schedules),

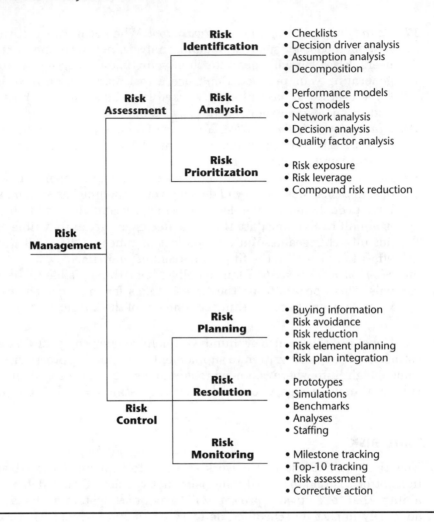

FIGURE 7.3 Software risk management steps/tools. *Source:* Barry W. Boehm, "Introduction and Overview," *Tutorial: Software Risk Management,* IEEE Computer Society, 1989, p. 2.

and prioritizes them so that you can monitor and work on removing the big swingers. Within the software field, a lot of attention has been given to the topic of risk management during the past decade. Several good books [18, 19] have been written on the topic, and courses on software risk management are being taught at the SEI and by the IEEE.

The process of risk control will be covered at length in Chapter 8. We will concentrate our attention in this chapter on the process of risk assessment so that you can complete your business plan. Risk assessment processes identify, analyze, and prioritize risks. Risk control monitors risk and resolves conflicts that occur. Figure 7.3 illustrates the steps involved and some of the tools available to help complete them.

Risk identification generates lists of potential risk items. Most of these are obvious. Many firms develop checklists to simplify the process based upon their experience. Others use their most experienced people during project startup to help identify risks. Table 7.6 identifies the 10 typical risks that occur on too many projects. We will use these a little later on in our discussion of how to prioritize risks. These 10 risk items can be classified into five categories—resources, commitments, management, technical performance, and technology—as follows:

Risk Category	*Risk Item*
Resources	Reuse schedule may be too aggressive
	The skills needed for reuse take a lot of time and effort to develop
	Reusable assets cost more
	New methods and tools are needed
Commitments	Assuming the firm will develop the reuse infrastructure may prove untrue
Management	The incentive structure needs to be changed to reward reuse
	The liability associated with reusing assets needs to be limited
	Processes need to be changed for reuse
Technical performance	Reuse makes achieving tight performance goals hard
Technology	Technology used for reuse may be immature and/or unproven

TABLE 7.6 Typical Risks

Risk Item	*Chances*	*Cost*	*Dependencies*	*Ranking*
1. Aggressive schedule	90%	High	Risk items 2, 6, and 8	2
2. Wrong skills	75%	Moderate	None	6
3. Costs more	90%	High	Risk item 6	3
4. New methods and tools	75%	High	Risk item 8	4
5. Infrastructure assumed in place	25%	Low	None	10
6. New incentive structure	100%	High	Risk item 5	1
7. Increased liability	50%	Moderate	None	8
8. New processes	75%	High	Risk item 5	5
9. Performance goals	50%	Moderate	Risk item 5	7
10. Immature technology	50%	Moderate	None	9

The primary goal of risk assessment is to identify the threats that can hurt you the most. Mature organizations do this through a set of processes that assess the probability of loss to develop priorities. As shown in Figure 7.3, the cost models talked about in the last chapter are helpful because they let you vary their cost drivers (staff experience, degree of tooling, etc.) to determine their impact on cost and schedule. However, you may not have a cost model. Instead, you might use a simple decision table, as shown in Table 7.6, to develop priorities and examine cause and effects.

The rankings that appear in Table 7.6 were probably counterintuitive. They were determined by looking primarily at probabilities and dependencies. For example, *new incentive structure* ranked first because it had a 100-percent probability of occurrence. Without rewards, there is no way that you will be able to motivate others to spend the extra dollars needed to build assets to be reusable. *Aggressive schedule* ranked second even though it was tied in probability with others due to its dependency on three related risk items. If you don't have the people, incentives, and processes in place when you need them, you will most probably not deliver on schedule. Management likes seeing a top-10 list like this in project plans. It shows them that you understand what the risks are and that you are in control of the situation.

EXECUTIVE PRESENTATION

You are now ready to give your plan to management. You have done your homework and pulled together your business plan. You are really proud of the document and are anxious to get approval to start. The document follows the outline provided in Plan of Action 7.1 and is brief and to the point. You believe it is well written. Realize that your boss is a busy person. Such a document takes a good deal of time to read and digest. Be aware that any document that contains more than three pages does not get immediate attention. It is just too big to swallow at one brief sitting. As a consequence, the plan will probably sit in your boss's in basket waiting for time to become available either in the evenings or on the weekend. Worse yet, your plan may fall victim to some crises that occurred that took time away from your boss's busy schedule.

While there may be a desire to read your plan, there might not be time. To counteract this trend, you must make time available for the review of your plan on your boss's calendar. The best way to do this is to schedule an executive presentation. This will give your boss a compelling reason to get involved in preparing the presentation. As the two of you work together, you will be able to communicate the guts of the plan to your boss and get his blessing, support, and help in getting it through the approval barriers.

The executive briefing should follow the outline of the plan. Don't be afraid of providing some refresher materials in the pitch. Executives are busy people and some of them may have forgotten some of the key concepts you presented when you made your initial briefing (see Figure 2.1 in Chapter 2). Try to do the presentation in, at most, one hour. Getting more than an hour might be difficult because of scheduling conflicts. You should be able to boil down what you have to say to at most 25 to 30 charts. You might prepare your charts to correspond with the 25 topics in the plan outline. However, don't skimp when it comes to discussing the task plan. Use several charts to provide detail on what needs to be done, when, and by whom. Don't approach the briefing as informational. You are making the presentation for two reasons. First and foremost, you want to get approval to implement your plan. Second, you want help in reducing some of the risks you've identified that are outside of your control. Let your audience know what you are after right up front. Push for approval and help as you brief and I guarantee that you will get a response. If the response is negative, ask your critics what rework needs to done to get their support or approval. Place the burden on their backs. Push again to get answers, or all of your hard work may have been for nothing. Be positive and stay cool, calm, and collected.

Some of the tricks you might use as you prepare your pitch to executive management might include:

- Use graphics whenever possible to communicate key concepts and points.
- Keep your charts simple (put at most five bullets on nongraphical charts).
- Anticipate the tough questions and be ready for them (have lots of backup charts to answer the questions that always seem to arise in such briefings).
- State what you are after up front and make sure you try to get it in your summary (e.g., a "what next" or "we need your concurrence" chart at the end of the briefing does this nicely).
- Emphasize the business issues in all of your discussions (this works especially well when you can supplement your points with solid marketing data).
- Focus your discussions on risks that are outside of your control, because this is the group of people who can possibly do something to alleviate them.
- Remember, you are the reuse expert and they are looking to you for answers, not vice versa.

In some organizations, you will have to go before some executive council to get a plan of this sort approved and funded. Such councils tend to be very political and you must presell your plan to its key members well before you come before them to ask for support. You still need to present your plan to the more general executive audience, because you are using the executive presentation as a forcing function to get your boss and others to buy into your plan. However, you may now need to do this earlier in the cycle, especially if you want to solidify your support with various members of the executive council. Your boss should be able to provide guidance as to the best path through this political maze. Again, use the business case developed in the last chapter to justify how the effort helps everyone. Get the key people on the council on your side, but don't forget to sell your boss on the plan first. You will be amazed at how much can be accomplished when your boss supports your cause.

CASE STUDY

The firm is about to mount an opportunistic reuse initiative within a classical information management system organization. The Information Systems (IS) shop is a centralized group that provides software support to the company's more than 500 sites throughout the world. Its over 300 software professionals develop applications for its six IBM 3890 computers running MVS/CICS connected to about 600 midrange, and more than 5000 IBM/PCs running Windows via a number of communications networks. Human Resources support (payroll, employee benefits, etc.) is provided via commercial off-the-shelf packages that run on the mainframes. Operations support for billing/collections, marketing/sales, and operations is provided via custom packages that run via a client/server architecture on all platforms. Funding for the information services is provided via a 10-percent tax levied on the 500 organizations that use its services. The IS shop is migrating to a full client/server architecture and is distributing its processing across networks at this moment.

The IS shop's current focus is on enterprise modeling, distribution, and generation. They believe the modeling techniques they should consider for domain analysis should be able to permit analysts to relate their application domain to their enterprise model so that data planning and standardization will be possible. Their software engineering group is developing processes and implementing tool strategies. Their focus is on applications generation using fourth-generation languages and modern CASE tools. They believe reuse should take the form of automatic generation of screens and application program classes (menu, directory, inquiry, and entry classes), in a manner that is supportive of their mainframe and midrange usability standards. They are trying to distribute their processing via their client/server architecture using APPC (application program-to-program communications) packages supplied by their primary hardware vendors.

They have identified the need to create a repository to store their reusable assets as the main focus of their reuse program. They need tools and are using the reuse initiative to help justify the purchase of a much broader software engineering environment. They have justified the costs to acquire and set up this environment based upon the high degree of sharing of their application program class libraries. They have developed their business plan and are ready to submit it for approval. As part of this plan, they have performed a risk analysis, whose results are shown in Table 7.7.

This case study is instructive of what not to do. The risk matrix highlights the fact that there is considerable cost and schedule risk associated with getting the environment to work. The risk is so large that management might opt to disapprove go-ahead under the condition that the group looks for a safer course of action. In this case, using reuse to justify a broader environment effort has seriously jeopardized the approval of the reuse library acquisition. Perhaps, a better course of action would have been to plan out the environment purchase as a spi-

TABLE 7.7 Example Risk Matrix

Importance	Risk	Probability	Cost
	Software Engineering Environment		
1	System hardware failure	90%	High
1	System software failure	90%	High
1	Individual tools don't work properly	90%	High
1	Lack of appreciable tool integration (especially with the repository)	90%	High
3	Needed tools not available	90%	Low
3	Lack of hard disk space	Unknown	Medium
	System Administration		
1	Loss of in-house support contractor	50%	High
1	Understaffed/overworked	90%	High
1	Poor backup/recovery procedures	75%	High
	General Risk Areas		
1	Loss of data	90%	High
2	Loss of personnel	90%	High
2	Lack of experience and training	75%	High
2	Loss of integration support for tools	75%	Low
1	Lack of a unified repository	90%	High
2	Inexperience with environment	75%	High
2	Automated process inefficient	75%	Medium
3	Lack of adequate test tool support	50%	Medium
3	Lack of mature object-oriented tools	50%	Medium
3	Incomplete automated certification process	10%	Medium

ral development, and show how incremental acquisition would have reduced the risk. The reuse library could then be incorporated in one of the early spirals, and time to reduce the risk could have been woven into the schedule.

Management did not approve this project. As a matter of fact, the proposal never made it to the executive council because middle management stopped the effort before it was elevated to that level. The team took another tack for the reuse library. Instead of purchasing the tool as a new purchase, they bought it as an add-on to one of their existing repository systems. They then used existing staff to develop the processes and operating procedures needed to use it. In other words, they ate the costs. They did this because they felt that the library could save them lots of time and effort. So far, data collected indicates they were right. The reuse of their class libraries has reduced cost by about 15 to 20 percent and cut development time in half. However, it is important to note that such reuse would have been impossible if they did not subscribe to a common usability standard across the 500 organizations that make up the firm. This standard defined the common ground that made broad-scale reuse possible for this firm.

SUMMARY

- The business plan is used to pull together your reuse program and communicate its important points to interested parties.
- You can approach reuse from either an opportunistic or systematic manner.
- When viewing your reuse plan, it is important to understand who the producers and consumers are and what their roles are.
- The real guts of the business plan revolve around the tasks you must complete in order to put your plan into action.
- Getting management to commit to implement the plan requires you to pay considerable attention to risk and to politics.

REFERENCES

1. Software Productivity Consortium, *Reuse Adoption Handbook,* SPC-92051-CMC, Version 02.00.05, November 1993.
2. Sentry Market Research, "Refreshing the Object Cupboard," *Software* magazine, August 1996.
3. Peter Coad, *Object Models, Strategies, Patterns, and Applications,* Yourdon Press, 1995.
4. Sidney Ballin, *KAPTURE user literature,* CTA, Inc., Rockville, MD, 1994.
5. Rueben Parieto-Diaz, *DARE-COTS marketing brochure,* reuse, Inc., Fairfax, VA, 1996.
6. John Boddie, *Crunch Mode,* Prentice-Hall, 1987.
7. Neal Whitten, *Managing Software Development Projects,* John Wiley & Sons, 1990.
8. David P. Youll, *Making Software Development Visible,* John Wiley & Sons, 1990.
9. Fred A. Maymir-Ducharme and S. Michael Webb, "Multiple Perspectives on Domain Engineering," *Reuse '96 Tutorial,* July 1996.
10. Ruben Parieto-Diaz and Gullermo Arrango, *Domain Analysis and Software System Modeling,* IEEE Computer Society, 1991.
11. Barry W. Boehm, "The COCOMO 2.0 Software Cost Estimation Model: A Status Report," *American Programmer,* July 1996.
12. Tom Parker, *Rules of Thumb,* Houghton Mifflin Company, 1987.
13. Donald J. Reifer, "The Economics of Software Reuse", *13th Annual Conference International Society of Parametric Analysts,* New Orleans, May 1991.

14. Jeffrey S. Poulin, Measuring Software Reuse, Addison-Wesley, 1997.
15. Frederick P. Brooks, Jr., *The Mythical Man-Month,* Addison-Wesley, 1975.
16. Donald J. Reifer, *Software Reuse Cost Study,* RCI-TR-095, May 1996.
17. Norman R. Augustine, *Augustine's Laws,* American Institute of Aeronautics and Astronautics, 1983.
18. Capers Jones, *Assessment and Control of Software Risks,* Yourdon Press, 1994.
19. Barry W. Boehm, *Tutorial: Software Risk Management,* IEEE Computer Society, 1989.

Part III

Operational Transition

Making reuse work requires time, talent and attention to detail especially in the process area.

8

Making the Transition

GETTING STARTED

Congratulations, you made it through the executive review with only a few scars. Things did not go pleasantly. They never do when money is involved. Management dug deeply at the meeting to test the soundness of your plan. Your boss came through when the going got tough and helped you to overcome some of the criticism and get approval of your plan. You were given one year to demonstrate the feasibility of your approach. As a result, you are under a lot of pressure to generate results quickly. You must get started right away. There is no time to wait. What do you do, when? How do you get started?

First, remain calm and recognize you are ready to start. Come to the table with an agreed-upon vision, a strategy, defined operational concepts, and a detailed plan. You have an approved budget and schedule. Most importantly, you have your management's commitment and support. Now you must take stock of your situation. Based upon your readiness, you can determine what to do to start your reuse program by answering the following 10 questions:

Getting Started Checklist

✔ What are the near-term milestones and deliverables that have been promised (e.g., the items scheduled for delivery within the first three months of the effort)?

✔ What form do these deliverables take (reports, demonstrations, etc.) and which work tasks need to be kicked off to generate them?

✔ Are any of these work tasks on the critical path through the schedule? If so, what are the task dependencies that must be satisfied?

✔ What are the long-lead items and how can you make them happen in a timely manner (e.g., it might take four to six weeks to process an order through your purchasing system for training needed during the second week of the effort)?

✔ What staff resources do you have at your disposal, and do they have the prerequisite skills, knowledge, and abilities to complete the near-term tasks? If not, what training will be needed and when can it be scheduled?

✔ What facilities, equipment, and tools does your staff need to get the reuse effort up and running?

✔ What parts of the management infrastructure have to be readied and put into place to support each of the near-term task deadlines (e.g., you may ask your process group to develop a set of asset management practices in parallel with your efforts to purchase, install, and ready your reuse library for use)?

✔ Because of conflicts, what tasks cannot be performed as scheduled and what can you do about them (e.g., delay a demonstration because the people needed to perform it are busy completing a task on the critical path)?

✔ What are your management's expectations and how do you measure success in terms of these in both the near and long term?

✔ What are the risks you have identified and what do you have to do to keep them under control as the reuse program unfolds?

What you must get done first will probably surface once you write down your answers to these questions. Like most good managers, your schedules have been developed from left to right (i.e., independent of imposed deadlines and their associated pressures) in your plans. To figure out how to implement these schedules, you now have to superimpose the risks you have identified on top of them from right to left, and readjust the task deadlines. You also have to make adjustments to accommodate unscheduled events (e.g., conduct a demo for visiting dignitaries) and real-world constraints (e.g., make deliveries before the end of the quarter so that your boss can get credit for the sale). In addition, you have other management activities that will take a lot of your time to perform. These activities, some of which are listed in the following, will consume as much as half of your time during the startup period. Unfortunately, most of them do not appear on your schedules, and you will have to make time available to get them done:

■ Organizing your reuse project team and recruiting the right talent to be part of it

■ Keeping your team motivated and focused as reuse becomes part of the culture

■ Kicking off, leading, and participating in those intergroup efforts that are impacted directly by reuse (process and/or quality improvement efforts, strategic planning groups, etc.)

■ Attending other intergroup meetings that may not have much to do with reuse (ISO preaudit task force, IR&D reviews, etc.)

■ Doing the many administrative functions managers have to do to support their people and organization (salary administration, reviews, management peer reviews, red teams, etc.)

■ Building alliances with projects, partners, and other organizations on which you depend for technical, management, and political support

■ Reviewing and helping to rewrite policies, standards, and practices that have recently been updated by others to incorporate reuse

■ Responding to urgent requests for information, briefings, and assistance in resolving high-level crises (i.e., what some of us call knee jerks)

The items on this list shouldn't surprise you. These items are the things managers get involved with and worry about when starting up any project of any size once they have been given the go-ahead. However, these items force managers to prioritize their time and place their attention on what's really important. You often start your day with plans to catch up. Then, all of a sudden your day is over and you wonder where all of your time went. The higher in management you go, the worse the situation becomes. There continue to be more and more demands for your time. To survive, you must learn to manage your time so that you get the really important things done when you are in the best shape to do them.

WHAT DO YOU DO?

Figuring out what to do, when, is your challenge. The management dos and don'ts that we will discuss in the paragraphs that follow are summarized in Plan of Action 8.1. For starters, you must put in place an organizational structure that facilitates getting the job done. Such a structure must be geared to the work that must be done, not the people you have to do it. Then, based upon the work, staff your organization with the people with the skills, knowledge, and abilities to get the job done. If your people don't have the required skills, try to develop them through a process of mentoring and training. Bring new people on board to cope with the staffing shortfalls. In parallel, provide your people with the facilities, equipment, and tools they need to work as efficiently as possible. Finally, orient

PLAN OF ACTION 8.1   Dos and Don'ts for Reuse Managers

Getting Organized

- *DO* place your early attention on organizing and staffing your team

- *DO* organize around the work you must get done

- *DO* focus your team's efforts on getting your reuse infrastructure in place

- *DON'T* tackle the job without clear definition of roles and responsibilities

- *DON'T* organize around the people you have to do this work because they will probably change

- *DON'T* forget to address your long-lead items as you start up the effort

Staffing Your Team

- *DO* view hiring competent people as your responsibility, not that of your human resources department

- *DO* recognize that staffing up under deadline pressures requires planning and innovation

- *DO* weave reuse into your firm's career paths and job requirements—this shows your staff where growth is possible

- *DON'T* blindside others by stealing their people; consult with them beforehand on the transfer

- *DON'T* be afraid to bring in outsiders to help start up the project and transfer their skills to your organization

- *DON'T* forget to define the skill, knowledge, and ability requirements for each of the positions identified

Work Efficiently

- *DO* colocate your team and provide them with the facilities, equipment, and tools needed to do the job

- *DO* provide your team with ample administrative and clerical support

- *DO* better manage your time (take a course or listen to a tape on the subject)

- *DON'T* assume that you will be able to get the tools and equipment you need in a timely manner

- *DON'T* have your people waste a lot of time on things they can (and should) off-load to support personnel

- *DON'T* let unproductive meetings drain your resources

Managing per Your Plan

- *DO* use your plan as your roadmap for getting the job done

- *DO* challenge your team to streamline processes as they gain experience using them

- *DO* use classical project management techniques to maintain visibility into and control over your reuse efforts

- *DON'T* let your plan get out of date; update it and maintain it as a living document

- *DON'T* be a micro-manager; delegate authority to those closest to the work

- *DON'T* be afraid to trust your people; they will come through for you when you empower them to get the job done

PLAN OF ACTION 8.1   *(Continued)*

Managing Risk

- *DO* assess the reuse risks you have identified using the approaches discussed in Chapter 7
- *DO* monitor risk and track resolution of your risk items to make sure that your plans are working properly
- *DO* get those impacted by your reuse risks involved in the process of risk management

- *DON'T* forget that risk management is an ongoing process; as soon as you close out a risk, a new one appears
- *DON'T* fail to factor reuse risk into your work plans and schedules; make the necessary adjustments
- *DON'T* forget to involve your user and those groups affected by the risk in figuring out what to do about it

Keeping Out of Trouble

- *DO* promote teamwork and team contributions in your every action
- *DO* reward team contributions in addition to those of individuals
- *DO* foster improved horizontal as well as vertical communications
- *DO* recognize that metrics, reviews, and reports can provide insights into your status and progress

- *DON'T* assume that teams can be built without careful preparation
- *DON'T* forget that social skills may need to be built before some people can function as team members
- *DON'T* let conflicts get out of hand
- *DON'T* forget your plan was devised to provide you with a framework for gaining visibility and control

your people and keep them focused on getting the job done. Build teams, provide them with direction, and maintain control at all times. Then come the challenges. You will have to address the people problems that always seem to occur on a project. You will have to strive for harmony knowing that deadline pressures and burnout will become demotivating forces on your project. You will have to arbitrate problems and deal with egos, many times suppressing your own inner desire to force closure and provide input for the good of the project. Management of people is by no means a simple task. Yet, when the team is successful, it can provide a sense of accomplishment that makes all the effort expended worthwhile.

Getting Organized

As we saw in Chapter 4, there are numerous ways to organize your reuse effort. What will work best for you tends to be a function of your culture, strategy, and the job needs. You can stay out of trouble by organizing around the work in a manner compatible with the culture. For example, you might form a core reuse team to put a reuse library in place within a firm whose culture is matrix management oriented (i.e., project groups manage the work, while the functional groups provide them with the needed skilled people and technology [1]). This is one of the many ways that an opportunistic reuse strategy that consists of the following five tasks might be approached:

- Acquire reuse library software
- Identify candidate reusable assets
- Develop reuse library standards and practices
- Populate the reuse library with existing assets
- Operate the reuse library

This core team will focus on acquiring the library software. You will create a working group to get key engineers from the projects to both identify candidate reusable assets that are already in use within the firm, and decide how they will be documented and classified for ease of access. In parallel, the core team will develop a draft set of asset qualification and library metric standards for use based upon examples taken from available sources [2]. The working group will then review, rewrite, and approve these drafts. The core team will install, populate and operate the library using the practices and standards derived for that purpose. The working group will evolve to become a shared resource change-control board charged with the responsibility of maintaining configuration integrity of assets reused across projects.

As another example, let's assume you are pursuing a more systematic reuse initiative consisting of the following 13 tasks:

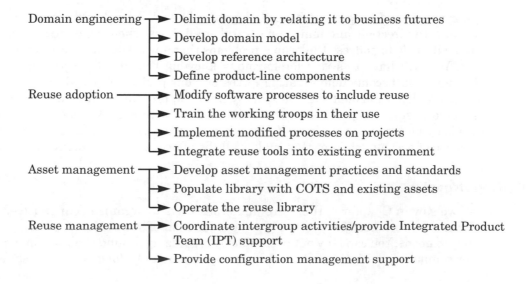

Domain engineering
- Delimit domain by relating it to business futures
- Develop domain model
- Develop reference architecture
- Define product-line components

Reuse adoption
- Modify software processes to include reuse
- Train the working troops in their use
- Implement modified processes on projects
- Integrate reuse tools into existing environment

Asset management
- Develop asset management practices and standards
- Populate library with COTS and existing assets
- Operate the reuse library

Reuse management
- Coordinate intergroup activities/provide Integrated Product Team (IPT) support
- Provide configuration management support

The way you might approach organizing your workforce to get the increased reuse workload done might involve the following three separate groups: a core reuse team, an integrated product team, and a reuse working group. As suggested in earlier chapters, you might want to establish some form of a management council to provide your team with direction and keep your key executives involved with your efforts and informed of your progress.

You might start by forming an IPT consisting of engineers from a number of functional disciplines (hardware, software, systems, etc.). You will charge this team with the task of performing the domain engineering and defining the elements of your product-line architecture. You might even task the team to go further and define the hardware and software components (processors, programs, buses, etc.) that comprise the product line. The team will work as a dedicated unit full time to define all three views of the architecture: technical, systems, and operational. They will use your business plan as a guide to develop a family of products designed specifically to satisfy your customer's requirements, now and into the future.

In parallel, your core reuse group will work to make software reuse concepts a part of the practices it uses to build software for elements of your product-line families. In addition, the team will look for opportunities to automate these practices and incorporate software reuse tools into the software engineering environment that your software engineers will use to develop their products.

As your third parallel thrust, set up your software reuse library so that your engineers can take full advantage of the reusable assets once they are made available by the other tasks. This activity will primarily be aimed at creating, populating, and promoting the reuse library that was made a part of your software engineering environment. Library processes will be perfected as reusable assets are acquired, and an index of holdings will be published. Assets will have to be qualified prior to being baselined and put under version control.

Staffing Your Team

Recruiting and keeping good people for your reuse team is a tough job. To attract them, you will have to make them feel that what you are planning to accomplish is exciting. You have to show them how they will grow, learn, and prosper once they become a member of the reuse staff. You will have to convince them that what they will do will help them realize their career objectives. You will have to reward them when they perform well and fulfill the promises you made when you hired them to keep them satisfied. You will have to develop new skills, knowledge, and abilities and keep them focused on achieving project goals. You may also have to develop social skills, especially if you are dedicated to using team approaches to getting the job done.

The types of functions these individuals will perform will vary, depending on the reuse strategy you select. For example, you will probably want to recruit staff to perform each of the following five functions if you selected one of the systematic approaches to reuse for implementation:

1. *Change Agent*—Work with projects, partners, and managers to create the business environment and successes needed to make reuse happen in practice.
2. *Chief Architect*—Develop, perfect, and refine the product-line architecture, become its chief advocate and provide the technical leadership needed to make its realization a reality.
3. *Process Engineer*—Modify existing technical and management processes the firm uses for software development to incorporate software reuse as a natural part of the way the organization does business.
4. *Reuse Methodologist*—Modify the technical model-based methods the firm uses to develop requirements and designs (object-oriented requirements analysis, model-based designs, etc.) to incorporate reuse considerations.
5. *Reuse Librarian*—Operate the reuse library in such a way that it provides value-added services for software development projects within the firm.

In a small organization, one person could be held responsible for all of these functions. In a larger institution, you might assign one or more individuals to address each of these specialties.

Because software reuse is an emerging technology, developing skills, knowledge, and abilities is a tough job. For example, Table 8.1 identifies the skill requirements for the five job functions just described. As you can see, it is unlikely that many of your software engineers possess all of the skills needed to get the job done. Of course, you plan to train your people and develop these skills. However, time now becomes your enemy. You have made commitments and your schedules don't always accommodate the learning curves involved in bringing people up to speed in a new technology. What do you do?

The three approaches that others have used to develop staff as they have tried to deal with deadline pressures include the rolling wave, a startup team and the sprinkle approach.

Rolling Wave   This approach assumes that you are using a spiral development paradigm. Train key staff members to perform reuse tasks during the first spiral. As part of the next spiral, have them mentor and train the next group to perform similar tasks. The process continues until all of the people you have targeted have been trained in reuse concepts. This approach seems to work best when an opportunistic strategy is being pursued.

Startup Team   This approach seeds your organization with experienced people who can mentor and coach those assigned the responsibility for performing reuse tasks. Hire consultants to assist and work with newly trained personnel to complete their startup tasks. Have the startup team leave once your people feel capa-

TABLE 8.1 Software Reuse Skill, Knowledge, and Ability Requirements

	Skills	Knowledge	Abilities
Change	Matches solutions to problems	Change management methods and models	Communicates well in writing/verbally
Agent	Organized Sees the big picture Technically current and competent	Reuse concepts Software engineering technology Technology transfer methods and models	Problem solver Thinks and plans strategically Works well with people/teams
Chief Architect	Analytical and pays attention to details Good modeling, design, and synthesis expertise	Formal methods Modeling methods Object-oriented techniques Reuse concepts	Achieves consensus Captures different architectural views Problem solver Technical leader
Process Engineer	Can model process from multiple views Understands what it takes to produce quality software	Reuse concepts SEI capability maturity models Software engineering technology	Can generate needed improvements Problem solver Understands user's views
Reuse Methodologist	Can model domains, product lines, and user requirements and designs	Domain engineering Reuse concepts Requirements and design methods	Captures experience and requirements in model base Problem solver
Reuse Librarian	Can administer a library and the system it runs on Evaluates assets and qualifies them prior to making them available for use Tunes the system and makes it perform well Works with users to help solve their requirements	Library organization schemes Library search and access methods Multimedia concepts and markup languages (HTML) Software protection schemes (copyrights) User requirements for library services World Wide Web capabilities	Able to use the many available library search engines Good writer Can organize library contents/collections Understands what is being made available by the library to the user community

ble of doing the job without any help. Use the concept of consultative education for startup, when applicable. Under this concept, you retain the trainer to work with the team to put the concepts they have learned in the classroom into action during the startup period. This approach seems to work best when a systematic approach is being pursued.

Sprinkle Approach   This approach puts one or more of the experienced people who have been working as part of your reuse planning team into each of the groups working the project. They become twin hatted. They work with the project to put the concepts you've formulated into action. They work with you to refine your plans, capture metrics and lessons learned, and propagate results to other projects. This approach assumes you have enough people to handle both hats. The approach works equally well when either an opportunistic or systematic strategy is being pursued. Having reuse skilled and dedicated staff assigned to work the reuse tasks on a project makes a noticeable difference.

There are a lot of good books on the topics of organizing, staffing, and building a project team [3,4,5]. I have listed several citations in the "References" section of this chapter. These references will provide you insights into the general management principles and techniques. Within this paragraph, I have tried to provide you with some tricks of the trade aimed at staffing up your reuse effort.

Working Efficiently

As you are bringing your team aboard, consider what it will take to get them producing at their peak efficiency. You will probably have to fight to get your people colocated in office space near those they will be supporting. You will also have to fight for equipment and tools, especially if you don't have a project or a current year budget allocated for them. Both of these items should be on the long-lead item list in your business plan. You should know what facilities, equipment, and tools you will need to get the job done well in advance of when you need them so that you will have enough time to acquire them. However, getting what you need often becomes tricky even when you have timed events properly. Be prepared for delays. Have contingency plans ready for execution, because space and equipment are often at a premium. Do whatever you have to do to provide your people with the right environment. Your staff cannot produce effectively when sharing desks and using archaic equipment and tools. Show your engineers you care for them by fighting for what they feel is important. They, in turn, will surprise you with their increased productivity.

You also have to establish an environment in which your staff can devote its time toward getting the important tasks done. Most people waste a lot of time and energy on what can be considered marginally useful work. For example, does your senior staff seem to spend hours at the copy machine? Do they prepare their own graphical briefing charts? Wouldn't it be more productive to off-load such tasks to your administrative and clerical support personnel? Of course, getting approval to hire support staff and finding someone good tends to present another set of challenges. Perhaps, you could bring on support personnel as part of your reuse library staff. Adding such functions to the library charter may make sense. They also make it easier to get the slots for the people approved. These are some of the things you need to think about to start up your reuse effort.

Other time wasters may be meetings. In some organizations it seems that all people do is attend meeting after meeting. Ask what the outputs of these gatherings are and nobody seems to know. Meetings should be held only if they can be expected to pay for themselves. They should have a goal, an agenda, and a focus. They should generate some useful output. The chair should start them on time and end them on time. They should be brought to closure when they've met their objective, and the results should be summarized and recorded. Guidelines for running productive meetings have been published [6]. From a reuse point of view, such guidelines should be expanded to include reuse checklists to highlight the reuse issues and to identify the reuse metrics data you want collected.

Like most managers, you also could do simple things to improve your efficiency. Probably the most important is to get control of your time. For example, do you answer every phone call? As an option, you might batch the nonurgent ones and answer them later in the day. Do you attend all meetings or have you learned to say no to those you really cannot contribute to? Do you schedule your time to get your work done without interruption when you are most productive? Try it. Close your door for an hour or two and see what happens. There are lots of books, courses, and even audio or video tapes that you can purchase to help you improve your time management [7,8]. You might consider having a course taught in-house, which provides your people with time organizers so that they can write down their to-do lists and prioritize their actions during the next week or two.

Managing per Your Plan

Your next challenge is figuring out how to generate visible results quickly. You have invested a lot of time and effort to develop your plan. You have briefed it to your management and made commitments based upon its contents. You have organized your staff around the work in the plan, and have brought your team aboard to attack the long-lead and critical path items in your schedule. Your plan provides you with a roadmap. It tells you what to do, when, and in what order. However, things never go smoothly at first and your original plan can quickly get out of date.

To set your team off on the right foot, make an effort to clarify the steps and procedures its members will use to accomplish key tasks in your work plan. Let them know what you expect them to do. Then, let them tell you how they will satisfy your expectations. Be flexible. If you have to, change your plans to reflect the combined wisdom of the group. Remember that there are many paths to the end point. You want your plan to reflect an agreeable path.

Challenge your team to identify ways to streamline your reuse processes. Give your team the authority to make the improvements to processes you've outlined in your plan. However, put in place a procedure as you start the effort to force your team to justify each change and document the rationale that led to its implementation.

Delegate authority to accomplish the work at the lowest level possible. Let the people closest to the job figure out how best to get it done. When encountering problems, ask your people for advice and to explain the root cause. Don't try to second-guess them! In other words, trust your people to do a good job and tell you when things are getting out of hand. Manage the work and motivate your people to do the best they can. You can't expect them to do more than they are capable of doing.

Have your people set their own deadlines and then hold them accountable except in the rare situations where slippages are clearly justified. If milestones are missed, schedule new dates with your people. Don't be afraid to alter your plans based upon events that happen as the reuse effort unfolds. The only constant we have in our business is change. To succeed, you must learn to manage change, or it will become your master.

Touch base regularly with your people. Use your plan as the baseline to assess your status and progress. If the plan is wrong, change it to reflect reality. Replan when you have to, but do so within the context of your original plan. Use your work breakdown structure as your framework for relating the three Ps (people, process, and product). Alter your schedules when you have to, and update your budgets periodically by looking at what it will cost to complete the job. Maintain your plan as a living document. Keep it up to date. It will quickly repay your effort.

Again, there are many good books on this topic [9,10,11]. Most of the advice that has been offered in this paragraph can be grouped under the heading of good software management. Treat what I have told you as a refresher. The important thing to recognize is that the concepts work in practice.

Managing Risk

In your plan, you defined the processes you planned to use to manage risk. You identified your potential risk items and performed a preliminary risk assessment to analyze and prioritize the hazards that could hurt you the most. As shown in Figure 7.3 in Chapter 7, you must take control of risk by planning, monitoring, and resolving conflicts as they occur when you start up your reuse effort. As an example, you might put the risk mitigation plan, shown in Table 8.2, into effect during startup to deal with the 10 reuse risk items listed in Chapter 7.

After you figure out what to do about risk, you must monitor your actions and track the hazards you have identified to assess whether your risk mitigation plans are working as planned. To manage risk effectively, you should have at your disposal the following:

- Standards against which performance can be measured
- Information to monitor actual performance
- Empowered workers with the authority to make the adjustments needed to deal with risks
- Competence to implement the best solution available

TABLE 8.2 Risk Mitigation Plan

Risk Category	Risk Item	Risk Management Technique
Resources	Too aggressive a schedule	Use spiral development approach; address long-lead items via prescheduling; push difficult requirements to late builds
	Wrong skills for the job	Offer training and mentoring program; use consultative education approach
	Reusable assets cost more	Get managers to buy in early; offset costs through external sales; make sure that assets have at least three potential users
	New methods and tools	Select only mature methods and tools; introduce them carefully; get proper training
Commitments	Assuming firm will develop the reuse infrastructure	Develop needed processes just in time; add new tasks to WBS; adjust schedule based upon the staff that you have to do work
Management	New incentive structure needed	Get executives to endorse; educate everyone on the need to change; make reuse a priority
	Increased liability	Develop a standard license that limits your liability; employ higher levels of quality assurance and testing on reusable assets
	New processes	Prototype processes and use them on a trial project before adopting; introduce processes in a just-in-time manner
Technical performance	Difficult performance goals	Develop a prototype; use simulation; do dynamic modeling; look at trades
Technology	Unproven and/or immature technology	Switch to more stable technology; bound risk and prove under controlled situations (e.g., on a nonrisky build or a prototype)

The information that you will be gathering should be compared against the performance standards you have set to determine whether you are eliminating the risk. As you attack the hazards, your people should be empowered to make the solution fit the problem at hand. This is an important consideration, because situations change as risk mitigation plans are implemented. In response, your people must be given the flexibility to cope with new and related problems as they arise.

As the risks are resolved, new ones will undoubtedly appear. As a consequence, you will have to plan to make sure your risk management process continuously assesses risk and identifies those new items you will have to place on your top-10 list. One management technique that has proven effective is to form a risk council to assess risks and develop risk mitigation plans. Because of the need to get a broad consensus as you change your reuse effort, members of such a council should include user representatives, systems engineers, software developers, and members of your reuse team.

Risk resolution can be monitored using existing tracking processes when you put the appropriate risk milestones into your current work plan and its associated schedules. Your risk council could serve as your governing board. It can help assess risks as they occur and then agree on plans to get them under control. The chances that these plans will be successfully implemented by members of the group are high once a consensus is reached and everyone buys into the approach.

Again, there are many good books on the topic of risk management [12,13,14]. The purpose of this short paragraph is to tell you how to use the techniques discussed in these books to control the risks associated with your reuse program.

Keeping Out of Trouble

You should realize that most of the problems that occur during startup of any project can be traced to one of the following five underlying causes: poor planning, poor requirements, poor teamwork, poor communications, and poor controls. We have adequately addressed planning and requirements in the work products we have generated so far. What can we do to improve our teamwork, communications, and control as the reuse effort gets underway?

We have talked a lot about teams throughout this book. However, we have not spent a lot of time discussing how to build them and make them productive. The key to making teams work for you is to promote group performance instead of individual accomplishments. You can foster this attitude in the following subtle ways:

- Encourage cooperation instead of competition when dealing with subordinates.
- Give the teams authority to act on their decisions and hold them accountable for their results.
- Celebrate team accomplishment by making a point to acknowledge their contributions in meetings and in correspondence.
- Reward successful team contributions, as well as those of the individual performers, through awards and the merit system.
- Show by example what it takes to be an effective team leader and member.
- Get the team involved with the user so that members will understand the user's needs firsthand.

Building teams requires you to plan to build relationships as you start up the effort. To build such relationships, you will often have to work to improve the social skills of the individual contributors. To establish an atmosphere of trust, encourage interaction between group members and value all contributions. Also, get members to talk and share their ideas. You must develop team leaders who can stimulate closure and consensus. You must foster open communications and encourage people to listen to others in the group. You must recognize conflicts and do your best to reduce their negative effects on the group as they arise. Most importantly, you must establish the sense of camaraderie based upon a sense of common purpose.

The use of teams is an essential ingredient to the success of any reuse effort. Because reuse involves many people from many disciplines, teams are employed to build a consensus about what should be done. Reuse efforts require you to manage teams of teams. As a change agent, one of your primary tasks is to plan to coordinate the team efforts so that their products will be available when you need them, and keep the communications channels open between organizations.

With regard to communications, you must cultivate speaking, writing, and listening skills within the team. You also must open the communications between teams and with other groups. In other words, increase the bandwidth horizontally and vertically to permit information to flow up, down, and across the organization. Some of the things you can plan to do to improve communications during startup include:

- Have reuse team members frequently present their findings and recommendations to outside groups. This builds their presentation skills as it exposes them to the broader community.
- Get your tool vendors and suppliers to present what they are doing to the general community. This lets people know that you are connected to the outside world.
- Publish a reuse newsletter to let people know what is happening and to give recognition to those individuals and teams who do a good job.
- Create a home page on the Web to allow those interested in reuse to review news and publications of interest (current listing of library holdings, your business plan and case, reuse guidelines, reuse training materials, etc.).
- Create an information clearinghouse containing reuse reference and training materials that you will make readily available to interested parties.
- Give frequent presentations about what you are doing to groups up, down, and across the organization. Keep people informed to reduce the chances of misunderstanding.
- Hold an annual reuse conference to share your experience across your organization and with your users/customers. Invite others outside your group to speak. Hold user forums and panels in conjunction with the conference to get feedback from those in attendance.

Our final discussion topic is control, which is the process of making things happen in an ordered manner or according to plan. The basic control process involves setting standards, measuring performance against these standards, identifying deviations, and taking corrective action. Control requires managers to take action at the right times so that things get done when they are supposed to. Feedback from process gates identifies what action is needed, when, and why. New or adjusted plans may result, as the situation warrants, to address the changes that occur as things progress.

Improved visibility and control builds on your planning and team-building efforts. To gain control, use your plan and some of the tools listed in Table 8.3. As noted in the table, the primary tools you have at your disposal for control are metrics, reviews, and reports. As we will discuss in Chapter 9, these tools allow you to status where you are and predict whether you will get where you want to be on your reuse project. Reviews are held when major milestones are reached or pivotal products are generated.

An example of such an event is when you establish your initial operational capability for your reuse library. For this example, hold a readiness review to determine if the capability that your reuse team plans to put online is ready for full-scale operational use. Ensure that the library has been thoroughly tested by user representatives, and then look over the library's holdings to make sure they are really the items that your user community wants. Inspect the metrics data and test results to determine whether there were any open problem reports that needed to be closed before you went operational with the library. In other words, do everything you can think of to make sure you are not prematurely releasing the reuse library to your user community. As we will discuss in Chapter 9, you will then optimize the performance of the library and add to its holding using the metrics data you were collecting after you had gone operational.

Again, the techniques discussed in this paragraph can be put under the heading of good management. As with the other topics covered, there are many good books, seminars, and educational videos available [15,16,17]. I have put a reuse spin on the material. The message you should be getting from my discussion so far in this chapter is that *good management techniques work for any technical discipline including software reuse,* especially when you apply them with consistency and rigor across the organization.

MANAGE CUTOVER TO OPERATIONS

The cutover point in a reuse program is that moment in time when you are ready to declare yourself operational. Startup activities have been successfully completed, a trained and experienced reuse team is in place, your processes and operational procedures have been optimized based upon your early experiences, and the benefits of your reuse program have been fully demonstrated.

You may not recognize that organizations must change to reflect the work that needs to be performed as a technology like reuse becomes institutionalized within your firm. At the start of your reuse effort, you documented your transition/migration concepts in your operational concept document. During startup, you focused on developing the people, processes, and products to do the job. Your main goal during startup was to prove your concepts and show management that you added value. Once you go operational, your focus changes to optimization. You and your users are comfortable with the reuse processes and standards that you

TABLE 8.3 Control Tools

Category	Type of Control	Examples	Purpose
Metrics	Management	Indicators	Provide indicators by assessing trends and metrics data (error rates, productivity, etc.)
	Library	Utilization data	Provide insight into who is using what from the library
			Provide performance indicators (access time, wait time, etc.)
Reviews	People	Performance reviews	Rate and rank performance of reuse team members
	Process	End of phase reviews (design, coding, etc.)	Assess readiness to move on to the next phase in the life cycle
		Software inspections	Build team; assess rework; and improve quality
	Product	Architecture reviews	Assess if proposed product meets architecture standards
		Release reviews	Assess if product is ready to release to user community
		Improvement reviews	Assess product performance and figure out how to tune it and make it work better
	Management	Oversight reviews	Keep informed of status and progress of key projects
		Change control board meetings	Disposition changes and assess their impacts
Reports	Management	Status reports	Document status of project relative to indicators of technical performance
		Progress reports	Document progress relative to plans and explain deviations
	Supporting Information	Configuration management	Document status of errors and changes in the system
		Quality evaluation	Document independent audit findings and the status of actions taken to address them

have developed. Your worth has been proven and you can now concentrate on customer satisfaction goals. The main task you have to perform is to restructure your organization to get ready to move to operations. The amount of time and management attention you will spend on the restructure will depend on how much of a change you plan. Assuming that you are ready to cutover to operations, the three primary options that you probably should consider are as follows:

- *Do nothing differently.* Continue to perform the reuse work you have planned using your core team to perform library functions, and your working groups and/or teams to support requirements, optimization, and promotion tasks. Optimize your processes and work on raising the level of maturity of those organizations using them through an expanded education and training program. Keep pushing and maintain the momentum you have created during the startup period. Increase your outreach activities as you try to get more and more people to embrace the concepts you are promoting.

- *Transition your reuse functions into other existing organizations.* Make reuse part of everyone's business by transitioning your software reuse functions to other organizations. Perhaps, maintain some top-level group to manage the shared assets in your reuse library and to coordinate resolution of common reuse concerns across affected groups. Get rid of your central reuse group, because it may be perceived to be nonaligned with business unit goals and out of the mainstream. Develop a transfer plan to move your people and your reuse responsibilities during cutover. Manage the transfer and cutover to operations when all the elements of this transition plan have been successfully completed.

- *Reorganize and make reuse a separate service organization.* Make reuse a separate business by transitioning your software reuse functions to a new business unit. Make the organization pay for itself by marketing products and services of value to your own and/or outside organizations. Use market forces to keep it lean and mean. Develop a transfer plan that may conduct parallel operations until the new unit is strong enough to pay for your people and provide your users with the level of service that they expect. Manage the transition and transition to operations when all the elements of this plan have been completed.

It should be apparent that each of these three approaches places different demands on your organization. The first option is the least burdensome because it essentially advocates a business-as-usual philosophy. It works well in organizations that are aggressively pursuing improving their level of process maturity. As stated many times in earlier chapters, aligning with a process improvement initiative, and even making reuse the responsibility of the process group, makes a lot of sense because of the apparent economies of scale. Establishing an operational capability is simple in this situation. It represents the point in time when you believe you are best able to make the move.

The second option is more troublesome. It calls for a planned and well-coordinated transfer of people and reuse responsibilities from one organization to another. It requires time, talent, and leadership to pull off. The option can become very frustrating, especially when decisions relative to organizational roles and responsibilities get bogged down in politics. It works well in organizations that don't like central groups, and where functional groups are king. Cutover to operations becomes difficult only when the people who are working the reuse initiative are not properly prepared for the change. The transfer to operations typically takes place over a period of several months as the functions of the existing reuse organization are taken on by other groups.

Although attractive, the third option is the most difficult to implement. It calls for the reuse team to pay its own way. This forces them to market their products and services. Unfortunately, good technical people don't always make good marketeers. As a consequence, you will probably have to supplement the team with additional resources during the transition to figure out what the market is and how to penetrate it. This function, in turn, will add a great deal of time to the transition period. In addition, you will have to make sure that the change in orientation doesn't cause problems relative to current service levels. You can make this option work when the internal market for software reuse is strong enough to carry the program through the transition period. But, the cutover period tends to take as much as one to two years when the external market has to be cultivated.

For any of the three options, you will manage cutover to operations via a transition plan that you should prepare as you start up your reuse effort. This plan outlines the tasks involved in cutover, provides milestone schedules, and sets expectations. If multiple groups are involved, the plan will contain signed *memoranda of understanding,* which record agreements between parties about their respective roles and responsibilities. To manage the plan, you will use the metrics, reviews, and reports shown in Table 8.3. These will enable you to control the activities being performed. Establish the success criteria for the cutover in your plan, and conduct a review to determine whether they have been satisfied at an appropriate time in the schedule.

MEASURE SUCCESS

You are now ready to define how you will measure the success of your reuse effort. You defined your initial measures of success in your operational concept document (OCD). You refined and added meat to these definitions in your business plan. As you plan how you will transition to operations, you must assess your performance relative to these measures.

Figure 8.1 provides some example measures of success, along with their mappings from the OCD to your business plan. As you can see in this chart, victory has been defined as a function of both business and transition goals. To be successful, you should emphasize demonstrating that reuse reduces both your time to market and product development cost in half. The metrics gathered once you start up for each of the products contained within your scope should be geared to convincing management that you can indeed achieve these goals once you go operational.

The next two measures of success are more tactically oriented. The first is aimed at showing management the virtue of moving to an open architecture (i.e., one where software is standards based and portable). Its goal is to show what a

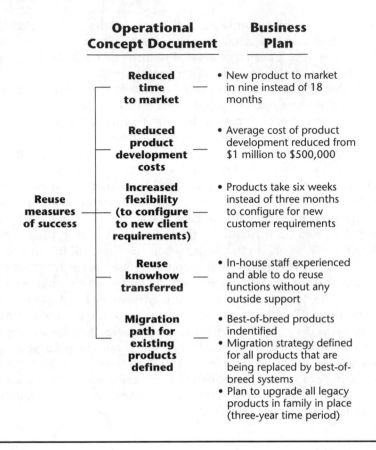

	Operational Concept Document	**Business Plan**
Reuse measures of success	**Reduced time to market**	• New product to market in nine instead of 18 months
	Reduced product development costs	• Average cost of product development reduced from $1 million to $500,000
	Increased flexibility (to configure to new client requirements)	• Products take six weeks instead of three months to configure for new customer requirements
	Reuse knowhow transferred	• In-house staff experienced and able to do reuse functions without any outside support
	Migration path for existing products defined	• Best-of-breed products indentified • Migration strategy defined for all products that are being replaced by best-of-breed systems • Plan to upgrade all legacy products in family in place (three-year time period)

FIGURE 8.1 Example measures of success.

product-line architecture can do for the organization. The other measure is more aligned with your transition goals. Its aim is to make sure that the reuse staff is fully capable of performing all tasks assigned to it independently of the outside sources that were brought in to develop knowhow (consultants, subcontractors, etc.). Both require you to collect metrics data to demonstrate convincingly that these tactical goals have been met.

The last measure of success is aimed at your legacy. This measure suggests that you will fail with your reuse effort unless you are able to figure out how to upgrade your existing products to satisfy your architectural requirements. After you fully analyze the situation, these legacy reengineering measures will probably force you to add the following tasks to your work plan:

- Define a best-of-breed product (i.e., assumes you have several candidates)
- Develop migration strategy (i.e., your approach for replacing any similar systems with the best-of-breed product)
- Develop upgrade strategy for legacy products (i.e., those elements of the product line being upgraded to comply with the architecture you have established for product family)

If you were smarter when you began the effort, you would have included these tasks in your business plan. However, you were flexible enough to realign your resources to get this work done once you recognized the omission. These omissions became apparent once you asked which criteria should be used during cutover to show that your reuse effort was successful. This forced you to replan as you related your work to your measures of success.

Now you have everything you need in place to start. You have your plans. You have organized your team and initiated staffing it with the talent you need to get the work you've planned done on schedule and within budget. You have the space you need to colocate your team with those developing the applications. You have initiated the long-lead process of acquiring the equipment and tools your team will need to work efficiently. You have recognized your need to manage your time better, and are planning to take a one-day seminar to do something about it. You have reviewed your plan and updated it to better address risk and cutover. You have selected your control tools and have defined in more detail the metrics, reviews, and reports you will use to gain visibility into and command over the reuse effort. You understand how your success will be measured and have factored assessment considerations into your work plan. You have been very busy and have accomplished a lot. You are now ready to make an impact by starting to execute your plan.

As you will see in Chapter 9, there is still a lot for you to do as you manage the change to a reuse culture. The excitement starts as you begin your journey. You won't be bored as the journey takes its many turns. Have fun and focus on achieving your vision. If you are even partially successful, you will feel a sense of satisfaction that makes all the effort worthwhile.

CASE STUDY

This *Fortune* 500 firm initiated a reuse effort two years ago. It manufactures computerized equipment used by manufacturing organizations to keep their production lines operational 24 hours a day, seven days a week. The firm has 25,000 employees and sales in excess of $25 billion. Engineering is centralized and performed using team approaches at the corporate headquarters located on one campus. Marketing and sales are distributed and done in district offices worldwide.

A previous reuse effort had been led by the research group. It wasn't successful because its results did not filter to the business units. This effort created a lot of bad will. Based upon the lack of results, many project managers and some software engineers believed it was premature to pursue reuse. They preferred to wait for the technology to become more mature.

To move the reuse effort forward, a corporate team composed of five representatives from the following three business groups was formed: instrumentation and test equipment, process control and assembly-line automation equipment, and manufacturing requirements planning (MRP) systems. Each business group has a number of existing product lines. However, there had been little sharing of either software or hardware assets across business units, and systems made by one group didn't necessarily interoperate with those produced by another group.

Management challenged the team made of superstars to figure out how to break down the walls that existed and build an architecture that facilitated sharing across business units. The team defined an open architecture specification that all of the business units could live with, which would permit software to be shared across widely available commercial off-the-shelf controllers and workstations. To verify that the proposed architecture would respond to their future requirements, the team held focus-group meetings with customers and suppliers.

The team created a vision, operational concepts, a business case, and a business plan. The plan called for chartering of the reuse groups displayed in Plan for Action 8.2. As shown, there was a lot of work to do and but a few people to do it. The team assumed they could get specific people for the slots.

The team briefed the proposed plan to an executive committee and was given the go-ahead. However, management warned that they expected to see results and would keep on top of things. Everyone on the team felt fine about the briefing because the reuse effort was planned down to the smallest detail. However, the research group's failure with reuse in the past seemed to have created a continued credibility problem with management.

The headaches began when the team held their kickoff meeting. Only two of the nine people they had counted on to work on the job showed up. After panic phone calls, it was discovered that the other seven were either on crash projects or vacation. While management was sympathetic when the team asked for help, they estimated it would take a minimum of six months to transition the promised key people to the reuse organizations. After all, these people were the high performers and everyone wanted them to work on their efforts. As an alternative, management offered the team five less skilled people who could be made available during the next two weeks. The sixth person, one of the pros the team wanted, would report when he got back from vacation in four weeks. Unfortunately, two of the candidates were new hires who were joining the firm right out of college. Another was nearing retirement and had a poor track record. The other two candidates were average performers, not the superstars the team was counting on to perform the job. The team was told to mold together this group and do the best that it could with the resources that were available.

Luckily, the team had anticipated the staffing problem and had devised a risk mitigation strategy to deal with it. The team had prenegotiated a subcontract with a small firm in the vicinity to make skilled reuse people available as a con-

PLAN FOR ACTION 8.2   Manufacturing Case Study Reuse Organization

Group	*Functions*
Corporate Reuse Group (five people)	Coordinate the total reuse effort Maintain the interface with executive management Develop and update corporate reuse business plan Maintain the open system architecture specification Acquire assets common to the architecture that all of the business units can use (buy them, contract for them, or fund business unit to develop them) Develop reuse standards and processes Acquire generic reuse training Set up and run the reuse library Identify research and development needs to labs Provide advocacy for reuse with business units Establish strategic partnerships with vendors Chair the shared resource board
Business Unit Reuse Group (three people each)	Maintain the interface with line-of-business managers Educate project managers on the benefits of reuse Develop business unit reuse standards and processes Manage product-line architecture(s) in a manner compatible with the open system specification Acquire business unit specific reusable assets and make them available to anyone via the reuse library (buy them, partner to develop them, or stimulate a project to generate them on their own) Develop approach to upgrade legacy products Acquire specific reuse training (for projects) Provide advocacy for reuse within the line of business Establish partnerships with projects and customers Participate as a member of the shared resource board Participate on reuse teams as a working member
Research Laboratories (no additional resources required)	Address identified reuse research and development needs in ongoing programs Demonstrate innovative solutions to architectural issues annually at the annual corporate research and development (R&D) conference Stimulate research community to address reuse technology needs through existing grant program

tingency. Unfortunately, two of the more senior of these people were currently committed to jobs, and it would take a month to phase them into the effort. In addition, contracting had made an issue of the rates and the buyer was not sure that she could get the firm under subcontract without upper management intervention in less than six weeks.

Space had also become an issue. The only facilities available for the people working at two of the business units was a trailer in the back of the parking lot. The offices the team was promised were occupied by accounting because their space was being renovated. The team was told that the space would become available in two months when accounting was expected to move back. Because the construction firm that was being used was slow, the team knew not to put a lot of faith in the schedule.

The saga continued as the team worked to resolve the people issues. The net result of all of the fracas was that the team was about a month behind when it actually started the job because of its staffing problems. The team might have been better off to assume that the people it was counting on would not be available when they were needed. In anticipation of its needs, the team might also have negotiated a transfer agreement with the projects these key people were working on to phase them onto the reuse job over a period of perhaps two to three months.

The problems in this case are typical of those that occur when you start up a reuse effort. They should not surprise you. Getting good people continues to be a challenge for most of us. The purpose of this chapter is to help you identify problems like these before you start your effort. This will hopefully provide you with the additional time you need to deal with them effectively.

SUMMARY

- Getting started forces you to organize and staff your team and acquire the space, equipment, and software it needs to get the job done effectively and efficiently.
- Organize around the work you have to perform, not the people you have to perform it.
- Startup also forces you to define your controls and develop your contingency plans to deal with the risks you have identified.
- Focus your early efforts on building teams and keeping them focused on the job at hand.
- The approach you use to cutover to operations can dramatically influence your plans and cause you to realign resources.
- The measures of success you select can also impact the structure and content of your plan.
- Be prepared for the unexpected during startup.

REFERENCES

1. Donald J. Reifer, *Software Management (Fourth Edition)*, IEEE Computer Society, 1993.
2. Defense Information Systems Agency, *Virtual Reuse Library Assessment and Library Infrastructure Report,* DCA100-93-D-0066, September 1994.

3. Tom DeMarco and Timothy Lister, *Peopleware,* Dorset House Publishing Co., 1987.

4. Harry T. Roman, *Building Internal Team Partnerships,* IEEE Press, 1993.

5. Philip C. Semprevivo, *Teams in Information Systems Development,* Yourdon Press, 1980.

6. William Carnes, *Effective Meetings for Busy People: Let's Decide It and Go Home,* IEEE Press, 1987.

7. Lester R. Bittle, *Right on Time! The Complete Guide for Time-Pressured Managers,* McGraw-Hill, 1991.

8. Brian L. Davis, Carole J. Skube, Lowell W. Hellervik, Susan H. Gebelein, and James L. Sheard, *Successful Manager's Handbook,* Personnel Decisions, Inc., 1992.

9. Robert Block, *The Politics of Projects,* Yourdon Press, 1983.

10. Milton D. Rosenau, Jr., *Successful Project Management,* Lifetime Learning Publications, 1981.

11. Capers Jones, *Programming Productivity,* McGraw-Hill, 1986.

12. Barry W. Boehm, *Tutorial: Software Risk Management,* IEEE Computer Society, April 1988.

13. Robert N. Charette, *Software Engineering Risk Analysis and Management,* McGraw-Hill, 1989.

14. Dale W. Karolak, *Software Engineering Risk Management,* IEEE Computer Society Press, 1996.

15. Thomas D. Floyd, Stu Levy and Arnold B. Wolfman, *Winning the New Product Development Battle,* IEEE Press, 1993.

16. Wess Roberts, *Leadership Secrets of Attila the Hun,* Warner Books, 1987.

17. Neal Whitten, *Managing Software Development Projects,* John Wiley & Sons, 1990.

Managing the
Transition

9

HOW WELL IS YOUR PROCESS WORKING?

You have spent a lot of time and effort setting up your reuse processes. While they looked fine on paper, they may not work well in practice. In response, you will have to alter, mature, and optimize your processes based upon the measurement data you gather over a period of time. From a process point of view, the four primary questions you want to answer when assessing this data are:

- Do your people follow the process or do they seem to go out of their way to avoid using it? Going around the process is a sure sign that it is not working. Ask those close to the process what they would do to correct its deficiencies. Then, alter the process and monitor it to see whether the change made a difference.

- Do your people seem very busy but continue to miss their milestones? Process can again be the culprit. People could be so concerned with adhering to a new process that they forget about generating the results. This problem can be avoided if you focus on the work in terms of the results it generates instead of the activity it involves.

- Have your costs gone down as your overall staff productivity has risen? If they haven't, something is wrong. Typically, inefficient processes are the cause of such a phenomenon. Look at your rework rates. If they are high, focus on improving your training. If this doesn't help, change your processes. Just as a reminder, don't interchange productivity with cost. Many groups

211

achieve high levels of software productivity by producing the wrong thing. Such high productivity often results in high cost because of the large rework factor.

■ Have your defect rates declined? Again, something is wrong if they have not gone down. Often, processes are again the culprits. Look at other indicators of product quality, such as defect densities and customer complaints to determine where the problem lies. Examine the selection, specification, test, and qualification processes you are using to see if the defects can be linked with the reusable assets you are using. Then, make the needed improvements.

The interrelationships among the three Ps introduced in Chapter 4 should come to mind. The *process* should be designed to make it easy for your *people* to generate their *products* efficiently using the best *technology* available. Either of the following two types of management can be used to determine whether your process is working:

■ *WBS-Based Management*—Adjusts tasking based upon your answer to the question: How well am I doing relative to my plan? Assesses your schedule and budgetary performance relative to the tasks in your work breakdown structure (WBS) using management indicators. These indicators in turn relate cost and schedule expenditures to measures of technical performance (e.g., number of design complete milestones achieved per specified technical criterion). Modifies your process based upon the experience you gain using it over a period of time.

■ *Metrics-Based Management*—Adjusts the process you are using, quantitatively using metrics data gathered specifically to the question: How well am I doing relative to my overall reuse goals? Provides insight into how well your processes are working, using hard measurement data and statistical techniques, as available.

The difference between the two approaches is dramatic. The WBS-based approach focuses on making sure you manage your plan. It is milestone-oriented and assesses goodness based upon your ability to meet your schedule and budgetary goals. It determines trends based upon your current rate of progress. Periodically, you have to perform a cost-to-complete and schedule-to-complete to determine whether your plan is still valid.

Assess whether your process is working based upon your ability to deliver acceptable products on time and within budget. Use management indicators to relate your schedule and/or budget expenditures to your measures of technical performance. An example management indicator [1] that you might use to determine whether you are making acceptable progress on a grouping of tasks associ-

Reuse Asset Acquisition Progress

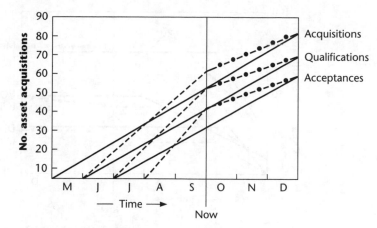

Budget Performance

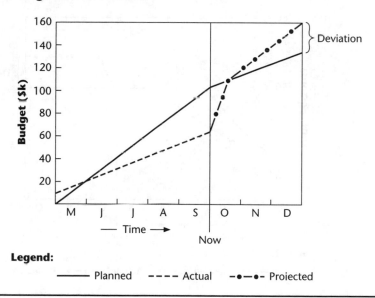

Legend:

——— Planned   - - - - Actual   -•—•- Projected

FIGURE 9.1a WBS-based management indicators.

ated with the acquisition of reusable assets is shown in Figures 9.1a and b. For this example, you are planning to acquire, qualify, and accept 10 assets a month. The technical performance measures that you are using to control quality revolve around your milestone-completion criteria. A milestone is considered completed only when the following requirements have been satisfied:

Computer Resource Performance

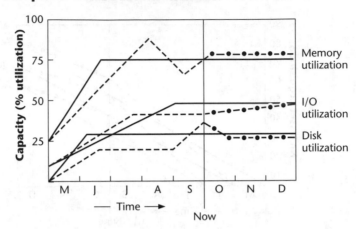

Staffing Performance

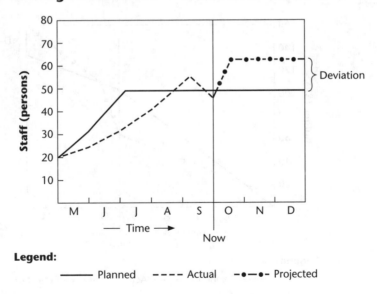

Legend:

——— Planned   - - - - Actual   -•—•- Projected

FIGURE 9.1b WBS-based management indicators.

- ■ The asset has three potential sponsors for its development.
- ■ The asset is packaged and documented per your reuse standards.
- ■ The asset is qualified through a series of approved developer and user tests.
- ■ The asset is readied for turnover to the reuse library. It has already been placed under version control and any open trouble reports were closed prior to its being accepted and turned over for use within the reuse library.

These three rate of progress lines in Figure 9.1a compares actual milestone completions to those planned as a function of time to identify trends and deviations from the plan. The example assumes all milestones take 30 days to complete. Milestones pictured in the chart include the following:

- *Reusable Asset Acquisitions*—Number of reusable assets that have been acquired by the engineering team as a function of time
- *Reusable Asset Qualifications*—Number of reusable assets that have passed their planned qualification tests as a function of time
- *Reusable Asset Acceptances*—Number of reusable assets that have been accepted by and turned over to the reuse library staff as a function of time

Trend lines like those portrayed in the figures can be deceptive. Your natural inclination is probably to extend the trend line based upon the current rate of progress to forecast the completion date. Such a projection does not take into account the startup problems illustrated in the chart. Once things get underway, the activities converge to what was originally planned.

Three additional WBS-based management indicators that you might consider using are defined in Table 9.1. These indicators, which are also displayed in Figure 9.1, are primarily concerned with resource utilization (staff, schedules, dollars, etc.). As shown, you track actuals versus planned to determine if you are having problems. If you are, take corrective action. Underutilization of resources means that you are probably behind in staffing. Overutilization simply means that the work is taking more resources than originally planned. In either case,

TABLE 9.1 WBS-Based Management Indicators

Indicator	Explanation	Definitions
Budget Performance	Compares actual expenditures to that planned by WBS activity as a function of time. Trend line indicates whether the group is over- or underspending.	*Actual* - staff hours or dollars spent on the activity *Planned* - staff hours or dollars planned to be spent at that time
Computer Resource Performance	Compares actual memory, I/O, and disk utilized to that planned by WBS activity. Trend line indicates whether you are going to run out of resources.	*Actual* - resources utilized by the activity *Planned* - resources planned to be utilized at that point in time
Staffing Performance	Compares staff levels to that planned by WBS activity as a function of time. Trend line indicates lack of people is becoming a problem.	*Actual* - number of people onboard and working in the group *Planned* - number of people planned to be available

modify your existing plan to reflect the actions you are going to take to correct problems.

Your metrics-based management indicators use measurement data and statistical techniques to assess quantitatively whether your process is working. You use your metrics data and management indicators to answer questions posed relative to the goals your users are trying to achieve. For example, the following goal-question-metrics tree might be used to partially assess how well your reuse library processes are working:

GOAL - Make it easy for engineers to reuse assets taken from your reuse library

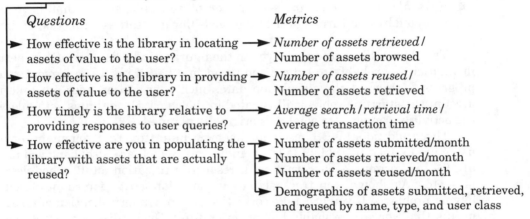

Questions	Metrics
How effective is the library in locating assets of value to the user?	*Number of assets retrieved /* Number of assets browsed
How effective is the library in providing assets of value to the user?	*Number of assets reused /* Number of assets retrieved
How timely is the library relative to providing responses to user queries?	*Average search / retrieval time /* Average transaction time
How effective are you in populating the library with assets that are actually reused?	Number of assets submitted/month Number of assets retrieved/month Number of assets reused/month Demographics of assets submitted, retrieved, and reused by name, type, and user class

Four commonly used metrics-based management indicators are defined in Table 9.2. Each of these indicators helps you determine how well your architectural engineering, asset management, and applications engineering processes are working. Each is illustrated in Figures 9.2a and b. In addition, you can use statistical techniques to help monitor and control your processes, putting the metrics data from these and other indicators to work for you via some form of closed-loop feedback system.

HOW GOOD ARE YOUR PRODUCTS?

Just having good reuse processes is not enough. To succeed, your products must be superior in quality to those offered by your competition. At a minimum, they should provide your clients with better price/performance. As we saw in Chapter 1, many engineers don't trust the quality of third-party assets, which is why they are reluctant to use them to build their products. All it takes is one negative experience to turn them off completely to the concept of reusing others' work.

You can use metrics-based management indicators to assess the quality of your reusable assets. However, you must recognize that defining metrics presents a challenge, because the types of assets that are candidates for reuse include much more than code. Unfortunately, most of the results of research in software quality have resulted in metrics just for code. The more popular of these code met-

TABLE 9.2 Metrics-Based Management Indicators

Indicator	Explanation	Definitions
Architecture Stability	Compares actual number of trouble reports to that planned as a function of time. Trend line shows whether error rate is leveling out.	*Actual* - number of trouble reports during this time period *Planned* - planned number of trouble reports by release
Asset Availability	Compares actual number of assets available to that planned as a function of time. Trend line indicates whether productivity of assets is falling behind.	*Actual* - number of assets in the reuse library by category *Planned* - number of assets planned to be available
Asset Utilization	Compares actual reuse level achieved to that planned by WBS activity as a function of time. Trend line shows if the staff is achieving the level of reuse expected.	*Actual* - number of assets taken from the library and reused *Planned* - the planned level of reuse (number of reused assets as a percentage of total assets)
Cycle Time Reduction	Compares actual time through spirals by product group as a function of time. Trend line shows whether cycle times are getting shorter.	*Actual* - number of weeks through a development spiral *Planned* - target number of weeks through a cycle

rics are tied to *ilities,* such as maintainability, portability, reliability, and testability. Quality is determined by analyzing the code and scoring the ility using a set of predefined weighted criteria that have been defined for that purpose. For example, maintainability can be scored using the following formula for the six prescribed criteria listed after the formula by assigning either zero or one point to each attribute, depending on whether it was found by inspecting the code:

$$\text{Maintainability Score} = \sum_{i=1}^{n} (\text{criteria score})_i$$

where i = the index of the score for each criterion ($i = 1$; n = number of criteria).

Maintainability Criteria

■ Code is self-descriptive (ratio of comments to program statements is one to one)
■ Programs have a single entry and single exit
■ There are no unreachable code segments
■ There is no unauthorized recursion
■ Interfaces are simple (i.e., no global variables and parameters of simple type)
■ Complexity is limited (i.e., as measured by some metric such as McCabe or Halstead)

Architecture Stability

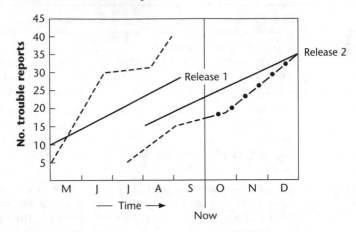

Asset Availability

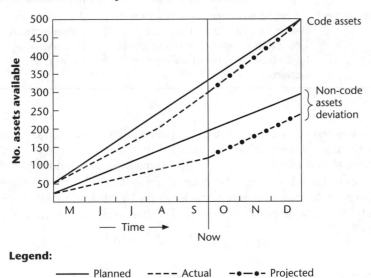

FIGURE 9.2a Metrics-based management indicators.

There are static analysis tools that automate checking against criteria such as those specified in the preceding list [2]. There are other tools that instrument the code and examine it as it executes to assess test coverage and identify unreachable code segments [3]. Many reuse libraries use such tools to automate the labor-prone, tedious processes associated with their assessing quality of assets.

Asset Utilization

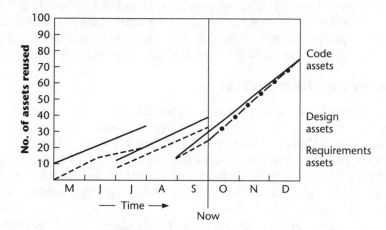

Cycle Time Reduction

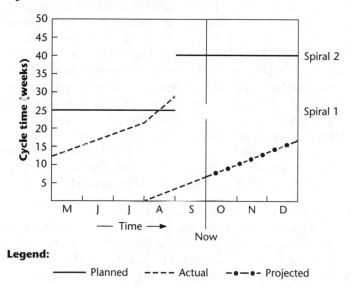

Legend:

——— Planned   - - - - Actual   -•-•- Projected

FIGURE 9.2b Metrics-based management indicators.

While useful, such metrics have only limited utility when the reuse library's population contains other assets in addition to code. Plan of Action 9.1 defines metrics for assessing the quality of several types of assets, but even these may not be sufficient. For example, while reliable, the program may not compile or may have open problem reports. While portable, the program may not run on your platform. While accurate, the algorithm may not converge to an answer within the allowable time. While comprehensive, the plan may not be achievable. These are some of the reasons you must task your staff to define qualification standards for assets you put in your library. In such standards, quality would be a necessary but not a sufficient condition for qualifying an asset.

HOW HAPPY ARE YOUR PEOPLE?

Good people use good processes to produce great products. As stated many times in earlier chapters, people are the key to productivity. Happy people are productive people. Motivate your staff and watch them overcome any obstacle. Inspire them and they can accomplish the impossible. Get them working together and observe the synergy. Build teams and see them become things of beauty. However, let conflicts proceed unabated and watch progress grind to a halt as people battle over the most trivial issues.

Needless to say, you must keep tabs on the mood of your team. Again, metrics-based management approaches can provide some advance warning of potential problems, but don't rely on them exclusively. You must sense the conflict in order to do something about it. You can accomplish this by observing the little things. For example, one person goes out of his way to avoid another. Another may glare at a teammate while he is talking. A third may have that glassy eyed look that indicates she is either bored to death or overwhelmed. Burnout, boredom, and bedlam are problems that are always present in a high-intensity situation.

Table 9.3 identifies three metrics-based indicators that can help you determine whether you are having problems with your people. Losing staff to sickness or other organizations is a sure sign something is wrong. Friction can develop between team members, or morale can be at an all-time low. If your team consistently misses its planned milestones, something can be amiss. The team can be fragmented or just out of gas. Ask yourself if the following other signs of trouble are present:

- You don't see people smile or laugh often.
- Everyone is too busy to go out for lunch or pizza after work.
- Nobody is around when you walk the halls after six o'clock at night.
- Your people keep looking at their watches at the end of the day.
- Everyone seems to be bellyaching about something.
- People seem to be making the same silly mistakes again and again.

If the indicators show signs of trouble, find the root cause. As you started your effort, there was wild enthusiasm. As you built your team and started up the effort, the situation tempered. Then, conflicts between people, and between people and the organization, started to occur just as deadlines neared and the pressure to deliver increased. Don't be discouraged; these things are normal and happen in the best of places. However, good managers do something about them. They know that happy people are productive people. They do whatever they can to reduce conflict and to make the work situation palatable and the job fun.

PLAN OF ACTION 9.1   Product Quality Metrics and Measures

Asset	*Metric*	*Measure*

Architecture (reusable asset is the model and knowledge base that goes along with it)

- Complete ⟶ All static and dynamic relationships between elements are specified along with characteristics of all components
- Consistent ⟶ Uniform notation is used to describe the architecture
- Model based ⟶ All three views of the architecture are modeled
- Verifiable ⟶ The requirements established for the architecture (openness, etc.) are verified and evidence is available

Requirements (reusable asset is the model along with trade studies and rationale for its construction)

- Complete ⟶ All requirements are fully specified along with performance goals and design constraints
- Consistent ⟶ Uniform notation is used to describe the requirements
- Model based ⟶ Performance goals are developed based upon prototypes or simulations
- Traceable ⟶ All requirements are traced to their source(s)
- Verifiable ⟶ All requirements are verified and evidence is available

Algorithms

- Complete ⟶ Algorithm properties such as initial, post, and exception conditions are stated along with their requirements
- Consistent ⟶ Uniform notation is used to specify the mathematics
- Correct ⟶ The code is validated to ensure that the algorithm as specified is implemented without alteration
- Verifiable ⟶ Properties such as fidelity, accuracy, and convergence are verified

Plans (reusable asset is the document and analysis upon which its contents are formulated)

- Complete ⟶ All paragraphs of the document are complete
- Comprehensive ⟶ What is planned is detailed to a level that makes it simple to understand what the tasks are and how they relate
- Readable ⟶ The language and construction of the document is aimed at making it easy for a reader to understand what is planned
- Verifiable ⟶ There is convincing evidence that the plan was followed

PLAN OF ACTION 9.1 *(Continued)*

Code (the source/object code from which the product is built)

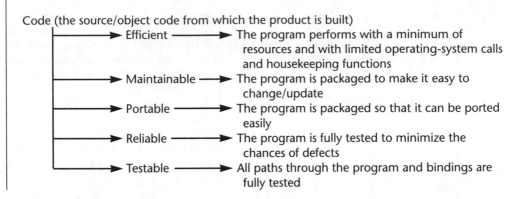

Efficient	The program performs with a minimum of resources and with limited operating-system calls and housekeeping functions
Maintainable	The program is packaged to make it easy to change/update
Portable	The program is packaged so that it can be ported easily
Reliable	The program is fully tested to minimize the chances of defects
Testable	All paths through the program and bindings are fully tested

When dealing with disputes, begin your effort by identifying the source of the conflict. Talk with your people and help them through the crises. Here are a few tidbits of advice to follow when handling conflicts between subordinates:

- Attack the conflict by getting people to vent their anger and talk to you about the problem.
- Encourage your people to depersonalize conflicts; have them look at the situation as a clash of ideas or approaches.

TABLE 9.3 People-Based Management Indicators

Indicator	Explanation	Definitions
Absentee Rate	Compares the average number of days a month that your staff is absent from work due to illness or causes other than vacation to industry norms	*Actual*—Average number of days staff is absent from work *Norm*—Norm for the industry or organization
Milestone Completion Rate	Compares the actual number of milestones your team completes to that planned for the time period	*Actual*—Number of milestones achieved as a percentage during a period of time *Planned*—Total number of milestones planned that period
Staff Attrition Rate	Compares monthly the average number of people that move on to other career opportunities within and outside your firm to industry norms	*Actual*—Average number of people lost per time period *Norm*—Norm for the industry or organization

- Never take sides; act as a neutral third party.
- If the conflict continues out of control, call for reenforcements. Get professional help, or the conflict may escalate as the team takes sides.

Keep your people happy by providing them with an opportunity to excel on the job. Search out conflict and keep it under control, recognizing that nothing you can do will eliminate it entirely. Keep the team informed and involved in decision making. Maintain the Asian concept of face by never making your people look bad. Remember, there is nothing you cannot accomplish as long as you give credit where credit is due. Understand the factors that drive your software engineers and use them to your advantage. Provide your people with the opportunity to do all they can do, and they will do it. Again, most of these concepts can be classified as good management. Books and articles on the topic of software psychology are plentiful [4,5]. My goal is to stimulate you to promote trust and teamwork, and keep your people happy. Hopefully, these ideas will help limit the conflicts that can make working on a job gone askew a living hell.

ARE YOU MAKING PROGRESS?

The management indicators provide you with a lot of WBS- and metrics-based status and trend information. Your job is to take these facts and figure out whether you are making suitable progress toward your goals. If you aren't, there are two things you can do: Either try to motivate your people to achieve higher levels of productivity, or recognize that your original approach was unsatisfactory and it is time to modify your plan.

The primary tools that you have at your disposal to make your assessment are metrics, reviews, and reports. We have shown you several graphs that portray the metrics data you have collected, which let you know if your process is working, if your products are any good, and if your people are happy. The trick is to keep these graphs up to date and use them to identify suspicious events. For example, your budget-performance graph shows your actual spending right on target. However, you know that you are about two weeks behind in publishing a key document. As another example, your quality indicators show asset reliability to be well in the bounds of acceptability. Yet, your primary customer for these assets is complaining loudly about their quality.

You may need to probe deeper to find out what is really going on. However, be careful because you can antagonize your team if you move too quickly. Sometimes, the best solution to a problem is to do nothing. Let your people handle it, and resist the temptation to interfere. Isn't experience the best way to grow their management judgment? However, leaving a problem unchecked too long may cause it to escalate and get out of hand. A careful balance must be reached, whereby your people work out the problem but keep you informed of the progress. This is often accomplished through weekly reviews and progress reports.

The three types of reviews, along with candidate meetings, that you might hold for your reuse effort are listed in Table 9.4. Major milestone reviews are typically held at the end of a cycle, or when a major event or delivery occurs, to determine whether you are ready to move into the next phase of the program. While not necessarily reuse specific, these reviews are held to make sure that you don't move ahead unless you are ready (i.e., they gate the process). Management reviews are held to keep your sponsors informed of your progress and let them know when you need help. Project reviews are held periodically to assess progress, work out problems, and assess the technical integrity of the assets you will reuse across your products and product lines. Chapter 10 will discuss the process changes that you should consider when moving to a reuse paradigm. To help you conduct successful meetings, I have included the essential points in Plan of Action 9.2 for the four starred reuse-essential reviews shown in Table 9.4.

All sorts of reports are generated to keep everyone involved informed of your progress. Your people should prepare weekly reports describing their progress relative to their task plans and outstanding issues. Using these individual reports as your basis, prepare a monthly progress report summarizing your status, progress, and problems relative to your plans at the activity level and circulate it throughout the organization. To keep your users informed, publish a newsletter and set up a news group online so that you can broadcast when new products and services become available. Keep everyone informed and they will remain your allies.

Often, your people will argue that generating so many reports is counterproductive. Wouldn't you rather me spend my time doing more productive work like coding? they might ask. Yet, ask anyone who has managed the generation of software under deadline pressures whether such reports are valuable. I'm sure you can guess the answer. The way to make your reporting requirements less burdensome is the use of the following three principles:

- *The simpler the better.* Design your progress reports so that they are easy to fill out and provide insights. Put a template online and ask your people to spend at most 30 minutes telling you what they did, what they plan to do, and what problems they are having. Include an instantiated template to give your people an idea of how you want it filled out.
- *Leave it alone if it isn't broken.* Leave things alone when they are progressing as planned. However, question to make sure that things are really as they are being reported. Sometimes, your people may view the current situation through rose-colored glasses.
- *Progressive detail.* When things seem to be getting out of line, ask for more and more details. Remember that software projects get late one day at a time, not all at once. The sooner you take corrective action, the better for all parties concerned.

TABLE 9.4 Candidate Reuse Reviews

Type of Review	Candidate Reviews	Purpose
Major Milestone Reviews	System Architecture Review*	Determine if the architecture for your product lines is stable and if you are ready to develop requirements for a product family member
	Requirements Review	Determine if the requirements are solid enough to start product design and implementation
	Software Architecture Review*	Determine if the design is stable enough to start product fabrication (assumes you have reduced technical risk using prototypes, etc.)
	Test Readiness Review	Determine if you are ready to start product integration and test
	Acceptance Review	Determine if you are ready to ship the product to its intended users and consumers
Management Reviews	Executive Committee Review	Keep executives informed of your progress and get their help in resolving problems
	Line-of-Business (LOB) Management Reviews	Keep LOB managers informed of your progress and get their commitment to help institutionalize such changes as reuse within their business unit
	Shared Resources Council Review*	Coordinate and determine the effectivity of proposed changes to those assets used by multiple business groups
Project Reviews	Progress Reviews	Determine task progress and work problems in real time with supervisory staff
	Design and Code Inspections	Assess the technical quality of design and code products, eliminating defects as early as possible in the cycle
	Third-Party Software Inspections*	Assess the functionality and quality of candidate third-party and COTS software assets prior to their acquisition and use
	Problem Solving Reviews	Special reviews held to assess progress of teams working studies and on special assignments

Again, the message of this chapter continues to be that good project management techniques are necessary for software reuse. Many articles and good books on the subject are available [6,7,8]. The suggestions offered within this and other chapters have been directed to making them work when you are pursuing a reuse initiative.

PLAN OF ACTION 9.2   Reuse-Specific Review Points

System Architecture Review

Has a domain analysis been performed and the results documented in the form of a reference architecture and lessons-learned report?

Have all three views of the architecture (i.e., technical, system, and operational) been factored into the derivation of the recommended model?

Does the model provide a static and behavioral look at how the wide range of user requirements can be accommodated in both hardware and software?

Have all of the functional, performance, interface, and design requirements established for the product line been validated and allocated to hardware, software, and operational procedures?

Have the performance requirements been validated via either prototyping or simulation?

Has the architecture been validated using execution threads that were defined via use cases formulated to replicate how a potential user would employ the system operationally?

Have the scaling, security, and interoperability constraints imposed on the system been factored into the reference architecture design?

Software Architecture Review

Has a software-specific architecture been developed to realize the allocated requirements for both the product and the product line?

Have the system requirements been mapped to the software architecture, and is their traceability between systems and software?

Is the architecture modeled around functional or data abstractions? For either case, have the rules associated with encapsulation and layering of services been made explicit?

Has the recommended architecture been validated by comparing it to acceptable architectural styles and templates?

Has the data architecture been mapped to that used for data flow and control, and can both be operated concurrently to meet the performance demands of the user?

NOTE: These are only a few of the questions you should be asking at these reviews. We recommend that you take these checklists and add more specifics to them.

PLAN OF ACTION 9.2   *(Continued)*

Shared Resources Council Review

Are the roles and responsibilities of the charter fully understood, and are they being followed by council members and the chair?

Are the procedures to determine the effectivity of the proposed changes to assets shared across product lines being complied with, and has an impact assessment been conducted?

Have all product managers who are potentially impacted by the proposed change been consulted about its desirability?

Have the suppliers of the affected reusable assets, both internal and external to the firm, been asked to estimate what resources it would take to implement the proposed change?

Are the supplier's proposed costs, schedules, and technical responses to the change request acceptable?

Can the impacts associated with the change be absorbed without causing major customer dissatisfaction?

Third-Party Software Inspections

Has the third-party package been delivered in acceptable form (i.e., with run modules, source code, libraries, build instructions, patches, user documentation, etc.)?

Can it be installed and operated on the platform of interest easily?

When run with your test cases, does it perform all advertised functions as expected?

When tested against your qualification criteria, does it pass?

When run with your performance benchmark, does it meet all of your timing and execution criteria?

Have you talked with users of the software to see what they like and don't like about it?

Have you reviewed the potential staying power of the supplier, and taken precautions should they go out of business (e.g., establish an escrow account for the source code)?

NOTE: Again, these are only a few of the questions you should be asking at these reviews. We recommend that you take these checklists and add more specifics to them.

IS TECHNOLOGY WORKING FOR YOU?

The last set of questions you are probably asking deals with whether the technology you have decided to insert into your organization is working for or against you. In earlier chapters, we stated that banking on new technology may be risky because it and the tools that support it may be neither scalable nor mature. As a consequence, your people may spend most of their time maturing the technology and/or tools instead of using it to achieve your reuse goals. In addition, new innovations and alternative technologies may become available as your reuse initiative is unfolding, which you may want to consider for adoption. How do you know if the technology that you are using is helping or hurting your team? How do you evaluate alternatives that come to your attention?

You want to continue to look at the potential impact of the technology on your bottom line, and the degree of risk you want to take to realize it. You can argue about the up- or downside of technology all day. What makes technology inviting is its ability to help you realize your goals. With reuse, your aspirations are clear. You documented your goals and how you were going to achieve them in your vision-and-strategy document. If the technology you are using can help you accomplish these goals quicker and easier, use it. If the alternative seems to be a better solution, use it instead. But, manage the risks by continuously monitoring how well the technology is working. Move away from the technology when its use becomes unprofitable.

These are easy words to say, but hard to implement. While there are no unique metrics that you could use to assess the use of technology, there are indicators that provide insight into whether it is working for or against you. As examples, indicators for the five criteria are provided in Table 9.5 for evaluating the use of new tools, new techniques, or innovations:

Depending upon your tolerance for risk, you might try to use some of the new reuse technologies as they appear under controlled situations. Although there may be problems, the use of the technology may provide an advantage if you harness it before your competitors.

LESSONS LEARNED IN PROGRESS MEASUREMENT

The last two chapters discussed how to make and manage the transition from concept to reality. We have discussed tracking status and determining progress. While not unique to software reuse, the following lessons have been learned relative to using the techniques and measures recommended for progress measurement activities:

■ Focus on getting your architecture for your products and product lines under control early in your reuse effort. The chances that you will experience delays in your reuse program will increase proportionately to the amount of time you take to baseline the technical framework you will use for determining what assets make the most sense to reuse.

TABLE 9.5 Assess the Use of Technology

Criteria	New Tool	New Technique	Innovation
Adequate	Helps you get your work done quicker.	Helps you structure a solution to a problem.	Has the potential to save time and effort.
Mature	New versions aren't provided on a weekly basis because of errors.	Doesn't require you to develop your own guidelines for use.	Utility has already been demonstrated on pilot projects.
Robust	Doesn't seem to break whenever you use it.	Doesn't require you to develop rules for use as you use it on the job.	Rules for use have been prepared and tried successfully.
Scalable	Doesn't crash when you move to larger problems.	The technique can be adapted for use on large problems.	Ability to scale to large projects has been demonstrated.
Usable	Your software people can use the tool without reading the manual or attending a seminar.	Your software people can use the technique with limited coaching.	Seems compatible with your people and paradigm.
	Comes with an online tutorial and help.	The technique is fully compatible with your reuse paradigm.	Has been tested by your people.

- As your reuse effort unfolds, change your emphasis to earned-value reporting. Earned value provides a valid measure of budgetary performance by relating actual expenditures to technical achievements, as determined by milestone completions. When the milestones are well defined and quantitative, they can act as gates that let you determine whether required quality criteria have been satisfied.
- Be forward looking in your measurement. Figure out what it will take to finish. View past expenditures as sunk costs. Learn from your past mistakes. Build bridges to the future by periodically performing a cost-to-complete and schedule-to-complete exercise.
- Recognize that metrics can provide valuable insight into the reasons why you might not be performing as anticipated. Metrics help by allowing you to examine the relationships that exist between your rate of progress and the primary variables that influence it.
- Make progress reporting easy by keeping the forms simple and putting report templates online for your people to use.
- Take the time to read and react to your people's progress report. Allow your people to use their reports to communicate issues to you informally. Show them that you care by taking appropriate action based upon their recommendations on the things they believe impact their and their team's performance.

■ Timing is strategy. The reason for progress measurement is to pinpoint problems early so that you can take appropriate action. Take action at the appropriate time. Recognize that taking no immediate action is a reasonable option in some cases.

These are just a few of the lessons that we have learned by applying good progress measurement techniques in practice on actual software development efforts [9,10]. They summarize some of the key points made in the last two chapters.

CASE STUDY

As part of reuse initiative, the Defense Information Systems Agency (DISA) went operational with a software reuse library in 1993. This library was actually a network of nine homogeneous reuse libraries located at military bases throughout the United States and interconnected via the Internet. Each of the services (i.e., Army, Navy, Air Force) and several agencies (Defense Logistics Agency, National Security Agency, etc.) created a reuse library under DISA sponsorship for their users. Each library used a common software package, called the Defense Software Repository System (DSRS), to make reusable assets available to authorized users via a common user interface. While each library maintained different collections of assets, all used similar standards and conventions to identify, evaluate, prepare, classify, install, and qualify them. The libraries were seamlessly interconnected so that a user could access the total library's holdings via a single query from one node on the network.

Assets placed in the DSRS by reuse librarians were qualified using the following four-level scheme [11], which incorporated quality metrics like those illustrated in Plan of Action 9.1.

Level 1 This initial level of qualification identifies the asset as approved for installation, based upon customer demand only. It may not have received any measurement, testing, or documentation beyond that originally provided by the donor. The completeness and functionality of the asset are unknown. While a Level-1 asset can be provided to the users quickly, the library offers them a relatively low level of confidence in its quality. Basically, this level takes assets into the library as is, and makes them available to potential users.

Level 2 This second level of qualification identifies the asset as released to users and verified for completeness. Many COTS software products and software items delivered to the government fall into this category. Assets for which the library has source code must compile to be eligible for Level 2. For Ada assets, the AdaMAT tool is used to score quality and count source lines of code. Results of the AdaMAT run are made available to the user on the screen. While this level offers greater confidence than Level 1, there is still little specific guidance or documentation to help the potential reuser.

Level 3 This third level of qualification identifies the asset as having met the requirements of Level 2, and also having compiled with its functions being validated and verified. Specifically, the asset is tested, and related test data and test results are captured. When a user extracts the asset, the test results are transmitted along with it and the test data, and made available as a file. In many cases, a Level-3 qualification is the best compromise between cost and timely library population, because it represents reasonable quality at an affordable price.

Level 4 This fourth and final level of qualification adds a reuser's manual to Level-3 requirements. When a user extracts a Level-4 asset, the reuser's manual is transmitted along with the asset. Level 4 offers the highest level of assurance to quality, completeness, and reusability criteria. The effort associated with certifying an asset at Level 4 is significant, and may be comparable to developing a new asset of similar size and functionality. Therefore, it is recommended only for those assets that have high potential reuse.

The Air Force Reuse Center [12] is one of the sites that employs the AdaMAT metrics tool as part of its qualification process to analyze Ada source code for assets that are candidates for its reuse library. AdaMAT breaks down the metrics and scores quality on a 0 to 100-percent scale using the following five categories of measurement data.

Source Lines of Code This first category examines measurements of physical lines of code (number of nonblank, noncomment carriage returns) and logical lines of code (roughly equivalent to the number of terminal semicolons in the code). When combined, these measurements give the user some indication of how large the application is and how many functions or objects it contains.

Reliability This next category looks at measurements of anomaly management and simplicity. Anomaly management looks at error handling, exception processing, and other indicators of error tolerance to measure how efficiently code can recover from errors. Simplicity looks at style and measures how clean and structured the code is by looking at such things as naming conventions and access types. When viewed together, these metrics tell you how free from error the code is and whether it will hold up under heavy user traffic.

Maintainability This third category investigates measurements of simplicity, system clarity, self-descriptiveness, modularity, and exactness. Simplicity has been described. System clarity measures how understandable the code is. Self-descriptiveness determines if the code is self-documenting. Modularity measures how independent the modules are from one another. Exactness measures whether the software contains only the code that it needs to perform its desired functions, without extraneous or useless segments. As a composite, these measurements tell you how easy it would be to change the software.

Portability   This fourth category examines measurements of modularity, self-descriptiveness, and independence. The modularity and self-descriptiveness measurements have already been described. Independence measures the degree of machine and software independence, and examines such things as mathematical precision and implementation-dependent calls. It looks at how easy it would be to move the software from one platform to another even when they differ greatly in architecture.

Reusability   This last measurement category is reusability. It examines all of the secondary metrics listed previously to provide a inclusive look at all of the software's metrics measurements (e.g., anomaly management, independence, modularity, self-descriptiveness, simplicity, exactness, and system clarity). These measurements are rolled up and reported as a composite view of how reusable the software under evaluation is, and who can use it under what circumstances. Generally, measurements such as portability and maintainability tell you when it might pay to reuse an asset. Reliability gives you insight into when to make the effort.

The U. S. Air Force and others such as DISA have reported great success with this qualification approach. In addition to using the AdaMAT tool to analyze Ada assets that are candidates for their software reuse library, they are offering the use of AdaMAT to their users as a service. They are also extending the concept for use with code assets written in other languages such as C and C++. While we certainly don't want to endorse any specific tool, we do advocate using tools of this class to make detailed quality metrics reports part of the qualification process for reusable assets.

The challenge that remains is to figure out how to apply these concepts as you qualify other types of assets. Users want to make sure that their reuse repositories are populated with noncode assets (architectures, designs, algorithms, tests and test data, etc.) that have been qualified according to meaningful criteria, and whose quality has been measured hopefully automatically using a metrics tool. Work is being pursued in this area by researchers and tool vendors. Hopefully, useful results will appear in the near term.

SUMMARY

- The *process* should be designed to make it easy for *people* to generate their *product* using the best *technology* available.
- WBS-based and metrics-based management indicators can provide insight into whether your process is working well.
- Product quality metrics and measures give you some indication as to whether your products are any good.
- People-based management indicators can identify if your people are happy and productive.

- Metrics, reviews, and reports can help you determine whether you are making suitable progress.
- Technology usage should be monitored to make sure that it is working for you.

REFERENCES

1. U. S. Air Force, *Software Management Indicators,* Air Force Systems Command Pamphlet 800-43, January 1986.
2. G. Gordon Schulmeyer, *Zero Defect Software,* McGraw-Hill, 1990.
3. Donald J. Reifer, Richard W. Knudson and Jerry Smith, *Final Report: Software Quality Survey,* American Society for Quality Control, 1987.
4. Daniel J. Couger and Robert A. Zawacki, *Motivating and Managing Computer Personnel,* John Wiley & Sons, 1980.
5. Gerald M. Weinberg, *Understanding the Professional Programmer,* Dorset House, 1982.
6. John Boddie, *Crunch Mode,* Prentice-Hall, 1987.
7. Tom DeMarco, *Controlling Software Projects,* Yourdon Press, 1982.
8. Donald J. Reifer, *Software Management (4th Edition),* IEEE Computer Society, 1993.
9. Department of Defense, *The Program Manager's Guide to Software Acquisition Best Practices,* 1995.
10. John J. Marciniak and Donald J. Reifer, *Software Acquisition Management,* John Wiley & Sons, 1990.
11. SofTech, Inc. (now part of CACI), *Reusable Software Component Certification Guidelines for Ada Implementation Component Types,* Defense Information Systems Agency, February 1993.
12. Air Force Reuse Center, *Newsletter,* Volume 2, Issue 3, Third Quarter 1996.

10

Key Reuse Process Areas

MANAGEMENT OF PRODUCT LINES, ARCHITECTURE, AND REUSE

A key process area (KPA) is defined by the SEI [1] to be a cluster of activities that, when performed collectively, achieve a set of goals considered to be important for establishing a software process capability. As such, the key process areas are the primary building blocks at a single maturity level that define the software process capability of an organization, and the improvements they need to make in order to advance to higher maturity levels.

As stated many times, the SEI has not currently adequately addressed management of product lines, architecture, and reuse in either the Capability Maturity Model (CMM) or the People Capability Maturity Model (P-CMM). This omission was not a conscious oversight on their part. Rather, the technology associated with reuse was just not mature enough to be included when the models were devised several years ago.

This chapter tries to fill the gap as the SEI ponders how to address reuse as it revises the CMM and P-CMM. It recommends a new KPA for managing product lines, architectures, and reuse. It also recommends changes to the existing KPAs that comprise the CMM and P-CMM to make them compatible with this recommended reuse management KPA. These changes are important because they provide the input you need to put the ideas in this book into practice as your organization updates its processes to address reuse.

We have already discussed the SEI CMM at length in earlier chapters. It represents a model of the stages through which software organizations evolve as they define, implement, measure, control, and improve their software processes. The higher the level, the more mature the organization. The SEI model contains the following 18 KPAs, each of which is assigned to a different maturity level:

Level-2 KPAs

Requirements management

Software project planning

Software project tracking and oversight

Software subcontract management

Software quality assurance

Software configuration management

Level-3 KPAs

Organizational process focus

Organizational process definition

Training program

Integrated software management

Software product engineering

Intergroup coordination

Peer reviews

Level-4 KPAs

Quantitative process management

Software quality management

Level-5 KPAs

Defect prevention

Technology change management

Process change management

We have not discussed the P-CMM. This newer model was developed by the SEI to guide organizations in establishing and improving their workforce practices. As shown in Table 10.1, the P-CMM organizes its twenty KPAs around the five maturity levels of the SEI model in a manner complementary to the CMM using the same architecture (see Figure 5.2).

Plan of Action 10.1 describes the recommended new KPA for reuse, the *management of product lines, architecture, and reuse* [1]. This is a key process area that should be considered for Level 3, the Defined level of process maturity. The purpose of this KPA is to integrate software product line, architecture, and reuse considerations into the organization's standard, tailorable software process so that families of quality software products can be developed quickly, efficiently, and economically by a highly motivated workforce.

Management of product lines, architecture, and reuse involves performing the engineering and management tasks that build and maintain software with a large reuse component, using a tailored version of your defined software process that you have modified with reuse in mind.

The software engineering and management tasks performed as part of this new KPA include: software reuse vision-and-strategy definition, software reuse planning, software reuse requirements and operational concept development, software reuse business case formulation, domain engineering and reference architecture establishment, applications development with reuse in mind, and asset management. These tasks may be performed at any or all of the following organizational levels: line of business, product line, and project.

The management infrastructure used to guide the cognizant organization's tailoring of the standard software process is assumed to be available as products

TABLE 10.1 Key Process Areas of the CMM and P-CMM by Maturity Level

Level	CMM KPAs[1]	P-CMM KPAs[2]
Optimizing (5)	Defect prevention Technology change management Process change management	Continuous workforce innovation Coaching Personal competency development
Managed (4)	Quantitative process management Software quality management	Organizational performance alignment Organizational competency management Team-based practices Team building Mentoring
Defined (3)	Organization process focus Organizational process definition Training program Integrated software management Software product engineering Intergroup coordination Peer reviews	Participatory culture Competency-based practices Career development Competency development Workforce planning Knowledge and skill analysis
Repeatable (2)	Requirements management Software project planning Software project tracking and oversight Software subcontract management Software quality assurance Software configuration management	Compensation Training Performance management Staffing Communication Work environment
Initial (1)		

References
1. Mark C. Paulk, Charles V. Weber, Bill Curtis, and Mary Beth Chrisses, *The Capability Maturity Model,* Addison-Wesley, 1995.
2. Bill Curtis, William E. Hefley, and Sally Miller, *People Capability Maturity Model,* Software Engineering Institute, CMU/SEI-95-MM-02, September 1995.

are developed. The infrastructure defines the managerial structure, processes, standards, and guidelines to be used to guide the implementation of selected reuse concepts in a manner compatible with the way the organization conducts its software business. The infrastructure creates a policy and decision framework for use in determining what process tailoring makes sense under what circumstances.

We have identified 27 process areas to support the introduction of product line, architecture, and reuse concepts within your organization. These are organized under the following three headings to make the changes to the CMM and P-CMM more understandable:

PLAN OF ACTION 10.1   Proposed Management of Product Lines, Architecture, and Reuse Key Process Area (KPA)

Goals

Goal 1   Integrate software product-line, architecture, and reuse concepts into the organization's standard, tailorable software process so that families of quality software products can be developed quickly, efficiently, and economically by a highly motivated workforce.

Goal 2   Establish and maintain product-line management techniques to manage the commonality and control the variability of the content of systems across the organization.

Goal 3   Establish and employ a reference software architecture to select the components that will be the standard building blocks for the product line.

Goal 4   Manage software reuse activities across the organization.

Goal 5   Manage product lines to support a quantitatively managed process.

Commitment to Perform

Commitment 1   Establish and maintain a written policy for managing product lines, architecture, and reuse.

Commitment 2   Senior management sponsors and rewards the organization's product-line management and reuse activities.

Abilities to Perform

Ability 1   Establish and maintain a plan for managing product lines, architecture and reuse.

Ability 2   Modify the management infrastructure as necessary for managing product lines, architecture, and reuse policy.

Ability 3   Obtain adequate resources and funding for managing product lines, architecture, and reuse.

Ability 4   Assign responsibility and authority for managing product lines, architecture and reuse.

Ability 5   Obtain required training as appropriate for the individuals performing or supporting product line, architecture, and reuse activities.

Activities to Perform

Activity 1   Manage product lines to support a quantitatively managed process.

Activity 2   Plan software reuse in a manner consistent with the organization's overall reuse vision and strategy.
This typically includes:
1. Putting your reuse strategy (either opportunistic or systematic) to work operationally.
2. Ensuring that project plans align with, and take advantage of, product lines.
3. Ensuring that each project exploits potential reuse opportunities.
4. Reporting results of software reuse at product-line levels and above.

PLAN OF ACTION 10.1 *(Continued)*

Activity 3 Establish and maintain a software reuse vision and strategy which provides a roadmap for introducing software product line, architecture, and reuse concepts into the organization in a planned and ordered manner.
This typically includes:
1. Identifying expertise and business opportunities.
2. Leveraging previous, comparable experience exploiting similar opportunities.
3. Defining product characteristics of each product line.
4. Aligning the vision and strategy with the business opportunities.
5. Aligning the projects with the product lines.

Activity 4 Realize requirements achieved in a manner compatible with aligned reuse operational concepts.
This typically includes:
1. Developing and specifying reuse requirements including those for the architecture and use of COTS and other third-party software.
2. Implementing selected reuse management, technical, and transition approaches as these requirements are being satisfied.
3. Using the reference architecture to guide the reuse selection and implementation activities.
4. Formulating and implementing plans to overcome management resistance and barriers associated with transitioning to reuse (legal, contractual, reward systems, etc.).

Activity 5 Realize the promises made in your business plan.

This typically includes:
1. Defining reuse expectations at a line-of-business, product-line, and/or project level in a business plan.
2. Justifying all required investments in terms of cost/benefits, competitive advantage, and/or other like measures.

Activity 6 Perform domain engineering to model past experience and develop the reference architecture for the product line.
This typically includes:
1. Performing domain analysis.
2. Performing domain design architecture.
3. Developing a reference architecture.
4. Specifying high-leverage, reusable assets to populate the architecture.
5. Populating the reference architecture with high-leverage reusable software assets.
6. Capturing the knowledge base of experience associated with building similar systems.

Activity 7 Establish and maintain product-line architectures.
This typically includes:
1. Designating components to serve as standard building blocks for the product line.

PLAN OF ACTION 10.1   *(Continued)*

> 2. Ensuring asset reuse is achievable.
> 3. Establishing interface/integration requirements for the software assets.

Activity 8   Modify applications engineering processes to be consistent with the domain engineering processes.
This typically includes:
> 1. Modifying engineering processes, methods, and tools to handle reuse considerations.
> 2. Developing specified reusable assets and packaging them according to documented standards.
> 3. Employing reusable assets whenever it is deemed beneficial to do so. Reusable assets include COTS, third-party software, and other assets (designs, algorithms, etc.) that provide added value to the project.

Activity 9   Establish and maintain a reuse repository and related asset management processes.
This typically includes:
> 1. Identifying and evaluating candidate assets.
> 2. Specifying how these assets will be organized, classified, documented, quality assured, and configuration managed.
> 3. Specifying how COTS and other reusable software assets are acquired, documented, quality assured, and configuration managed.
> 4. Acquiring, deploying, operating, and maintaining a reuse library and its associated population of reusable assets.
> 5. Exploiting the assets in this library on software projects.
> 6. Deploying reusable assets to projects.

Activity 10   Integrate the reuse repository and associated tools into your software engineering environments.
Reuse tools considered include:
> 1. Modeling tools for domain engineering.
> 2. A reuse library system for asset management.
> 3. Generators for producing reusable software as part of applications engineering activities.
> 4. Browsers and other search engines for finding reusable assets of interest locally or on the network.

Activity 11   Modify the organization's standard software process to support the reuse infrastructure.

Activity 12   Alter personnel policies to support incentives and rewards established for reuse.

Activity 13   Establish and maintain a software reuse infrastructure which creates the management structure, processes, and standards needed to implement product-line concepts.
This procedure typically specifies:
> 1. Creating a product-line and/or line-of-business organization.

PLAN OF ACTION 10.1   *(Continued)*

    2. Modifying your standard software process to support domain engineering, applications engineering, and asset management activities.
    3. Creating a management policy and decision framework for guiding implementation of reuse actions.
    4. Conducting periodic reuse and architectural review.
    5. Publishing periodic reuse status and progress reports.

Measurement and Analysis

Measurement 1   Use measurement to determine the functionality and quality of reusable assets used to populate products and product lines.

Measurement 2   Use measurement to obtain insight into the status and effectiveness of managing product lines and reuse.

Verifying Implementation

Verification 1   Objectively review designated activities of organizational product lines for adherence to the quantitatively managed process.

Verification 2   Objectively review designated software work products of organizational product lines for adherence to applicable standards and requirements.

Verification 3   Periodically review the activities of organizational product lines with senior management.

Product-Line Management

Architecture management

Incentives and rewards

Integrated product teams

Resource management

Strategic partnerships

Reviews and approvals

Technical Practices

Domain engineering

Architectural engineering

Applications engineering

Asset management

Interface management

Test management

Management practices

Configuration management

Education and training management

Intergroup coordination

Metrics and measurement

Patents management

Personnel management

Process management

Project management

Quality management

Requirements management

Reuse management

Risk management

Subcontractor management

Supplier management

Technology management

Each of these process areas and the practices that support them will be explained more fully in the paragraphs that follow.

PRODUCT-LINE MANAGEMENT

Product lines are families of similar software products that are developed to service the market needs of a particular business area. The idea of a product line is not new. The concept has been used by industry for years to define classes of offerings for everything from automobiles to televisions. Products within a product line share common characteristics and features (e.g., a line of copiers). Typically, increased price means added functionality and performance (e.g., more copies per minute and perhaps a sorter). Within the software field, product lines have been defined to accommodate markets for applications (inventory control, oil exploration, payroll, etc.), customers (government, consumer, international, etc.), technologies (networking technologies such as the World Wide Web, object-oriented methods and tools, etc.), and platforms (desktop, workstation, etc.).

Product-line management is a business function that manages the definition, development, evaluation, use, and evolution of product-line software assets over time. It is strategic in nature and typically performed at a level above an individual project organization. Product-line organizations develop the requirements for product families based upon market needs, and coordinate their timely development through a series of software product releases. They sponsor the development of the software reuse infrastructure, and often defray the additional costs associated with development of reusable assets through subsidies and workload balancing. Projects develop the components of the product-line family to satisfy the requirements. Components are designed to take full advantage of the opportunities that exist for reuse. Architectures are developed for use for the family. Reusable assets are developed to be used to populate the product-line architecture. Projects are held accountable for both building reusable assets and realizing reuse goals.

Product-line management concepts require that new, reuse-oriented processes be inserted above the project level. These are normally put into place within a line-of-business organization. Such organizations are held responsible for satisfying the needs of a specific market area. They pursue reuse in order to reduce their time to market or to reduce development cost. The six new reuse process areas used to identify best practices include: architecture management, incentives and rewards, integrated product teams, resource management, strategic partnerships and reviews and approvals.

Architecture Management

Practices that establish a policy and decision framework to support the systematic development, maintenance, and use of product-line architectures within a business unit. Examples of such practices include:

- Creating the standards and building codes for the reference architecture and inventory of reusable assets needed to build up your product line
- Populating the architecture with the assets that are responsible for most of the reuse
- Evaluating products to make sure that established standards and building codes are being followed as reusable assets are being fully exploited by individual projects

Incentives and Rewards

Practices that alter the organization's overall reward structure to foster the development and use of COTS, third-party, and reusable software assets, some or all of which are architecture based. Examples of such practices include:

- Making reuse a visible corporate goal
- Encouraging reuse at all levels of the organization through the use of tangible incentives (promotion and merit pay systems, bonuses, etc.)
- Encouraging reuse at all levels of the organization through the use of non-monetary rewards (recognition awards, etc.)

Integrated Product Teams

Practices that take advantage of concurrent engineering and multidisciplinary team approaches to develop the reference architecture and define the reuse opportunities across the product line. Examples of such practices include:

- Using teams to get all affected groups, suppliers, partners, and customers to develop an acceptable architecture for the product line
- Involving suppliers in reuse decisions and viewing them as strategic partners
- Developing the instinct to both create reuse opportunities and fill them in a manner that broadens the market for related goods and services across the product line

Resource Management

Practices that fund product-line developments rather than individual projects one at a time. Examples of such practices include:

- Requiring projects to justify any plans to deviate from the reference architecture
- Capitalizing work performed to develop and maintain the product-line architecture, its population of reusable assets, and the related reuse management infrastructure
- Funding reuse developments based upon product line instead of individual project considerations

Strategic Partnerships

Practices that establish long-term partnerships with software suppliers so that the costs and opportunities associated with the product-line developments are shared, and all involved parties benefit during the relationship. Examples of such practices include:

- Stimulating investments by partners in product-line developments
- Involving suppliers in the engineering and design of the product-line architecture
- Providing a business base that justifies evolution of third-party products that can be reused with no changes to requirements

Reviews and Approvals

Practices that reinforce the use of the reuse management infrastructure and building codes as components of the product line are developed, maintained, and supported in the field. Examples of such practices include:

- Performing make-buy reviews early in the product life cycle
- Conducting architectural reviews to ensure that product developments use the reference architecture and exploit opportunities identified for reuse
- Incorporating reuse considerations into other reviews held at the line-of-business level to assess progress and work marketing issues

Table 10.2 shows where these process areas can be addressed in the existing versions of the CMM and P-CMM. In addition to adopting the proposed new *management of product lines, architecture, and reuse KPA,* abilities and activities need to be added to both versions of the CMM to address the process needs of product-line management.

TECHNICAL PROCESSES

The engineering processes you use often change when product-line management techniques are transitioned into use by your firm. This is especially true if you pursue an architecturally based strategy that employs the dual life-cycle paradigm discussed in earlier chapters. As part of this paradigm, the following new processes have to be inserted to operate in parallel with those used for software engineering: domain engineering, architectural engineering, and asset management. In addition, your interface management, test management, and applications engineering processes have to be changed at the product-line management level to address reuse requirements. Practices for these three additional process areas are not currently treated by the CMM or the P-CMM.

TABLE 10.2 Reuse Process Areas/CMM KPA Cross-Reference Matrix

Reuse Process Areas	CMM KPAs	P-CMM KPAs
Product Line Management		
Architecture management	Software product engineering	Not applicable
Incentives and rewards	Software product engineering	Organizational performance alignment
	Intergroup coordination	Competency-based practices Compensation Performance management
Integrated product teams	Software product engineering Intergroup coordination	Participatory culture Team-based practices Team building
Resources management	Intergroup coordination	Not applicable
Strategic partnerships	Intergroup coordination	Participatory culture
Reviews and approvals	Intergroup coordination	Not applicable
Technical Practices		
Domain engineering	New	Not applicable
Architectural engineering	New	Not applicable
Asset management	New	Not applicable
Applications engineering	New	Not applicable
Interface management	New	Not applicable
Test management	New	Not applicable
Management Practices		
Configuration management	Software configuration management	Not applicable
Education and training	Training program	Career development Competency development Workforce planning Knowledge and skill analysis Training
Intergroup coordination	Intergroup coordination	Communication
Metrics and measurement	Quantitative process management Software project planning Software project tracking and oversight	Performance management
Patents management	New	Not applicable
Personnel management	Not applicable	Coaching Mentoring

TABLE 10.2 *(Continued)*

Reuse Process Areas	CMM KPAs	P-CMM KPAs
		Staffing Work environment
Process management	Process change management Quantitative process management Organizational process focus	Continuous workforce innovation
Project management	Software project planning Software project tracking and oversight	Staffing
Quality management	Defect prevention Software quality management Software quality assurance Peer reviews	Not applicable
Requirements management	Requirements management	Not applicable
Reuse management	Organizational process focus Organizational process definition Integrated software management Intergroup coordination	Personal competency development Organizational competency management Career development
Risk management	Software project planning Software project tracking and oversight	Not applicable
Subcontractor management	Software subcontract management	Participatory culture
Supplier management	New	Participatory culture
Technology management	Technology change management	Not applicable

It is important to realize that you still have to modify your processes even when you pursue an opportunistic reuse strategy. You must insert asset management practices as you put your software reuse library into operation. Again, interface management, test management, and applications engineering processes have to be modified to address reuse considerations. As a consequence, these six new reuse process areas are used to identify best technical or engineering practices.

Domain Engineering

Practices that define the domain's scope, model its structure, codify the domain's knowledge base based upon past experience, and define and stimulate the development of an asset population that exploits identified reuse opportunities. Examples of such practices include:

- Scoping the domain to establish its boundaries based upon market or other factors
- Conducting domain analysis to codify the knowledge base of past engineering experience with similar systems
- Creating a domain model for candidate architectures
- Specifying a reference product-line architecture based upon analysis of alternatives
- Acquiring the assets to populate the architecture and demonstrating their form, fit, and function, as appropriate

Architectural Engineering

Practices that develop, maintain, and evolve a reference architecture for the product line using the domain model as the basis of its definition. Examples of such practices include:

- Employing viewpoint models (i.e., operational, technical, and systems) to explore the trade-offs that exist to define the architecture
- Encapsulating generality and variability within the architecture to support scaling, performance, and the wide range of other market requirements
- Mapping requirements to both the architecture and the domain model to show how they were satisfied
- Identifying architecture-based, high-leverage reuse opportunities

Applications Engineering

Practices that stimulate the workforce to take full advantage of product-line concepts, reference architectures, and reusable software assets as they specify, design, develop, and test solutions to user requirements throughout the entire product life cycle. Examples of such practices include:

- Proposing 90-percent solutions that meet user requirements based upon reuse of architectures and other reusable software assets
- Generating large amounts of reusable code directly from a specification for well-bounded parts of the reference architecture (e.g., generating screen templates)

- Using qualified assets from a reuse library to populate elements of the reference architecture (e.g., the controller used to manage the screen logic)
- Using COTS, whenever possible, to minimize the overall cost of ownership

Asset Management

Practices that control the use of reusable assets and make them available to potential users in quality form. Examples of such practices include:

- Providing the access controls needed to ensure that only authorized users can view, browse, and/or retrieve candidate reusable assets from a software reuse library
- Establishing the standards used to classify reusable assets so that candidates for specific applications are easy to locate
- Documenting reusable assets so that their capabilities can be fully understood
- Establishing the quality of reusable assets stored within a reuse library by applying different usage-oriented levels of testing and quality control

Interface Management

Practices that ensure that hardware and software interfaces are properly documented and controlled at all levels of the reference architecture. Examples of such practices include:

- Demonstrating that asset suppliers provide those standards-based architectural services that are specified as part of the reference architecture
- Documenting application program interfaces (APIs) and controlling their changes via an interface control working group (ICWG)
- Establishing guidelines for integrating new applications into the product-line architecture
- Developing the wrappers needed to migrate legacy applications into the mainstream

Test Management

Practices that demonstrate the functionality, performance, quality, and integrity of COTS, third-party, and other reusable software assets that are being incorporated into a product or product line. Examples of such practices include:

- Requiring COTS to be adequately tested before they are acquired and used within a product or product line

■ Encouraging the review of historical error data to determine the relative quality of candidate reusable software assets

Table 10.2 shows how these reuse process areas can be addressed in the existing versions of the CMM and P-CMM. In addition to adopting the proposed new *management of product lines, architecture, and reuse KPA,* abilities and activities must be added to both versions of the CMM to address the process needs of product-line management.

MANAGEMENT PROCESSES

Management processes also change when product-line management techniques are transitioned into use in your firm. Modification of existing key processes are needed to stimulate sharing of reusable assets across project boundaries independently of reuse adoption strategy. Processes in 12 process areas must be changed to address reuse requirements imposed by new life-cycle paradigms. In addition, practices for three new process areas have to be developed to provide reuse-specific legal and contractual (Patents Management, Level 2), COTS and strategic partnership (Supplier Management, Level 2), and reuse integration (Reuse Management, Level 3) guidance at the designated levels of process maturity.

Modification of processes is needed to support the product-line management push to establish processes for reuse-oriented processes at the line-of-business level. Such changes are pervasive because they change how an organization does business. For example, it is likely that practices for well-established disciplines, such as configuration management, will have to be updated to address change control of reusable assets used by projects across several different business units. There are 15 reuse process areas recommended to be used to identify best management practices.

Configuration Management

Existing practices that are modified to address the reuse of shared software assets across product lines and/or business units. Examples of such modified practices include:

■ Creating architectural baselines for products and product lines
■ Defining how architectural and reuse baselines are documented
■ Maintaining a reusable software asset's unique identification using a numbering system
■ Establishing a change-control board that assesses the desirability of enhancing, perfecting, and/or modifying reusable assets when they are shared across business units

- Providing archival and distribution procedures for controlling different releases of COTS, third-party, and other reusable software assets
- Verifying that the configuration integrity of reusable assets (architectures, COTS, etc.) is being maintained operationally through the use of audits and inspections

Education and Training

Existing practices that are modified to develop, maintain, and support the skills, knowledge, and abilities needed to sustain product lines and associated architectural and reuse core competencies. Examples of such modified practices include:

- Identifying the job requirements in terms of core competencies for new reuse positions (e.g., product-line manager, chief architect, reuse librarian)
- Defining how these core competencies and their related skills, knowledge, and abilities are developed, maintained, and managed across functional groups (systems engineering, software engineering, test and evaluation, etc.)
- Describing the educational requirements for these job requirements and techniques to be used to build the prerequisite skills, knowledge, and abilities (distance learning, after hours courses, on-the-job training, mentoring, coaching, etc.)

Intergroup Coordination

Existing practices that are modified to ensure that all potential stakeholders are involved in the definition, implementation, and evolution of the reuse vision and strategy. Examples of such modified practices include:

- Encouraging the use of consensus-building, concurrent engineering, and innovative team approaches to develop the reuse vision and strategy
- Getting affected groups involved in the development of a product-line architecture and/or reuse library system (i.e., depends on the strategy adopted)
- Making the suppliers, vendors, and customers fully vested members of the reuse team
- Maintaining communications across affected groups as the strategy unfolds

Metrics and Measurement

Existing practices that are modified to support reuse measurement goals. Examples of such modified practices include:

- Defining measures of success to be utilized to determine whether the goals established for the reuse effort are being fully realized at different organizational levels

- Capturing the measurement data needed to assess the goodness of the product-line architecture and/or the reusable assets selected to populate it
- Establishing the metrics to assess the quality of reusable assets selected to populate the software reuse library
- Developing reuse estimating models and capturing the historical data needed to accurately calibrate them based upon actual past performance

Patents Management

Practices that resolve contractual, ownership, and legal issues associated with the use of COTS, third-party, and reusable software in products and product lines. Examples of such practices include:

- Providing guidance on reuse legal, licensing, and contractual issues
- Developing model contracts and licenses that limit exposure, risk, and/or liability when COTS, third-party, and reusable assets are bought or sold
- Establishing the means to protect your rights in software and technical data (copyrights, copylefts, trademarks, patents, etc.)
- Developing the means to derive revenue streams from the reuse of protected assets through royalties and/or other financial arrangements

Personnel Management

Existing practices that are modified to fill reuse positions with qualified staff, train and retain, and create a reward structure designed to motivate everyone in the organization to achieve high levels of reuse as they perform their jobs. Examples of such modified practices include:

- Establishing career ladders and job description needed to support the new product line, architectural, and reuse positions
- Altering personnel rating and ranking practices used for raises and promotions to emphasize the realization of reuse objectives
- Providing financial and nonmonctary rewards to foster development and use of reusable software assets

Process Management

Existing practices that are modified to make sure that feedback from product-line initiatives is used to help improve and optimize practices adopted as part of the process improvement activities. Examples of such modified practices include:

- Incorporating product-line, architecture, and software reuse considerations into the organization's software process development and improvement plans

- Stimulating the process group to coordinate their activities with line-of-business groups as part of their organizational focus practices
- Modifying the organization's standard software process to take into account experience with product lines, architecture, and reuse
- Expanding the process library to provide example product-line, architecture, and reuse documentation

Project Management

Existing planning, tracking, and oversight practices that are modified to address product-line, architecture, and reuse considerations. Examples of such modified practices include:

- Reporting reuse progress periodically to product-line or line-of-business management
- Altering the standard work breakdown structure (WBS) to address product-line, architecture, and reuse work tasks
- Utilizing the modified WBS to provide reuse project-planning guidance, controls, and performance measurement
- Modifying estimating procedures to determine what additional resources are needed to successfully complete reuse work tasks
- Providing the tailoring guidance to adapt product-line requirements to project needs

Quality Management

Existing practices that are modified to address product-line, architecture, and reuse quality considerations. Examples of such practices include:

- Addressing quality considerations for product lines at the line-of-business level
- Establishing evaluation criteria for determining the quality of COTS, third-party, and reusable software assets prior to their acquisition for use
- Creating checklists for evaluating the quality of COTS, third-party, and reusable assets during audits, inspections, and reviews
- Defining statistical quality controls for monitoring the quality of reuse processes

Requirements Management

Existing practices that are modified to incorporate reuse considerations into requirements specifications for products and product lines, and to address trade-offs that occur when COTS, third-party software, and reusable assets are extensively used. Examples of such modified practices include:

- Ensuring that the reference architecture is used as a basis for requirements trade-offs
- Looking to relax the requirements in order to find a 90-percent solution to the customer's needs (hopefully at 50 percent of the price)
- Identifying potential reuse opportunities and investigating the reuse of COTS, third-party software, and reusable assets
- Conducting the functionality/cost/performance trade-offs necessary to determine whether reusable software assets can be reused as is to satisfy market requirements
- Addressing the traceability of requirements to COTS, third-party software, and reusable assets

Reuse Management

Practices that foster the development of an integrated process framework for managing product lines, architecture, and software reuse. Examples of such practices include:

- Integrating reuse concerns into the practices used to run the business organization
- Making sure that each project software development plan addresses reuse and those intergroup relationships established to put the product line's reuse strategy to work
- Providing tailoring guidance for use with the organization's standard process based upon the degree of reuse to be practiced

Risk Management

Existing project management practices that are modified to address the risks associated with utilizing product-line, architecture, and software reuse concepts. Examples of such modified practices include:

- Identifying risk issues associated with reuse and determining their relative priorities (e.g., using COTS, upgrading legacy, and migrating to the reference architecture)
- Developing risk mitigation plans that are coordinated with business, product-line, and project management
- Rewarding risk takers and innovators who are pushing to quickly adopt reuse

Subcontractor Management

Existing practices that are modified to address the issues associated with having subcontractors adhere to your product-line, architecture, and software reuse requirements. Examples of such modified practices include:

- Selecting subcontractors who are qualified in architectures and reuse
- Ensuring that subcontractors build their products so that they interface with and operate as part of the reference architecture
- Establishing quantitative reuse goals in subcontract agreements and contracts
- Providing subcontractors with financial rewards to stimulate reuse
- Limiting the legal liability associated with having your subcontractors use your architecture, reusable software assets, and COTS
- Flowing reuse requirements down from primes to subcontractors

Supplier Management

Practices that are aimed at managing and motivating suppliers to invest, integrate, and innovate when it comes to reuse. Examples of such practices include:

- Involving suppliers in the development of the reference architecture
- Stimulating suppliers to invest in developing assets to populate the reference architecture
- Providing suppliers with business opportunities that justify their reuse investments
- Ensuring that reusable software assets supplied by strategic partners are compatible with the reference architecture, satisfy requirements, and are kept well maintained
- Evaluating the quality, functionality, and performance of COTS, third-party software, and reusable assets prior to integrating it into your product line
- Ensuring that adequate maintenance is provided for COTS and third-party software

Technology Management

Existing practices that are modified to quicken the introduction of product-line, architecture, and software reuse technology into operations. Examples of such modified processes include:

- Developing the knowhow needed to expedite widespread adoption of technology
- Establishing a long-range technology roadmap to guide the timely acquisition of needed reuse technologies
- Using collaborative practices to involve stakeholders in harnessing technology

Table 10.2 shows how these reuse process areas can be addressed in the existing versions of the CMM and P-CMM. In addition to adopting the proposed new *management of product lines, architecture, and reuse KPA*, abilities and activities need to be added to both versions of the CMM to address the process needs of product-line management.

PUTTING THE PROCESSES TO WORK

While we have talked a lot about software reuse-based processes in this and earlier chapters, we haven't explained them to the depth needed to put them to work within your organization. You really need to understand more about the activities that must be performed, their products, and their interrelationships in order to integrate the reuse-based processes we've talked about into your way of doing business. Chapter 7 discussed such reuse-based activities from a planning context for both the opportunistic and systematic approach. In these discussions, we assumed that you had readied your organization for software reuse, and had put a management infrastructure into place that was responsive to the requirements laid out as part of our reuse KPA. We described two new activities, asset management and domain engineering, that were conducted in parallel and had to be interfaced to your reuse-based applications engineering, management, and marketing activities.

In the paragraphs that follow, let's assume that you have decided to pursue a systematic reuse strategy. This seems reasonable when viewing process implementation, because it is based upon the premise that you are going to implement most of the new reuse-based activities. Continuing along these lines, let's look at the reuse-oriented work you must accomplish to be successful with your domain engineering, application engineering, and asset management activities.

Domain Engineering

The systematic approach to reuse is product-line oriented and architecture based. As such, domain engineering tasks are conducted in parallel with applications development to use past experience to define what assets should be built to be reusable. The product-line approach often tasks some separate group to bound the domain, model it, develop a reference architecture using the model, and generate the reusable assets to populate the architecture. This separation makes sense when domain engineering tasks are performed by some systems or marketing organization at a level higher than an individual project. As we saw in Chapter 7, the typical task breakouts for the domain engineering activity and their primary products are as follows:

Domain engineering

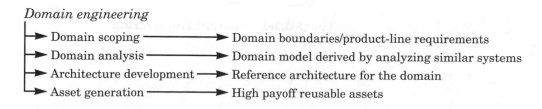

Domain scoping	Domain boundaries/product-line requirements
Domain analysis	Domain model derived by analyzing similar systems
Architecture development	Reference architecture for the domain
Asset generation	High payoff reusable assets

A series of data flow diagrams developed to set the context and describe the task and subtask relationships are presented in Figure 10.1. The data dictionary that accompanies this figure and defines the data items used within it is provided as Table 10.3.

Domain Scoping

As shown in Figure 10.1, domain scoping involves bounding and developing requirements for perceived product lines. The goals of domain scoping are to characterize and understand the problem space so that requirements for the solution

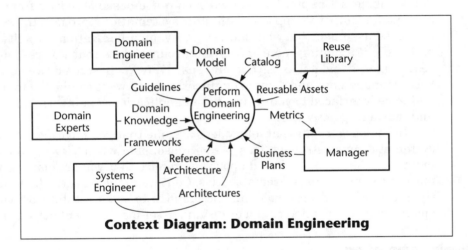

Context Diagram: Domain Engineering

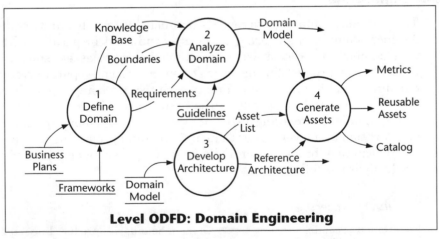

Level ODFD: Domain Engineering

FIGURE 10.1 Domain engineering data flow diagrams.

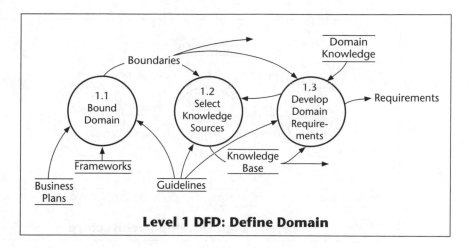

Level 1 DFD: Define Domain

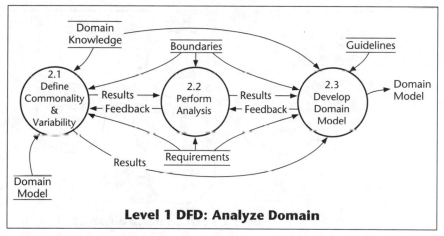

Level 1 DFD: Analyze Domain

FIGURE 10.1 *(Continued)*

space can be derived. Various frameworks [2] for scoping domains have been pro-posed. Some of these bound domains based upon business/marketing, manage-ment/organizational, and technical factors. Others are more functional in nature. For example, a computer firm may decide to develop a product line of Java offer-ings for its networking line-of-business organization based upon market forecasts, a strategic partnering agreement that provides marketing channels, and server requirements. Independent of the criteria used, a clear boundary for the domain, a knowledge base of past experience, and a detailed set of requirements for prod-ucts that are part of the product family are the expected outputs from the domain scoping tasks.

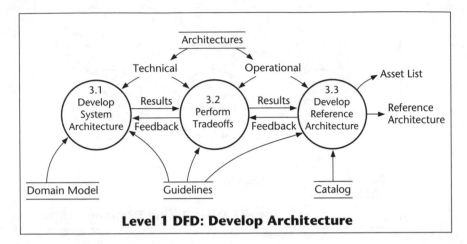

Level 1 DFD: Develop Architecture

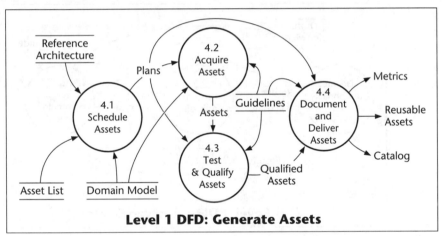

Level 1 DFD: Generate Assets

FIGURE 10.1 *(Continued)*

Domain Analysis

Domain analysis develops a model for the domain based upon your knowledge base of past experience [3]. As shown in Figure 10.1, domain analysis identifies common features in the knowledge base to define a generic model of the domain's static and dynamic structure. Any of a number of different methods, some functional and others object oriented, can be used to develop the model. The three keys to success in a domain analysis are: select a precedented domain, involve the right people, and make sure the model abstractions allow you to address the variability

TABLE 10.3 Domain Engineering Data Dictionary

Data Item	Definition
Architectures	Refers to the technical architecture that is based upon a standards profile, and the operational architecture that is based on a use case
Assets	Assets that are candidates for software reuse, including COTS and third-party packages
Asset List	A list of candidate assets for populating the reference architecture
Boundaries	The limits or extent of a domain
Business Plans	The plans established at the line-of-business level, which identify top-level requirements for the product lines and a business case for reuse
Catalog	A centralized source of information about the assets in a reuse library
Domain Knowledge	The knowledge base that characterizes the domain
Domain Model	An image of the domain's contents, structure, and internal relationships
Feedback	The return of data about the result of an activity
Frameworks	Various taxonomies used for different evaluation purposes
Guidelines	A handbook of information about the topic of interest
Knowledge Base	A codification of past engineering experience with similar systems
Metrics	Quantitative standards set for measurement
Plans	Roadmaps that detail what assets will be developed, when, why, and by whom
Qualified Assets	Assets that are candidates for reuse, which have been tested and qualified but have not been documented and prepared for delivery
Reference Architecture	A software architecture defined to serve as the point of departure for a product line or family of similar systems
Requirements	The functional, performance, interface, and quality specification established for a system or family of systems
Results	The outcome of a specific action
Reusable Assets	An asset that has been tested, cataloged, and stored in a reuse library (this term implies that a reusable asset is more valuable than other assets because potential users can find it and have confidence in its quality)

needed to satisfy requirements across the product line. As noted, the primary output of this task is the model.

The generation of the domain model involves many people and a lot of work. The team developing the model codifies experience and lessons learned by getting engineers who were involved in developing the original system (the domain experts) to reflect on the results of their engineering decisions. Then, based upon hindsight and actual field experience, they can determine what worked and what did not. The more systems analyzed, the better the conclusions. That's the reason for emphasizing the use of domain analysis for precedented domains. The resulting knowledge base provides the team with the practical insight they need to build a comprehensive model. This model defines the static and dynamic structure (the model's generality) that facilitates the design of a family of systems that fulfill a wide range of requirements (the model's variability). This model provides those developing the reference architecture for the product line with a framework for engineering decision making.

Architecture Development

The domain model may be used as a blueprint to bound an architecture for one or more product lines. For example, a copier firm may use the same basis architecture across all of its small office and home products to achieve economies of scale. As another example, common middleware may be defined across diverse business applications (payroll, inventory control, logistics support, etc.) that can be viewed as the glue that makes a generic architecture possible. In reality, the reference architecture you develop for your product line is an instantiation of the domain model. This is done by trading off elements of your operational, technical, and system architecture to realize specific requirements established by your customers for products and product families. The reference architecture results in a specific design that dictates how products that comply with it are built, sustained, and evolved over time. For example, the architecture may use messaging for inter-process communication, forcing designers to address real-time performance issues associated with an operating system such as POSIX. As noted in Figure 10.1, the primary outputs of this task are the candidate reusable software asset list and the reference architecture.

Asset Generation

From a domain engineering viewpoint, asset generation populates the reference architecture by acquiring those assets on the candidate assets list for which a strong business case can be made. Assets may be obtained via purchase, partnership, and/or development. They are systematically acquired to fulfill specific product-line needs according to a plan. Some organizations use third parties to develop assets and off-load the extra work involved from the applications engineering shop. Other organizations task projects to build the reusable assets as part of their normal workload. They may or may not off-load the extra work involved. In either case, the shop responsible for obtaining the assets must do something to help projects satisfy their requirements under deadline pressures. Assets can include the full range of software artifacts associated with the reference architecture (benchmarks, tests and test cases, algorithms and designs, code—both coarse-grain and fine-grain components—documentation, training materials, etc.). As a result, this activity outputs a wealth of architecturally compatible reusable assets, each of which has a high potential for reuse. In other words, the process should permit you to promote previously developed assets to reusable status.

Applications Engineering

The systematic approach to reuse integrates product-line, architecture, and software reuse considerations into the processes software engineers use to develop and maintain their products. New and radical ways of doing business are avoided. Instead, the organization's standard software process is augmented to address the architecturally based dual life-cycle paradigm. Interfaces with domain engineering and asset management activities are controlled so that assets flowing between tasks can be properly managed. Changes made to the organizational structures that impact roles and responsibilities are also handled. For example, in addition to making assets provided by those responsible for domain engineering reusable, the process should be able to promote assets developed as applications are engineered to reusable status.

As we saw in Chapter 7, the typical task breakouts for the applications engineering activity (from a reuse viewpoint) and their primary products are:

Applications development (from a reuse viewpoint)

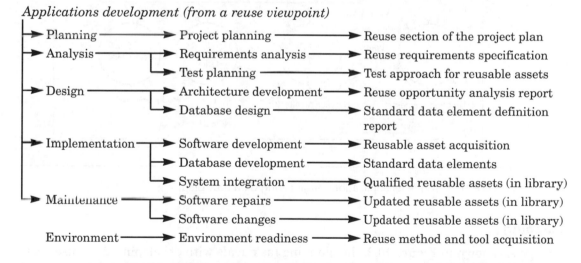

A top-level data flow diagram that sets the context and describes the reuse aspects of the task relationships is pictured in Figure 10.2. The data dictionary that accompanies this figure and defines the reuse-specific data items used within it is provided as Table 10.4. Because this is a pretty standard life cycle, we did not feel that a detailed decomposition of the process is warranted. For those of you who want more detail, we refer you to some excellent references [4,5] on the topic.

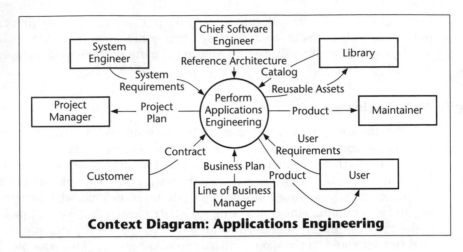

Context Diagram: Applications Engineering

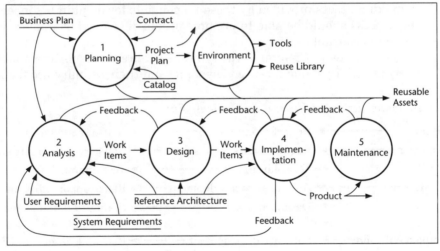

FIGURE 10.2 Top-level applications engineering data flow diagrams.

Planning

As shown in Figure 10.2, the planning task deals with developing the reuse parts of the project plan. Such plans are by design compatible with those developed at the line-of-business or product-line level. The plan summarizes the reuse opportunities that exist and how they will be exploited on the project. In order to exploit these opportunities, it adjusts budgets and schedules accordingly. It also identifies any COTS and strategic partnerships that have been formed and discusses how they will be managed. Last, it analyzes and discusses how to mitigate the risks, if they exist, associated with using these components.

TABLE 10.4 Applications Engineering Data Dictionary

Data Item	Definition
Business Plan	The plans established at the line of business level, which identify top-level requirements for product lines and a business case for reuse.
Catalog	A centralized source of information about the assets in a reuse library.
Contract	The legal instrument used to acquire a system. A contract specifies the obligations and the terms and conditions agreed upon by both parties.
Feedback	The return of data about the result of an action.
Product	The deliverable for this effort (it could be a total system, such as a telephone switch or a software package). Normally includes the software and all associated documentation (user's manuals, etc.) and training materials.
Project Plan	A management document describing the approach that will be taken to meet a project's goals. The plan typically describes the work to be done, the resources required, the organization, the schedules, the methods to be used, and the tailoring of the organization's standard process.
Reference Architecture	A software architecture defined to serve as a point of departure for a product line or family of similar systems.
Reusable Assets	An asset that has been tested, cataloged, and stored in a reuse library. This term implies that a reusable asset is more valuable than other assets because potential users can find it and have confidence in its quality.
Reuse Library	The element of the software engineering environment where reusable software assets are stored, maintained, and made accessible to potential users. The reuse library is much more than a normal library. It has browsing and many other user-oriented capabilities.
System Requirements	The functional, performance, and interface requirements allocated to software for the system. These tend to be feature oriented.
Tools	Software used to help develop, test, analyze, or maintain other software products and/or its documentation (e.g., compilers, test analyzers).
User Requirements	The operationally oriented requirements specified by the user, which are capability and performance oriented.
Work Items	The interim work products that are generated as by-products of ongoing engineering activities (design specifications, prototypes, code, test plans, listings, etc.).

Analysis

Requirements analysis is conducted using the reference architecture as a basis for departure. The goal is to figure out how to use the reference architecture and its population of reusable software assets to satisfy the customer's requirements quickly and in the most economical manner. If this can be done, existing requirements and test plans will be reusable. Even though such solutions do not always provide either all of the desired functionality or performance, they may be viewed with favor if they can be fielded at a fraction of the estimated price. As an option, you can work with your customers to evolve your reference architecture to their requirements, especially if you can establish a broader market for the derived product that justifies your investment. The primary output of this task is a requirements specification. Test plans are also generated, which address how COTS and other reusable software assets will be tested.

Design

If the requirements don't change radically, the existing designs can be carried over as is from project to project. Because they have been laid out with reuse in mind, they can be easily adapted to the particular requirements of the customer. It is here where the extra effort you put into the architectural design pays off. By focusing on packaging, you've made it possible to add and remove components (modules, data files, etc.) with a minimum of impact. In addition, the domain model can be used to determine how proposed changes impact performance as the reference architecture is manipulated to extend its capabilities. After all the trade-offs have been evaluated, the product of this task is the updated architectural design, including that for the database (i.e., its logical schema). Under many circumstances, this design can be treated as a reusable software asset.

Implementation

Once the design has been stabilized, implementation can start in earnest. Reusable assets, data, COTS, and newly created components can be integrated together incrementally to build up the desired deliverable capability. As reuse opportunities that were not evident during earlier stages of the development become apparent, additional reusable assets can be produced. Each component will be qualified as the system gets built up using a variety of means (development test, beta test, independent verification and validation, etc.). Finally, the product will be delivered along with prescribed documentation and training to the end user. The outputs of these tasks are the reusable assets that were acquired during the development for use with the reference architecture.

Maintenance

After the product is fielded, it will undoubtedly be updated and changed. Software is the change element of the system. It is often updated to provide users with new features and functions (enhancements), perform better (perfective changes), and/or fix bugs (repairs). The output of these maintenance tasks are updated reusable assets.

Needless to say, the COTS and reusable software that make up the product may have to be changed as well. However, this is not as simple a task as changing software used on this and this project only. The impact of the change may be pervasive because it may cross product lines. After analyzing the situation, you may want to resist the change.

Environment

The final task in our list is associated with readying the software engineering environment. The goal here is to make it easy for the software engineers to perform their reuse-oriented tasks. Reuse must be made part of the methodology used by your software engineers and programmers. Tools that support these methods and are an integral part of the software engineering environment must be provided. Just because a method is more reuse oriented doesn't mean your people can use it without guidance and tool support. In addition, a software reuse library must be acquired and made part of the environment. The output of this task is the set of software reuse tools and methods that form a part of the software engineering environment used on the project. In the best of worlds, this software environment would itself be a reusable software asset.

Asset Management

The systematic approach to reuse employs a software reuse library to store, control, distribute, and manage the reusable software assets that you acquired to support the reference architectures that form the basis of your product lines. Assets in this context include much more than just code. In the best of all possible worlds, this software reuse library will be an integral part of your software engineering environment. Such an environment will enable your software engineers to find, browse, and access reusable assets as they are performing their applications engineering work tasks. It is important to note that an online software reuse library is a desire, not a requirement. Organizations can perform the asset management function manually without it. However, the burden associated with a manual library system increases proportionally with both the number of users and assets that populate it.

The typical task breakouts for the asset management activity and their primary products are:

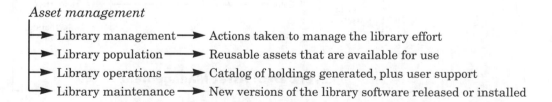

Asset management

— Library management → Actions taken to manage the library effort
— Library population → Reusable assets that are available for use
— Library operations → Catalog of holdings generated, plus user support
— Library maintenance → New versions of the library software released or installed

A series of data flow diagrams developed to set the context and describe the task and subtask relationships are presented in Figure 10.3. The data dictionary that accompanies this figure and defines the data items used within it is provided as Table 10.5

Library Management

Library management is conducted to administer the reuse library, maintain access control, and manage the day-to-day operations. The amount of work involved

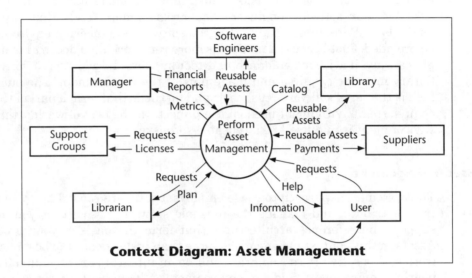

Context Diagram: Asset Management

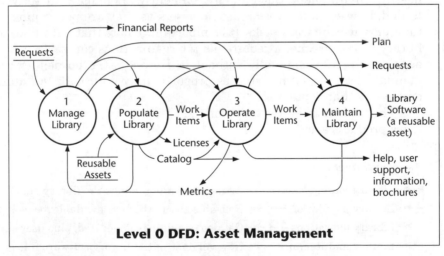

Level 0 DFD: Asset Management

FIGURE 10.3 Asset management data flow diagrams.

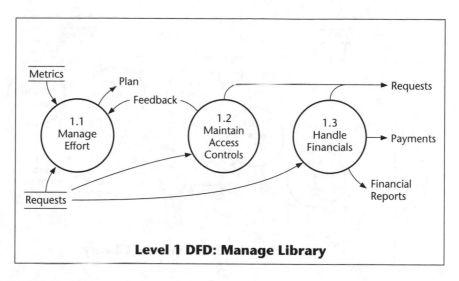

Level 1 DFD: Manage Library

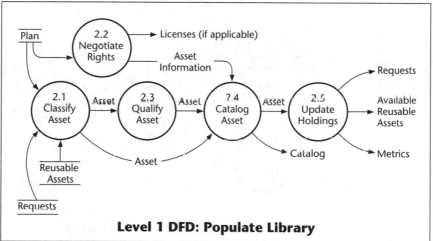

Level 1 DFD: Populate Library

FIGURE 10.3 *(Continued)*

depends heavily on the operational concept employed, the number of users, and the size of the library population. For example, library management can be a simple system administration task if the software reuse library is part of the software engineering environment, and access to it is controlled as part of the overall system administration workload. However, the amount of work grows tremendously when you offer various goods and services on a fee-for-service basis if you put the reuse library online as part of an electronics shopping mall.

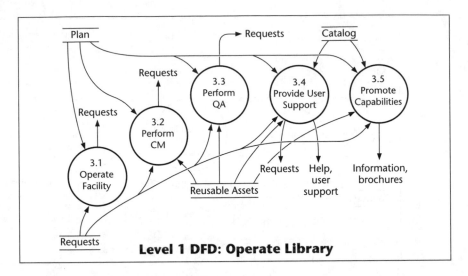

Level 1 DFD: Operate Library

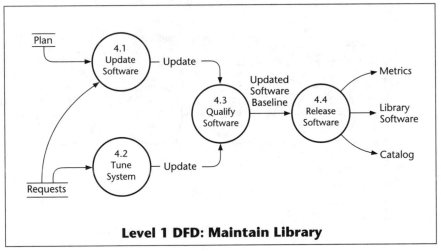

Level 1 DFD: Maintain Library

FIGURE 10.3 *(Continued)*

Library Population

Populating the software reuse library is another potentially large and tedious task. This is especially true when you are trying to make reusable assets of varying levels of quality a part of your reuse library's holdings. Each asset must be abstracted, classified, and qualified based upon predefined criteria before it is made available to potential users. In some cases, reengineering of assets may be in order. Again, the amount of work involved depends on your operational concepts and the num-

TABLE 10.5 Asset Management Data Dictionary

Data Item	Definition
Assets	Assets that are candidates for inclusion in the software reuse library, including COTS and third-party packages
Asset Information	A description of the asset suitable for inclusion in the library catalog
Available Reusable Assets	A listing of the reusable assets available at any point in time (i.e., assets that have been classified, qualified, and cataloged)
Brochures	Sales literature for potential new reuse library subscribers
Catalog	A centralized source of information about the assets in a reuse library
Feedback	The return of data about the result of an action
Financial Reports	Summaries of financial transactions issued for accounting purposes
Help	Both online assistance and a hot line that assists users and provides them answers to their questions in a timely manner
Information	Information (both written and online) answering potential subscribers' questions and providing them facts about capabilities
Library Software	The current released version of the reuse library software
Licenses	Legal agreements outlining the legal limitations associated with use of a software package
Metrics	Quantitative standards set for measurement
Payments	Compensation paid to third parties whose software the reuse library makes available to its users on a fee-for-service basis
Plan	Refers to an operationally oriented management plan for the reuse library
Requests	A system of work orders used to manage the orderly completion of different types of service requests
Reusable Assets	An asset that has been tested, cataloged, and stored in a reuse library
Updates	Updated versions of the reuse library software
Updated Software Baseline	A baselined version of the new qualified version of the reuse library software
Work Items	The interim work products that are generated as by-products of ongoing engineering activities

ber of assets you have in the queue. The primary product of this task is a listing of qualified assets. In cases where you have implemented a virtual reuse library (i.e., a library of libraries), the product is the combined index of holdings.

Library Operations

Your next asset management task is to operate the library and provide advertised goods and services to its users. As part of this effort, you must keep users informed by periodically publishing a catalog. You must baseline assets and maintain them under configuration control. You must maintain quality control by keeping track of problems and purging troublesome assets. You must staff a help desk to answer user questions when they arise. You must publicize and promote your capabilities in an attempt to get more of your staff to utilize your capabilities. The primary products of this task are a catalog of library holdings, promotion brochures, and operating and metrics reports summarizing who is using the reuse library and what assets are being heavily reused.

Library Maintenance

Maintaining the reuse library software and keeping it up to date is your final task. This becomes especially difficult when you integrate a third-party product to become part of your software engineering environment. You must do this because there are few environments on the market today that can provide you with the desired set of needed capabilities (browser, search engine, knowledge-base front end, tight repository interfaces, etc.). You most likely will bind your reuse library to your database management and configuration management systems. These bindings will change when any of the three packages described change. Keeping your software current takes time and effort. The product of this task is the library software itself.

CASE STUDY

A large aerospace firm is in the midst of a software process improvement exercise. This firm was rated a Level 3 in 1989 in an SEL-assisted appraisal. This was prior to adoption of the Capability Maturity Model (CMM) as the standard used by the rest of their industry. The firm plans to conduct its reassessment using the CMM-based appraisal for internal process improvement (CBA IPI) method. This is an important event for this firm, because the government may use its score during future source selections to determine whether it is qualified to bid on competitive contracts.

The team formed to work process started its effort by sending its members to be trained in the CMM at the SEI. The SEI offers frequent courses and the group members wanted to understand the changes. In parallel, the team conducted a quick-look internal assessment using personnel from other operating groups who had already gone through a CBA IPI. Like most large firms, the team had a large number of sister organizations who were also in the midst of reassessments.

The team was very critical of the current efforts to institutionalize the process when it briefed its findings to executive management. While good work was being done, the team felt that not enough attention was being placed on getting the projects to use the organization's standard software process as a starting point. While some members of the group were devastated by the findings, others felt the team's remarks were on the mark. Because management was pressuring the group to publish processes, little time was being devoted to project liaison. The group felt that the briefing provided a needed reprieve.

The results of the preliminary assessment went as expected. Executive management asked the process group to address the findings and implement its recommendations. They asked for a briefing containing an updated plan for the process improvement effort within a week. Several members of the process group viewed this occurrence as an opportunity to get the approval and budget to do several necessary things. The item of particular interest dealt with incorporating support within the process for managing product lines, architecture, and software reuse. One of the members of the group had recently attended a course on the topic and came back with materials that could be used to address known deficiencies in the CMM relative to software reuse.

After considerable debate, the process group decided to incorporate support for reuse into its revamped processes on a KPA-by-KPA basis as it got ready for the reassessment. The group started by preparing a sales pitch for executive management about reuse. This was put into the briefing to management on the updated process improvement plan. Management loved the pitch. Inserting support for product lines, architecture, and software reuse into the process for a seemingly small additional cost was difficult for them to say no to. During the briefing, management told the process team members that they could do almost anything they wanted, as long as it made sense and didn't impact the schedules, which were said to be fixed, and their ability to be awarded an SEI Level 3. The group later learned that the reason behind this push was that the general manager got 6 points out of 100 toward his bonus based upon achievement of this milestone in his incentive plan.

The process group had nine months to get ready for the reassessment. It was in relatively good shape because they had a trained and experienced team in place and weren't starting from scratch. However, expectations were high and group members felt they had seriously underestimated the work involved in getting projects to use the revamped process. Luckily, the assessment team pointed out this problem. Plans were in place to correct the situation. Several projects had volunteered to be pathfinders for use of the process, and people in the trenches wanted to use it.

Working groups were formed to get people from the project involved as the process was being developed. In essence, members of these working groups extended the capabilities of the process group and became a force multiplier. They volunteered hundreds of hours of their own time to work specific process-related issues. For example, the education and training working group coordinated with local universities and training firms to try to fill the training requirements. In several instances, members of this working group developed and ran process training sessions on their own time because there wasn't time to get it done any other way.

A reuse working group was formed to address process-related issues and to define the overall infrastructure needed to insert reuse into the projects. While the process group revised practices, the reuse working group reviewed them and added the detail needed to make sharing of assets a reality. It soon became apparent that major organizational changes at the line-of-business level were needed to make their architecture-based reuse initiative a reality. But, such changes were very difficult to make happen, because people were very comfortable with the way that the business was currently being run. This group was told repeatedly by its management to practice evolution, not revolution. Being volunteers, they quickly reoriented what they were doing toward things that they could accomplish with minimum pain and effort.

The reuse working group opted to get four things accomplished during its first three months of operation. First, they tried to make reuse part of the practices that were developed for each SEI KPA. Things that were missing were added wherever they seemed to make sense. For example, each project would address reuse in its project plan. Reuse management was addressed as part of integrated software management because it was easy and seemed a likely place to satisfy the requirements. Patent, legal, and ownership issues were tackled as part of the quality assurance function. Asset management functions were handled as part of configuration management.

Second, the reuse working group tried to convince line-of-business management that they needed a chief software engineer. In addition to working software issues with the customers, the chief software engineer would be responsible for the architecture and product integrity. Software management liked the idea because they were looking for ways to increase the software competency of its business units. They were also looking for allies within these organizations, especially those who understood what it took to field a software product.

Third, the working group cataloged available reusable assets and identified which of them could be shared. This effort was eventually expanded to include COTS and other third-party software packages that were used across the firm.

Fourth and finally, the working group interfaced with other groups and got them, whenever they could, to address their needs. For example, they identified the need for a reuse library to the tools working group, and got them to recommend a package that filled requirements that were jointly established by both groups.

The reuse function that seemed impossible to get started was domain engineering. Some of the questions hurled by opponents included: Why create a separate group to develop architectures and build reusable assets? How do you justify its cost? Doesn't systems engineering already perform this function? Doesn't our existing architecture establish the standard? Finally, in frustration, the group gave up. They felt good because they had won a partial victory when they got the line of businesses to bring a chief software engineer on board. They would have to rely on the chief software engineer to both define a suitable reference architecture for the product line, and continue to push for domain engineering. Perhaps, members of the group could try to introduce domain analysis again with the support of the chief engineer when the time seemed ripe.

As you can gather, the implementation of product lines, architecture, and reuse as part of this process improvement initiative became a series of compromises. Not everything that was desired could be implemented. There just wasn't enough time and some of the changes proposed were too radical. However, the initiative succeeded in changing the infrastructure to provide a lot of support for software reuse. This was done by getting those affected by the processes involved in their development. The net result was that everyone who participated in the development of the revamped processes wanted to use them. The payoff was that most of the processes were being used by projects as they were being finalized and published. Putting the chief software engineer in the line-of-business organization also helped. It focused attention on architecture and gave responsibility for its development to someone with the authority to make sure the related processes were utilized.

This case continues and the final results are pending. As of this writing, we don't know if the firm will get its SEI Level 3 (or hopefully Level 4) rating. However, we do know that people are enthused and the organization's reuse-based standard process is being used by many projects. We also are encouraged by the emphasis placed by this firm on making product lines, architectures, and software reuse part of the process. Much of the work that is included within this chapter was developed as part of this process-improvement effort.

As a side comment, one of the major difficulties this firm had to cope with was in the areas of methodology and software tools. Many vendors asserted that their methods and tools were reuse oriented. However, their claims were not substantiated when the process group evaluated their offerings. Most of the methods investigated had been used in a research setting and were not yet industrial strength. Even more disappointing, most of the software tools that were assessed could not be easily integrated into the software engineering environment. The tools that were acquired seemed to be constantly causing trouble. For example, the firm tried to use the viewpoint capability of its software engineering environment to create its software reuse library. This capability allowed users of the environment to reorient the contents of its repository based upon facets of interest (degree of reuse, quality rating, etc.). The standard search, browsing, and access mechanisms could then be used to support reuse-based applications development processes. For awhile, everything was fine, but response time became a problem as the number of software assets in the library grew. When the vendor was contacted, he expressed amazement. Nobody had ever experienced delays like this before. After considerable analysis, the vendor responded with a fix. Because this was the first time that anyone had stressed the environment to this degree, the firm paid the price.

SUMMARY

- A new SEI Level-3 key process area, named *"Management of Product lines, Architecture, and Reuse,"* has been proposed in this chapter for software reuse.

- Twenty-seven process areas have been defined under the headings of product-line management, technical processes, and management process to support the introduction of reuse concepts into organizations.
- In addition to affecting 12 existing CMM KPAs, we have proposed three new management-oriented process areas: patents management, supplier management, and reuse management.
- We have included a series of data flow diagrams to help you put the following reuse-based processes to work as you pursue a systematic reuse strategy: domain engineering, applications engineering, and asset management.
- Our case study discusses the typical compromises organizations have to make as they try to take our reuse KPA recommendations and transition them into use operationally.
- The hardest reuse process to implement is domain engineering.

REFERENCES

1. Donald J. Reifer, "Experience in Making the Transition to Product Lines as Part of a Process Improvement Program," *Conference on Software Process Improvement,* Irvine Research Unit in Software, University of California, Irvine, January 1997.
2. Department of Defense, *Proceedings DoD Domain Scoping Workshop,* Defense Information Systems Agency, September 1995.
3. Ruben Prieto-Diaz, "Domain Analysis for Reusability," *Proceedings of COMPSAC'87,* IEEE Computer Society, September 1987, pp. 23–29.
4. Software Productivity Consortium, *Reuse Adoption Guidebook,* SPC-92051-CMC, November 1993.
5. Software Productivity Consortium, *Process Definition and Modeling Guidebook,* SPC-92041-CMC, December 1992

Future Directions

HOW WILL REUSE BE AFFECTED BY NEW TECHNOLOGIES?

There is a lot of technology that can influence the software reuse strategy you select. Many people believe that a revolution in computing is occurring with a shift from the desktop to a network-centric programming paradigm [1]. Many believe that increased reuse will be stimulated by object-oriented methods and better software engineering environments. Others believe that advances in visualization and multimedia will usher in a new era of user-oriented programming. Still others argue that new interoperable client/server architectures, advances in open systems standardization, and intelligent agents will make enterprise-wide computing the rage in the foreseeable future. There are those from the artificial intelligence schools who brag that rule-based paradigms will soon come of age and be ripe for transition.

You should view technology advances as an opportunity. Each new development has the potential to make software reuse easier and more economical to accomplish. We will try to understand how technology potentially impacts reuse using the cause-and-effect diagraming techniques developed by Kaoru Ishikawa [2]. These fishbone diagrams shown in Figure 11.1 can be used to show how technologies relate to an organization's standard software process when it is aimed at realizing some goal, such as institutionalizing software reuse.

The main spines fanning in on the left of the fishbone portray the major enabling technologies that are driving, or whose absence is constraining, software reuse. Each technological development that contributes to the improvement of

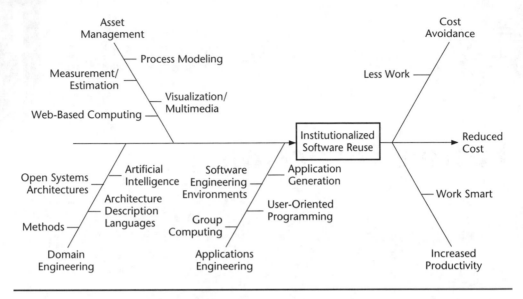

FIGURE 11.1 How technologies relate to an organization's standard software process.

these processes is shown as a horizontal spike that intersects the spines. The order in which the factors are presented has no significance. The ultimate effects or benefits are shown as spines fanning out to the top right of the fishbone.

Fishbone diagrams that look in detail at technologies that impact the activities that make up the process areas in the top-level diagrams are shown in Figures 11.2, 11.3, and 11.4. These diagrams build on the technology roadmap published last year by the DoD Software Reuse Initiative [3,4].

The 12 technologies listed along with their impacts in Table 11.1 seem to be the primary reuse enablers based upon our analysis of the current literature. The current status of each of these technologies is summarized along with an assessment of its future impact on software reuse in the paragraphs that follow.

Application Generation

Software systems can be generated using either a composition or generative approach. Composition refers to a megaprogramming concept that develops new applications primarily from libraries of reusable software building blocks. These building blocks can be either fine grained (data structures, mathematical subroutines, etc.) or coarse grained (entire subsystems, COTS packages, etc.). They can be either active (filters, scanners, etc.) or passive.

Generative approaches rely on reusable patterns in addition to building blocks. Executable code is generated directly using a very high-level language to

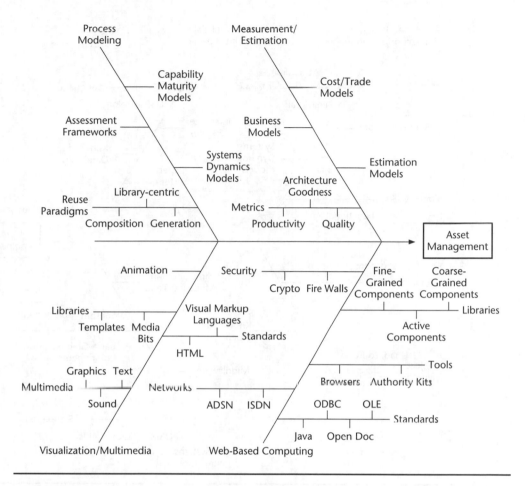

FIGURE 11.2 Asset management fishbone diagram.

specify the requirements for such patterns. Hybrid systems, such as the University of Texas's GenVoca [5] environment, have been developed to synthesize complex software systems from libraries of reusable components. Use of knowledge of semantic patterns, such as frames, assists in generating responsive solutions to user specifications. When perfected, the impact of such generators will be pervasive and will make software reuse easier.

Current Practice   The reuse of small, self-contained building blocks is common. Building entire systems consisting of off-the-shelf building blocks is not. Generators are being used to produce small applications for well-defined and behaved problems within mature domains such as manufacturing or accounting. They are

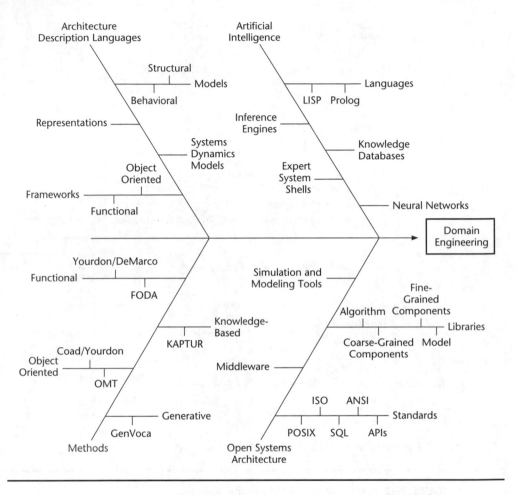

FIGURE 11.3 Domain engineering fishbone diagram.

not frequently used to generate large systems because of the large degree of variability involved. However, some positive experience has been reported when generators were used in conjunction with product-line architectures [6]. In addition, products such as Template Software's SNAP are entering the marketplace, which can be used to generate almost entire applications within targeted domains.

A reuse library system always seems to come first. As its use matures, the library contains the assets needed to create products from building blocks that can include components, frameworks, patterns, or generators. Generation is accomplished by specializing/instantiating building blocks using frameworks, patterns, and glue code based upon the domain model, the reference architecture, design decisions, and other information in the library.

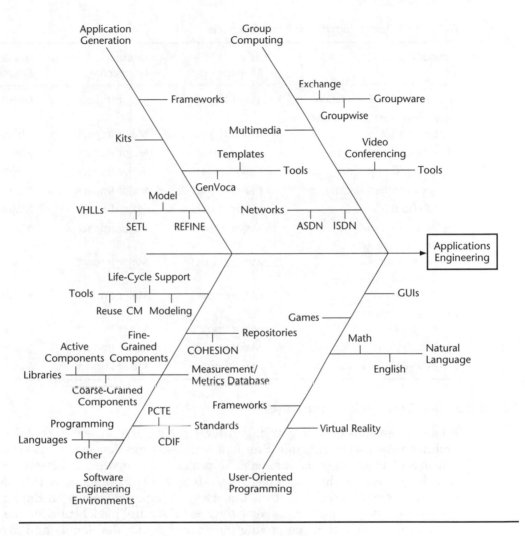

FIGURE 11.4 Applications engineering fishbone diagram.

Emphasis Areas As open or standards-based architectures become more prevalent, both forms of application generation discussed will eventually become more popular. This is especially true in distributed environments where the major computer and software vendors are making tool-building tools such as ActiveX readily available to system developers. Increased use of scripting languages such as Visual Basic will make composition of systems from building blocks easier. Generative approaches based upon patterns [7,8] hold a lot of promise.

TABLE 11.1 Technology/Reuse Process Impacts

Technology	Asset Management	Domain Engineering	Applications Engineering
1. Application Generation	Major Impact	Major Impact	Major Impact
2. Architecture Description Languages	Minor Impact	Major Impact	Minor Impact
3. Artificial Intelligence	Minor Impact	Major Impact	Minor Impact
4. Group Computing	Major Impact	Major Impact	Major Impact
5. Measurement/Estimation	Major Impact	Major Impact	Major Impact
6. Methods	Major Impact	Major Impact	Major Impact
7. Process Modeling	Major Impact	Major Impact	Major Impact
8. Open Systems Architectures	Minor Impact	Major Impact	Major Impact
9. Software Engineering Environments	Major Impact	Major Impact	Major Impact
10. User-Oriented Programming	Major Impact	Minor Impact	Major Impact
11. Visualization/Multimedia	Major Impact	Major Impact	Major Impact
12. Web-Based Computing	Major Impact	Major Impact	Major Impact

Architecture Description Languages

A lot of research is underway trying to develop ways to represent or model software architectures. As one example, Stanford University has developed an event-based, concurrent, object-oriented language for prototyping software architectures, called Rapide [9]. As another example, interesting work on languages that describe dynamic software architectures is underway at Imperial College in England [10]. This work is very important because these architectural models provide the underlying framework within the product-line paradigm for developing and exploiting reusable assets. Its future impact on domain engineering could be major.

Current Practice   There are many formalisms being proposed today for use in representing software architectural models within the universities. Unfortunately, most of these are tied to a specific methodology or research project. No standard representation currently exists that makes it possible for architectures to be shared. Most architects use requirements modeling systems that support these methodologies to perform their analyses and trades.

Emphasis Areas   Efforts to standardize architectural representations are important because they directly influence whether the assets that populate the associated structural framework can be reused. Research in such description languages will start to be tapped as more and more industry groups try to reach agreement on standards, such as CORBA [11] and ODBC [12], which can influence profoundly the client/server architectures of products sold competitively by the computer vendors (HP, IBM, Silicon Graphics, Sun, etc.).

Artificial Intelligence (Knowledge-Based and Expert Systems)

Artificial intelligence has been, and remains, the domain of researchers whose aims are to reproduce aspects of human intelligence on computers and thereby learn something about its nature [13]. This research has generated several languages (LISP, Prolog, etc.), tools (rule-based inference engines, frame-based templating systems, etc.), and techniques (automatic induction, self-explanation, etc.) that have proved useful in acquiring, structuring, analyzing, and exploiting knowledge. Work in neural networks and expert system shells has also matured. As currently used, artificial intelligence could have a major impact on domain engineering.

Current Practice Artificial intelligence technology has had but a limited impact on the software engineering community. The reasons for this are debatable. However, the results are not. Domain engineering is one of the few areas where some concentrated efforts have been mounted to use inference engines and artificial intelligence techniques to make sense out of domain knowledge. These efforts capitalize on experience with previous systems and designs [14] to derive rules that form the basis of the behavior of a domain model.

Emphasis Areas Using artificial intelligence techniques to understand the knowledge base and build domain models is important. So is the potential use of rule-based techniques to structure and optimize the contents of a reuse library, especially if it is network based. Frame-based techniques could have a major impact on applications engineering if their domains of applicability can be broadened, and they can be tied to advances in automatic programming.

Group Computing

A great deal of current research has been devoted to developing Internet-based tools, services, protocols, and design methodologies to allow teams of specialists from different locations and organizations to collaborate online to solve engineering problems on projects as the needs arise. Systems such as Argo [15] and Madefast [16] are examples of how government, industry, and academia researchers can partner to use the Internet to collaborate on projects, jointly develop work products, and archive results via the World Wide Web. As the paradigm shifts to network-based development, such groupware will have a major impact on how software is developed. Therefore, this technology can have a large potential impact on all three of our reuse process areas.

Current Practice   Currently, a messaging model is used for group collaboration via the Internet. Messages are sent as discussion groups are formed to solve specific engineering problems. Little use of multimedia is made and online hyperlinks to information and tools are practical only within the research community. Knowledge bases are not exploited and rapid prototyping of ideas is currently impractical due to resource limitations. Research is currently being pursued to figure out ways to overcome these problems.

Emphasis Areas   To permit teams to collaborate on development of software architectures and designs, access to virtual repositories of knowledge is needed. So are client/server tools that allow users to access catalogs of components, and rapidly build or model prototypes of their evolving designs online. Exploitation of multimedia technologies is also needed to enhance understanding through visualization. Animation and other forms of personalized communication are also needed to make interacting fun.

Measurement/Estimation

The switch over to object-oriented methods, increased focus on process improvement, and the drive to systematically reuse existing software assets has stimulated a lot of research in the fields of software measurement and estimation [17]. New cost-estimating models, such as COCOMO 2.0, and new metrics, such as object points, are being proposed [18]; which call for us to rethink the metrics we use to estimate cost, schedule, and technical performance. The use of COTS and emphasis on reengineering of legacy systems are changing the way we make our cost/benefit trade-offs. These changes can have a major impact on all three of the software reuse process areas under investigation.

Current Practice   In the late 1980s, measurement was the craze. During that time, many firms instituted metrics programs to improve software predictability and control. Now that software process improvement is the rage, most of these programs have been realigned to help measure the cost/benefits associated with the SEI ratings. Metrics-based management is one of the themes of SEI process improvement. Lots of good books and courses are available on the topic [19,20]. Measurement/estimation methods [21,22] and tools are available for those who wish to capitalize on what others have learned and commercialized. Unfortunately, most of what is available does not always work well for new technologies such as software reuse. As a consequence, many organizations are looking for new metrics and models that provide better insight into the cost/benefits associated with software reuse.

Emphasis Areas   New metrics and models for reuse are needed. These must provide support to the concept that more than just code is being reused. In addition, new technical measures that look at the goodness of such assets as architectures and *complexity* of object-oriented designs are needed. Probably the most overlooked area where additional effort is needed is legacy. We need better metrics to help us make decisions relative to the cost and desirability of reengineering versus rebuilding existing systems and their components.

Methods

Methods are important to software reuse. They convey the steps, representations, and rules that engineers follow to accomplish such tasks as domain analysis and design with reuse in mind. They structure the task and provide guidance on what to do, when, and how to evaluate the goodness of the products. These are pragmatic because they build on what works and discard what doesn't. Definition is needed to provide structure and order to reuse such processes as domain engineering and asset management. As such, progress in methodology development has a potential major impact on all of the process areas under investigation.

Current Practice   Quite a lot has been written on domain analysis methods [23]. Courses are available at the SEI and other places for those who want to learn the specifics of using one of the alternatives. The same holds true for applications engineering methods. Many of these methods are aimed at developing reusable components using specific languages [24], methods [25], or design approaches [26]. Some are functionally based, while others are object oriented. In the area of asset management, a wealth of methodology experience has been published on the topics of asset classification (using faceted and other schemes, etc.) and qualification [27,28].

Emphasis Areas   The software engineering field seems to have a surplus of methods, but guidelines for their selection and use and experience reports are lacking. We need to better understand which method to use to solve what problem. In addition, most of the methods used are not formally grounded. As progress is made in the area of architectural description languages, application of formal methods in reuse to address problems of security, privacy, and data integrity may be warranted, especially for distributed or network-based systems.

Process Modeling

Inserting software reuse into your existing systems/software processes is a delicate activity. You want to improve your processes, not disturb them. Models are needed to understand how the proposed reuse-based processes will work for you under a variety of conditions. These models should allow you to experiment with different options and operational concepts. They should let you try different scenarios and examine the results. They let you simulate the interactions of players so that you can decide on implementation tactics.

Current Practice   In conjunction with their process improvement programs, several organizations have built executable models to answer questions about the effectiveness of their proposed processes [29]. Several others have built repositories that store information about project experience with their process and process assets [30]. These organizations hope to optimize their process and move to higher levels of SEI process maturity based upon an analysis of the results and experience gathered from these activities over time.

Emphasis Areas   Because of the high degree of interaction between processes, new and innovative modeling techniques are needed to quantify impacts of optional selections on cost, productivity, quality, and time to market. The pioneering work of Forrester [31,32] and the application of system dynamics modeling concepts [33] might provide some of the insights needed to get a handle on the implications of process improvement decisions. Some of the experience gained in modeling processes for dynamic manufacturing applications might also provide useful insight within the software field.

Open Systems Architectures (Including Client/Server)

The move to open systems has been stimulated in recent years by the widespread adoption by the primary hardware vendors of standards and middleware. The availability of a full range of highly capable computer and communications hardware with good price/performance and user-friendly desktop software has stimulated the push toward client/server computing. The adoption of standards, such as POSIX, SQL, and CORBA, by the vendors has made it easier for application developers to port their systems from one platform to another. The availability of middleware and component libraries has accelerated the shift to distributed computing. Visual scripting languages, such as PowerBuilder and Visual Basic, have made reuse easier because they permit users to assemble applications from off-the-shelf building blocks that employ standard application program interfaces (APIs) [34]. Such APIs are important because they provide a wealth of distributed processing services (remote file access, remote procedure calls, etc.) that are transparent to their users. Impacts of the move to such distributed architectures could be pervasive, especially in the domain and applications engineering process areas.

Current Practice   Open systems and client/server architectures are in widespread use today in a variety of user shops. To take full advantage of these architecture, many firms are continuing to migrate their mainframe-oriented applications to client/server configurations. To free the applications from their platform dependencies, the underlying architecture for these configurations is segmented into layers using a service hierarchy. Middleware that rides on top of the operating system is used to provide basic distributed processing services (database, networking, security, etc.) and standard interfaces between the applications and the platforms. Libraries of standard components, tools, and building blocks are used to populate each layer of the architecture. When used as such, middleware personifies software building-block reuse at its utmost, because every application uses its services to perform their functions. Of course, others would debate this statement because they would argue that frameworks, patterns, and generators have higher potential yields. I agree and hope in the future that they will be right.

Emphasis Areas   Using service-layered architectures and middleware has its advantages and disadvantages. As software reuse is increased through the use of generalized building blocks, performance degrades. As the system grows and becomes more distributed, overhead may increase and response may take longer due to the effects of layering. Incorporating performance attributes as part of the asset description and building active rather than passive components are ways to address some of these performance issues.

Software Engineering Environments

Tools continue to be an important consideration because, in addition to automating tedious manual processes, they provide an effective means for technology transfer. While CASE tools have not lived up to all of their promises, they did deliver important repository technology that many of the vendors are using to integrate their products together and provide a wide range of support to developers across the software life cycle (support for analysis, design, coding, testing, maintenance, etc.).

In addition to productivity packages, such as Rational's ROSE [35] and Excel Software's WinA&D [36], several of the major tool vendors have linked their libraries to their repositories and provided bindings to POSIX and Windows. Others have created open interfaces so that third-party vendors could integrate their products with their repository. Better tools have the potential to make a major impact on all three of the software reuse process areas under examination.

Current Practice   There are lots of tools in the marketplace. Unfortunately, most of the packages that are available are methodology specific and provide limited support for software reuse. In addition, most of what is available for software reuse is not industrial grade. To automate software reuse functions, you will most likely have to use the first wave of research tools coming to market in a standalone manner. The major exceptions are component libraries. As already noted, such vendors as IBM, Microsoft, Oracle, and Sun are making libraries of active components available to support their clients who are using their products to develop software primarily for distributed, client/server applications.

Emphasis Areas   Integrating software reuse tools into the repository, and incorporating a reuse library that interfaces directly across the Internet (or intranet) with other libraries used for configuration management, knowledge exploitation, and version/release control, is imperative. Providing industrial-strength tools as part of an integrated software environment to support software reuse modeling, process improvement, domain analysis, application composition, and generation functions would add value to the process. Providing access to a wide range of reusable software assets, both fine and coarse grained, which your engineers can use to develop their products quickly and expertly is essential. Finally, providing integrated visual tools, animation, and multimedia capabilities along with those that support operating on Java applets is highly recommended.

User-Oriented Programming

The ultimate goal of user-oriented programming is to ease the professional programmer out of the loop. To accomplish this, vendors are arming users with context-sensitive tools to develop their applications. The vendors are employing visual languages, animation, and multimedia capabilities (see next paragraph) to make their products more user friendly and easier to use. Such tools enable users to employ voice recognition (especially when they can't type), exploit the power of natural languages (English, etc.), and use graphical/sound-bite libraries containing reusable building blocks. These techniques could have a major impact if they make it easier to find reusable assets and put them to work for applications written and fielded by nonprogrammers.

Current Practice   Visual languages, animation, and multimedia tools are just starting to be used in applications engineering. The authoring tools to create and use these techniques are just starting to be introduced to the market as part of the packages systems/software engineers use to create their products. For example, Corel has just provided an HTML (Hypertext Markup Language) editor and browser as part of Release 7.0 of WordPerfect. These capabilities are making it easier for engineers to prepare documentation that is accessible across networks. The visual and animation capabilities of desktop packages are also being used to provide context-sensitive help to confused users.

Emphasis Areas   Using natural languages and visual tools as part of your software engineering environment to take potential users by the hand through your software reuse processes and standards has merit. Providing visual and sound prompts tied to use cases does as well. Using templates to permit users to specialize frameworks for their specific needs is also highly recommended. Experience recently published about developing software from components without programming using a manufacturing application framework and templates reinforces this point [37]. Persistency permits users to capitalize on your underlying tools in language-independent ways.

Visualization/Multimedia

As already noted, visualization, animation, and the use of multimedia are providing the community with state-of-the-art delivery mechanisms that make the job of developing software easier. Standard visual markup languages are being proposed that permit application developers to exploit the power of graphics and sound across the Internet. Libraries of multimedia components (sound bits, video clips, animation demons, etc.) are just starting to come to market that make the task of production easier. Because this technology opens the software reuse door to nonprogrammers, advances have the potential to dramatically impact all three reuse process areas.

Current Practice   The use of visualization, animation, and multimedia is relatively new. Software vendors such as Microsoft and Oracle are using it to make their packages easier to understand and use. They are also teaming with large entertainment and publishing firms to create new markets for consumer products on the Internet. Application developers are just starting to use this technology to make their products more user friendly and provide context-sensitive help. As already noted, use has not been high because the multimedia authoring tools and associated libraries were not readily available until recently.

Emphasis Areas   This technology creates two types of opportunities. In its fundamental form, increased use of multimedia creates a demand for development of visual and sound-bite libraries that are highly reusable. These libraries make software development easier and more fun. Libraries of application frameworks, templates, frames, and other means of abstracting your users' views of their needs at higher levels are also possible. The second type of opportunity is in simplifying the reuse process. As noted previously, visualization/multimedia enables you to provide your potential users with a variety of context-sensitive help about the reuse process.

Web-Based Computing

The Internet (and intranets) has sparked a wave of activity in the computing community. These networks, some public and some private, act as highways that tie together consumers and suppliers of information technology in a value-added manner. Of course, there are many problems associated with the use of the Internet, because it is still in its infancy. However, use of this information highway accentuates software reuse because it provides its users with an economic means to promote, distribute, and lever the use of reusable assets across boundaries (physical, organizational, etc.). As such, this technology has major potential impact on the three reuse process areas under review.

Current Practice   A war is raging between the major suppliers of software for the Internet. On the client side, Microsoft and its allies are pushing to provide users with more Windows-based desktop capabilities and cheaper personal computers (PCs). On the server side, Sun and its allies are promoting the use of Java technology to handle much of the processing. Both camps are creating more opportunities for software reuse. Both call for the increased use of libraries of prebuilt reusable assets, including patterns for visual tools and generators, as part of their underlying operational concept [38,39]. However, assets for such libraries have been slow to appear on the market, because suppliers are reluctant to develop products for proprietary standards endorsed by such combatants as Java, ODBC, OLE, and OpenDoc. The vendors have responded by making these standards more open.

There is another interesting school of thought about the future impact of NCs on reuse. This pay-for-use school popularized by Brad Cox [40] argues that the shift to network boxes will make it more economical for software engineers to pay for the software they need to do their jobs (tools, libraries, reusable assets, etc.) on a per-use instead of a per-copy basis. Such a shift would make the move to an electronic shopping mall an eventuality. In addition, such a move would open up large markets on the Internet for reuse goods and services to small businesses and entrepreneurs.

Emphasis Areas   Siding with either of the combatants could be counterproductive. You must preserve your options as the battle rages. Undoubtedly, building-block libraries for your Internet, intranet, and desktop applications will appear as the market matures. Collections of active components (graphical viewers, filters, etc.) developed for specific client/server applications (inventory, publishing, etc.), called frameworks, will also appear on the market. As part of your reuse strategy, you might consider pursuing a dual-use strategy that calls for selling the component libraries you develop for internal use. Of course, you wouldn't do this if these frameworks provided you with some competitive advantage. As a cost-cutting tool, you might explore teaming or partnering with suppliers who would develop frameworks for your applications and market them openly.

These assessments were made by looking five years into the future. By then, the material in this book will probably be outdated. Hopefully, the research community will spawn new and more innovative technology to take its place. Your challenge is to take these technological advances and put them to work. Let's look at how you might go about doing this.

IMPACT OF TECHNOLOGY ON PRODUCT LINES

These 12 technologies have made a major impact on the movement to product lines. Open systems architectures have provided developers with the freedom to move their applications from one platform to another with relative ease. Architecture description languages, knowledge databases/inference engines, and such methods as domain engineering have made it simpler for domain analysts to specify architectures responsive to the wide range of requirements established for the product line. Application generators, metrics/measurement tools, object-oriented methods, process modeling, and modern software engineering environments have made it easier for applications engineers to generate software assets to populate these architectures. Visualization and user-oriented programming have gotten the users of the application involved in the development. Group and Web-based computing have made it possible for geographically dispersed teams of specialists to cooperate, coordinate, and jointly develop applications across the network. As one can infer from these trends, the major challenge firms face as they move to product lines is not the technology itself. Instead, it is putting in place the processes they need to harness the technology and put it to work within both its culture and an industry that is constantly going through paradigm shifts.

The major paradigm shift that is occurring that has the most potential impact on the move to product-line architectures is the network computers (NC) and the TV model of network distribution (i.e., push technology). These low-cost machines have the potential to alter the manner in which we process our application workload. Two decades ago, we saw the move to decentralized processing begin when personal computers appeared on the scene. A decade ago, we saw the transition accelerate even further as firms started to shift their processing from their mainframes (or minicomputers) to client/server architectures. As networking technology and the price/performance of PCs improved in the late 1980s, we saw firms distribute their applications further across enterprise-wide networks to personal computers acting as smart clients on the desktop, and workstations acting as local servers. Applications were partitioned and distributed in such a manner that they could be executed efficiently on both the server and the desktop. As the shift continues, we now see substantial portions of the application logic being centralized on the server in order to increase performance, reliability, manageability, and security within a client/server environment. We will also see networks being segmented into many parallel pipelines using new channelized distribution models to increase throughput.

NCs accelerate the trend toward centralization and Web-based computing even further by making simpler, low-cost computing devices that preserve a customer's investment in software available to replace the PC on the desktop. Software investments are preserved by deploying even more of the applications to the server, and allowing users to access them transparently from NCs via HTML browsers and Internet protocols. As previously noted, NCs pit the Sun Microsystem/Oracle JavaStation against the Microsoft/Intel/existing PC manufacturer's low-cost PC, which they call the reference platform [41]. Microsoft is discussing improvements to its Windows operating systems, which could include new ways for storing applications on servers connected to these low-cost reference platform PCs via the Internet (or intranets) as part of this initiative. Independently of who wins this looming battle in the future, architectures designed to segment the processing workload between the client and the server must be altered to reflect the trend toward increased centralization.

IMPACT OF THE WORLD WIDE WEB

As already discussed, another technology that is changing the way firms do business is the Internet. Many firms are evaluating using enterprise-wide and global networks both to overcome the obstacles associated with client/server computing and to move toward electronic commerce. Others are viewing the move toward network computing as a business opportunity. As an example of a firm that is harnessing the Web's power, National Semiconductor recently enhanced its customers' ability to download information about any of its over 30,000 products at anytime and from anywhere in the world by creating a Web site that provides fast, intuitive access to published data [42]. As an example of a firm trying to cash in on the movement to network computing, CyberCash is one of the hundreds of firms that have sprung up that are trying to capitalize on the opportunities to perform electronic commerce. Its mission is aimed at providing safe, convenient, and immediate payment systems for banks, businesses, customers, and individuals on the Internet [43]. As an example of potential widespread use, President Clinton promised to have the government attach every school in the United States to the Internet during the 1996 election campaign.

As with any new technology, the Internet has its problems. Its three biggest limitations are: security, bandwidth, and simplicity. Security is a major problem on the Internet. Once rejected as science fiction, the threat of hackers and sabotage looms larger and larger as firms depend more and more on computers to perform critical functions. Nobody can be sure that credit cards and other forms of financial information are protected. Vulnerabilities are pervasive and many firms are now employing techniques like key codes and crypto cards to ward off potential compromises. Firewalls are used to prevent messages from being intercepted. Yet, more research is needed because crafty hackers can defeat any of these measures.

Bandwidth impacts the user's ability to exploit the visualization and multimedia advances discussed earlier in this chapter. One second of compressed video takes as much as five minutes to download even when using a 28.8 or 33.6Kbps fast modem. As the Internet continues to get more and more popular, packet delays caused by growing traffic will increasingly limit its effective use. You can actually get more than 128Kbps with ISDN (Integrated Services Digital Networks) with compression techniques. Cable promises modem speeds of 3Mbps and better. However, use of ADSN (Asynchronous Digital Subscriber Networks) will probably be available along with cable, and it is also capable of data connection in the megahertz range.

Creating a site on the World Wide Web is a quite straightforward affair, but getting people to visit it is another matter. While would-be entrepreneurs are busy developing financing, marketing, and distribution models for electronic commerce, few are thinking of developing markets for reusable software assets. In addition, tool vendors are just starting to augment their software environments to provide network-based development and distribution support for reuse. The ASSET software reuse library has paved the way for electronic commerce in reuse across the Internet. Under government sponsorship, ASSET has been determining how to use existing technology to develop an electronic shopping mall for reuse. They have put their reuse catalog online and are marketing a variety of reuse services across the Internet. You can reach them at http://source.asset.com.

EDUCATION AND TRAINING IMPLICATIONS

Technology is reordering the economy. Alan Greenspan, Chairman of the U.S. Federal Reserve Board, calls the shift to the information age "one of those rare, perhaps once-in-a-century events." The WWW is dramatically altering how the workplace is structured and how it functions. As noted previously, the WWW is creating new opportunities for electronic commerce in the specialized area of reusable software assets. This switch over to Web-based computing is heralding a major paradigm shift in software development that must be supported by our education system. Setting up a Web site is just the beginning. Those who use the site must be armed with new skills, knowledge, and abilities. Job requirements are changing as new positions, such as network administrator and reuse coordinator, are being introduced into the workforce. Teachers are starting to incorporate the WWW and related new technologies into their curriculum and lesson plans. A concentrated effort is being mounted to increase the use of technologies, such as distance learning and collaboration across the Web, to deliver quality education and training.

University curriculums must be changed to address the needs of industry relative to reuse. Most colleges recognize that the SEI curriculum archetype [44] published in 1987 is out of date. Many schools have taken action to address the shortfalls. For example, the University of Houston-Clear Lake, working to meet the needs of NASA and industry, has updated its curriculum [45] to incorporate the following six recent advances in the body of knowledge, practice, and technology of software engineering into its graduate offerings:

- Increasing importance of process modeling, control, and improvement
- Increasing importance of formal methods
- Explosion in the manipulation, storage, and communication of information, particularly in connection with WWW and the so-called information highway
- Rising problem of legacy software systems and the associated reengineering needs
- Use of software for ever more demanding and critical applications
- Success of the object-oriented paradigm and the move toward methods that cover the full development cycle

As part of their curriculum-updating effort, the University of Houston-Clear Lake has incorporated the following two courses in their current catalog: Software Architecture, and Reuse and Reengineering. As the reuse knowledge base solidifies and good textbooks on the topic come to market, more colleges will follow suit. In the interim, the market for educating and training engineers in industry has been filled by several training firms. In addition, good training material is available free on the WWW via ASSET and the other points of contact listed in the appendices.

The Software Engineering Institute is also offering public courses for practitioners on the topics of open systems and domain engineering in 1997. Their goal is to transition courses to improve the practice of software engineering [46].

KEYS TO EXPLOITING NEW TECHNOLOGY

It is always fun to forecast the future. If you are wrong, nobody can fault you. After all, unpredictable things can happen in the near term that can make what appears obvious today irrelevant tomorrow. However, you don't want to be wrong when it comes to technology in which you are making major investments and on which you are counting to solve specific technical problems. Therefore, you want to make sure that the technology you are nurturing has a high probability of being successful (i.e., at least within the context that you hope to use it). The four things you can do to increase your odds of being victorious are:

- *Build Bridges*—Technology transfer has been described as a contact sport. People, not papers, transfer technology [47]. Practitioners work with researchers to take their results and mold them into products others want to buy. Compromises are made as team members collaborate with each other to develop the market demand and technology pushes needed to make research successful.
- *Increase Understanding*—You need to make sure that you and your staff fully understand the technology being considered and how you intend to use it to solve problems. You should counter the hype that goes along with any technology by realistically assessing the chances of success through the use of prototyping and other proven risk-reduction methods [48].
- *Emphasize Technology Transfer*—Lots of technology sits on the shelf and doesn't get incorporated into products [49]. To counter this phenomenon as you transfer the technology, consider the business environment into which the results of the research will be deployed as you try to take full advantage of the technical merits of the technology [50].
- *Time Transfer Properly*—Finally, make sure that the research results are available when you need them, or they will have little utility and go unused. Missed opportunities are nothing more than opportunities bungled.

CASE STUDY

When I took over the DoD Software Reuse Initiative in 1994, I sponsored an effort to develop a software reuse technology roadmap [3,4]. My goal was to define a software reuse technology investment plan that would:

- Identify those technologies that are critical to implementing software reuse in the DoD
- Assess the current and projected maturation of these critical technologies
- Recommend investments in specific technologies aimed at accelerating their maturation
- Make sure that the recommendations were consistent with the software technology plan being developed by another office within the Department of Defense

The process used to accomplish these three goals worked well. I had my support contractors develop the first version of the roadmap. To get cooperation and approval from the academic, industrial, and the research communities, I enlisted the support of experts and created a group of distinguished reviewers. As a separate action, I also got warfighters (service representatives with operational responsibilities; e.g., tank commanders, fighter pilots, etc.) involved in the exercise via an online chat group on the Internet. As the roadmap was developed, the authors refined their work based upon the comments by the distinguished reviewers. In parallel, I had the warfighters assess whether the roadmap met their needs and was on the mark. Their concerns, and those of my trusted advisors, allowed me to redirect the effort so that it was mission oriented.

Within a cause/effect framework, the analysis that led to the conclusions in the roadmap document were developed at three levels. First, the technologies judged to be critical to software reuse were identified by polling reuse experts from government and industry in a structured manner. To validate the findings, I asked my distinguished reviewers to evaluate the results. They looked over the findings, pointed out inconsistencies, discussed key points, and solicited additional input from the outside experts to reach a consensus. Second, maturity levels for these technologies were developed using the general maturation pattern and timeframe described by Redwine and Riddle in their classic paper [51]. These findings were again validated by my distinguished reviewers who gathered, reviewed the recommended maturity levels, and argued the results until agreement was reached on the output. Third, the technologies that were lagging and would best respond to DoD investment were defined based upon the following three criteria:

- Feasibility of use of the technology for software reuse within the targeted timeframe had been demonstrated.

■ Substantial evidence showed that the technology had value and was applicable to the mission of its targeted user community.

■ The technology was judged by experts to be at a point where it had been propagated to about 40 percent of its targeted user community.

As you can tell from these criteria, we were looking for technology with which we could get the most return from a near-term investment. Because of the softness of the evaluation criteria, considerable dialog between the experts from academia, industry, and the government was needed to reach consensus on the findings. Our distinguished reviewers and warfighters helped by providing insight into what made sense. While this process took a lot of time, the resulting recommendations were supported by all parties involved, including the warfighters. I am very proud of the team that developed this document, and feel it is a quality product. I encourage you to get a copy.

SUMMARY

■ The following 12 technologies have the potential to influence the software reuse strategy you select:

Application Generation	Process Modeling
Architecture Description	Open Systems Architectures
Languages	Software Engineering Environments
Artificial Intelligence	User-Oriented Programming
Group Computing	Visualization/Multimedia
Measurement/Estimation	Web-Based Computing
Methods	

■ Impact of these technologies on product lines was explained along with their education and training implications.

■ Impact of the movement to the Internet and adoption of the World Wide Web was explored.

■ The following four keys to exploiting these technologies for reuse were explained:

Build Bridges	Emphasize Tech Transfer
Increase Understanding	Time Transfer Properly

REFERENCES

1. Sun Microsystems, *Java Computing in the Enterprise,* White Paper, available online at http://www.sun.com/jav, 1996.
2. Kaoru Ishikawa, *Guide to Quality Control,* Quality Resources, 1982.

3. Software Reuse Initiative, *Technology Roadmap, Version 2.2, Volume 1: Technology Assessment,* Department of Defense, March 1995.
4. Software Reuse Initiative, *Technology Roadmap, Version 2.2, Volume 1: Implementation Plan,* Department of Defense, March 1995.
5. Don Batory, Vivek Singhal, Jeff Thomas, Sankar Dasari, Bart Geraci, and Marty Sirkin, "The GenVoca Model of Software-System Generators," *Software,* IEEE, September 1994, pp. 89–94.
6. James O'Connor, Catherine Mansour, Jerri Turner-Harris and Grady H. Campbell, Jr., "Reuse in Command-and-Control Systems," *Software,* IEEE, September 1994, pp. 70–79.
7. Paul G. Bassett, *Framing Software Reuse,* Yourdon Press, 1997.
8. Texas Instruments, *Assembling Components of Public Value,* Advertizing Brochure, 1996.
9. David C. Lukham, John J. Kenney, Larry M. Augustin, James Vera, Doug Bryan, and Walter Mann, "Specification and Analysis of System Architecture Using Rapide," *IEEE Transactions on Software Engineering,* Vol. 21, No. 4, April 1995, pp. 336–355.
10. Jeff Magee and Jeff Kramer, "Dynamic Structure in Software Architectures," *Software Engineering Notes,* Vol. 21, No. 6, November 1996, pp. 3–14.
11. Object Management Group, *CORBA 2.0 Standard,* Draft, 1995.
12. Microsoft, *ODBC Specification,* Draft, 1995,
13. John J. Marciniak (Editor), "Artificial Intelligence in Software Engineering," *Encyclopedia of Software Engineering, Volume 1,* John Wilcy & Sons, 1994, pp. 49–58.
14. Ted J. Biggerstaff and Alan J. Perlis (Editors), *Software Reusability* (e.g., see Section IIIB. for several related articles), ACM Press, 1989.
15. H. Gajewska, J. Kistler, M. Manasse and D. D. Redell, "Argo: A system for distributed collaboration," Proceedings of Multimedia 1994, Association for Computing Machinery, pp. 433–440.
16. Mark R. Cutkowsky, Jay M. Tenenbaum, and Jay Glickman, "Madefast: Collaborative Engineering over the Internet," *Communications of the ACM,* Vol. 39, No. 9, September 1996, pp. 78–87.
17. Shari L. Pfleeger, "Measuring Reuse—A Cautionary Tale," *Software,* IEEE, July 1996, pp. 118–127.
18. Center for Software Engineering, *Proceedings 11th International Forum on COCOMO and Software Cost Modeling,* University of Southern California, October 1996.
19. Lawrence H. Putnam and Ware Myers, *Measures for Excellence,* Yourdon Press, 1992.
20. Capers Jones, *Applied Software Measurement,* McGraw-Hill, 1991.
21. Center for Systems and Software Engineering, *ami Handbook,* South Bank Polytechnic, 1995.

22. Robert B. Grady and Deborah L. Caswell, *Software Metrics,* Prentice-Hall, 1987.
23. Ruben Prieto-Diaz and Guillermo Arango, *Domain Analysis and Software Systems Modeling,* IEEE, 1991.
24. Jerry D. Smith, *Reusability and Software Construction: C and C++,* John Wiley & Sons, 1990.
25. Bertrand Myer, *Reusable Software: The Base Object-Oriented Component Libraries,* Prentice Hall, 1994.
26. Balachander Krishnamurthy (Editor), *Practical Reusable UNIX Software,* John Wiley & Sons, 1995.
27. SoftTech, *RAPID Center Reusable Software Component Procedures,* Report 3451-4-326/4, available from the Army Reuse Center, June 1990.
28. Tung X. Bui, James C. Emery, Gerald Harms, Myung Suh, and Tina Van Hook, *A Clearinghouse for Software Reuse: Lessons Learned from the RAPID/DSRS Initiatives,* Naval Postgraduate School, Case Study Series on Implementation Practices, October 1992.
29. Software Productivity Consortium, *Improving the Software Process through Process Definition and Modeling,* International Thomson Publishing, October 1995.
30. Richard T. Bechtold, "Goal-Driven, Incremental Construction of Process Asset Repositories," *Proceedings of the Software Technology Conference,* April 1996.
31. Jay W. Forrester, *Principles of Systems,* Wright-Allen Press, 1968.
32. Jorgen Randers (Editor), *Elements of the System Dynamics Method,* The MIT Press, 1980.
33. Edward R. Roberts, *Managerial Applications of System Dynamics,* The MIT Press, 1978.
34. Shawn Butler, David Diskin, Norman Howes, and Kathleen Jordan, "Architectural Design of a Common Operating Environment," *Software,* IEEE, November 1996, pp. 57–65.
35. Rational, *ROSE Brochure,* 1996.
36. Excel software, *WinA&D Brochure,* 1996.
37. Hans A. Schmid, "Creating Applications from Components: A Manufacturing Framework Design," *Software,* IEEE, November 1996, pp. 67–75.
38. Eva Freeman, "Microsoft Stakes Out ActiveX Position," *Application Development Trends,* July 1996, pp. 76–81.
39. Michael W. Bucken, "Window of Opportunity," *Application Development Trends,* July 1996, pp. 82–85.
40. Brad Cox, "Market Processes: A New Foundation for Software Engineering," *unpublished paper,* available at http://www.virtualschool.edu/mon/cox.
41. Don Clark, "Microsoft, Allies to Propose Simpler PC," *Wall Street Journal Europe,* October 28, 1996, p. 6.
42. John Kador, "National Semiconductor Combined Java and a Search Engine to Find a Needle in a Haystack," *Internet Development Trends,* June 1996, p. 21.

43. Bill Pike, "CyberCash: the Net is money from secure electronic commerce," *Internet Development Trends,* June 1996, pp. 10–11.

44. Software Engineering Institute, *Proceedings of the 1987 SEI Conference on Software Engineering Education,* brochure, 1987.

45. Colin Atkinson, David Eichmann, and Charles McKay, *An Evolution of a Software Engineering Curriculum,* University of Houston-Clear Lake, available online from http://ricis.cl.uh/SE, 1996.

46. Software Engineering Institute, *1996-97 SEI Public Courses,* brochure, August 1996.

47. Jim Foley, "Technology Transfer from University to Industry," *Communications of the ACM,* Vol. 39, No. 9, September 1996, pp. 30–31.

48. Jean Scholz, "Technology Transfer through Prototypes," *Communications of the ACM,* Vol. 39, No. 9, September 1996, pp. 26–27.

49. Ellen A. Isaacs and John C. Tang, "Technology Transfer: So Much Research, So Few Good Products," *Communications of the ACM,* Vol. 39, No. 9, September 1996, pp. 23–25.

50. Allan Kuchinsky, "Transfer Means More Than Just Technology," *Communications of the ACM,* Vol. 39, No. 9, September 1996, pp. 28–29.

51. Sam Redwine and William E. Riddle, "Software Technology Maturation," *Proceedings of the Eighth International Conference on Software Engineering,* IEEE, 1985, pp. 189–200.

Special Topics in Software Reuse

This last chapter will discuss special topics pertinent to software reuse primarily in the area of government contracting and acquisition management. Commercial firms that acquire their software through partnering, subcontracting, and third parties will also find this material pertinent.

IMPLICATIONS OF COTS SOFTWARE

Commercial off-the-shelf (COTS) software is supplied by a third party who retains responsibility for its continued development and life-cycle support of the package. COTS software is used as is without change. It typically is a compromise solution that provides as much as 90 percent of what the user wants at a substantial cost savings. The government has stressed the use of COTS in its recent procurements and policy statements. The reasons for this emphasis are:

- Although it may not totally satisfy the user's requirements, COTS software can provide an acceptable solution for most problems.
- Because the supplier maintains responsibility for development and life-cycle support of the package, COTS software has a substantial cost advantage over its life cycle.
- Lots of COTS software is readily available to solve a variety of needs.

Use of COTS is a form of software reuse. Many COTS packages have been designed with reuse in mind. They are targeted for use by a general community, but can be specialized for use by a few. The main difference between COTS packages and reusable software assets is the manner in which they are managed. Reusable software assets are managed as a shared resource, while COTS software is managed as a purchased item. This means that when consensus is reached that change is warranted, reusable software assets can be changed much more easily than COTS.

The use of COTS by industry and government organizations has not been without its difficulties [1]. The majority of problems experienced to date could have been avoided by proper management. Let us take a look at some of the major difficulties and at ways of overcoming them.

COTS Software Doesn't Come Free

In earlier chapters, we saw that considerable effort had to be expended to evaluate, select, acquire, and manage COTS as part of your solution. The COTS lifecycle process was discussed and reviews and deliverables were highlighted. To get an adequate budget (e.g., time, people, and dollars), you probably will have to educate your management about the work that must be performed. To make sure shortcuts are not taken as COTS is assessed, selected, acquired, and deployed, you will have to incorporate steps, reviews, and practices into your organization's software process. Finally, you will have to hire smart buyers. These are purchasing agents who can work with your software engineers to put into practice the licensing and contractual innovations given in the next few paragraphs.

Entry Costs Low/License Costs High

The license fees for the first site using the package are reasonable. However, the fees mount as you scale up production or roll out the package for use by the rest of the enterprise. As the number of units or sites goes up, so does your bill. This is especially true for COTS packages that are licensed on a seat-by-seat basis. In addition, you may have to pay the fees over and over again when the vendor releases new versions of the package.

One way to reduce fees is to negotiate a basic ordering agreement or an enterprise-wide license with the vendor right up front [2]. These license fees are typically structured to give you deep discounts based upon usage or number of seats. Such discounts can be negotiated on a lot basis after you agree to purchase a minimum number of units. For example, you might get a 20-percent discount if you order between 50 and 100 units, and a 40-percent discount if the quantity is between 100 and 500. You can even negotiate a lid on the license fees. This means that after you acquire, say, 1000 seats, additional seats come free. Another approach that works well for large lot purchases is enterprise-wide licenses with which you handle the distribution onsite. You make the copies of the package from a master and distribute them along with copies of documentation to your users electronically.

Package Incapable of Meeting User's Needs

You select a COTS package that seems to be capable of satisfying most of your user's needs. You did a detailed analysis and reviewed the literature to make sure the capabilities of the package was on the mark. However, you soon find out from your users that the package doesn't perform as well as you thought it would after you purchase it. The features are there, but the performance isn't as the number of users increase. Most problems of this sort can be avoided by proper evaluation, benchmarking, and talking to users before you buy the package. Evaluators should continue to compare product features. They are important to your users. However, be sure to supplement the evaluation with a reference check with users. You will be surprised by how few people call existing users to discuss how they view the product. You'll also be surprised by the amount of advice you can get via an inquiry through one of the many news and chat groups that have sprung up on the Internet. Another technique that has worked well in the past is the trial license. Get your vendor to give you a three-month evaluation license for the package. Have your users try it before you buy it. Make sure that you and your users have defined evaluation criteria and that there is a plan in place. You will be glad you did.

Vendors May Go Out of Business

Be extremely cautious when dealing with COTS vendors who may not have the staying power or financial resources to continue in business. This caution is not limited to just small firms. Large firms that expand too fast, extend their resources, and have a cash-flow problem are just as suspect. But, you can't do a financial analysis on all the firms from which you buy COTS software. You don't have either the time or resources, and many of the vendors hold their financial information closely. However, take precautions when you exercise large package buys. For example, make sure that you have access to the source code via some escrow account should the vendor go out of business or stop supporting the product. You should also negotiate a *right to use another party* clause should you elect to contract for support with some other firm if your vendor's assets get tied up in the courts by some lawsuit.

Vendor Is Inflexible

You select a COTS package. After using it successfully, you identify a number of enhancements that your users need to perform their jobs. However, the vendor is reluctant to commit to a firm schedule for providing these capabilities. When you ask why, you get the following response: We have lots of users who want features. We prioritize what we put into our versions based upon usage or market demand. In other words, their biggest customers get what they want in the package first. That seems all right because that's good business.

But, let's say that your users say that the proposed functions/features are essential. How do you exert pressure, accelerate schedules, and gain leverage? After all, the option of replacing the package or acquiring a unique version for your users is unacceptable. Providing some sort of financial incentive seems to be the technique that works best. Show the vendor that you are serious by offering money or people. Reinforce the fact that you are an important customer in your market segment. Show them how the functions/features you are pursuing will increase appeal for their product within your market area. However, get commitments from the top, because salespeople will always promise you that the needed feature will be in the next version.

Vendor Support Is Unsatisfactory

Your users complain that COTS vendor support is poor. Every time they call, they get put off. Questions are left open and calls are not returned. Worse yet, the number of defects experienced when new versions are released are unacceptable. Your people are complaining that they have better things to do than debug the vendor's package. To avoid such problems, make sure that you consider past service records when you select your vendor. If the package is central to what your organization does, consider negotiating the level of service as part of your licensing agreement. For example, it is not unreasonable to ask for 24-hour response time to a user query. This can be easily satisfied by the vendor service representative saying: I don't know the answer but I will get an answer and get back to you by close of business tomorrow. If you are a large enough account, get your vendor to provide a dedicated customer service engineer that your users can call. There is nothing like personalized service. Protect yourself against latent defects in their products by negotiating some form of reliability warranty. This gives your vendors a limited time to correct a problem before you hold them liable for damages.

Package Addresses Your Core Competencies

Most firms avoid using COTS to perform their core competency functions. They develop their own packages for a competitive advantage. For example, an oil firm would gain little advantage using COTS software for exploration. Instead, it would build its own exploration software to increase its probability of finding oil before its competitors. As you can see, COTS software is primarily used for general business functions such as payroll and accounting.

Sometimes, growth, schedules, and other factors may force a firm to perform some of its core competency functions using COTS software. For example, a firm may elect to use COTS when setting up a factory because other options may be infeasible. Again, extreme care must be taken to ensure that whatever competitive advantage you are gaining due to processes and people is not jeopardized. You should negotiate some form of protection against disclosure of what you consider privileged information [3] or trade secrets [4] into your license agreements.

CHANGES IN GOVERNMENT CONTRACTING ARE NEEDED

The current business practices within government discourage software reuse. Software is typically acquired under contract, and contractors are paid either a fixed fee or by the hour to develop and/or maintain it. Focus is placed on the individual project, and the fee earned is used to motivate the contractor to deliver acceptable products, of which software is normally part, on-time and within agreed-to cost targets [5]. The more money spent, the more profit the contractor earns. If there is business volume, the contractor can make money even if the government reduces the fee because the contractor is behind schedule and/or overspending. Unless other incentives are offered, software reuse provides negative incentives to those doing the work, because fee is calculated based upon a reduced volume of work. In other words, why should contractors reuse when they can make considerably more money if they continue to do business as usual.

Three major changes are needed in order to correct this unacceptable situation. First, the government's focus must be changed from individual systems to product lines. What is optimal for a single project may not be appropriate for an entire product line. For example, all Army tactical systems use movement control software. This software directs resources (troops, tanks, artillery, etc.) to different locations on the battlefield based upon existing doctrine and need. In the current environment, each major tactical system would implement movement control separately even though a single system may make better business sense. The reason for this occurrence is that each Army system is funded separately by Congress, and the product-line manager for tactical systems, the program executive officer (PEO), has no budget to fund shared items. The only leverage the PEO has is his influence over the program managers (PMs) who control each project's budget. If the PEO can convince the PMs that building shared resources makes sense and is not risky for their project and to their careers, he may get someone to develop a common movement system. Of course, that doesn't mean that others would use it. To correct the situation, product-line managers need to be given a budget and more control over the projects within their purview. Such changes would enable the PEO to make the tough reuse decisions, fund their implementation, and enforce their continued use across the product line.

The second thing that must be changed is the process the government uses to acquire its software. These must stimulate software reuse by making it in both the government's and the contractor's best interest. Luckily, several groups have been working to resolve this issue for the past three years. The DoD Software Reuse Initiative sponsored the development of a business model for reuse[6]. This model incorporates reuse principles into the acquisition cycle of software-intensive systems within the DoD. In a separate but coordinated activity, the Reuse Acquisition Action Team (RAAT), working in conjunction with the DoD's Management Issues Working Group (MIWG) and the Industry Reuse Advisory Group (IRAG), has published a set of scenarios [7] whose aim is to demonstrate how to change the software acquisition process to stimulate and encourage systematic reuse within military procurements. Each of the 11 scenarios, which are briefly characterized in Table 12.1, serves as a basis for discussion between business and government leaders on how to acquire systems to take advantage of software reuse within the context of government procurements, using either a systematic or an opportunistic strategy.

The third set of changes that must be made are legal and contractually oriented. They revolve around changes in how the Defense Federal Acquisition Regulation Supplement (DFARS) is interpreted and invoked, especially in conjunction with their treatment of reuse of computer software and software documentation. The most important point to make to superiors about the DFARS is that the "Rights in Data and Computer Software" section supports software reuse as currently practiced [8]. Negotiation of terms and conditions of software use is a policy objective of the DoD. Moreover, the minimum data rights required in any acquisition of reusable software developed at private expense or mixed funding are adequate beginning points for negotiation between the government and industry. In other words, contracting officers could, if they desired, pursue any of the 11 acquisition scenarios listed in Table 12.1. You are probably asking, Why don't they? The answer is simple: precedence. Contracting officers are by their nature and training conservative people. Their job is to protect their clients from litigation. They deal with the law and are not risk takers. As a result, few of the contracting officers I've worked with have been willing to pursue reuse, because they feel they are paving new legal ground in the areas of intellectual property and liability. The problem that seems to surround software reuse is the impression that *legal issues* or *regulatory aspects* bar use of innovative practices. As just discussed, this notion is false.

Let's look at how we would go about adapting the DFARS for software reuse. The Software Development Agreement (SDA) is the mechanism used for addressing the intellectual property and rights in data issues. A draft is normally issued during the source selection, and the final is negotiated with the winning contractor team. As shown in the following, an SDA is organized as six articles and contains negotiated price schedules:

Article I—Definitions and Agreements	Article V—Payments
Article II—License and Warranty	Article VI—Installation
Article III—Software Maintenance	Schedule I
Article IV—Operating Environment	Schedule II

The SDA is characterized by the bargain achieved through arms-length negotiation with the contractor. It identifies the tasks each party is responsible to perform, payments and payment schedules, the rights of each party in the event of default or dispute over any of the terms of the contract, the mechanism to resolve disputes, and, most importantly, the terms and conditions associated with acquiring and maintaining reusable assets. To negotiate the SDA from a position of

TABLE 12.1 Software Reuse Acquisition Scenarios

Scenario	Characterization
1. Share Cost of Development	Develop system and assets under shared cost contract; government can reuse the architecture; contractor retains rights to market the reusable assets commercially
2. Provide Suitable Market Incentive	Government provides a large enough market to stimulate contractor to provide system and reusable assets that satisfies requirements at no cost to the government; contractor retains rights to market reusable assets
3. Develop via Shadow Project	Develop needed reusable assets through a separately funded and managed shadow project; separate funding line established; award fee used as incentive; rights negotiable
4. Develop via Reuse Libraries—I	Develop system from reusable assets in government reuse library; contractors generate reusable assets for libraries that when used earn them either a royalty or fee
5. Develop via Reuse Libraries—II	Develop system from reusable assets in government reuse library; stimulate reuse via incentive fees derived from savings due to reuse
6. Build Based on Proprietary Architecture	Procure based solely on contractor-owned, proprietary software architecture; contractor retains rights to the reusable assets developed under contract and domain model; government owns delivered system
7. Upgrade Based on Legacy Software	Upgrade system based upon legacy software; reengineer legacy to fit architecture; contractor retains rights to new reusable assets developed as incentive; government gets rights for delivered system
8. Develop under Security Concerns	Develop classified systems using a large, multicontractor team; sharing restricted to *inside the program;* government retains rights; outside use of architecture/assets not practical due to security concerns
9. Develop Prototype Using COTS/GOTS	Develop prototype system composed of COTS and GOTS software assets within an existing architecture; devise strategy for full-scale development based upon results; use of award fee as incentive
10. Develop System Using COTS/GOTS	Develop system using COTS and GOTS software for multiple government agencies; system cost is fixed price and is adjusted based upon the number of users; contractor gets maintenance job as incentive
11. Pursue Product-Line System Developments	Develop system to government-owned and managed product-line architecture; separate contractor teams develop the architecture/assets and application; government owns architecture/assets but provides contractor commercial rights as an incentive

strength, the team writing it should be familiar with the DFARS Data Rights Section 227.7013 and the relevant data rights contract clauses and policy provisions. In all, there are about 20 provisions in this section that are vital to any effort involving substantial software reuse. Negotiating the SDA is an exercise in risk management. You want to provide rewards for innovation and a lid on risk [9]. The basis for sound negotiation strategy for software reuse exists in the Data Rights provision of the DFARS (Sections 227.403-11(a)(3) and 227.401(17)). Further guidance in using the DFARS to support your SDA reuse acquisition strategy is found in the DLA handbook on the topic [10].

GET YOUR CONTRACTORS/SUBCONTRACTORS TO COMMIT

Software reuse should be considered early in the program as part of the acquisition strategy. This permits those acquiring the system to factor reuse concerns into their requirements, instructions for bidders, deliverables, schedules, and cost estimates. Considerations, such as those that follow, attract the bidders' attention and get both sides to commit to a reasonable reuse plan during negotiations.

Requirements

In the statement of work (SOW), have the contractor perform such reuse tasks as domain analysis and asset management. State your preference for COTS and reuse in the performance specifications that you use to communicate your users' needs to your bidders. Instruct the contractors to discuss their software reuse approach in both the technical and managerial volumes. Have them list their qualifications and those of their people to perform the proposed reuse tasks. Have them write up their reuse plans as part of the draft software development plan that they will submit with their proposals. Have them price their COTS separately and demonstrate its performance during the source evaluation process. Ask them to provide draft SDAs as part of their response to outline the terms and conditions associated with their proposed use of the COTS. After negotiations, make these part of the contract.

Instructions for Bidders

Make software reuse one of the primary factors (subfactors) you use to rate and rank proposals. Get the bidders' attention by stating in the Information for Bidders section that you are willing to negotiate your rights in technical data and computer software, and relax some of the normal contractual terms and conditions of the solicitation when it comes to use of COTS and software reuse to get concessions and save money. Require the contractors to flow the reuse requirements down to their subcontractors, teammates, and suppliers. Put the burden of proof on the contractors to propose an acceptable technical approach that satisfies your requirements while minimizing your risk. Consider using one of the software reuse acquisition approaches discussed earlier in this chapter to stimulate increased reuse by providing the contractor with financial incentives (increased fee, royalties for usage, etc.) to produce less software. Require the contractors to finalize any negotiations for the use of COTS prior to the award (e.g., get their suppliers to sign basic ordering agreements that offer deep discounts on their packages).

Deliverables

Have the bidders put their software reuse proposals in writing during the proposal evaluation phase. Then, make what the winner proposes part of his contract. This gives you legal recourse should the contractor fail to fulfill his obligations as the contract unfolds. Schedule delivery of reuse plans and reports called for in the SOW on the contract data requirements list (CDRL). Get the bidders to propose delivery schedules for assets. Consider requiring COTS demonstrations during source selection and at critical times during the program. Call for results of make/buy trade studies. Make sure that you put enabling clauses into the contract, which enable third-party experts of your choosing to review draft deliverables and to perform independent testing and analysis. Else, they may have to wait to do their job until after the final deliverables are approved. Do whatever you can contractually to get visibility into and control over the winning contractor's/subcontractor's reuse processes.

Schedules

Consider conducting either a CBA IPI (CMM-based appraisal for internal process improvement) or SDCCR (software development capability/capacity review) as part of the source selection process to make sure that the bidders have acceptable software reuse capabilities and a set of reuse practices that are in widespread use throughout the firm. In addition to scheduling the reuse deliverables called out by the SOW, require your contractors to conduct a software architecture review early in the program. The purpose of this review is to make sure that the architecture is stable and that the proposals for the use of COTS and development and use of reusable assets are justified. Require your contractors to periodically deliver reusable assets to a government software reuse library during the contract. If you don't, you may have to wait until the end of the contract to take such delivery. Make the contractors commit to dates, then hold the winner to the schedule proposed.

Cost Estimates

Depending on your acquisition strategy, set definitive reuse goals and have your contractors estimate the range of costs that can be saved if their plans are realized. Then, propose a fee schedule that rewards the winner for generating less software. Because you need to establish a should-cost estimate, generate a range of costs based upon levels of reuse using one of the models discussed in Chapter 6. This should create a fair basis for comparing offers from different bidders. Make sure that you precisely define what you mean by reuse in the solicitation, and specify the bounds for the estimates so that there is no confusion over what is meant by terms and SOW taskings. For example, define what you mean by a source line of code. Specify the term for a COTS license. Do everything you can to minimize the liberties different bidders take with definitions to make their offers look good.

The only commitments that contractors make that hold up in a court of law are those that are part of the contract. As a consequence, you must do everything you can to get contractors to put into writing what they proposed during the source selection process. You also must specify your requirements as completely as you can in the solicitation so that the contractor has no recourse but to keep his promises. With these items in hand, you have the legal backing you need to get your contractors to fulfill the commitments they made in the contract. For those interested in this topic, further guidance can be found in the DoD Software Reuse Initiative's *Program Manager's Reuse Issues Handbook* [11].

MANAGE REUSE IN A CONTRACTUAL ENVIRONMENT

Software acquisition management is the process of ensuring that software that is being developed for you under contract satisfies your specification. Your job is to tell your contractors what you want, not how it should be developed. Your contractor's task is figure out how best to meet your requirements. They can accomplish this in any number of ways. That's their decision. What's important to you is that the product fulfills your requirements, works, and is delivered on time and within agreed-upon cost targets. To ensure you get what you want, you set in place systems and procedures to oversee what they do, and review their work in process. The primary tools you have at your disposal are your specifications and contract. These spell out exactly what your contractors have committed to do, what will be delivered, when, and how disputes will be adjudicated.

When I think of acquisition management, I think of hiring a general contractor to manage the building of a house. You start by furnishing the plans (specifications) and agreeing on a price and schedule. The general contractor will then subcontract to get the right people (plumbers, roofers, electricians, etc.) involved at the right times to realize your plans. If you change the plans, the cost and schedule may be altered. As the house is built, you may visit the construction site many times to make sure shortcuts aren't being taken, the work is not poorly done, and the materials that you've specified are being used. The house is also inspected periodically by the local authorities, who make sure that the house is being built per approved plans and that building codes are being followed. If the house is late or exceeds cost estimates, you use the contract as the basis of settlement. You might have to accept the delay if it was caused by circumstances outside of the contractor's control.

Needless to say, the house analogy seems to hold true for software as well. Unfortunately, measuring software progress is much harder to do than determining how far you've advanced as you build a house. You can see the house coming together. That isn't always the case for software. Luckily, we have made some progress in software acquisition management during the past few years. Some of the tricks that we've learned that you can use to make a better assessment of your software reuse progress follow.

Make Software Progress Visible

Break the reuse work defined in your WBS down into small pieces. For each task, define a deliverable (document, demonstration, etc.) that shows that the task has been satisfactorily completed. Keep track of the deliverables. Plot trends and investigate variances associated with them. Understand that reuse projects get into trouble a little at a time, not all at once. Seek out the problems and resolve them head on.

Hold Frequent Reviews

Have the developers show you their progress at critical points in the reuse process. Make sure that the products of one stage of development (requirements, architecture, etc.) are stable before you move into the next stage. Talk frequently with the developers to gain insights into where they think the reuse problems are. Try to distinguish between fact and fiction by digging into the details when you suspect something is amiss.

Use Earned Value Concepts

Actual spend lines can be deceptive because the only thing they tell you is how much money you actually expended against your budget. Earned value techniques let you find out the truth by relating actual expenditures to technical achievements, as determined by milestone completions [12]. You can use milestone completion frequency and volume data to plot the trends and determine your current rate of progress.

Collect Meaningful Metrics Data

Relying on milestone completion rates alone may be a mistake. Other measures of performance are needed to supplement and confirm earned value predictions for reuse tasks. For example, completion of a work package may be in trouble because of staffing or budget difficulties. You may have found it difficult to find people with reuse experience, or you may have not budgeted enough to cover the true costs of reengineering legacy code. In both cases, you might have been able to predict the problems if you captured data on metrics, such as staffing rate, rework rate, or change rate.

Remember, the specification and contract are the basis for settling disputes. If they don't support your argument, give them up. Instead, place your attention on negotiating equitable changes to these documents to support your case. After all, they form the legal basis of everything you can reasonably expect your contractor to perform. For those interested in more information on this topic, further guidance can be found in my and John Marciniak's text on acquisition management [5].

MEASURE PERFORMANCE AND ALLOCATE FEE

The contract establishes how and when fees will be allocated and distributed. The type of contract and terms and conditions negotiated during source selection determine how performance will be measured and fees dispersed. There are two basic types of contracts used in government procurements: fixed price and cost reimbursement. Under a fixed-price contract, the government pays the contractor a fixed sum for the goods and/or services agreed upon. Because the price is fixed, the contractor assumes the risk. Profit is a direct function of his ability to keep costs under control and deliver an acceptable product for less than the price paid.

Under a cost-type contract, risk is shared because the government agrees to reimburse the contractor's allowable costs, plus a reasonable profit. Different fee schemes are used to motivate the contractor to keep down costs and deliver an acceptable product. The four primary types of fee schemes that are commonly used include fixed fee (you earn based upon what you spend), incentive fee (your fee can vary based on how well you manage your costs), award fee (your fee varies based upon how well you perform against subjective evaluation criteria), and cost sharing (you earn no fee). As you might expect, most contracts that require software reuse are of the cost-reimbursable type.

The contractor is responsible for satisfactory performance relative to the work called out in the contract. The acquisition agent closely monitors the contractor's progress to ensure that the requirements are being satisfied and problems that occur during development are eliminated. The acquisition agent maintains visibility into and control over the contractor's performance, using controls like those noted in the previous paragraph and Chapter 8. Cost, schedule, earned value, and other technical performance information is used by evaluators to determine what percentage of the fee the contractor has earned. If overall performance is unacceptable, the fee for a period can be zero. If performance is superior, the fee could be set to its maximum level.

Some of the criteria organizations have used in the past to measure software reuse performance as part of the fee-determination process include:

- Level of reuse achieved (actual percentages versus planned by project or product)
- Rate of reuse progress (actual percentages achieved versus planned)

- Cost (or schedule) savings attributable to software reuse (actual savings versus planned)
- Improvement to software quality attributable to reuse (actual gain versus planned)

CASE STUDY

In early 1994, a government agency ventured forth to acquire a prototype of a sensor system that would be used in the next generation of aircraft, such as the U.S. Joint Strike Fighter (JSF). The agency didn't have much money, but created a lot of interest on the part of the avionics houses because the requirements for this sensor were considered state of the art. A technical demonstration was planned early in the project. The agency wanted to prove that a COTS processor, such as a DEC Alpha or a Sun machine running a standards-based operating systems based upon POSIX, could handle the high-performance, mode-dependent data processing requirements of the sensor. They hoped to use a militarized version of one of these COTS processors to control their next-generation sensor. They also wanted the winning contractor to establish a testbed so that they could evaluate several candidate approaches for addressing their avionics legacy problem. They had a large quantity of existing avionics software written in a variety of programming languages for proprietary machines that they wanted to reuse with the minimum amount of rework possible.

The agency issued a broad area announcement (BAA) in the *Commerce Business Daily,* requesting interested firms to submit a 10-page white paper summarizing their technical approach. In addition to specifying the top-level requirements, the BAA established that this project would explore use of networks/groupware for management and require cost sharing. More than 10 white papers were received. However, only two of them were deemed worthy of further exploration. The government invited both contractors to submit a proposal that detailed their concepts. The six criteria against which the proposals would be evaluated in their rank order were:

1. Responsiveness to requirements
2. Soundness of technical approach
3. Degree of software reuse
4. Qualifications of technical team
5. Risk to the government
6. Degree of cost sharing

Both contractors came back with excellent proposals. However, the winning proposal had the following seven innovative ideas relative to software reuse.

Software Architecture First

Instead of focusing on hardware evaluations, the contractor proposed to spend much of the early effort defining a suitable software architecture (from a domain model based upon past experiences in the sensor field). Because there was a requirement to preserve previous software investments, they preferred placing an emphasis on architecture. The designers argued that they could experiment with the hardware later when they knew more about what was required to solve the software problems.

Rapid Prototyping on Both a Simulator and a Bench

The contractor also proposed using simulation to experiment with the architecture before a hardware prototype was built. He felt that this would make it easier to look at such trade-offs as the effect of different cache sizes on performance. In parallel, he also developed a rapid prototype to assess the quality of the COTS-supplied tools that the hardware vendors supplied before they were used to develop the actual prototype. In retrospect, this is an often overlooked item that can have a major impact on software productivity. The most capable hardware is useless if it can't be easily programmed to perform its intended functions.

Feasibility Demonstration of Architecture

The contractor also proposed to use the Universal Network Architecture Services (UNAS) system [13] developed by TRW and marketed by Rational Software to build rapid prototypes of candidate architectural configurations on the testbench. This was deemed very important because a number of system architectures were being considered to satisfy the peak loading performance requirements of different weapon systems. The contractor proposed to simulate first to configure the architecture to the problem, and then to benchmark performance on the UNAS prototypes using MATLAB math models and target generators to determine what worked best under different loading scenarios. As an option, a man-in-the-loop simulator could be added, in which the pilot would interact with the system through a mockup of his actual controls and displays.

Hard Performance Data

The contractor also proposed to instrument the testbench to capture performance data in real time using fast associative memory devices wired to the bus, which would not load down the COTS processors under loading conditions. Again, this capability was believed to be important because nobody wanted to allow measurement processes or devices to bias the test results. While associative memory data recorders are not a proven technology, the contractor presented enough field evidence in his proposal to make evaluators think that the concept had merit and warranted further exploration.

Innovative Legacy Approach

When it came to the avionics software legacy problem, the contractor proposed an innovative approach. Instead of using traditional reengineering approaches that are based upon reverse engineering of graph models of the software's structure, the contractor proposed to use a frame-based conversion approach. Because most sensor software can be conceived as a large number of cooperating processes interacting and communicating in real time to process large quantities of data, the contractor felt they could repackage processes using frames to develop new packages that were nothing more than encapsulations of the data that were being operated upon. As communication between packages was handled by message passing, these packages would be perceived as object-oriented collections of mathematical routines that could be mechanized in a straightforward manner using object-based languages such as C++ or Ada 95.

Reconfigurable Software Engineering Environment

The contractor proposed using a secure intranet to tie together his geographically dispersed team and the government during the development. The government would have access to the work in process. All deliveries would be electronic (i.e., paperless). Groupware would be used along with video-teleconferencing across the network to cut down on travel costs. Most importantly, the environment itself was rich and robust. Although it was built using COTS tools and repositories, it was configurable based upon the software engineering processes used. When either a reuse- or legacy-based process was instantiated, the environment could be configured with tools and libraries to support it. When test and performance analyses were invoked, the environment could be tied to the test-bench and reconfigured to provide drivers and other forms of assistance. Use of this configurable approach seemed to simplify tool integration, and permitted engineers from different disciplines to operate with the same software versions and on the same test data.

Dual-Use Approach

The contractor also demonstrated how his solution could be adapted and sold to commercial airplane companies. Planes today have many sensors aboard (GPS, airborne radar, etc.). Commercial pilots, like their military counterparts, need to be able to fuse sensor data quickly to react to it, especially when passenger safety is involved. Use of COTS processors and software could reduce the cost of such sensor fusion systems so that they were affordable for small aircraft (executive jets, commuter planes, etc.). Because such aircraft represent a large and potential lucrative market for such developments as those called for in the BAA, the contractor was able to generate a business case, justifying joint investment in the technology. As part of the business case, the contractor enclosed three letters from aircraft manufacturers, stating that they would buy such systems and flight test them for potential sale should the government fund the development. In other words, the contractor showed the government how the proposed development would solve its and industry's needs at the same time (i.e., dual use). As the capstone, the contractor proposed to do the job in three phases using the following formulas, which he justified based upon risk sharing:

Phase I—Feasibility Demo	Government 100 percent
Phase II—Preproduction	Contractor 50 percent, Government 50 percent
Phase III—Commercialization	Contractor 100 percent, Government 0 percent

Negotiating the contract with the contractor was fun. Of course, there was considerable give and take on both sides during the sessions. But, the atmosphere was constructive, not combative, and everyone was excited about the prospects for success. The government had a very forward-looking contracting officer (the buyer) involved. He was not afraid to try new contracting approaches based upon the spirit of acquisition reform. The type of contract negotiated for Phase I of the effort was CPAF (cost plus award fee). It was selected because it provides suitable financial incentives for subjective topics. Under this form of contract, the buyer establishes a number of performance criteria in areas that are hard to measure (ease of use, degree of reuse, software quality, etc.). The buyer and contractor then agree on a fee structure based upon ratings of these factors. There is typically a base fee and an award amount. The base fee is fixed and does not vary as a function of performance. However, the award fee does and can be used to motivate the contractor to excel in specified areas, such as reuse, using the criteria of performance established through negotiation.

The base profit in this case was set to 2 percent of the target cost. The maximum profit that could be earned was set to 20 percent of the target cost. To maximize the incentive, the fee was set much higher than allowed by law in a comparable cost-plus-incentive-fee (CPIF) contract using the CPAF approach. The actual award would be determined through a quarterly evaluation by an award-fee board, using criteria established for each of the proposal evaluation factors. In the case of degree of software reuse, a 10-percent goal was established as nominal. Then, targets were set and fees assigned as follows: 20 percent reuse/5 percent fee; 30 percent reuse/8 percent fee; 40 percent reuse/10 percent fee; 50 percent reuse/12 percent fee; 60 percent reuse/15 percent fee; and 70 percent reuse/maximum fee. Assets that could be reused included architectures, requirements, designs/algorithms, code/libraries, tests/test cases, and models/tools/instrumentation. Measurement of reuse would be done using a scheme to be negotiated. The contractor was to propose such a scheme within 30 days in the update of his draft software development plan. The government would either approve or counter with proposed modifications.

This contract is currently under way. Of course, I have taken liberties with the facts presented to keep the identity of the government agency and the contractor team private. Not everything stated happened as discussed. But, many of the facts and ideas in this case study are true and presented in the spirit of showing how one can innovate to put a lot of the principles discussed in this book into practice in a government contractual environment. The use of secure networks to tie together the contractor and government into a paperless environment with video teleconferencing is singled out because it worked extremely well. Many of the delays experienced on similar projects of this size waiting for delivery by couriers of key documents were avoided.

The major problem that always seems to occur in contracts of this type revolves around measurement issues. Disputes tend to occur when award fee is based upon subjective factors such as software reuse. Jointly solidifying the measurement scheme for such factors right up front goes a long way to reduce the eventual friction, but it doesn't eliminate it entirely. This is especially true on jobs such as this one, where the profit earned can vary between 2 and 20 percent. My recommendation is to work with your customer in the beginning to establish the best measurement scheme you can. You will find the effort expended worth the pain experienced.

SUMMARY

- Government contracting that involves the management of the acquisition of software through third parties poses several unique challenges when it comes to software reuse.
- Although its use can be potentially beneficial, COTS software must be managed carefully to overcome known difficulties.
- The three major changes that must be made in government contracting to support reuse include: Increase the focus on product lines, use reuse-based acquisition scenarios, and adapt the existing DFARS for software reuse.
- To get the contractors' attention and commitment, software reuse considerations must be incorporated into both the solicitation and any contract that results from it.
- You can manage software reuse effectively and allocate fee in a contractual environment using your existing control tools (earned value, reviews, etc.).

REFERENCES

1. R. L. Langley, "COTS Integration Issues, Risks, and Approaches," *Technology Review*, TRW Systems Integration Group, Vol. 2, No. 2, Winter 1994, pp. 4–14.
2. John J. McGonagle, Jr., *Business Agreements*, Chilton Book Company, 1982.

3. Tobey B. Marzouk, *Protecting Your Proprietary Rights,* IEEE Computer Society, 1976.

4. James H. A. Pooley, *Trade Secrets,* American Management Association, 1987.

5. John J. Marciniak and Donald J. Reifer, *Software Acquisition Management,* John Wiley & Sons, 1990.

6. DoD Software Reuse Initiative, *Software Reuse Business Model Technical Report,* U. S. Army Space and Strategic Defense Command, January 1995.

7. Reuse Acquisition Action Team, *Software Reuse Acquisition Scenarios: A Discussion Paper,* Association for Computing Machinery, July 1994.

8. DoD Software Reuse Initiative, *Policies, Laws, and Regulations Affecting Software Reuse in DoD Instructor Manual,* Defense Information Systems Agency, 1995.

9. DoD Software Reuse Initiative, *Risk Assessment and Mitigation Procedure (RAMP) Final Technical Progress Report,* U.S. Army Space and Strategic Defense Command, January 1995.

10. Defense Logistics Agency, *Software Reuse Handbook, Version 1.0,* Office of Counsel Columbus Region, October 1994.

11. DoD Software Reuse Initiative, *Program Manager's Reuse Issues Handbook,* Defense Information Systems Agency, August 1995.

12. Donald J. Reifer, *Software Management, Fourth Edition,* IEEE Computer Society, 1993.

13. Rational Software, *Universal Network Architecture Services,* brochure, 1996.

Exercises and Student Projects

CHAPTER 2

Exercises

1. Explain why you believe a vision and strategy needs to be written for your organization.
2. Which strategy would you select? Why did you select it? What were the selection criteria you used?
3. Develop an annotated outline for a white paper you would prepare to communicate your vision and strategy. Provide more detail than that contained within the chapter.
4. What approach would you use to sell reuse in your firm?
5. How would you modify the sales presentation in Figure 2.1 to support your vision and strategy? Suggest modifications and new charts.
6. Under what circumstances would you generate a white paper? Explain why you do not believe all of the recommended documentation is needed.

Student Project

This project was written to help you understand what was presented in this chapter more fully. Instead of asking questions, it directs you to develop a product as a learning exercise. This product could be generated by individuals or a team either as a class project or for fun.

You are convinced that reuse makes sense for your firm. You've done your homework and believe that you could save as much as one staff year of effort during the first year on your project alone just by putting a reuse library in place to facilitate sharing of existing software assets. You are developing a lot of screens and reports for an online application. You have decided to generate each of these as an object from class libraries. You have developed an object manager to dispatch and schedule objects. This piece of software was designed to be portable across platforms. It runs on top of both Windows and POSIX, and was designed using client/server concepts to be highly portable across workstations and the desktop. You believe the object manager and your human interface architecture to be highly reusable as well. Two other projects are currently using it as is.

Unfortunately, your boss is not a fan of doing anything new. He is very schedule driven and continues to warn you to focus on the job at hand. You need to get him into your camp. Else, you will never be allowed to take your concepts further.

Create a presentation aimed at convincing your boss of the merits of reuse on a broader scale than just his project. Make sure you tell him what he will gain personally if he cooperates. You have 30 minutes on his calendar tomorrow afternoon. You want him to reassign you to a task to develop a reuse library that all projects within your software shop can use. This will mean he will have to find a replacement to take over your current job. You are positive he will resist reassigning you right away. You will have to work hard to convince him of the merits of your proposal.

The key to a compelling argument is to show your boss how what you propose will help everyone. Make a strong case and give him reason to agree with you. This will make reassigning you to the reuse task more palatable.

CHAPTER 3

Exercises

1. Explain why an operational concept document needs to be written for your organization.
2. What paradigm would you select? Why did you select it? What were the selection criteria you used?
3. Develop an annotated outline for a white paper you would prepare to communicate your operational concepts. Why did you elect to develop a white paper instead of an OCD?
4. What additional technical, managerial, or technology fanout factors would you add to the OCD outline that appears as Plan of Action 3.1? Why? If you have none, why not?
5. Why is it important to focus on key process areas in your discussions? Why are they important? Why is it important to scope revisions to them and not to the practices that implement them?

6. What technical concepts would you advocate to implement a middleware paradigm?
7. What management concepts would you utilize to implement the middleware paradigm?
8. How would you go about applying results from a pilot project to the rest of your product line? How would you build the required knowhow?
9. How would you address issues associated with updating an existing product line to a preferred architecture in your OCD? Will dual operations be involved? How would you get the customers/users on-board?
10. What did you or did you not like about the 11 principles and the tactics suggested for instituting change? Can you suggest a better approach? If so, do so.

Student Project

Congratulations, your briefing to your boss was very successful. He liked your taking the initiative. He believed the climate was ripe for implementing what you proposed. He loved it when you told him that the reuse library would make him stand out and give him an edge for promotion. He liked what he heard but wanted more details before he would give you the go-ahead for your proposal. During the briefing, he asked you to provide him with the following information:

■ Describe the steps you will follow to figure out what assets to put into the library. Who would you involve and how would you get consensus on the decisions?
■ Describe the steps you will follow to take assets from a project and make them available for widespread use via the reuse library. Tie these steps to the typical actions a reuse library user would follow to put assets into the library, and take assets from the library. Identify the subsidiary processes and their inputs and outputs (asset classification, qualification, etc.).
■ Describe the steps you will follow to make what you have in the library widely known.
■ How will you pay for the library? Will you acquire the library tools using your capital budget? Is one of the projects willing to pay to set it up and get it running? Will you tax projects to keep it going once it goes operational? Will you charge users on a fee-for-service basis to recoup your operational costs?

When asked what he wanted, your boss said: For the three processes, provide me with a set of data-flow diagrams or something equivalent that shows the steps you will take, what the inputs and outputs will be, and what the dependencies are between activities. For the last question, draft a short memo providing me the options and your recommendation.

In essence, what your boss has asked you to prepare is the nucleus of your OCD. He wants to know how you would use, operate, and pay for the library once you got approval to develop it.

CHAPTER 4

Exercises

1. How would you attack management issues in your firm?
2. How would you handle reuse technical issues in your firm?
3. What are the three Ps and why is viewing the relationships between them important?
4. Is taking an applications development perspective the right approach? If not, why not?
5. What organizational option would you use to mount your initiative? Why? List what groups you would make part of the initiative. Discuss their roles and responsibilities.
6. Develop a list of the tools you will need to support domain engineering and architectural initiatives that your firm is mounting.
7. Why is it important to incorporate tool support for your methods in your software engineering environment?
8. What incentives would you use to motivate your troops to use assets developed by others?
9. How would you stimulate program managers to build reusable assets for others?
10. How would you go about transitioning early project successes across your firm? Define the process you would use and justify it based upon results.

Student Project

Your answers to your boss's questions were just right. He liked them. Of course, he quizzed you for about an hour, but you passed the test with flying colors. He gave you an idea that he wants you to run with. He said: Why don't we see if we can get Sandra to help us? Sandra runs the biggest line of business in the firm. If you can get her support, resources will not be a problem.

As you are about to leave your boss's office, you ask him what the next steps are. He says, Let's schedule a meeting with Sandra tomorrow. Her hot button is the World Wide Web. Prepare a briefing that takes your vision statement and operational concepts and goes the next step. Show her how she can use the reuse library on the Internet to increase customer satisfaction. Make news about new products and beta versions of them available across the network to her customers.

Wow, you are thinking. We really can have a lot of fun with this idea if we can get Sandra to buy into supporting it. Go off and prepare your briefing to Sandra. Be sure to tell her what you want to do, why you want to do it, how you will go about doing it, what the people implications are, and what technologies are involved. In essence, tell her what the ingredients for success are in your estimation. Don't forget to make your boss look good. You know what it takes to keep him in your corner. Make a lot of what you are suggesting sound like his idea. Sandra is smart enough to see through the facade and give credit where credit is due.

CHAPTER 5

Exercises

1. Discuss how you would assess the readiness of an organization to accept software reuse technology.
2. How would you use the SEI Capability Maturity Model (CMM) to help firms sell reuse internally within a company?
3. What factors would you use to build your case for reuse? Why?
4. What would you offer your chief competitors to get them to participate in a benchmarking exercise?
5. What benchmarking data would be the most valuable to you, and why?
6. Many people feel that source lines of code/staff-month of effort is a terrible measure of software productivity. What are your thoughts on this topic?
7. When and why would you conduct a capability evaluation?
8. What change tactics would you weave into your action plan, and why?
9. Why pursue developing all of these plans? Would it not be more profitable to focus on achieving some results?
10. Draw a diagram showing how all of the documents generated to date relate to one another.

Student Project

Sandra loved your presentation. She understood what you wanted to do. She liked your vision and complimented your boss when you provided the detailed concept of operations. However, she asked a lot of questions. Most of these were business related. In addition, she didn't seem sure that the time was right for action. However, she expressed her willingness to be convinced otherwise.

Your boss helped you by asking Sandra what it would take to get her support. In response, she asked for the following items:

- A competitive assessment showing how reuse would help her increase her sales and penetrate new markets
- An evaluation of the impact the initiative would have on her existing capability to perform (i.e., Would the reassignment of personnel create instead of relieve schedule problems?)
- Your assessment of the staff's ability to adopt reuse (Are they ready?)

When you finished, she said: "Don't be discouraged. Give me the ammunition I need and I will support you when you pitch this upstairs." As you are walking out of the room, your boss said: "She's one tough lady. I'd suggest that you use the competitive edge to sell her. Joe Green is in the midst of a benchmarking study involving most of your customers and five of your major competitors. I'm sure he wouldn't mind trying to get the data you need to answer Sandra's questions and get her into *our* camp."

You call Joe. He says: "I wish you had called me two weeks ago. The benchmarking exercise is nearing completion and I just can't go back and ask for more data." However, Joe was more than willing to provide you the following data that he has assembled for Sandra's business area:

- *Workload*—New product releases are scheduled for fifteen months/product; Sandra has seven products in her product line; each product has about 300 features/functions; it takes about 500 source lines of code (SLOC) to implement each feature/function.
- *Workforce*—You have 100 software engineers and 40 support personnel (configuration management personnel, quality assurance professionals, etc.) to handle Sandra's workload. Most of the engineers are young and dynamic. In addition to having an undergraduate degree, about 50 percent of the workforce has masters degrees in computer science or a related field. Most are interested in software technology, and most are Web fanatics.
- *Time to Market*—Your product releases are running about six months behind schedule; your competitors are issuing new releases on schedule for competitive products on an eighteen-month cycle.
- *Software Cost*—Your costs are averaging about $4,500,000/release or $30/SLOC; your competitors are reporting costs of about $2,500,000/release or $25/SLOC. Their releases are smaller than yours because they already contain reusable libraries that are counted only once, when developed, so that they don't distort the totals.
- *Product Quality*—Your customer complaint rate is averaging five defects/thousand source lines of code (KSLOC) during the first year after a product is released; your competitors are reporting just three defects/KSLOC.

In addition to the hard data, Joe's team developed the following list of issues by talking with your key customer account representatives:

1. Your customers want better price/performance (i.e., more functions/features for their money).
2. Your customers feel your products are too hardware dependent. They want your products to be more portable so they can move platforms more easily.
3. Your customers want new product releases quicker (i.e., reduced to a year). They feel you are taking too long to get them the functions/features they need to do their jobs.
4. Your customers seem concerned about quality. They seem to feel they are debugging your products for you.
5. Your customers are moving to desktops, and are looking to you to provide them support for their Windows/POSIX applications running on client/server architectures. They are confused by the battles being waged among their operating-system suppliers. However, they expect you to remain neutral and be able to interact with both combatants.

Formulate an action plan showing Sandra how software reuse helps her address each of these five issues. Do it in briefing form using the outline in Plan of Action 5.1 as a guide. Don't worry about the economic arguments too much. That will be the subject of Chapter 6. However, use the facts and figures provided as you need to in order to formulate answers to her questions. Don't forget to brief your boss first. Keep him in your camp. Ask for his suggestions. They've been very good so far. Be prepared to answer the question about readiness.

CHAPTER 6

Exercises

1. Where would you go to get financial and marketing data on your competitors?
2. Compute the net present worth of the following six-year investment, assuming the cost of money is 6 percent and there are no tax implications.

	Costs	Benefits		Costs	Benefits
Year 1	$250,000	None	Year 4	$200,000	$600,000
Year 2	200,000	$150,000	Year 5	200,000	800,000
Year 3	200,000	500,000	Year 6	200,000	900,000

3. What is the benefit/cost ratio (BCR)?
4. What is the breakeven point for the investment (the point in time the benefits recover the costs expended to date)?
5. How would these figures change if you added a $500,000 startup cost in the first year?
6. How would you take the tax implications into account in your cash flow analysis?
7. Use the SPC reuse cost model shown in Figure 6.3 to compute the cost of developing a common communications handler that will be reused at least 50 times once it is placed in inventory ($b=20\%$, $R=50\%$, $E=130\%$).
8. Compute the cost of developing the common communications handles, assuming that the number of reuses drops to 20, and the relative cost of developing the assets skyrockets by 20 percent ($E=156\%$).
9. Prepare a balance sheet for personal household, and state in essay form whether or not you think it is useful.
10. Are there other financial metrics your organization feels are important? If so, what are they? Define them and show their value using the financial data provided in question 2.

Student Project

Well, you bombed. At least you feel like you did. Sandra did not think you went far enough with your briefing. She felt that you failed to make a strong enough business case for your proposal. Two of her project managers who attended the briefing were antagonistic. They argued that the money you were asking for would be better spent on their projects. Apparently, both of them were behind schedule and needed additional resources to catch up. She sent you back to the drawing board and told you to come back with hard numbers. Your boss agreed with her, never mentioning the fact that you had previously ran the briefing through him.

Your assignment is to prepare two to five additional charts that provide justification for your reuse initiative. The data supplied in Chapter 5, supplemented by the following information, should be all you need to build your business case:

- You estimate that it will cost about $600,000 to buy the tools and libraries you need to kick off the initiative. Normally, accounting treats such expenditures as expenses and writes it off. However, your friend in accounting says that you can capitalize R&D expenditures and write them off into a depreciation account for five years using the straight line method with zero salvage value. Because of the tax implications, you are thinking about this option.
- Your main competitor has staffed an equivalent initiative with five people. The annual cost of personnel is estimated to be $750,000 if you assume the cost of a staff-year of labor costs $150,000 a year, including burden (i.e., with overhead and general and administrative costs). You think you will need this full team for a minimum of two years. By then, you will either have proved your worth or been sent back to the salt mines.
- The current cost of money (i) is about 5 percent. The minimum attractive rate of return for an investment is about 20 percent. This means that management will not even consider a proposal unless it yields at least a 20-percent return on investment.
- Your chief software engineer believes that you can mine assets from existing libraries to build your reuse library quickly. Unfortunately, some reengineering will be required. However, this can be done if the assets are selected properly at 50-percent less cost than building the assets anew. He believes that there are about 500 candidate assets in inventory that have potential applicability to Sandra's product line.

You might consider using the SPC model to perform a breakeven analysis once you've analyzed the cost/benefits. The following worst-case assumptions seem reasonable to your accounting folks:

$b = 0.2$	Relative cost to reuse software
$E = 1.4$	Relative cost to develop reusable software
$R = 0.5$	Proportion of reused code in the product

Make any other assumptions that you like. However, be sure to record them. You will be surprised at the number of questions management will raise at a meeting about the assumptions upon which your estimates were based.

CHAPTER 7 EXERCISES

1. Where would you get the information needed to fill out each of the sections in the business plan outline? What documents have we produced that would be your sources? What other documents would you have to look at?
2. Under what circumstances would it make sense to pursue the opportunistic approach? Identify the factors you would use in making the decision, and explain how you arrived at your conclusion.
3. Under the opportunistic approach, we suggested that reuse planning should be included within the project plan. Do you think this is a good idea? If not, why not?
4. Identify the requirements you would place on a reuse library from a user point of view? How do these impact the work identified under asset management in this chapter?
5. What subtasks would have to be performed to consummate a strategic partnership?
6. Under the systematic approach, we identified a task called domain scoping. How would you go about performing this job?
7. Earlier in the book, we discussed three views of architecture: technical, system, and operational. Where and how would you use each of these to perform different tasks under the systematic approach?
8. Explain why Brook's other law holds true: "Adding manpower to a late project makes it later."
9. How would you go about identifying risk? Define the process and tools you would use (hint: perhaps interviews).
10. If you were asked to shorten your executive briefing to 20 minutes, what would you put in it and why?

Student Project

Things seem a lot better. Sandra liked the business-case materials you added to your briefing. She got excited and was very supportive. She even offered to partially fund the initiative if you could get the executive council to ante up the funds to develop the infrastructure. However, she expressed a concern that you had too much material. In response, Sandra suggested that you reorganize your briefing as follows:

1. Why the briefing?
2. Why pursue reuse?
   —Top-level cost/benefits
   —Competitive analysis
3. Vision and Strategy
4. Operational concepts
   —Organization
   —Management
   —Technical
   —Transition
5. Plan of attack
   —Work elements
   —Deliverables
   —Milestones
   —Dependencies
   —Products

6. What we need?
   —Budget
   —People
   —Support
7. Market analysis
8. Business case
9. Competitive assessment
10. Elements of success

11. Strategic partnerships
12. Risks and risk management
13. Next steps
14. Where we need your help
    Backup Charts
    —Market survey
    —Cost/benefit analysis
    —Competitive analysis

Sandra's suggestions made a lot of sense. To get your audience's attention, she recommended that you hit them early with the justification for your effort (item 2). Later in the presentation, she suggested that you could solidify your hold on the audience by summarizing the market survey, cost/benefit analysis, and competitive assessment (items 8, 9, and 10) that you had completed.

Your current task is to prepare this briefing. You need to take the materials that you have generated to date and repackage them for an executive audience. Pay special attention to eliminating inconsistencies and making sure that all of the materials are at about the same level of detail. Don't forget to double-check your spelling, numbers, and calculations. Having an executive correct you during your presentation can be very unsettling. Keep things as simple as possible. Don't put too much information on your charts (e.g., five to six bullets at most). Realize that you are dealing with busy people whose attention span is limited.

You also need to fill in the holes in the briefing. The most important item missing from the pitch is your risk matrix. Make any assumptions you have to in order to generate your top-10 list and any other items that you might need to complete your presentation. As always, jot your assumptions down on a piece of paper before you forget them.

Just before Sandra is ready to leave, she pulls you aside and offers you the following words of wisdom:

■ Don't ask for more than $750,000 to kick off this effort. That's all the money that corporate has available for discretionary projects this year.
■ Synchronize your funding requests with your firm's budgetary cycle. The fiscal year for your company begins on the first of April. As a consequence, requests for capital and research expenditures must be submitted in the fall of each year.
■ Ask the line-of-business managers to ante up part of the needed funds. Partner with them to get things rolling. Show them what they will get for their money.

Again, have fun and use your imagination on this exercise. It is fairly similar to what happens in the real world.

CHAPTER 8

Exercises

1. How would you start up a systematic strategy that was placing its early emphasis on developing a reference architecture? Would you use a team? If so, who would you invite to be members of it?
2. What is the difference between an integrated product team and an interdisciplinary task team? Do they have different goals? Would they be structured differently?
3. You are setting up an architecture group. What job positions would you create? What are the skills, knowledge, and abilities needed for each of these positions?
4. What techniques would you employ to develop knowhow? Are the tactics you plan on using different from those in your OCD? If so, why are they different?
5. How would you go about improving the way your people run meetings? List the rules you would set and the guidelines you would establish to eliminate time wasters.
6. The work breakdown structure (WBS) for your project represents how you relate your people to the work. How would you use the WBS to monitor task status and assess progress?
7. Managing risk requires that you monitor your actions and track hazards. Sketch the process you would use to accomplish this activity. What are the inputs and outputs of this process?
8. Give five examples of the types of rewards you can give for team performance.
9. Why must you plan for cutover prior to starting your reuse effort? If you waited, what could happen?
10. Identify the data you would have to collect to quantify the management indicators shown in Figure 8.1. Would collecting the data require extra work on the part of your people?

Student Project—Managing Your Time Better

As mentioned in this chapter, time can seem to be your scarcest resource. For the next week, keep a log of where you spend your time. When you are finished, classify where you spent your time into the following categories:

A—The few things you do that have a large impact on getting the work done (interview and select key personnel, prepare plans, review major problems and develop recovery plans, etc.)

B—Items whose effect on the outcome of your effort is proportional to amount of time you spent on them (coordinate interfaces, hold a readiness review, etc.)

C—The many things you do that have little influence on your work (respond to momentary crises, read all mail, answer every phone call, read all of your e-mail, attend informative meetings, interview applicants who will not report directly to you, etc.)

Note: the time you spend on *A* items can be 20 to 25 times more productive than time spent on *C* work [1].

After looking over the results, identify those items that can be delegated or handled in a more efficient manner. Prepare a report documenting your findings and recommending what you are going to do in the future to improve the way you manage your time. For example, write down the five things you have to get done today, and schedule uninterrupted time to do them.

CHAPTER 9

Exercises

1. In Figure 9.1, the budget performance indicator shows the project under-spending its budget but forecasting an overrun. Why can this be true?
2. What gating criteria would you use to govern the completion of the milestone *asset available* for the following two noncode assets: architecture and tests?
3. How can you be sure that an asset is actually reused? List the criteria you would use to come up with your determination and findings.
4. In Plan of Action 9.1, correctness is one of the metrics used to assess the quality of an algorithm. Why can an algorithm be correct even though it doesn't execute when implemented?
5. Most books on the topic of motivation say that money is not a motivator for most technical people. Instead, it is viewed as a hygiene factor (i.e., it becomes important only when you are not being paid what your peers are making). They argue that interesting work, the opportunity for advancement, respect by one's peers, and work challenge are the most important stimulants. Do you believe these arguments? Explain why you agree or disagree.
6. In Table 9.3, why is milestone completion rate an indicator of how happy your people are?
7. Would you do anything different at the major milestone reviews listed in Table 9.4? Explain what reuse products you would look at and why.
8. Why would new technology be viewed as risky? When would you use new technology for reuse and why?
9. The Air Force Reuse Center currently has over 1,200 reusable assets in its reuse library. Most of these assets are qualified at Level 1. Why do you think this is the case?

10. If you have access to a Web browser, look at the Air Force Reuse Center's Web site at the following address: http://www.ssc.af.mil/EN/ENSD/AFRC. What do you think?

Student Project

Develop a checklist like those in Plan of Action 9.2 for assessing reuse topics at your requirements and test-readiness review. Be sure to phrase the inputs as questions to be asked at the reviews. Make the following assumptions as you develop your checklists:

- *Requirements Review*
  - A system architecture review has been held and a reference architecture for your product line has been or is being developed.
  - Functional, performance, interface, and design requirements have been allocated to software via a system design document.
  - A draft user's manual for your product has been developed, which keys to a common user interface that you have been directed to reuse (i.e., a Windows-based set of software that includes an object manager, screen and report templating facility, and related libraries).
  - An operational concept has been developed by your customer community, which identifies several usage scenarios for the product.

- *Test-Readiness Review*
  - A use case consisting of a user-defined sequence of typical actions that your customer will follow has been defined to guide your test program. Tests will be automatically generated per these scripts using an existing tool that you plan to modify and reuse.
  - A set of benchmarks tests has been developed for validating product performance.
  - The test cases, data, and results for the user interface software exist and can be reused.

For those of you who are industrious, generate an acceptance-review checklist for extra credit. Recognize that satisfying the requirements is necessary, but not a necessary and sufficient condition for acceptance. For example, your product may meet requirements but not work in the intended operational environment. Some of the things you might put in your checklist to protect against such an occurrence include:

- Have all open trouble reports been closed satisfactorily?
- Have all approved change requests been completed along with related testing?
- Does the product work as the user expects (verified via alpha and beta testing)?

CHAPTER 10

Exercises

1. In Plan of Action 10.1, how would you incorporate software reuse requirements into a requirements specification to comply with the criteria outlined under Activity 3?
2. In Plan of Action 10.1, what additional tools would you consider for incorporation into your software engineering environment under Activity 8?
3. Why did we break out six new process areas under product-line management? Couldn't they be handled under the current CMM architecture?
4. Why did we separate technical from managerial processes? Couldn't we accommodate them by adding an activity for each of these processes to each CMM and P-CMM KPA?
5. Under what circumstances would you want to strategically partner with a supplier who was providing you software that would form part of your product?
6. How do you distinguish between COTS and reusable software? Aren't they the same thing?
7. After reading the section on domain engineering, what additional detail, if any, would you put under Activity 5 in Plan of Action 10.1 to make the criteria for this procedure more specific?
8. After reading the section on applications engineering, what additional detail, if any, would you put under Activity 6 in Plan of Action 10.1 to make the criteria for this procedure more specific?
9. After reading the section on asset management, what additional detail, if any, would you put under Activity 7 in Plan of Action 10.1 to make the criteria for this procedure more specific?
10. If you have access to your organization's standard software process, look it over and generate a summary of its reuse practices. After reading this chapter, are these sufficient? Will they help you institutionalize reuse?

Student Project

There is an active debate underway about the structure of the software CMM. In its current version, the structure as shown in Planning Guide 10.1 is:

Maturity level
    —— contain ➤ *Key process areas*
        —— organized by ➤ *Common features*
            —— contain ➤ *Key practices*
                Activities or infrastructure ◄ describe ——

However, the SEI Systems Engineering Capability Maturity Model (SE-CMM) employs a different architecture*. Its dual-path structure is illustrated as follows:

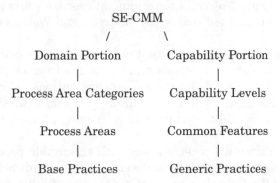

The SE-CMM separates systems engineering process areas (on the domain side) from generic characteristics (on the capability side) related to increasing levels of process capability as a function of maturity level.

While there have been some attempts to interrelate these architectures**, the net result has been confusion. The SEI is trying to resolve the clashes and will most likely make the structures more consistent in the very near term.

Your assignment is to take the domain engineering process and propose how it fits under both architectures. We know you are somewhat at a disadvantage when it comes to the SE-CMM because we haven't fully explained it. The question we are really trying to get you to answer is, Which architecture seems to be the best fit for tasks performed at the product-line level?

---

*R. Bate, D. Kuhn, C. Wells, J. Armitage, G. Clark, K. Cusick, S. Garcia, M. Hanna, R. Jones, P. Malpass, I. Minnich, H. Pierson, T. Powell, and A. Reichner, *A Systems Engineering Capability Maturity Model, Version 1.1,* CMU/SEI-95-MM-003, November 1995.

**J. Giannuzzi and S. Garcia, *Relationships between the Systems Engineering Capability Maturity Model and Other Products, Version 1.0,* CMU/SEI-94-TR-26, November 1995.

CHAPTER 11

Exercises

1. If you could insert one new technology right away, which of the 12 listed in this chapter would you choose and why?
2. Prepare a table comparing the pros and the cons of the generative versus the composition approaches to software reuse. Which approach would you use, when?
3. Artificial intelligence as a technology has been oversold. Yet, expert system techniques and shells can be used with great advantage when the problems

are small and scaling is not an issue. How would you use artificial intelligence techniques to benefit reuse?

4. Discuss how group computing can help organizations like yours get reuse more quickly adopted via expanded use of the Internet and Web-based computing paradigm.

5. Much of the literature promises increased reuse when object-oriented methods and languages are used. Such methods and languages focus on packaging software using data instead of functional encapsulations. Communications between software packages is handled through message passing instead of procedure calls. Why should this change in packaging philosophy make a difference?

6. How would you use simulation techniques with executable process models to assess the goodness of a proposed software reuse procedure? Goodness is defined in terms of the following three criteria: compatibility with your organization's software process, ease of adoption, and ability to increase reuse/ decrease costs.

7. Why are reuse tools so important? What function do they serve and how do they make it easier to transfer technology?

8. Is Web-based computing and the power of the Internet being oversold?

Student Project

Your organization has recently made the decision to move to the use of the C++ programming language and object-oriented techniques for a safety-critical health-care application. As the technical lead, you have been asked to complete the cause and effect, or Ishikawa, diagram in Figure S.1 to show what technology you plan to use in conjunction with these decisions to achieve your goal of increasing software reuse by 40 percent a year.

The diagram was developed by a team composed of engineers, marketers, users, and customers. It focuses primarily on technology needed to achieve mission-specific instead of process-oriented needs. These needs, which appear as the spines in the diagram, were defined by your health-care customers. They represent the technical considerations your customers feel will drive your products during the next 10 years.

You may make any assumptions that you think are pertinent. The only thing we ask of you is that you write them down. Make sure that you consider the impact of at least the 12 technologies covered in this chapter.

CHAPTER 12

Exercises

1. Develop a risk matrix for COTS that identifies the things you have to worry about in one column, and how you plan to address them in a second.

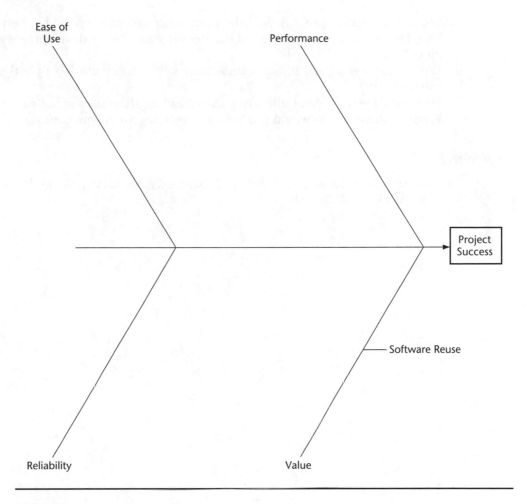

FIGURE S.1 Student project fishbone diagram.

2. When would you pay a vendor to modify COTS? Would the package still be considered COTS after it was modified?
3. Assuming you have access to the source code, what do you do when your COTS vendor goes out of business? Do you really want to assume responsibility for the COTS software?
4. Which of the 11 reuse acquisition scenarios listed in Table 12.1 appeals to you? Why?

5. When you purchase COTS, does the license agreement supplied by the vendor with the package address most of the items by a software development agreement?
6. When does and doesn't it make sense to make the contractor's proposal part of the contract?
7. How would you go about allocating the award fee discussed in the case study? What measurements would you take and metrics would you use?

REFERENCES

1. Bertram N. Abramson and Robert D. Kennedy, *Managing Small Projects for Fun & Profit,* TRW, 1980.

Appendix A

ACRONYM LIST

ADSN	Asynchronous digital subscriber networks
ANSI	American National Standards Institute
API	Application program interface
ARC	Army Reuse Center
ASQC	American Society for Quality Control
ASSET	Asset Source for Software Engineering Technology
AT&T	American Telephone & Telegraph
BAA	Broad area announcement
CAMP	Common Ada missile parts
CARDS	Central Archive for Reusable Defense Software
CASE	Computer-aided software engineering
CBA IPI	CMM-based appraisal for internal process improvement
CDRL	Contract Data Requirements List
CM	Configuration management
CMM	Capability Maturity Model
CMVC	Configuration management and version control
COCOMO	COnstructive COst Model
COE	Common operating environment

CORBA	Common Object Request Broker Architecture
COSMOS	Cost management with metrics of specification
COTS	Commercial Off-The-Shelf
CPAF	Cost Plus Award Fee
CPIF	Cost Plus Incentive Fee
DARPA	Defense Advanced Research Projects Agency
DEC	Digital Equipment Corporation
DFARS	Defense Federal Acquisition Regulation Supplement
DISA	Defense Information Systems Agency
DoD	Department of Defense
DOS	Disk operating system
DSRS	Defense Software Repository System
DSSA	Domain Specific Software Architecture
EUROWARE	Enabling users to reuse over wide areas
EUVE	Extreme Ultra Violet Explorer
FODA	Feature-oriented domain analysis
GE	General Electric
GOTS	Government off-the-shelf
GUI	Graphical user interface
HP	Hewlett-Packard
HTML	Hypertext markup language
IBM	International Business Machines
IBM/PCs	IBM personal computers (or compatibles)
ICWG	Interface control working group
IEEE	Institute of Electrical and Electronics Engineers
IPT	Integrated product team
IR&D	Internal Research and Development
IRAG	Industry Reuse Advisory Group
IS	Information Systems
ISDN	Integrated Services Digital Networks
ISO	International Standards Organization
JAD	Joint application design
JIT	Just in time
JSF	Joint Strike Fighter
KPA	Key Process Area
LAN	Local Area Network
LOADS	Landfill Operations And Disposal System

MCC	Microelectronics Computer technology Corporation
MIWG	Management Issues Working Group
NASA	National Aeronautics and Space Administration
NC	Network Computers
NIH	Not Invented Here
NISMC	Naval Information Systems Management Center
NIST	National Institute of Science and Technology
OCD	Operational Concept Document
ODBC	Open DataBase Connectivity
OLE	Object Linking and Embedding
OMG	Object Management Group
OMT	Object Modeling Technique
OO	Object Oriented
OOD	Object-Oriented Design
OOP	Object-Oriented Programming
OORA	Object-Oriented Requirements Analysis
PC	Personal Computer
PCTE	Portable Common Tool Environment
PEO	Program Executive Officer
PM	Program Manager
PMP	Program Management Plan
PSE	Project System Engineer
PSL	Project System Leader
RAD	Rapid Application Development
RAAT	Reuse Acquisition Action Team
RAMP	Risk Assessment and Mitigation Procedure
RBSE	Repository-Based Software Engineering
REBOOT	REuse Based on Object-Oriented Techniques
RIAT	Reuse Action Team
RICIS	Research Institute for Computing and Information Systems
RIG	Reuse Library Interoperability Group
RMM	Reuse Maturity Model
ROTS	Research Off-The-Shelf
RSA	Reusable Software Asset
RSRG	Reusable Software Research Group
SAMPLEX	Solar, Anomalous, and Magnetospheric Particle Explorer
SCALE	System Composition And Large-grain component Reuse

SDA	Software Development Agreement
SDCCR	Software Development Capability/Capacity Review
SEI	Software Engineering Institute
SET	System Engineering Team
SORT	Software Optimization and Reuse Technology
SOW	Statement Of Work
SPC	Software Productivity Consortium
SQL	System Query Language
SRB	Software Review Board
SRI	Software Reuse Initiative
SRL	Software Reuse Library
SSE	Software Support Environment
STARS	Software Technology for Adaptable, Reliable, and maintainable Systems
STSC	Software Technology Support Center
3Ps	Process, product, and people
UARS	Upper Atmospheric Research Satellite
UNAS	Universal Network Architecture Services
VCOE	Virginia Center of Excellence
VHLL	Very High-Level Language
WAN	Wide Area Network
WSRD	Worldwide Software Resources Discovery
WVHTC	West Virginia High Technology Consortium
WWW	World Wide Web

Appendix B

POINTERS TO FREE INFORMATION

Professional Groups

> ***Reuse Action Team (RIAT)*** The RIAT is a reuse group that supports and promotes the integration of software reuse into the software and systems engineering processes that are used by government and industry. It is sponsored by the SIGAda Reuse Working Group of the Association for Computing Machinery.
>
> | Contact: | LTC Gene Glasser | Dr. Harry Joiner |
> |---|---|---|
> | | USAISSC ASQB-IRC Stop C-2 | Telos Corporation |
> | | 6000 6th St., Suite S122A | 55 N. Gilbert St. |
> | | Fort Belvoir, VA 22060-5576 | Shrewsbury, NJ 07702 |
> | | Phone: (703) 806-4300/3680 | Phone: (908) 842-8647 |
> | | glasser@issc.belvoir.army.mil | harry.joiner@telos.com |
>
> ***Reuse Interoperability Group (RIG)—Web Address: http://www.aecorp .com/ae*** The RIG is a reuse standards group that is part of the IEEE Software Engineering Standards Committee. The RIG has developed an entity-relationship data model that defines classes of assets (IEEE Std. 1420.1).

Academic and Research Groups

Esprit—Web Address: http://www.newcastle.research.ec.org Esprit is the European Union's information technologies research program. The following relevant software projects are being pursued: COSMOS (cost management with metrics of specification), EUROBANQUET (support for effective software evolution in European banks), EUROWARE (enabling users to reuse over wide areas), PROTEUS (support for system evolution), REBOOT (reuse based on object-oriented techniques), RECYCLE, and SCALE (system composition and large-grain component reuse).

Process Reuse Study—Web Address: http://softeng.cs.mcgil This IBM Toronto Software Solution Laboratory research project funds Columbia University, McGill University, the Software Engineering Institute, University of Maryland, and University of Southern California to explore innovative software reuse methods, tools, and process paradigms.

Reusable Software Research Group (RSRG)—Web Address: http://www .cis.ohio-state.edu The work of this joint Ohio State University and University of West Virginia project is focused on reusable software components. Most of its work is related to the development of the RESOLVE framework for understanding component-based software systems.

Software Evolution and Reuse (SER)—Web Address: http://www.sema.es This server is used to promote and deploy the software evolution and reuse solutions produced by the following Esprit reuse projects. It provides information and up-to-date news.

Software Systems Generator Research Group—Web Address: http://www. cs.utexas.edu The work of this University of Texas-sponsored group is concerned with software system generators. The work is based on GenVoca: a domain-independent model of software construction that describes components and their composition.

Visual Programming-Software Engineering Group—Web Address: http://cuiwww.unige.ch The work of this University of Geneva-sponsored group is concerned with developing environments that make visual programming practical. Its ROSA project aims to provide more user-friendly and effective support for software reuse.

Industry Sponsored Groups

Virginia Center of Excellence (VCOE)—Web Address: http://www.software.org/vcoe The VCOE was jointly established by the Software Productivity

Consortium and Virginia's Center for Innovative Technology to help organizations institutionalize software reuse as part of their systems development processes. They have a variety of products (guidebooks, training courses, videos, etc.) available to help transfer this potentially beneficial technology.

Government Sponsored Groups

DoD-Asset Source for Software Engineering Technology (ASSET)—Web Address: http://source.asset.com ASSET serves as an online broker of digital products for the information technology and scientific communities. It provides Web access to both its Worldwide Software Resources Discovery (WSRD) components systems and publications library database. ASSET also provides up-to-date information and an electronic marketplace for software and related products (training materials, etc.).

DoD and NASA-Comprehensive Approach to Reusable Defense Software (CARDS)—Web Address: http://www.cards.com The CARDS program provides available information, technology, and techniques to facilitate the use by its partners of a product-line approach supported by a systematic reuse-based systems engineering approach. CARDS's goal is to put reuse technology to work. As currently structured, its products are aimed at technology transfer.

DoD-Reuse Information Clearinghouse—Web Address: http://sw-eng.falls-church.va.us The Reuse Information Clearinghouse serves as a focal point within the DoD for reuse information. It provides information on software reuse news and events, source code repositories, publications, lessons learned, successes, methodologies, working group results, policy, and history. It provides convenient links to other reuse Internet resources.

DoD-Software Engineering Institute (SEI)—Web Address: http://www.sei.cmu.edu The SEI, operated by Carnegie Mellon University for the Department of Defense, is pursuing a number of reuse-oriented projects under its product-line systems technology program. Assisting DoD components in transferring the results from these and other investigations is its primary mission.

DoD-U.S. Air Force-Air Force Reuse Center—Web Address: http://www.ssc.af.mil/EN/ENSD This Reuse Center provides Air Force users with access to management information system reuse products and services, including a variety of components (via its reuse library), education, and success stories.

DoD-U.S. Air Force-Software Technology Support Center (STSC)—Web Address: http://stsc.hill.ad.mil The STSC is an in-house technical resource that helps U.S. Air Force organizations identify, evaluate, and adopt technologies such as reuse, which are aimed at improving their overall software capabilities and capacity.

DoD-U.S. Army-Army Reuse Center (ARC)—Web Address: http://arc_www. belvoir.army.mil   The ARC provides online resources for U.S. Army organizations to access its extensive reuse library, customer support, educational, and technology transfer services.

DoD-U.S. Navy-Naval Information Systems Management Center (NISMC)— Web Address: http://www.nismc.navy.mil   NISMC is responsible for managing Navy information resources and serves as the Software Executive Official endorsing reuse policies and practices for use across Navy and Marine Corps units.

NASA-Repository Based Software Engineering (RBSE)—Web Address: http://rbse.jsc.nasa.gov   The RBSE program is a research and development effort whose mission is to provide state-of-the-art technology transfer mechanisms to improve NASA's software capabilities. The RBSE program operates the ELSA repository as its public interface. The project is administered by NASA Johnson Space Center and the Research Institute for Computing and Information Systems (RICIS), a part of the University of Houston at Clear Lake.

NASA-Software Optimization and Reuse Technology (SORT)—Web Address: http://soft.ivv.nasa.gov   The SORT Program was created through a cooperative agreement between NASA and West Virginia High Technology Consortium (WVHTC) Foundation to apply the vision of software reuse to selected NASA centers, and build upon the experience to transition the technology into widespread use. The effort is leveraging on current work to nurture the adoption of systematic reuse techniques.

NASA-The Software Engineering Laboratory—Web Address: http://fdd. gsfc.nasa.gov   The Software Engineering Laboratory's mission is to continuously improve software products and processes, including those for reuse. The Laboratory is a partnership between NASA, the University of Maryland, and Computer Sciences Corporation. Its focus is on measurement and approaches for technology transition.

Glossary

The following definitions are offered for terms used in this report. Whenever possible, the *NIST Glossary of Software Reuse Terms* [1] was used as the source of these definitions. However, other referenced sources for defining terms were used whenever the need arose.

Activity: A major unit of work to be completed. An activity has precise starting and ending dates, includes a set of tasks, consumes resources, and results in work products.

Ad hoc reuse: No defined processes for identifying and exploiting reuse opportunities. Success relies on individual initiative.

Application engineering: The processes/practices firms use to guide the disciplined development, test, and life-cycle support of their applications software.

Application framework: A framework that provides preassembled generic application code that a developer can modify to create a real application.

Application program interface: The classes, types, functions, and other programming constructs used by software engineers to take advantage of the services provided by a particular layer of the programming environment.

Architecture: The structure of components, their interrelationships, and the principles and guidelines governing their design and evolution over time.

Architecture-centric reuse strategy: Product lines form the basis for identifying software assets whose reuse potential justifies investment in their productization.

Asset: Any product of the software life cycle that can be potentially reused. This includes: architectures, requirements, designs, code, lessons learned, and so on.

Asset management: The processes/practices firms use to manage their assets and make them readily available in quality form to their potential users.

Attribute: An important characteristic attributable to an asset, object, or object class.

Authority: In project management, the right to give direction and allocate resources.

Baseline: A work product that has been formally reviewed and agreed upon, and that can be changed only through formal change control procedures.

Behavioral model: A view of the problem domain that portrays the important relationships (control, performance, etc.) between objects that are part of a domain.

Benchmark: An industry-wide or organizational standard against which performance measurements or improvement comparisons are made.

Browsing: The ability to skim through both the assets and their descriptors within a software reuse library.

Budget: A statement of expected results expressed in numerical terms.

Build: An operational version of a software product that contains a specified subset of the capabilities provided by the final product.

Business area: A coherent market created by consumers who have similar needs. May be organized by customer, geography, product, or some other characteristic.

Business area manager: The person or organization responsible for managing the definition, use, and evolution of assets within a business area.

Catalog: A centralized source of information about the assets in a reuse library.

Class: A group of objects with similar properties, common behavior, common relationships to other objects, and common semantics.

Classification: The manner in which the assets are organized for ease of search and extraction within a reuse library.

Client: In client/server systems, a program that uses services provided by one or more server programs.

Collection: A like grouping of similar developmental assets within a domain.

Commercial off-the-shelf software: Software that is supplied by a third party who retains responsibility for continued development and life-cycle support of the package. COTS software is used as is (i.e., the version is not changed to address the unique needs of the user).

Commonality: Those features that are prevalent in the great majority of applications within a domain.

Component-based development: The process of building systems by combining and integrating pretested and preengineered fine-grained software objects often taken from some framework or class library.

Context: The usage environment in which a particular system operates.

Core competency: Those capabilities of the firm deemed essential for its continued survival.

Cost/benefit analysis: Analysis conducted to determine whether the benefits that accrue to alternatives are worth the costs involved.

Critical path: In a network diagram, the longest path from start to finish, or the path that does not have any slack; thus the path corresponding to the shortest time in which the project can be completed.

Critical success factors: Those characteristics, conditions, or variables that have a direct influence on your customers' satisfaction with the products and services of your business processes.

Deliverable: A product developed, packaged, and provided to satisfy the customer's needs/requirements.

Domain: A distinct functional area that can be supported by a class of systems with similar requirements and capabilities (avionics, command centers, etc.).

Domain analysis: The process of identifying, collecting, organizing, analyzing, and representing the relevant information in a domain based on the study of existing systems and their development histories, knowledge captured from domain experts, underlying theory, and emerging technology within the domain.

Domain engineering: The reuse-based processes/practices firms use to define the scope (domain definition), specify the structure (domain model), and build the assets for a class of systems, subsystems, or applications. Domain engineering can include the activities of domain analysis and domain implementation.

Domain expert: A person who is intimately familiar with the elements of, and speaks the language of, the problem domain.

Domain model: An image of the domain's contents, structure, and internal relationships.

Earned value: A measure of budgetary performance, which relates actual expenditures to technical achievements as determined by milestone completions.

Facet: Perspectives, viewpoints, or dimensions of a particular domain that can be represented via the classification taxonomy.

Feature: A viable aspect, quality, or characteristic of a software system.

Framework: An extensible library of cooperating classes that make up a reusable design solution for a given problem domain.

Horizontal domain: A domain that provides information or services to more than one application area (e.g., communications, human interfaces, etc.).

Hyperlink: The device that drives intuitive navigation on the World Wide Web. Click on a hyperlink and you will jump to a related page.

Hypertext markup language: The coding method used to format documents on the World Wide Web. Browsers display text, graphics, and links on Web pages by translating HTML tags that appear in the file.

Infrastructure: The underlying framework used by management for making decisions and allocating resources.

Inheritance: A relationship between classes, where one class shares the structure or behavior defined in one (single inheritance) or more classes (multiple inheritance). Inheritance defines a hierarchy among classes in which a subclass may inherit characteristics from one or more superclasses; a class often augments or redefines the inherited structure or behavior of its superclasses.

Institutionalization: The building of infrastructure and culture to support making whatever is changed a part of the ongoing way a firm does business.

Integrated Services Digital Network: Digital telephone scheme that allows simultaneous connections over the same wire. ISDN communications can include audio or data.

Intellectual property: An intangible output of rational thought processes, which has some intellectual or informational value.

Interoperability: The ability to exchange assets, asset descriptions, and other information among software reuse libraries.

Key process area: A cluster of related activities that, when performed collectively, achieve a set of goals considered to be important for establishing process capability.

Knowhow engineering: The ability to transfer the knowhow associated with a new technology in a manner that builds the skills, knowledge, and ability to do the job in a logical order.

Knowledge base: The codification of the organization's past engineering experience in building and sustaining similar systems

Legacy: Reusable software assets developed on one project that have the potential for use on another project. For example, algorithms developed for one program may be candidates for another if they were designed to be reused.

Library-centric reuse strategy: Reusable software assets are made generally available to potential users via an online library. Users can browse, search, and retrieve assets of interest remotely via this library, providing they have access privileges.

Life cycle: The period of time that starts when a software product is conceived and ends when that product is retired from use.

Line-of-business manager: The person put in charge of deciding how to fulfill consumer needs within a business area with some product or product line.

Localization: Packaging interfaces with their import and export mechanisms defined and placed within a common area.

Logical model: A view of the problem domain, which illustrates the structure of and relationships between objects that comprise it.

Management: Getting things done through the work of other people.

Matrix organization: A combination of functional and project forms of organization, in which the line is responsible for providing skills and doing the work, and the project is responsible for budgets and programmatic performance.

Measure: A unit of measurement (e.g., source lines of code of pages of design documentation).

Measurement: The process of collecting, analyzing, and reporting metrics data useful in assessing status, progress, and trends.

Metamodel: A set of rules for describing and building models.

Method: The steps, notation, rules, and examples used to structure the approach used to model or build a system.

Metric: A quantitative standard of measure used to represent and compare some process-or-product, process-or-people attribute (complexity, error rate, productivity, etc.).

Middleware: A layer of software that sits between the operating system and application that provides as a minimum the distributed computing services through a simple programming interface. Today's middleware may provide common development tools, deployment facilities, and an execution environment.

Milestone: A schedule event of significance.

Mining: The software engineering activities conducted to generate reusable software components (assets) by reengineering objects from existing libraries, whenever it is determined to be cost effective to do such.

Model: A representation of a real-world process, device, or concept.

Motivation: The act of influencing the behavior of others through the combined use of incentives and rewards.

Multifaceted: A library classification scheme that ranks facets by citation order according to their relevance to users of a collection. Instead of searching a library hierarchically, users specify an n-tuple of facets, which quickly lets them home in on items of interest.

Object: A concept, abstraction, or thing with crisp boundaries and meaning for the problem at hand.

Object-oriented method: A requirements or design method that uses objects and object classes as its underlying basis to encapsulate abstractions, identify associations, and describe behavior of a system.

Operation: A function or transformation that may be applied to or by an object in a class.

Operational architecture: The user's view of the system, expressed in terms of the operational sequences (threads) that will be exercised to provide the functions/features desired.

Opportunistic reuse: Reuse processes are geared to project-level reuse. Little sharing occurs across projects. Typically, projects employ a library-centric reuse strategy. Assets are not built to be shared across product areas or product lines. Reuse occurs as a function of people, not process.

Package: A coherent subset of the system containing tightly bound groups of functions (or classes) and their relationships.

Paradigm: A modeling approach for the software development process.

Peer review: A review of a software work product, following defined procedures, by peers of the producers of the product to identify defects and improvements.

Process: The sequence of steps followed to achieve a goal.

Process maturity: A relative assessment of an organization's ability to achieve its goals through the technical and managerial processes it uses to develop its products and services.

Product: A system and all its associated work products.

Product family: The realization of a product line, by which products are organized according to their similarities and differences.

Product line: A family of similar products that are developed to service the market needs of a particular business area.

Product-line management: The business function that manages the definition, development, evaluation, use, and evolution of product-line assets over time.

Project: An organized undertaking that uses human and physical resources, done once, to accomplish a specific goal.

Reengineer: The process of examining, altering, and reimplementing an existing software system and reconstituting it in a form acceptable to its new user.

Reference architecture: A software architecture defined to serve as a point of departure for a product line or family of similar systems.

Reusable: The extent to which reusable software assets can be applied across systems without modification. The difference between reusable software assets and commercial off-the-shelf (COTS) software packages is how they are developed and managed. To be reusable, assets should be acquired/designed with reuse in mind, and managed as a shared resource within/across product lines. Users must be willing to take whatever functions/features are provided by the vendor when using COTS software, because they don't want to take responsibility for either its maintenance or management.

Reusable software: Software designed and implemented for the specific purpose of being reused within a product line.

Reusable software asset: An asset that has been tested, cataloged, and stored in a reuse library. This term implies that a reusable asset is more valuable than other assets because potential users easily find it and can have confidence that its suitability has been checked.

Reuse: To use again. The process of implementing or updating software using existing assets.

Reuse advocate: The person(s) empowered to make reuse happen within an organization. This person champions reuse and provides its leadership and support.

Reuse engineering: The engineering activities performed to systematically develop, test, field, and maintain reusable software assets.

Reuse library: A software library specifically designed and built for reusable assets. Contains a controlled collection of assets together with the procedures and support functions required to satisfy its users' needs. In other words, the term library refers to both the collections of assets and the software tools that populate them.

Reuse management: The processes/practices firms use to manage their reuse initiatives and the elements that constitute them (pilot projects, practices, tool developments, etc.).

Risk: The probability that a software project will experience potential hazards that may adversely impact its scheduled delivery dates and budgets.

Role: A unit of defined responsibility that may be assumed by one or more persons.

Scenario: A usage-oriented, execution-order sequence of events developed to elicit some system behavior.

Server: In client/server systems, a program that provides services to one or more clients.

Service: In OO methods, the specific behavior that an object is responsible for exhibiting. In layered architectures, any remote functions available to the client.

Shared assets: Reusable software assets that are shared across business units and product lines (class libraries, bindings, tools, etc.).

Smart agent: A time- and energy-saving utility that scans various Internet resources and collects files pertinent to the search request.

Software architect: The person within the business area who is responsible for overseeing the definition and realization of the software architecture for the product line.

Software engineering environment: The supporting hardware, software, and firmware used in the production of software throughout its life cycle. Typical elements include computer equipment, compilers, assemblers, operating systems, debuggers, simulators, and other software tools.

Software life cycle: The period of time that begins when a software system is conceived and ends when the software is retired from use.

Software process: A set of activities, methods, practices, and transformations people employ to develop and maintain software and associated products.

Software repository: A permanent, archival storage place for software and related documentation.

Software reuse library: The element of the software engineering environment (SEE) where reusable software assets are stored, maintained, and made accessible to potential users. The reuse library is much more than a normal library. It has browsing and many other user-oriented capabilities.

Suitability testing: Testing to ensure that the product is appropriate for use in a product line. The component is tested against predefined suitability criteria developed as a function of the product-line architecture.

Systematic reuse: A product line approach to reuse has been institutionalized, under which individual projects use a common architecture and shared assets to satisfy their requirements.

Task: The smallest unit of work subject to management accountability. A task contains a well-defined work assignment for one or more team members. The specification of the work to be performed is documented in a work package. Related tasks are grouped to form activities.

Trade secret: Any formula, process, design, or tangible intellectual property that is protected by secrecy.

Vertical domain: A domain that addresses aspects of a single function or application area.

Well-defined process: A process that includes readiness criteria, inputs, standards, and procedures for performing the work, verification mechanisms (such as peer reviews), outputs, and completion criteria.

Work breakdown structure: A family tree that organizes, defines, and graphically illustrates the products, services, or tasks necessary to achieve project objectives.

[1]Katz, S., C. Dabrowski, K. Miles, and M. Law, *Glossary of Software Reuse Terms,* National Institute of Standards and Technology (NIST), NIST Special Publication 500-222, 1994.

Paulk, M. C. et al., *The Capability Maturity Model: Guidelines for Improving the Software Process,* Addison-Wesley, 1995.

Reifer, D. J., *Joint Integrated Avionics Working Group Glossary of Reuse Terms,* RCI-TN-438, Revision 1, February 26, 1990.

Reifer, D. J., *Software Management (4th Edition),* IEEE Computer Society, 1993.

Reuse Library Interoperability Group (RIG), *RIG Glossary,* RIG Technical Report RTR-0001, April 1, 1993.

Bibliography

This bibliography cites references for those seeking more insight into the topics related to software reuse.

GENERAL

1. James P. Adamczyk, "Strategy First, Reuse Benefits Later", *Client/Server Computing,* June 1995, p. 59–61.
2. James Baldo, Jr., *Reuse in Practice Workshop Summary,* Institute for Defense Analyses, D-754, April 1990.
3. Ted J. Biggerstaff and Alan J. Perlis, *Software Reusability (Volumes I and II),* ACM Press, 1989.
4. Christine Braun, *New Directions in Software Reuse,* Reuse 1996 Tutorial, July 1996.
5. Christine Braun, *Software Reuse,* ACM Professional Development Seminar Notes, November 1992.
6. A. Christie, L. Levine, E. Morris, D. Zubrow, T. Belton, L. Proctor, D. Cordelle, J. Ferotin, and J. Solvay, *Software Process Automation: Experiences from the Trenches,* Software Engineering Institute, CMU/SEI-96-TR-013, July 1996.
7. Brad J. Cox, "Planning the Software Industrial Revolution", *Software,* IEEE Computer Society, September 1990, p. 25–33.
8. Michael A. Cusumano (Editor), *Software Reuse in Japan,* Technology Transfer International, Inc., 1992.

9. G. T. Ferguson, Jr., "Reuse and Reengineering," *American Programmer,* Vol. 4, No. 3, March 1991, p. 39–43.

10. William Frakes and Christopher Fox, "Sixteen Questions about Software Reuse," *Communications of the ACM,* Vol. 38, No. 6, June 1995, p. 75–87.

11. William Frakes (Editor), *Software Reuse: Third International Conference on Advances in Software Reusability,* IEEE Computer Society Press, 1993.

12. William Frakes and Sadahiro Isoda, "Success Factors of Systematic Reuse," *Software,* IEEE Computer Society, September 1994, p. 14–19.

13. Peter Freeman, *Tutorial: Software Reusability,* IEEE Computer Society Press, 1987.

14. Ernesto Guerrieri, *Software Reuse and Software Quality Assurance: How Do They Work Together?* Reuse 1996 Tutorial, July 1996.

15. P. A. Hall (Editor), *Software Reuse and Reverse Engineering in Practice,* Chapman and Hall, 1992.

16. Brian W. Holmgren, *Software Reusability: A Study of Why Software Reuse Has Not Developed into a Viable Practice within the Department of Defense (Thesis),* Air Force Institute of Technology, Report AFIT/GSM/LSY/905-16, September 1990.

17. Ivar Jacobson, Martin L. Griss, and P. Jonsson, *Software Reuse, Architecture, Process, and Organization for Business Success,* Addison-Wesley, 1997.

18. Ivar Jacobson, "Succeeding with Objects: Reuse in Reality," *Object Magazine,* July 1996.

19. Even-Andre Karlsson, *Software Reuse: A Holistic Approach,* John Wiley & Sons, 1995.

20. Balachander Krishnamurthy (Editor), *Practical Reusable UNIX Software,* John Wiley & Sons, 1995.

21. Charles W. Krueger, "Software Reuse," *ACM Computing Surveys,* Vol. 24, No. 2, June 1992, p. 131–183.

22. Wayne C. Lim, *Managing Software Reuse,* Prentice-Hall, 1993.

23. Carma McClure, *The Three Rs of Software Automation,* Prentice-Hall, 1992.

24. John D. McGregor and David A. Sykes, "A Paradigm for Reuse," *American Programmer,* Vol. 4, No. 10, October 1991, p. 30–39.

25. Bertrand Meyer, *Reusable Software,* Prentice-Hall, 1994.

26. National Institute for Software Quality and Productivity, *Software Reuse and Reengineering,* National Symposium Proceedings, April 1991.

27. National Institute of Standards and Technology, *Glossary of Software Reuse Terms,* NIST Special Publication 500-22, 1994.

28. N. Plant and T. Wooding, "Starting with objects and managing reuse," *Object Manager,* July 1994, p. 5–8.

29. Jeff Poulin (Editor), *Proceedings of the Sixth Annual Workshop on Software Reuse,* IEEE Computer Society, November 1993.

30. Ruben Prieto-Diaz, "Issues and Experiences in Software Reuse," *American Programmer,* Vol. 6, No. 8, August 1993, p. 10–18.

31. Ruben Prieto-Diaz, "Software Reuse", *Communications of the ACM,* Vol. 34, No. 3, May 1991, p. 88–97.

32. Donald J. Reifer, *Tutorial: Software Management,* 4th Edition, IEEE Computer Society, 1993.

33. Donald J. Reifer, "Software Reuse: The Next Silver Bullet?" *American Programmer,* Vol. 6, No. 8, August 1993, p. 2–9.

34. Donald J. Reifer, "Tutorial: Introducing Software Reuse," *TRI-Ada/1992,* November 1992.

35. Donald J. Reifer, *Software Reuse Study: Findings and Conclusions,* April 1992.

36. Donald J. Reifer, *Software Reuse for TQM,* Reifer Consultants, Report RCI-TN-490, June 1991.

37. Donald J. Reifer, "Software Reuse: Myth or Reality," *American Programmer,* Vol. 4, No. 3, March 1991, p. 18–23.

38. Wilhelm Schafer, Ruben Prieto-Diaz and Masao Matsumoto, *Software Reusability,* Ellis Horwood, 1994.

39. Guttorm Sindre, Reidar Conradi, and Even-Andre Karlsson, "The REBOOT Approach to Software Reuse," *Journal of Systems and Software,* Vol. 30, No. 3, September 1995, p. 201–212.

40. Software Productivity Consortium, *Proceedings of Workshop on the Software Reuse,* SPC-TR-88-008, October 1987.

41. Will Tracz, *Confessions of a Used Program Salesman: Institutionalizing Software Reuse,* Addison-Wesley, 1995.

42. Will Tracz, "Software Reuse Myths," *ACM SIGSOFT Software Engineering Notes,* Vol. 13, No. 1, January 1988, p. 17–21.

43. Will Tracz, *Tutorial: Software Reuse Emerging Technology,* IEEE Computer Society, 1986.

44. Paul Walton and Neil Malden (Editors), *Integrated Software Reuse: Management and Techniques,* Ashgate Publishing Co., 1993.

45. Ed Yourdon (Editor), "Software Reuse," *Application Development Strategies,* Vol. VI, No. 12, December 1994.

46. Ed Yourdon, *Decline and Fall of the American Programmer,* Yourdon Press, 1992.

47. Mansour Zand and Mansur Samadzadeh, "Software Reuse: Current Status and Trends," *Journal of Systems and Software,* Vol. 30, No. 3, September 1995, p. 167–170.

ARCHITECTURE

1. Barry B. Boehm and William L. Scherlis, "Megaprogramming," *Proceedings DARPA Software Technology Conference,* April 1992.

2. Christine Braun and James Armitage, "Domain Specific Software Architectures: A Process for Architecture-Based Software Engineering," *Proceedings 11th Annual Conference on Ada Technology,* March 1993, p. 46–54.

3. Shawn Butler, David Diskin, Kathleen Jordan and Norman Howes, "Architectural Design of the Common Operating Environment," *Software,* IEEE, November 1996, pp. 57–66.

4. Alistair Cockburn, "The Interaction of Social Issues and Software Architecture," *Communications of the ACM,* Vol. 39, No. 10, October 1996, pp. 40–46.

5. David Garlan, Robert Allen and John Ockerbloom, "Architectural Mismatch: Why Reuse Is So Hard," *Software,* IEEE, November 1995, pp. 17–26.

6. DoD Software Reuse Initiative, *Minutes of DoD Technical Interchange Meeting for Product-Line Architectures,* Defense Information Systems Agency, June 1995.

7. William G. Griswold and David Notkin, "Architectural Tradeoffs for a Meaning-Preserving Program Restructuring Tool," *IEEE Transactions on Software Engineering,* Vol. 21, No. 4, April 1995, pp. 265–287.

8. Hassan Gomaa, "Reusable Software Requirements and Architectures for Families of Systems," *Journal of Systems and Software,* Vol. 28, 1995, pp. 189–202.

9. Frederick Hayes-Roth, *Architecture-Based Acquisition and Development of Software: Guidelines and Recommendations from the ARPA Domain-Specific Software Architecture Program,* Teknowledge Corp. October 1994.

10. Rick Kazman, Gregory Abowd, Len Bass, and Paul Clements, "Scenario-Based Analysis of Software Architecture," *Software,* IEEE, November 1996, pp. 47–56.

11. Lloyd K. Mosemann II, *Architecture and Acquisition,* Presentation to the SMC, November 1995.

12. Eberhardt Rechtin, *System Architecting,* Prentice Hall, 1991.

13. Donald J. Reifer, *Software Architecture Study,* Report RCI-TN-96-0004, February 1996.

14. Mary Shaw and David Garlan, *Software Architecture,* Prentice-Hall, 1996.

15. Mary Shaw, "Comparing Architectural Design Styles," *Software,* IEEE, November 1995, pp. 27–41.

16. Will Tracz, *Collection Overview Reports from the DSSA Project,* Loral Federal Systems, June 1995.

17. Frank Van Der Linden and Jurgen Muller, "Creating Architectures with Building Blocks," *Software,* IEEE, November 1995, pp. 51–60.

COMPONENT-BASED DEVELOPMENT

1. Paul G. Bassett, *Framing Software Reuse,* Yourdon Press, 1997.

2. Sean Cotter and Mike Potel, *Inside Taligen Technology,* Addison-Wesely, 1995.

3. Max Dolgicer, "The Object Infrastructure Challenge," *Application Development Trends,* Vol. 3, No. 10, October 1996, pp. 55–64.

4. Dan Kara, "Object-Oriented and Component-Based Development," *Application Development Trends,* Vol. 3, No. 6, June 1996, pp. 69–76.

5. Hans A. Schmid, "Creating Applications From Components: A Manufacturing Framework Design," *Software,* IEEE, November 1996, pp. 67–76.
6. Steve Sparks, Kevin Benner, and Chris Faris, "Managing Object-Oriented Framework Reuse," *Computer,* Vol. 29, No. 9, September 1996, pp. 52–62.
7. Texas Instruments, *Assembling the Components of Public Value,* brochure, 1996.

DOMAIN ENGINEERING

1. David V. Blue, *Joint Integrated Avionics Working Group (JIAWG) Domain Analysis Description,* CTA Corporation, September 30, 1991.
2. Defense Information Systems Agency, *Domain Analysis Workshop Proceedings,* September 1992.
3. Defense Information Systems Agency, *DoD Domain Definition Report,* July 1992.
4. Robert L. Glass and Iris Vessey, "Contemporary Application—Domain Taxonomies," *Software,* IEEE Computer Society, July 1995, p. 63–78.
5. Martin L. Griss and Kevin D. Wentzel, "Hybrid Domain-Specific Kits," *Journal of Systems and Software,* Vol. 30, No. 3, September 1995, p. 213–230.
6. James A. Hess, William E. Novak, Patrick C. Carroll, Sholom G. Cohen, Robert R. Holibaugh, Kyo C. Kang, and A. Spencer Peterson, *A Domain Analysis Bibliography,* Software Engineering Institute, CMU/SEI-90-SR-3, July 1990.
7. Alan Jaworski, Fred Hills, Thomas A. Durek, Stuart Faulk, and John E. Gaffney, Jr., *A Domain Analysis Process,* Software Productivity Consortium, Report 90001-N, January 1990.
8. Kyo C. Kang, Sholom G. Cohen, James A. Hess, William E. Novak, and A. Spencer Peterson, *Feature-Oriented Domain Analysis (FODA) Feasibility Study,* Software Engineering Institute, Report CMU/SEI-90-TR-21, November 1990.
9. Randall R. Macala, Lynn D. Stuckey, Jr., and David C. Gross, "Managing Domain-Specific, Product-Line Development," *Software,* IEEE Computer Society, May 1996, pp. 57–66.
10. Fred A. Maymir-Ducharme and S. Michael Webb, *Multiple Perspectives on Domain Engineering,* Reuse 1996 Tutorial, July 1996.
11. Jeff Poulin, "Populating Software Repositories: Incentives and Domain-Specific Software," *Journal of Systems and Software,* Vol. 30, No. 3, September 1995, p. 187–200.
12. Ruben Prieto-Diaz and Guillermo Arrango, *Domain Analysis and Software Systems Modeling,* IEEE Computer Society Press, 1991.
13. Ruben Prieto-Diaz, *Domain Analysis: Concepts and Research Directions,* Contel Technology Center, CTC-TN-89-021, November 1989.

14. Balasubramaniam Ramesh and Mitchell D. Lubars, *Domain Analysis for Service Order Processing,* MCC, STP-SQ-236-91, July 1991.

15. Software Productivity Solutions, *Impact of Domain Analysis on Reuse Methods,* November 1989.

GUIDELINES

1. American Institute of Aeronautics and Astronautics, *Reusable Ada Software: Assessment Criteria for Aerospace Applications,* Recommended Technical Practice (draft), April 1992.

2. Grady Booch, *Software Components with Ada: Structures, Tools, and Subsystems,* The Benjamin/Cummings Publishing Co., 1987.

3. Defense Information Systems Agency, *Domain Analysis Guidelines,* April 1992.

4. Department of the Air Force, *Guidelines for Successful Acquisition and Management of Software Intensive Systems,* Vol. 1, February 1995.

5. Jean Faget, *Reboot Reference Book,* ESPRIT Project 5327, Deliverable D6.1.B, April 1992.

6. Robert J. Gautier and Peter J. L. Wallis, *Software Reuse with Ada,* Peter Pereginus Ltd. Publishers, IEE Computing Series (UK), 1990.

7. James W. Hooper and Rowena O. Chester, *Software Reuse Guidelines and Methods,* Plenum Press, 1991.

8. Joint Logistics Commanders (JLC) Joint Policy Coordinating Group on Computer Resources Management (JPCG-CRM), *Reusable Software Acquisition Environment Guidebook,* December 1991.

9. McDonnell Douglas Missile Systems Company, *Developing and Using Ada Parts in Real-Time Applications,* CDRL No. A008, Contract No. F08635-88-C-0002, April 1990.

10. Donald J. Reifer, *Joint Integrated Avionics Working Group Reusable Software Handbook (Volumes 1–5),* 1991.

11. Jerry D. Smith, *Reusability and Software Construction: C & C++,* John Wiley & Sons, 1990.

12. Software Productivity Consortium, *Domain Engineering Guidebook,* SPC-92019-CMC, December 1992.

13. Software Productivity Consortium, *Process Definition and Modeling Guidebook,* SPC-92041-CMC, December 1992.

14. Software Productivity Consortium, *Using New Technologies: A Software Engineering Technology Transfer Guidebook,* SPC-92046-CMC, December 1992.

15. Software Productivity Consortium, *Software Measurement Guidebook,* SPC-91060-CMC, December 1992.

16. Software Productivity Consortium, *Reuse Adoption Guidebook,* SPC-92051-CMC, December 1992.

17. Robert H. Terry and Margaretha W. Price, "A Practical Guide for Ada Reuse," *Proceedings 11th National Conference on Ada Technology,* March 1993, p. 70–79.
18. U. S. Army, *Software Reuse Guidelines,* ASQB-GI-90-015, April 1990.

MANAGEMENT/BUSINESS ISSUES

1. James Baldo, Jr., Craig A. Will, and Dennis W. Fife, *Strategy and Mechanisms for Encouraging Reuse in the Acquisition of Strategic Defense Initiative Software,* Institute for Defense Analyses, P-2494, June 1990.
2. Thomas W. Bragg, "Nontechnical Barriers to Software Reuse," *American Programmer,* Vol. 6, No. 8, August 1993, p. 19–23.
3. Defense Information Systems Agency, *Legal/Acquisition Issues: A Technical Report,* November 1992.
4. DSD Labs, *Acquisition Handbook—Comprehensive Approach to Reusable Defense Software (CARDS),* March 1994.
5. DSD Labs, *Direction Level Handbook—Comprehensive Approach to Reusable Defense Software (CARDS),* March 1994.
6. Martin L. Griss, "The Reuse-Driven Software Engineering Case," *Object Magazine,* December 1996, pp. 67–70.
7. Danielle Fafchamps, "Organizational Factors and Reuse," *Software,* IEEE Computer Society, September 1994, p. 31–41.
8. Richard Fairley, Shari L. Pfleeger, Terry R. Bollinger, Alan Davis, A. J. Incorvaia, and Brian Springsteen, *Final Report: Incentives for Reuse of Ada Components (Volumes 1 through 5),* George Mason University, 1989.
9. Watts S. Humphrey, *Managing the Software Process,* Addison-Wesley, 1989.
10. Jenifer Jones, "Software Reuse Faces Barriers in Government Sector," *Federal Computer Week,* June 1996.
11. Kyo Kang, Sholom Cohen, Robert Holibaugh, James Perry, and A. Spencer Peterson, *A Reuse-Based Software Development Methodology,* Software Engineering Institute, CMU/SEI-92-SR-4, May 1992.
12. Wayne C. Lim, "Effects of Reuse on Quality, Productivity, and Economics," *Software,* IEEE Computer Society, September 1994, p. 23–30.
13. Steven L. Mandell, *Computers: Data Processing and the Law,* West Publishing Company, 1984.
14. Tobey B. Marzouk, *Protecting Your Proprietary Rights in the Computer and High-Technology Industries,* IEEE Computer Society, 1988.
15. John J. Marciniak and Donald J. Reifer, *Software Acquisition Management,* John Wiley & Sons, 1990.
16. William Z. Nasri, *Legal Issues for Library and Information Managers,* The Haworth Press, 1986.
17. National Security Industrial Association, *The Business Issues Associated with Software Reuse,* Letter Report, December 1990.

18. Office of Technology Assessment, *Finding a Balance: Computer Software, Intellectual Property, and the Challenge of Technological Change,* OTA Document S/N 052-003-01278-2, 1991.

19. Reuse Acquisition Action Team, *Software Reuse Acquisition Scenarios,* Association for Computing Machinery, July 1994.

20. Richard N. Peterson, *Software Reuse Management Issue Analysis,* RNP Development Corp., September 1992.

21. James H. A. Pooley, *Trade Secrets,* American Management Association, 1987.

22. Pamela Samuelson, Michel Denber, and Robert J. Glusko, "Developments on the Intellectual Property Front," *Communications of the ACM,* Vol. 35, No. 6, June 1992, p. 34–39.

23. Will Tracz, "Legal Obligations for Software Reuse: A Repository Scenario," *American Programmer,* Vol. 4, No. 3, March 1991, p. 12–17.

24. U. S. Army/Space and Strategic Defense Command, *Software Reuse Business Model,* Technical Report, January 1995.

25. Giuseppe Visaggio, "Process Improvement Through Reuse," *Software,* IEEE Computer Society, July 1994, p. 76–85.

26. Craig A. Will, James Baldo, Jr., and Dennis W. Fife, *Proceedings of the Workshop on Legal Issues in Software Reuse,* IDA, D-1004, July 1991.

MEASUREMENT AND METRICS

1. Victor Basili, Lionel C. Briand, and Walcelio L. Melo, "How Reuse Influences Productivity in OO Systems," *Communications of the ACM,* Vol. 39, No. 10, October 1996, pp. 104–116.

2. Bruce Barnes and Terry B. Bollinger, "Making Reuse Cost Effective," *Software,* IEEE Computer Society, January 1991, p. 13–24.

3. James Bieman and Santhi Karunanithi, "Measurement of Language-Supported Reuse in Object-Oriented and Object-Based Software," *Journal of Systems and Software,* Vol. 30, No. 3, September 1995, p. 271–294.

4. Barry W. Boehm, "The COCOMO 2.0 Software Cost Estimation Model: A Status Report," *American Programmer,* July 1996.

5. Barry W. Boehm, "Software Reuse Economics," *Fourth International Conference on Software Reuse,* April 1996.

6. Barry W. Boehm, *Software Engineering Economics,* Prentice-Hall, 1981.

7. Terry B. Bollinger and Bruce Barnes, *Making Software Reuse Cost Effective,* Contel Technology Center, CTC-TR-90-012, June 1990.

8. Terry B. Bollinger and Shari L. Pfleeger, *The Economics of Software Reuse,* Contel Technology Center, CTC-TR-89-014, December 1989.

9. Max Dolgicer, "Should Development Tools Dictate Middleware, or Vice Versa?" *Application Development Trends,* April 1996.

10. John E. Gaffney, Jr., *An Economics Foundation for Software Reuse,* Software Productivity Consortium, SW-REUSE-ECONOM-89040-N, July 1989.

11. John E. Gaffney, Jr. and Tom A. Durek, *Software Reuse—Key to Enhanced Productivity; Quantitative Models,* Software Productivity Consortium, SPC-TR-88-015, April 1988.

12. Robert B. Grady, Practical Software Metrics for Project Management and Process Improvement, Prentice Hall, 1992.

13. Robert B. Grady and Deborah L. Caswell, *Software Metrics: Establishing a Company-Wide Program,* Prentice Hall, 1987.

14. Capers Jones, "Economics of software reuse," *Computer,* IEEE Computer Society, Vol. 27, No. 7, July 1994, p. 106–7.

15. K. H. Moller and D. J. Paulish, *Software Metrics: A Practitioner's Guide to Improved Product Development,* IEEE Computer Society Press, 1993.

16. Simon Moser and Oscar Nierstrasz, "The Effect of Object-Oriented Frameworks on Developer Productivity," *Computer,* Vol. 29, No. 9, September 1996, pp. 45–51.

17. Shari L. Pfleeger and Terry B. Bollinger, *A Reuse-Oriented Survey of Software Cost Models,* Contel Technology Center, CTC-TR-90-002, January 1990.

18. Jeffrey S. Poulin, Measuring Software Reuse, Addison Wesley, 1997.

19. Jeffrey S. Poulin, *Software Reuse Metrics, Reusability Metrics, and Economic Models,* Reuse 1996 Tutorial, July 1996.

20. Jeff S. Poulin and J. M. Caruso, "Determining the Value of a Corporate Reuse Program," *Proceedings of First International Software Metrics Symposium,* IEEE Computer Society, 1993, p. 120–8.

21. Jeff S. Poulin, J. M. Caruso, and D. R. Hancock, "The business case for software reuse," *IBM Systems Journal,* Vol. 32, No. 4, January 1993, p. 567–94.

22. Lawrence H. Putnam and Ware Myers, *Measures for Excellence: Reliable Software on Time, within Budget,* Yourdon Press, 1992.

23. George E. Raymond and David M. Hollis, "Software Reuse Economic Model," *Washington Ada Symposium Proceedings,* June 1991.

24. Donald J. Reifer, *The Economics of Software Reuse,* Reifer Consultants, RCI-TN-488, March 1991.

25. Donald J. Reifer, *Joint Integrated Avionics Working Group Reuse Metrics and Measurement Concept Paper,* Reifer Consultants, RCI-TN-456B, September 1990.

METHODS AND TOOLS

1. Patrick Arnold, Sephanie Bodoff, Derek Coleman, Helena Gilchrist, and Fiona Hayes, *An Evaluation of Five Object-Oriented Development Methods,* Hewlett-Packard, HPL-91-52, Bristol, England, June 1991.

2. Colin Atkinson, *Object-Oriented Reuse, Concurrency, and Distribution: An Ada-Based Approach,* Addison-Wesley Publishing Co., 1991.

3. Grady Booch, *Object-Oriented Design with Applications,* The Benjamin/Cummings Publishing Co., 1991.

4. Grady Booch, *Software Engineering with Ada (Second Edition),* The Benjamin/Cummings Publishing Co., 1987.

5. Jeffrey D. Boyken, Brian K. Mitchell, and Michael J. O'Connor, "A Farmer's Guide to OOA: Harvesting Requirements," *Proceedings 11th Annual Conference on Ada Technology,* March 1993, p. 121–126.

6. Tilmann Bruckhaus, Nazim H. Madhavji, Ingrid Janssen, and John Henshaw, "The Impact of Tools on Software Productivity," *Software,* September 1996, pp. 29–38.

7. Dennis de Champeaux, *A Comparative Study of Object-Oriented Analysis Methods,* Hewlett-Packard, HPL-91-41, Penelope Faure da Nutech, France, April 1991.

8. Peter Coad and Edward Yourdon, *Object-Oriented Analysis (2nd Edition),* Yourdon Press, 1991.

9. Mary Anne Durnin, Kevin Terry and Rick Sullins, "Establishing a Repository for Enterprise-Wide Reuse," *Reuse 1996,* July 1996.

10. David R. Dunklee and Robert M. Rutherford, "Reuse on I-CASE," *Reuse 1996,* July 1996.

11. Scott Henninger, "Information Access Tools for Software Reuse," *Journal of Systems and Software,* Vol. 30, No. 3, September 1995, p. 231–248.

12. Scott Henninger, "Using Iterative Refinement to Find Reusable Software," *Software,* IEEE Computer Society, September 1994, p. 48–59.

13. Ivar Jacobson, Maria Ericsson, and Agneta Jacobson, *The Object Advantage,* Addison-Wesley, 1995.

14. Ivar Jacobson, *Object-Oriented Software Engineering,* Addison-Wesley, 1992.

15. Mark Lorenz, "Facilitating Reuse Using Object Technology," *American Programmer,* Vol. 6, No. 8, August 1993, p. 44–49.

16. Mitchell Lubars, Greg Meredith, Colin Potts, and Charles Richter, *Object-Oriented Analysis for Evolving Systems,* MCC Report STP-RQ-341-91, September 1991.

17. D. R. Reed, "Tools for software reuse," *Object Magazine,* Vol. 4, No. 9, February 1995, p. 63–67.

18. Reuse Information Clearinghouse, *Catalog of Software Reuse Products and Tools,* 1995.

19. Theodore B. Ruegsegger and Ernesto Guerrieri, "The RAPID Center Library as a CASE Tool," *Proceedings CASExpo,* Spring 1989, SofTech, TP289, May 1989.

20. James Rumbaugh, Michael Blaha, William Premerlani, Frederick Eddy, and Will Lorensen, *Object-Oriented Modeling and Design,* Prentice-Hall, 1991.

21. Sally Shaler and Stephen J. Mellor, *Object Life Cycles: Modeling the Real World in States,* Yourdon Press, 1992.

22. Sally Shaler and Stephen J. Mellor, *Object-Oriented Systems Analysis,* Yourdon Press, 1988.

23. John D. Williams, "Managing Iteration in OO Projects," *Computer,* Vo. 29, No. 9, September 1996.

24. Rebecca J. Wirfs-Brock, "Object-Oriented Frameworks," *American Programmer,* Vol. 4, No. 10, October 1991, p. 21–29.
25. Rebecca J. Wirfs-Brock and Ralph E. Johnson, "Surveying Current Research in Object-Oriented Design," *Communications of the ACM,* Vol. 33, No. 9, September 1990, p. 104–124.
26. David M. Weiss, *Reuse and Prototyping: A Methodology,* Software Productivity Consortium, SPC-TR-88-022, March 1988.
27. T. Wapper and K. P. Yglesias, "What a Reuse Tool Can Do for You," *Object Magazine,* Vol. 4, No. 8, January 1995, p. 42–45.
28. Xiu Xiaowen, "C++ Templates and Software Reuse," *Mini-Micro Systems,* Vol. 16, No. 3, March 1995, p. 17–22.

PROCESS MATURITY MODELS

1. Roger Bate, et al., *A Systems Engineering Capability Maturity Model (DRAFT), Version 1.1,* Software Engineering Institute, CMU/SEI-95-MM-003, November 1995.
2. Bill Curtis, William E. Hefley, and Sally Miller, *People Capability Maturity Model,* Software Engineering Institute, CMU/SEI-95-MM-02, September 1995.
3. Jack Ferguson, Jack Cooper, Michael Falat, Matthew Fisher, Anthony Guido, John Marciniak, Jordan Matejceck, and Robert Webster, *Software Acquisition Capability Maturity Model, Version 00.02,* Software Engineering Institute, February 1996.
4. Joseph Giannuzzi and Suzanne M. Garcia, *Relationships between the Systems Engineering Capability Maturity Model and Other Products, Version 1.0,* Software Engineering Institute, CMU/SEI-94-TR-26, November 1995.
5. Mark P. Ginsberg and Lauren H. Quinn, *Process Tailoring and the Software Capability Maturity Model,* Software Engineering Institute, CMU/SEI-94-TR-024, November 1995.
6. Mark C. Paulk, Charles V. Weber, Bill Curtis, and Mary Beth Chrisses, *The Capability Maturity Model,* Addison-Wesley, 1995.

PRODUCT LINES

1. Lisa Brownsword, Paul Clements, and Ulf Olsson, "Successful Product-Line Engineering: A Case Study," *Software Technology Conference,* April 1996.
2. Lisa Brownsword and Paul Clements, *A Case Study in Successful Product-Line Development,* Software Engineering Institute, CMU/SEI-96-TR-016, 1996.
3. Sholom Cohen, Seymour Friedman, Lorraine Martin, Nancy Solderitsch and Robert Webster, *Product-Line Identification for ESC-Hanscom,* Software Engineering Institute, CMU/SEI-95-SR-024, November 1995.
4. Gibbie Hart and Sholom Cohen, "Domain Engineering and Product Lines," *Software Technology Conference,* April 1996.

5. John Foreman, "Product Line-Based Software Development—Significant Results, Future Challenges," *Software Technology Conference,* April 1996.
6. Randall R. Macala, Lynn D. Stuckey, Jr., and David C. Gross, "Managing Domain-Specific Product-Line Developments," *Software,* IEEE Computer Society, July 1996, pp. 57–66.
7. Donald J. Reifer, *Making the Transition to Product Lines,* Reuse 1996 Tutorial, July 1996.
8. Dennis Turner and John Willison, "SMART Initiative," *Management Issues Working Group Presentation,* March 1996.
9. John Withey, "Product-Line Opportunity Analysis," *Software Technology Conference,* April 1996.

SOFTWARE REUSE INITIATIVE PUBLICATIONS

1. DoD Software Reuse Initiative (SRI), *Vision and Strategy (Draft),* September 1995.
2. DoD SRI, *Operational Management Plan (Draft),* September 1995.
3. DoD SRI, *Program Manager's Reuse Issues Handbook (Draft),* August 1995.
4. DoD SRI, *Strategic Plan (Draft),* June 1995.
5. DoD SRI, *Software Reuse Executive Primer,* May 1995.
6. DoD SRI, *Technology Roadmap (Version 1.0),* October 1993.
7. Donald J. Reifer, "DoD SRI Status, Achievements, and Lessons Learned," *Proceedings of the Software Technology Conference,* May 1995.

SUCCESS STORIES AND CASE STUDIES

1. D. Bauer, "A Reusable Parts Center," *IBM Systems Journal,* Vol. 32, No. 4, January 1993, p. 620–4.
2. Christine Braun and Alan B. Salisbury, *Software Reuse in Command and Control Systems,* Contel Technology Center, CTC-TN-90-029, August 1990.
3. Christine Braun and Mamie Liu, *Software Reuse in Network Applications,* Contel Technology Center, CTC-TN-90-030, August 1990.
4. Ted Davis, "Adopting a Policy of Reuse," *Spectrum,* IEEE Computer Society, Vol. 31, No. 6, June 1994, p. 44–48.
5. DSD Labs, *RRTTF Reuse Success Stories,* STARS-VC-AA12/002/00, February 1996.
6. Emmannuel Henry and Benoit Faller, "Large-Scale Industrial Reuse to Reduce Cost and Cycle Time," *Software,* IEEE Computer Society, September 1995, p. 47–53.
7. J. W. Hutchinson and P. G. Hindley, "A Preliminary Study of Large-Scale Software Reuse," *Software Engineering Journal,* Vol. 3, No. 5, September 1988, p. 208–212.

8. Sadahiro Isoda, "Experience Report on Software Reuse Project: Its Structure, Activities, and Statistical Results," *Proceedings of 15th ICSE,* May 1992, p. 320–324.

9. Sadahiro Isoda, "Experiences of a Software Reuse Project," *Journal of Systems and Software,* Vol. 30, No. 3, September 1995, p. 171–186.

10. Rebecca Joos, "Software Reuse at Motorola," *Software,* IEEE Computer Society, September 1994, p. 42–47.

11. Barbara Kitchenham, Lesley Pickard, and Shari Lawrence Pfleeger, "Case Studies for Method and Tool Evaluation," *Software,* IEEE Computer Society, July 1995, p. 52–62.

12. John A. Lewis, Sallie M. Henry, Dennis G. Kafura, and Robert S. Schulman, "An Empirical Study of the Object-Oriented Paradigm and Software Reuse," *Proceedings of OOPSLA 1991,* November 1991, p. 184–196.

13. Gary N. Mayes, "USASSDC's Software Reuse Program," *Proceedings STARS 1992,* December 1992.

14. James O'Connor, Catherine Mansour, Jerri Turner-Harris, and Grady Campbell, "Reuse in Command and Control Systems," *Software,* IEEE Computer Society, September 1994, p. 70–79.

15. William R. Stewart and William G. Vitaletti, "Domain Engineering: Establishing Large-Scale, Systematic Software Reuse," *Proceedings 11th Annual National Conference on Ada Technology,* March 1993, p. 55–69.

16. M. Wasmund, "Implementing Critical Success Factors in Software Reuse," *IBM Systems Journal,* Vol. 32, No. 4, January 1993, p. 595–611.

17. William Wessale, Donald J. Reifer, and David Weller, "Large Project Experiences with Object-Oriented Methods and Reuse," *Journal of Systems and Software,* Vol. 23, No. 2, November 1993, p. 151–161.

18. Harvey Wohlwend and Susan Rosenbaum, "Schlumberger's Software Improvement Program," *IEEE Transactions on Software Engineering,* Vol. 20, No. 11, November 1994, p. 833–839.

TECHNOLOGY TRANSFER

1. Victor Basili, M. K. Daskalantonabkis, and R. H. Yacobellis, "Technology Transfer at Motorola," *Software,* IEEE Computer Society, March 1994, pp. 70–76.

2. John L. Bennett, "Building Relationships for Technology Transfer," *Communications of the ACM,* Vol. 39, No. 9, September 1996, pp. 35–37.

3. Barbara M. Bouldin, *Agents of Change,* Yourdon Press, 1989.

4. Johnson A. Edosomwan, *Integrating Innovation and Technology Management,* John Wiley & Sons, 1989.

5. Jim Foley, "Technology Transfer from University to Industry," *Communications of the ACM,* Vol. 39, No. 9, September 1996, pp. 30–31.

6. General Accounting Office, *Technology Transfer, Copyright Law Constrains Commercialization of Some Federal Software,* GAO/RCED-90-145, June 1990.

7. Michael Hammer and James Champy, *Reengineering the Corporation,* HarperBusiness, 1993.

8. Jeff Johnson, "R<->D, not R&D," *Communications of the ACM,* Vol. 39, No. 9, September 1996, pp. 32–34.

9. Capers Jones, "Why Is Technology Transfer So Hard?" *Computer,* IEEE Computer Society, June 1995, pp. 86–87.

10. Allan Kuchinsky, "Transfer Means More Than Just Technology," *Communications of the ACM,* Vol. 39, No. 9, September 1996, pp. 28–29.

11. Geoffrey A. Moore, *Crossing the Chasm,* HarperBusiness, 1991.

12. Jean Scholtz, "Technology Transfer through Prototypes," *Communications of the ACM,* Vol. 39, No. 9, September 1996, pp. 26–27.

13. Karl Sveiby and Tom Lloyd, *Managing Knowhow,* Bloomsbury, 1987.

14. Robert H. Waterman, Jr., *The Renewal Factor,* Bantam Books, 1987.

Index